Hong Kong Overview

What is Hong Kong? It's a question that many artists, directors, writers and politicians have struggled to answer.

In a very broad sense, Hong Kong is a city of duality, an at-times schizophrenic place that is both Western and Chinese. On one side of the Harbour, British pubs blare rugby matches to their Western clientele, while across the water, lounges populated by lunching Chinese croon with singers belting out traditional Cantonese Opera. All the while, over on Graham Street, you can eat snake soup in one restaurant and Yorkshire pudding in another.

Yet, while there is a clear difference between the communities within the dried seafood-lined streets of the Western District and those of expat havens like Discovery Bay, Hong Kong has absorbed much of what the British brought and created a fusion of cultures that isn't Chinese or Western, but something else altogether. The tea and food halls (cha chaan teng; 茶餐廳), serving cheap meals of sandwiches, noodles, fried rice and curries, are the result of Hong Kongese combining Chinese and Western style cooking. Local musicians sing Chinese lyrics over Western melodies, while local Triad films blend the furious action of talented Chinese martial artists with Western-style "cops-n-robbers" crime action. Ancient rituals and festivals dance down Hollywood Road as trams whiz up historical mountains and subways roar below incense-filled temples, mingling a swirl of old and new into a unique local culture.

But it's more than just a juxtaposition of Western and Chinese cultures that defines Hong Kong. Truly, this city of multiplicity has so many fascinating characteristics born from countless corners of the world it eludes definition. Whether you're into soaring skyscrapers, country villages, Muslim prayer sessions, dim sum, tango, haggling for a new suit, catching a cricket match, having some deer penis wine along with your whiskey or discovering bizarre dried sea creatures, Hong Kong has more than enough for everyone within its dazzling energy.

A poll once attempted to discover whether Hong Kongers felt more Chinese or Western. Their ultimate answer? "Neither – Hong Kongese." In the end, the only answer to the question "What is Hong Kong?" is the one you find out for yourself. So get pumped, start packing those bags and come discover what Hong Kong is to you. One thing we guarantee: you will have a blast!

History

Early Settlers & the "Five Great Clans"

Human life in the Hong Kong area can be traced back to the Middle Neolithic era (4000 BCE – 2500 BCE), evidenced by relics like the Fan Lau stone circles on Lantau Island. In fact, Hong Kong is known to be particularly rich in artifacts from both the Neolithic and the Bronze Age (1500 – 220 BCE).

Traditional Chinese peoples didn't have a presence in Hong Kong until around 221 BCE, and much of this was characterized by conflicts between various clans and ethnic groups. There is evidence that the Che people were the earliest of the area's inhabitants and were soon followed by groups who moved in to take advantage of the area's abundant fishing potential. Many of them, such as the Tanka, who inhabit boats and stilt homes at Tai O Fishing Village, still call the area their home.

In fact, the Tanka fisherfolk were not originally boat dwellers, but were slowly forced offshore by the influx of several

Han Chinese groups who ironically called themselves "Punti" (本地 ; local). The Punti were made up of the Five Great Clans, a set of five powerful families who settled the area with a scattering of their own walled villages.

The first clan to settle the area was the Tang. Originally arriving in the 11th century, the Tang held the position as the most powerful of the new immigrants. The Hau and Pang soon followed, creating the first Han Cantonese culture in the Hong Kong area, and these three clans were joined by the Liu in the 14th century and the Man 100 years later. To this day the descendents of the "Five Great Clans" hold considerable political and social clout in Hong Kong.

Their settlements were little more than small villages, however, and the first major Han establishment in Hong Kong came when the the Southern Song Dynasty was driven to the area by the invading Mongols.

The Mongol Invasion & the Song's Establishment in Hong Kong

The Mongols tore into China in the beginning of the 13th century, choosing a time when resistence was particularly weakened, as the Southern Song Dynasty was competing for land with the Jin Dynasty to the north. An initial alliance was formed between the Song and the Mongols, who held a common enemy in the Jin. Once the Jin were defeated, however, the Song abandoned the alliance, allowing the Mongols to consolidate their territories in the west, including the Dali Kingdom in Yunnan, and quickly turn their full attention to the Song.

With a large population, a strong economy and advanced weaponry, the Song presented a great challenge to the Mongols. During the 1250s and 1260s, the Mongols slowly chipped away at the Song's territory and political support, with Kublai Khan exacerbating internal disputes by offering land to Song defectors. In 1268, Kublai began the siege of Xiangyang, a long struggle that ended in a Mongolian victory in 1273. The Song fell three years later, and its court soon fled to Hong Kong.

With the establishment of the Song court in Hong Kong, the economy prospered through salt, fishing and pearls as more and more Chinese came to escape conflict and famines. The last two of the Five Great Clans, the Liu and the Man, came during this time, and established villages in the New Territories that you can still visit today.

The Mongolians didn't hold onto China

for long, however, and by the 14th century the Ming Dynasty had taken control of the country. By the time the Qing Dynasty took power in 1644, the routed Ming Dynasty had fled to Taiwan. Ming loyalists were strong in the Hong Kong area, the greatest of them being Koxinga, a pirate who wreaked havoc on the Qing Dynasty coastlines for the two decades after the dynasty's founding.

Instead of continuing a losing war against Koxinga, the Qing eventually gave up on Hong Kong. In 1661, the Kangxi Emperor commissioned the Great Clearance, requiring 16,000 people to leave the area, banning any inhabitation until 1669. Less than 2,000 people returned when the ban was lifted, and though the Qing Dynasty tried to encourage Hakka (an ethnic group of Han Chinese) migrations to the area afterwards, Hong Kong didn't have a substantial population again until the British set up their colony.

Opium: A Prelude to War

Trade between China and Europe became regular after Portugal's 1557 establishment of their base in Macau, just 65 km (40 mi) west of Hong Kong. The British joined the show 130 years later, bouncing off their East India Company ports along concessions on India's east coast. By the 18th century, the British (and much of Europe) had accumulated a trade deficit with China due to their insatiable demand for Chinese products like porcelain, tea and silk; a trade demand that was not reciprocated by the Chinese. To counteract their growing trade deficit, the British introduced opium, a product the British had in endless supply from their holdings in India, and one that the Chinese soon became rabidly addicted to.

Though the Qing court issued major edicts in 1729 and 1799 banning the drug, they soon found themselves powerless to stop its import. In 1730, there were some 15 tons of opium traded. By 1773, the amount had increased to 70 tons per year, and by 1800 it was an astronomical 280 tons per year.

The insatiable demand for opium in China had spun the trade deficit on its head, with China seeing its silver tael reserves plummet. Even worse was the effect of the opium on the populace, making addicted court officials and soldiers lazy and ineffectual at their duties, severely weakening China's governing and military power.

The situation became dire in the 1830s as opium imports (per year) surpassed 1,400 tons. Emperor Dao Guang (reign 1820 – 1850) decided on a new course of action, first issuing arrest warrants for dozens of foreign opium merchants, and then appointing the honorable Lin Zexu – governor of Hubei and Hunan – to end the opium trade once and for all. The hard-nosed Lin arrested thousands of Chinese opium dealers and called the foreign merchants to hand over their inventories. When they refused, Lin put them under house arrest and proceeded to confiscate a massive cache of 20,283 chests of opium, equal to approximately 1,700 tons and valued at 2 million pounds. After he destroyed the narcotics, Lin demanded the British merchants sign agreements not to trade opium under punishment of death. The majority refused and were forced back to England.

China, Jardine began an aggressive lobbying campaign for war. He appealed directly to British Foreign Secretary Lord Palmerson and hired journalists and pamphleteers to push his case. Though war was opposed by Chartists in Parliament, Palmerson was convinced on military action. The narrow 271-261 pro-war majority was pushed over the edge when Sir G Thomas Staunton summarized British imperial sentiments: "If [we] submitted to insults from China, British ascendancy will collapse!"

The Opium Wars: Britain Takes Hong Kong

British warships arrived from India in 1840, and with their far superior technology captured Canton and easily routed the Chinese military. Figures cited by the historian Foster Stockwell put the British death toll at 500, compared to a staggering 20,000 in the Chinese. The next year, Captain Elliot took Hong Kong and proposed concession of the colony as the main condition for a peace treaty.

Lin Zexu destroying opium

Unfortunately for Lin and the Qing emperor, this was not the end of their opium problem. The British crown saw their expulsion from China as a major insult from a less advanced nation and labeled the Qing court as xenophobic. On the other side of the water, the Chinese equally felt themselves superior to the foreign "barbarians," and tensions brewed throughout the 1830s. After Chief Trade Superintendent Charles Elliot – who was sent to negotiate with the governor of Canton – was refused an audience and died of fever while exiled in Macau, British merchants angrily penned the Canton Petition, demanding the British government take a stand.

Among the 85 merchants who signed the petition, there was none more powerful than William Jardine. Jardine had graduated from medical school in 1802 and joined the East India Company as a surgeon's mate on a trade ship. On his journeys, he engaged in personal trade, and eventually quit medicine for commerce in 1817. In 1832, he founded Jardine, Matheson & Co with James Matheson and became one of the most loathsome and unscrupulous foreigners in China. When a 1837 edict called for "Jardine and others" to be expelled from

The British government was furious at first, seeing nothing of value in the small island. Elliot had been told to "obtain freedom for the British to live and trade at the five ports of Canton, Amoy, Foochow, Ningpo and Shanghai," but Palmerson wrote, "Instead... Elliot had obtained a barren island with hardly a house upon it."

Elliot was quickly dismissed from his position, and Britain eventually got everything it wanted with the 1842 Treaty of Nanking, including giving British citizens extraterritorial rights in Chinese ports, something not offered to Chinese in British lands. Though Palmerson thought of Hong Kong as a useless outpost that could be traded back to China for more concessions, subsequent governors of Hong Kong quickly developed the island to something worthy of a permanent interest.

Jardine's associate James Matheson understood the importance of Hong Kong early on. In a letter to an official arguing for retention of Hong Kong, he said, "It is by far the best harbour for large ships in the vicinity of the Canton River." A later correspondence from a Jardine, Matheson & Co representative concluded, "Many prefer the Kowloon Peninsula, but we ought to have both."

They would have both in 1860 when the Second Opium War resulted in China's concession of Kowloon, and in 1898, Britain was leased the New Territories for 99 years.

About 200 years later, the name of the warmongering profiteer Jardine continues to carry with it connotations of power and commerce in Hong Kong. His name adorns street signs, building names and mountains, and his former company, Jardine Matheson Holdings Ltd, has a huge presence in China, controlling companies like Hongkong Land, Jardine Motors Group and the Mandarin Oriental Hotel Group.

Early British Rule

The early years of Hong Kong required the British to essentially build from scratch as the area was full of little more than scattered fishing villages. Their first order of business was to clear out the pirate scourge, which didn't fare much better against modern British war ships than the Chinese navy did.

The British established the city center in Central, then called Victoria. The Canton Bazaar was one of the first buildings built in 1842 as the first major trade space. The Former French Mission Building on Government Hill, now housing the Court of Final Appeal, was the first building in which British legislators met, while Queen's Road and Hollywood Road became the city's first roads.

Land reclamation began in 1859 at Sheung Wan, and from 1864 to 1878, a major stretch of land, including present day Causeway Bay, Wan Chai and Kennedy Town, was pulled from under the ocean. The area that today is Queen's Road Central, a deep jungle of tall buildings, was little more than sandy coast 150 years ago.

Over its first few decades, Hong Kong struggled to grow as famines, an outbreak of the bubonic plague, and numerous typhoons rocked the area's property and population. The early years saw a number of criminals and shady characters take up residence as well, but over time the city began to blossom into a strong community.

Hong Kong reached a population of 33,000 in 1850, and just 46 years later it had climbed to a staggering 240,000. This number escalated even further as Chinese began immigrating from the Mainland, which had fallen into chaos under the failing Qing Dynasty. The Qing finally collapsed in 1912, bringing more fleeing immigrants to Hong Kong as a gaggle of war lords, the Nationalist Party (Kuomintang) and the Communist Party decimated the country in a bloody civil war.

World War II: Japanese Occupation

Six years after the Japanese invaded Manchuria in 1931, their complete takeover of Shanghai drove more Chinese south and caused the population of Hong Kong to increase from about 1 million to 1.6 million between 1937 and 1941. When the Japanese invaded Hong Kong in 1941, they took the city in 17 days, with a British surrender on December 25.

The Japanese military set the tone of their occupation from day one, storming the military hospital at St Stephens College, killing doctors, raping nurses and putting the bayonete to injured soldiers. The occupation of Hong Kong continued in this harsh manner for the remainder of the war, as Chinese civilians found themselves indiscriminately killed in the early weeks and foreign residents were imprisoned at a POW camp in Stanley. The Japanese Military Yen replaced the Hong Kong Dollar, and soon the economy tanked as local businesses were usurped. Long lines for rationed food meant severe malnourishment and starvation for many, and Hong Kong's population more than halved during these four years. After the Japanese surrender in 1945, the British tried 122 Japanese officers and soldiers in Hong Kong for war crimes, 108 of whom were convicted, and 21 given death sentences.

Post-War Boom

Hong Kong's dwindling population was down to 700,000 at the end of World War II, but a sharp rebound saw the city once again at 1.7 million by 1947.

The 1950s in China brought even more terror and social strife to the nation, setting the stage for Hong Kong's fast-paced growth in the second half of the 20th century. With the nation falling into communist hands, Mainland refugees began pouring into the city, increasing significantly as the Cultural Revolution ran amok in the 1960s.

Local authorities began to fear subversion by communist factions and a rise of CCP revolutionary zeal. Many communists set up "patriotic schools," whose curriculums ran hardline pro-communist agendas, most of which were quickly shut down. Riots sparked by communist furor hit the streets in 1956 and 1967, marked by young revolutionaries marching the streets under banners of Mao slogans.

At a time when Mainland and Hong Kong tensions were at their highest, a People's Liberation Army invasion force that was slated to enter Hong Kong was called off at the last minute by PRC Premier, Zhou Enlai.

The population boom meant that a great number of the new residents were impoverished refugees living in shanty towns in the hills on the fringes of Kowloon. Made of little more than wood, clothing and blankets densely packed into a relatively small area, these shanty towns saw tragedy when multiple fires took some 200,000 lives during the 1950s. Public housing became an obvious necessity and was seriously pursued after the 1953 Shek Kip Mei fire that left 53,000 people homeless. Today about 50% of the population lives in publicly subsidized housing. Shanty towns and squatter settlements can still be found on the edges of some of the country parks in the New Territories.

Hong Kong's first major economic boom began as manufacturing found its way into the city in the '50s. Toys and textiles took the majority of the production, which continued to increase through the '70s, and it was at this prosperous time that Hong Kong's economy began shifting towards finance. By the end of the decade, manufacturing made up about a quarter of the economy, continuing to decline through the years as white collar services came to the fore.

The increasing economy of the 1970s meant that more and more Hong Kongese were able to live middle class lives comparable to those in the West. Local restaurants quickly began developing their own fusions of Western and Chinese food, particularly at the *cha chaan teng* (tea and food halls), which began to serve up ramen-style spaghetti.

Entertainment also took off during the thriving '70s, as the growing middle class sat down in front of their television sets to watch news reports and dramas every night. The theme songs from many of these dramas gave rise to Cantopop music as stars like Roman Tam, "The Godfather of Cantopop," found their breaks and rose to fame.

Hong Kong found its place as the leading

film producing country in Asia with much help from talents like Bruce Lee and Jackie Chan, as the city's cinema began to take the world by storm.

The 1970s made way for wide development of Hong Kong's transportation infrastructure as well, punctuated by projects like the Cross-Harbour Tunnel in 1972, which allowed automobiles to drive between Hong Kong and Kowloon for the first time. The MTR opened its first subway lines in 1979.

The boom in the wake of WWII was not all rainbows and lollipops, however. The driving economy and swift development opened lucrative opportunities for corruption, especially among police, fire fighters and other civil servants, who were known to require kickbacks before taking action in an emergency. Police officers often protected Triad members and drug dealers in exchange for money, and many businesses factored police bribes into their budgets. Police corruption got so bad that in 1977, when the government busted up a large police corruption ring, they ended up giving amnesty to low level officers who committed crimes before 1977 out of fear they would hardly have a force left if they prosecuted all their crimes.

Since the formation of the Independent Commission Against Corruption in 1974, Hong Kong has made monumental strides against corruption. Transparency International ranked the city as the 14th least corrupt country or territory in the world in 2012, beating out both the United States and the United Kingdom and falling just short of Canada.

The 1980s and '90s would continue along the same upward trajectory as that of the previous decades. In fact, some have called the '80s and '90s Hong Kong's Golden Era. It was an especially rich time for cinema and music, and many of the best Chinese films of all time, as picked by the Hong Kong Film Association, were filmed during this Golden Era. The 1986 film *A Better Tomorrow* set the standard for gangster films, a standard that was emulated by 1990s Hollywood as well. Singers like Anita Mui and Leslie Cheung showed that they could act as convincingly and passionately as they could sing on their platinum-selling records.

The excitement of 1980s Hong Kong also sat side-by-side with an unnerving look at the uncertain future. In 1984 the Sino-British Joint Declaration was signed, requiring Hong Kong to be handed over to China in 1997.

As Britain's 99-year lease over the New Territories edged towards its 1997 expiration date, anxiety began to seep into the city. Hong Kong Governor Murray MacLehose went to Beijing in 1979 in an attempt to extend the lease. Instead he was greeted with Deng Xiaoping's staunch refusal. Discussions between the United Kingdom and China on the future of Hong Kong took place again in 1982, culminating in the December 19, 1984 signing of a declaration that would established Hong Kong as a Special Administrative Region of China in 1997. The government and civil rights were to be left unchanged for 50 years (in 2047), at which point it would become fully integrated into the People's Republic of China.

The people of Hong Kong had become used to a high level of social and political freedoms, albeit without full democracy, under British rule. Hong Kong had developed a vibrant, free marketplace of ideas, critical newspapers and rights to protest; liberties that are largely nonexistent in China. Many Mainland incidents, not least including a particularly notorious event in Beijing in 1989, gave the citizens of Hong Kong cause for great concern, and they now commemorate the events of Tian'anmen Square every year with a candlelight vigil.

Both sides in the handover tried to assuage the Hong Kong people that they would have autonomy. The British set the first legislative elections, and Deng Xiaoping, in a talk to visitors celebrating National Day on October 3, 1984, said:

"In the agreement we stated that no change would be made for 50 years, and we mean it. There will be no changes in my generation or in the next. And I doubt that 50 years after 1997, when the Mainland is developed, people will handle matters like this in a narrow-minded way. So don't worry, there won't be any changes."

"Besides, not all changes are bad. Some of them are good, and the question is what should be changed."

Though some Hong Kongers took comfort in Deng's statement, many may have had some concerns about changes under Chinese control. One particular concern came to light when in 2012 protests erupted against newly proposed curriculums that would teach what critics called an "indoctrinating version" of Chinese history.

Anticipating the eventual handover to China, the British government began slowly introducing democratic reforms to the city in 1985. That year, they hosted the first ever legislative council (LegCo) elections, but the indirect election only appointed 24 of the 46 members. In 1995 the first full elections were held and allowed half the members of the LegCo to be elected by geographic constituencies, and the other half to be elected by functional constituencies (FCs), including corporations and workers representing commercial, labor and social interest groups. Currently the Chief Executive is elected by an Election Committee composed mostly of FC members.

However, some Hong Kongers are even disatisfied with their own form of government, and protests for universal suffrage in the Chief Executive elections (which the territory does not have) still hit the streets on a regular basis. One Hong Kong University law professor is trying to organize a takeover of Central (Occupy Central) in 2014 if the city isn't granted universal suffrage.

Hong Kong in the 2000s

As the city enters the new millennium, some of Hong Kong's dynamism of the past two decades has slowed down. The population rose from 6.87 million in 2000 to just 7.07 million in 2014, and much of the increase has come from Mainland Chinese immigrants, as local Hong Kong birthrates have actually dropped.

Tragedy fell upon Hong Kong in 2003 when the SARS outbreak claimed 299 lives. That same year, two of the city's most beloved cultural icons, Leslie Cheung and his longtime friend and singing and acting partner, Anita Mui, passed away. For many Hong Kongese, the deaths of such beloved cultural icons signaled to many the end of an era and seemed to coincide with the coming of a concerning and unsure future under the rule of Mainland China.

Surveys done by the University of Hong Kong during the past decade have found that less than 30% of Hong Kongese identify themselves as Chinese citizens, while a majority identify themselves as Hong Kong citizens or "Hong Kong citizens plus Chinese citizens." In 2012, the survey found its most striking results yet when just 16.6% of respondents said they considered themselves Chinese citizens. This result garnered strong criticism by Mainland Chinese state-run media.

Friction between Hong Kongese and

Mainland Chinese rose to the forefront of controversy in January 2012 when a Hong Kong man and Mainland woman got into an argument on an MTR train after the man told the mother's child to stop eating on the train (which is not allowed in Hong Kong but common in the Mainland). The incident, which was filmed by another passenger, heated up quickly, and the video was soon shared online. In the aftermath, Professor Kong Qingdong of Peking University went on CCTV and called the Hong Kongese "imperialist running dogs." Hong Kongers responded by calling Mainlanders "locusts."

Many Hong Kongese oppose the trend of Mainland Chinese mothers coming to city to have babies in order for the children to obtain local citizenship. Others also resent the fact that Mainlanders, who gave birth to 37% of babies in Hong Kong in 2010, are crowding hospital beds and putting a burden on the social welfare system. Mainland citizens also like to come to Hong Kong to purchase milk powder, which is perceived to be much safer here than in Mainland China, where there have been a number of poisonous milk scandals. This prompted the Hong Kong government to put a customs limit on milk powder to prevent Hong Kong's own reserves from becoming depleted.

Though Hong Kong's future is uncertain, there are many who hold high hopes that, instead of the political and social climate tightening and becoming more repressed, perhaps the city

and its people's penchant for progress and free thought may inspire positive change on the Mainland. Only time will tell, though there is no doubt that the Hong Kongese won't lose their way of life without a fight.

Geography & Districts

Hong Kong is divided into 18 districts. For most travelers, the important distinction is between Hong Kong Island (香 港 島) and Kowloon (九龍半島). Hong Kong Island was the first area occupied by the British, and it was from here that much of modern Hong Kong developed. Across the Harbour sits Kowloon peninsula, and further north of Kowloon's main city center you'll find the area known as the New Territories (新 界). Whereas Kowloon is highly urbanized, the New Territories are far more rural. Though residents of Chinese heritage are found throughout all of Hong Kong's districts, it is Hong Kong Island that is the home to most of the city's expats (this area is generally more expensive than Kowloon). Off the coast, some 260 islands make up the Outlying Islands. Most of them are uninhabited, but those that are inhabited – of which Lantau (大嶼山) is the largest – offer some excellent excursions.

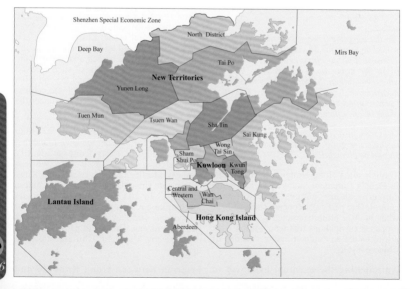

Hong Kong Island

Hong Kong Island is divided into four districts: Central and Western (中西區), Wan Chai (灣仔區), Eastern (東區) and Southern (南 區). Most of the development is on the northern side of the island around Central (中環). This was the first area of development and is currently where the main government buildings and financial institutions are located. On the western edge of Central around Sheung Wan (上環), you can still find some old Chinese areas with seafood markets and traditional medicine shops. This western edge is also home to Hong Kong University and the neighborhood of Shek Tong Tsui (石塘 咀), which used to be an entertainment district known for its Cantonese opera and opium dens. Up the hills south of Central are the Mid-Levels (半山區), where there are hip bars, quirky cafes and houses that get progressively more expensive as you get to the very top of Victoria Peak.

The neighborhood of Wan Chai marks the center of the island and includes the famous Causeway Bay (銅鑼灣) shopping area and some famous parks and sports grounds. This is where you'll find Happy Valley horse racing track and the nearby Hong Kong Stadium, where rugby matches are hosted.

The Eastern district starts on the east side of Causeway Bay. It isn't the most interesting part of Hong Kong from a traveler's perspective, but its most famous neighborhood, North Point (北角), has a fair amount of traditional charm.

The Southern district includes everything on the south side of Hong Kong Island. With a sparser population and clusters of mountains, this area is particularly scenic and includes plenty of great beaches and stunning vistas. Some of the best known are Repulse Bay and Big Wave Bay and the towns and villages of Stanley and Aberdeen.

Kowloon

Kowloon is the most crowded area of Hong Kong, while the first or second most crowded neighborhood in the world (depending on the source) is Mong Kok (旺 角). Mong Kok is the northernmost area in the frantic shopping, dining and lodging district of Yau Tsim Mong (油尖旺), named after the three areas it encompasses: Yau Ma Tei (油麻地), Tsim Sha Tsui (尖沙咀) and Mong Kok. Just about all ranges of accomodation can be found here, including some of the most expensive hotels (like the Langham and the Peninsula) and the cheap guesthouses and migrant trader shops of the Chungking Mansions. Yau Tsim Mong

is one of the most enticing areas of the city, but Kowloon has plenty of excitement in each of its five districts.

Just east of Yau Tsim Mong is Kowloon City. Much quieter than Yau Tsim Mong, Kowloon City is a more traditional Chinese area and is home to the site of the Kowloon Walled City, one of the most underappreciated parts of Kowloon. Venture away from Festival Walk – the upscale mall outside of Kowloon Tong MTR station – towards the roads south of Kowloon Walled City Park, and you find yourself on streets with a delicious array of restaurants, including Thai and Vietnam towns. While the large area that is Kowloon City extends to the Harbour near Hung Hum (紅磡) and Whampoa, it is the area north of Prince Edward Street that is considered the cultural heart of Kowloon City.

Farther east are the outskirt districts of Kwun Tong (觀 塘) and Wong Tai Sin (黃大 仙). Wong Tai Sin is home to the famous Wong Tai Sin Temple, but overall these areas are made up mostly of residences, and the farthest edges are home to great swathes of public housing; almost 90% of Wong Tai Sin's residents live in public housing.

New Territories

Farthest out from the city, the New Territories include a few urban areas and housing estates along rolling rural terrain and country parks. There are nine districts that make up the New Territories.

The main cities in the New Territories are Sha Tin (沙田), Yuen Long (元朗), Tuen Mun (屯 門), Tai Po (大 埔) and Sai Kung Town (西貢). Sha Tin (in Sha Tin district) is home to malls and public housing developments, a horse racing track and a theater that often hosts Cantonese opera. East of the urban area of Sha Tin is the Ma On Shan Country Park, and even further east you can find Sai Kung Country Park extending down a strip of land to the sea. This is where some of the most beautiful and secluded beaches in Hong Kong are located. The shore of Sai Kung district is lined with beaches and towns like Clear Water Bay (清水灣), Joss House Bay (大廟灣) and Hebe Haven (白沙灣).

To the west of Sha Tin, Tsuen Wan (荃 灣) and Tuen Mun border the southern tip of Hong Kong's western half. Places like Sham Tseng (深 井) town in Tsuen Wan include some of Hong Kong's tastiest roast goose. Continue down the road, and you arrive in Tuen Mun, where the Castle Peak Bay looks out on Lantau Island.

The three northernmost areas, Yuen Long, Tai Po and North District (北 區), are also three of the least densely populated. These places are known for their old walled cities and are worth a visit.

Islands

The Outlying Islands are all administered under one district called the Islands District (離 島 區). The largest island (larger than Hong Kong Island) is Lantau Island. Because Lantau is mostly country parks, it's a great place for hiking or biking. You can find some excellent beaches and fishing towns here as well, including Mui Wo (梅 窩), Pui O (貝 澳) and Tai O. Lantau also features some of Hong Kong's tallest mountains, which make for particularly rugged hikes. The Po Lin Monastery is alongside Lantau Peak, the tallest mountain on the island.

Film

For years, Hong Kong contained the world's third-largest film industry. The local cinema brings with it a special level of artistry, and the techniques and styles of Hong Kong's filmmaking masters have influenced directors around the world, including some of Hollywood's greatest. Martin Scorsese once said, "Hong Kong Cinema is something you can't duplicate in any way – you couldn't go near John Woo's *The Killer*, for example. My skills as a filmmaker just can't compete with that." Similarly, after watching *Chungking Express*, Quentin Tarantino gushed, "I just started crying. I'm just so happy to love a movie this much."

The cinema that inspired these and other Hollywood greats began in 1913 Hong Kong, when the city's first feature film, *Zhuangzi Tests His Wife*, was made and directed by Lai Man-wai. During this part of the 20th century, the Chinese film industry was actually concentrated in Shanghai, but things began to change when China fell into political turmoil, beginning with the Nationalist Party's (the Kuomintang) banning of martial arts films in 1931. Further problems came during World War II, when the Japanese occupation severely limited the film industry, and little improved after World War II as the Communist Party's stifling and castrating grip on the Chinese film industry subjugated it to nothing more than propaganda pieces that promoted the Party. This led to a massive exodus of artists and filmmakers to Hong Kong, who looked to escape the persecutions of the CCP.

Kung fu

Early Hong Kong films often relied on traditional stories. Cantonese opera stars made the transition into film, and many pictures borrowed stories from opera. One of the earliest bases for movies was *wuxia*, stories about "martial heroes" roaming the earth and using their fighting skills for noble causes. They emphasized the values of righteousness, honor and, in many cases, patriotism, mostly dealing with China's historical struggle against foreign powers and the internal strife of warring factions and warlords.

One of the longest running characters in *wuxia* began in 1949 when Kwan Tak-hing played the role of Wong Fei-hung (1847 – 1925), a real master of *hung gar* kung fu and instructor for Guangdong's militia. Wong became a constant character in *wuxia* and was depicted by Tak-hing in 77 films (later depictions included those by Jackie Chan and Jet Li).

These early Wong Fei-hung ficks sparked an interest in kung fu that was taken up by the Shaw Brothers Studio, which led the way in kung fu films throughout the '60s and '70s.

Notable Shaw Brothers kung fu films: *One-Armed Swordsman* (director: Chang Cheh, 1967); *36th Chamber of Shao Lin* (director: Lau Kar-leung, 1975)

Bruce Lee (李小龍)

By 1960, Bruce Lee had already appeared in 25 films. His father was a Cantonese Opera performer and, before he was two years old, Lee was carried on stage to play an infant in *Golden Gate Girl* (1941). With a history of street fights in Hong Kong, Lee went to the United States in 1959 and began teaching kung fu in California. He took roles in several TV series, most famously playing Kato in *The Green Hornet* from 1966 to '67, but struggled finding work in big Hollywood films. Lee soon returned to Hong Kong, where he got his big break with a new film studio: Golden Harvest.

Formed in 1970 by two Shaw Brothers executives, Golden Harvest allotted actors higher pay and more flexibility than the Shaw Brothers. The new studio started off strong after signing Bruce Lee to a two-film contract, the first of which was the 1971 box office smash hit *The Big Boss*. His next film, *Fist of Fury* (1972), was a turning point for kung fu movies because of its commercial success. In the patriotic tradition of *wuxia*, Bruce Lee fights with Japanese karate students in Shanghai during the Japanese occupation. The film helped the genre transition from scenes focused entirely on sword-fighting to those of hand-to-hand combat.

After Lee's unfortunate and sudden death in 1973 (the same year *Enter the Dragon* was released), Hong Kong entered a period of Bruceploitation. Similar to Mainland China's fake goods industry, Bruceploitation films

made use of actors with appearances similar to Bruce's, gave them names that mirrored his, and based their stories on those of the late actor's films. Among the most notorious Bruce imitators were Bruce Li (Ho Chung-tao), whose hits included *Exit the Dragon, Enter the Tiger* (1976), and Bruce Le (Huang Jian Long), who starred in *Enter the Game of Death* (1978) and *The Clones of Bruce Lee* (1981). The latter picture also included Dragon Lee and Bruce Lai as crime fighters cloned from Bruce Lee's brain tissue.

Jackie Chan (成龍)

Jackie Chan initially worked as a stuntman in several of Lee's films, and his first starring *wuxia* role was actually part of a Bruceploitation film as well: *New Fist of Fury* (1976). In 1978, he played the role of Wong Fei-hung in the hugely popular *Drunken Master*, which was a major box office success in Hong Kong, and established Chan's comedic action style. The 1980s saw Chan first test the waters in Hollywood with little success, though he remained successful domestically with *The Young Master* (1980), *Dragon Lord* (1982), and *Police Story* (1985). *Rumble in the Bronx* (1995) was his first movie of notoriety in the United States, and *Rush Hour* in 1998 catapulted him to international fame.

Triad Films

Another development to come out of *wuxia* was the "heroic bloodshed" style of movies emphasizing loyalty and brotherhood amongst criminals with a code of honor. The extreme choreography of the sword fights and gruesome bloodletting in Chang Cheh's earlier kung fu films like *One-Armed Swordsman* (1967) strongly influenced this burgeoning gangster genre. But as greater China moved away from its feudal past, the modern day warriors began swapping swords for machine guns, and running around on crowded city streets rather than country plains. These became the conerstones of the gangster-focused Triad films.

Director John Woo found some of his earliest

一個傳奇的誕生

INFERNAL AFFAIRS II

Notable triad films: *Triad Election* (director: Johnnie To, 2006); *Infernal Affairs* (directors: Andrew Lau and Alan Mak, 2002); *Long Arm of the Law* (director: Johnny Mak, 1984)

John Woo ultimately became the quintessential heroic bloodshed director, directing *Hard Boiled* (1992) and *The Killer* (1989), which Chow Yun-fat also starred in. Along with these three movies, Chow's most lauded works also include his roles in *City on Fire* (1987) and *Crouching Tiger, Hidden Dragon* (2000).

New Wave

In the 1970s, a number of directors started exploring alternative ways of storytelling and filming, bringing a more artistic feel to screen. These New Wave directors, led by Ann Hui and Allen Fong, also presented a more personal look into their characters, delving into more emotional and philosophical matters.

Ann Hui first came to prominence with her series about Vietnamese refugees that culminated with *Boat People* (1982), a film that would rank eighth of all time on the Hong Kong Film Association's list of best movies. Not shying away from the grisly details, *Boat People* presented a mother who resorts to prostitution to raise her children, who in turn have to scavenge through garbage and dead corpses to look for valuables, all while refugees are targeted by the guns of the coast guard. This kind of honest look at the social issues and personal stories of the time was a hallmark of the New Wave movement.

Allen Fong's film *Ah Ying* (1983) moved away from the darkness of *Boat People*, taking a close look at the life of a budding actress and her relationship with a teacher. Often seen throughout the film outside her drama class, Ah Ying has one of her most notable scenes when she helps her parents at a crowded and noisy fish market. The scene particularly showcases the film's use of natural cinematography, where the smooth and produced style of many other films' camera work is swapped for a bumpy and handheld feel.

These natural methods of cinematography became influential with later directors. In particular, Wong Kar-wai became well-known for his wild use of hand-held cameras. His piece *First Love the Litter on the Breeze* (1997) lightheartedly mocked the New Wave style as it followed one man through a dating video via the point of view of a swaying camera.

Second Wave

Wong Kar-wai actually made his debut in 1988 and is considered by many as the quintessential Second Wave filmmaker. Many

experience working with Cheh as an assistant director on some of his films, and he had already had moderate success directing several kung fu and action movies when, in 1986, New Wave director and producer Tsui Hark provided Woo with the funding for *A Better Tomorrow* (1986). The plot tells of an ex-mobster who is the brother of a rising police officer. After being released from jail, he tries to stay away from crime, but his brother won't forgive him for his actions, and his friends in the Triads won't let him move on with his life. With bullets flying and hard-nosed characters and dialogue, this movie set the standard for Triad films. It was rated by the Hong Kong Film Awards as the second best Chinese movie of all time on their 2005 top 100 list, and singlehandedly launched the careers of John Woo and Chow Yun-fat and the trajectory of the genre.

Notable New Wave films: *Made in Hong Kong* (director: Fruit Chan, 1997); Chungking Express (director: Wong Kar-wai, 1994); *Summer Snow* (女人四十) (director: Ann Hui, 1995)

critics of Wong blasted his work for having nothing actually happen. But Wong was quick to argue that this is exactly the point: most of his films focused more on the inner feelings of characters as they coped with problems of love and identity rather than on wild external storylines. Through discursive plot lines, Wong explored the human psyche, and most of his characters never find true love. Particularly representative of this style is Wong's 1997 *Happy Together*, which ends with one character heading to the airport alone after having broken up with his boyfriend as the song "Happy Together" plays in the background. One of the few Hong Kong films to include a gay relationship, the film took many audiences by surprise in its stirring exploration of the main characters' mindsets as they navigated their homosexual relationship in a less-than-accepting world.

Artistic films of the Second Wave began having some success in the market and were soon attracting top-tier actors. The cast members of Wong's film *Days of Being Wild* (1990) made up an all-star list of the '90's best actors, including Leslie Cheung and Tony Leung (whom Wong worked with in multiple films), as well as Andy Lau, Maggie Cheung, Carina Lau and Jacky Cheung.

Other independent directors like Fruit Chan stuck with little known actors. Chan filmed a number of quirky and humorous ficks, such as 2002's *Public Toilet*, the story of a man who was born in a toilet and who searches toilets of the world looking for his past.

The Golden Era: 1980s-90s

All of these developments in filmmaking came together in the Golden Era of the 1980s and '90s, when elements of different genres merged to create movies that represented the vivid culture of Hong Kong at a time when its economy was booming. From 1960 to 1980, the number of annual films made in Hong Kong jumped from 200 to 300.

Chief among the leaders of the trending New Wavers was Tsui Hark. He debuted with the 1979 piece *The Butterfly Murders,* which portrayed a *wuxia* story through a New Wave aesthetic. His 1980 work *Dangerous Encounters of the First Kind* firmly established him as one of the most controversial filmmakers after it was banned by the government for showing a bombing spree undertaken by high school students.

When he started his production company Film Workshop in 1984, Hark began backing blockbusters that were artistically appealing, including a number of gangster films and kung fu movies. After producing John Woo's films *A Better Tomorrow* and *The Killer,* he soon directed and produced *Once Upon a Time in China* (1991), which cast Jet Li as Wong Fei-hung. The latter spawned a six-film series, the first three of which earned over HK$20 million each.

Between the years 1980 and 2000, 34 of the top 100 Chinese films of all time (as chosen by the Hong Kong Film Awards in 2005) were produced in Hong Kong. That list includes six directed by Wong Kar-wai, five by Tsui Hark and four by Ann Hui. Because the Golden Era in film happened to coincide with the Golden Era in Cantopop music, some of the top movie actors were also the top singers, and the films featured beautiful themes from their performers. Singer-actors like Andy Lau, Jacky Cheung, Leslie Cheung and Anita Mui paired songs with their movies. At the end of *A Better Tomorrow III* (1989) – known in Chinese as *Song of Sunset* – Mui's rendition of "Song of Sunset" plays as she is whisked away from Saigon in a helicopter, dying in her lover's arms.

The 21st Century

Unfortunately, the popularity of Hong Kong movies has seen a notable decline as the

Notable Golden Era films: Days of Being Wild (Wong Kar-wai, 1990); A Chinese Ghost Story (Ching Siu-tung, 1987); Comrades: Almost a Love Story (Peter Chan, 1996)

20th century has progressed into the 21st, though not to the same degree as some more traditional cultural staples, like Cantonese Opera.

In 1993, Hong Kong produced 200 films, but by 2002, that number had fallen to 90, and in 2012, it reached only 53. There are a number of reasons for the decline. Some actors and directors began focusing on Hollywood after they reached fame, while others emigrated before the 1997 handover of Hong Kong to China. The financial problems that came with the Asian financial crisis and Hong Kong's rapid inflation further hurt the film industry, while reforms in Mainland China have opened up Beijing and Shanghai's movie industries, presenting steeper competition in the Asian market.

Cantonese Opera

With a history of over a millenium, opera is the fundamental traditional form of entertainment in China. Actors perform not only singing and acting, but also show off their superb skills in acrobatics and martial arts, offering both a visual and aural sense of entertainment. Each region of China has a somewhat different local style, but they all retain the basic tenets of actors in elaborate and colorful costumes and makeup as they act out traditional Chinese stories. The two most famous forms of opera in China are surely Peking Opera (from Beijing) and Cantonese Opera, the opera of Guangdong and Hong Kong.

Before movies and television came along, Cantonese Opera was the main form of mass entertainment. Although not as popular as before, there are still three theaters in Hong Kong that hold regular plays: the North Point Sunbeam Theatre, the Yau Ma Tei Theatre and the Sha Tin Assembly Hall Theatre. If you come to Hong Kong during a holiday or festival, look out for public celebrations where there are often Cantonese Opera performances.

Cantonese Opera performances usually follow traditional stories that often revolve around ancient scholars and soldiers. Plays fall into two main styles: *mou* (武 ; martial arts) and *man* (文 ; literature and culture). *Mou* focuses on generals and war, and one of this style's most famous stories is "Tale of the Three Kingdoms," based on the period when three warlord-run states fought for control of China. *Man* plays involve scholars and literati and usually delve into poetic themes.

A typical traditional play might be about four hours long and include 10 or 20 fixed tunes, known as *xiao qu* (small songs), that are sung to express events of the story. These fixed tunes are borrowed and reused with different lyrics, and there is a large repertoire of fixed tunes in Cantonese Opera (professional actors must know about 300 by heart). A suitable fixed tune can come from any kind of music and be adapted for Cantonese opera; some tunes in modern operas even come from popular Western music, and this has lead to Cantonese Opera being dubbed an "integrated genre."

Nearly everyone, including the majority of Chinese, find their opera (be it Peking, Cantonese or other) incomprehensible, largely because it utilizes extremely poetic language in antiquated dialects and Classical Chinese. Some theaters include English subtitles on screens, but even the acting can be confusing because there are many symbolic gestures that make up for a limited amount of props and settings.

Despite the elusiveness of the storyline, Cantonese Opera is a beautiful and wonderful experience. If you choose to see a performance, here are some elements to watch for:

Characters – There are four main categories of characters in Cantonese Opera: *sang* (生) represent the men, *daan* (旦) are the women, *zing* (淨) are characters with specially painted faces who often represent gods, and *cao* (丑) are the clowns. The characters within each category are further distinguished by age (young, middle aged, or old, with the middle aged usually representing the major roles) and profession (scholars, soldiers, royalty, or the extremely talented scholar-soldier). Female characters, once played exclusively by men, are now mostly played by women, and some women have even played male military generals. In the 1930s and '40s, Xue Jue-xian emphasized "Six Major Roles": the scholar-soldier (文武生), the beautiful female

Cantonese Opera

main character (正印花旦), the clown (丑生), the soldier (武生), the children (小生) and the secondary female character (二幫花旦). There are other character types, but these are the ones that are most commonly seen.

To identify the characters, you'll want to look out for their particular headwear. Scholars wear black hats with wings protruding on either side, while soldiers wear simple hats and generals wear helmets with tall pheasant feathers coming out like antennae. Unmarried women have their hair in buns. If a character is frustrated or ready to give up, they will often take off their hat.

Makeup – Most of the characters have what is called "white and red face" makeup, which is seen as a white face and pinkish-red makeup that surrounds the eyes and fades out over the rest of the face. You can tell a character is hot tempered if he has a red triangle covering the middle of his forehead starting from between his eyebrows. Eyebrows are emphasized in black, and eyes are surrounded in black makeup in what is called "phoenix eye" (鳳眼) style. Both men and women alike wear bright red lipstick. A completely red face usually indicates someone of extreme loyalty.

Costumes – The costumes are one of the most interesting parts of Cantonese opera. Generally consisting of gowns made of bright fabrics that are ornately adorned with patterns, flowers or dragons, these outfits are tantilizing to view, especially up close. Female characters, in particular princesses and queens, have a spectacular collection of jewels in their headwear.

Music – The band uses various kinds of traditional Chinese instruments, including several variations of Chinese zithers and violins. Some of the most common traditional Chinese stringed instruments used are the *er xian* (二弦), *san xian* (三弦), *yue qin* (月琴) and *er hu* (二胡). These instruments can often sound high pitched because they are usually tuned to a very high register. The *er hu* in particular is generally felt to be the most haunting and emotional of China's traditional instrument repetoire.

The three major styles of singing in Chinese opera are *ping hou* (平喉), *zi hou* (子喉), and *da hou* (大喉). *Ping hou* is known as the "real voice," *zi hou* is a falsetto voice used more often by females, and *da hou* is a "big voice" that combines *ping hou* and falsetto and is more often used by males.

Music

Classical

Hong Kong boasts a number of talented orchestras. The highest-regarded of them is the Hong Kong Philharmonic Orchestra, and you can also find the Hong Kong Sinfonietta, the Hong Kong Chamber Orchestra, the City Chamber Orchestra, the Hong Kong Festival Orchestra and the Metropolitan Youth Orchestra.

The Hong Kong Philharmonic Orchestra performs most Friday and Saturday nights at the Concert Hall of the Hong Kong Cultural Centre. Tickets start at about HK\$120 to HK\$160. With 150 or so performances a year, they also have shows from internationally renowned conductors. The Hong Kong Cultural Centre hosts brilliant musicians all year long.

The Sinfonietta is the second most frequently performing orchestra in Hong Kong. It puts on over 30 shows per year, nearly all of them at the Hong Kong City Hall Theatre. Along with traditional symphonies, they also have specially themed and age-group oriented performances, such as the charmingly named "Good Music for Babies."

The Hong Kong Chamber Orchestra performs about four to six large scale independent performances a year, and they also put on some collaborative and small scale performances that are set inside intimate community center settings and are usually free.

Among Hong Kong's domestic soloists, composer and pianist Man-Ching Donald Yu is a standout. His compositions are premiered by himself and others at universities and concert halls throughout Hong Kong.

Cantopop

Cantopop is the most popular genre of music in Hong Kong and, in many ways, the standard for popular music in China. The music takes influence from jazz, rock, R&B and lounge music and mixes them with Chinese memes. Though it has branched out to include different styles and fast paced songs, it has traditionally consisted mostly of ballads, which still make up many of the genre's best songs.

Cantopop began its rise to prominence in the 1960s. Previously, Chinese popular music had been dominated by opera and *shidaiqu* (時代曲), an early relative of Cantopop with a more traditional sound. Cantopop owes much of its early success to Teresa Teng (邓丽君), who was a leader in popularizing the new style of Chinese pop music throughout Asia and, although many of her songs were in Mandarin, she still had a major impact in Hong Kong. Dropping out of high school to begin singing, this Taiwanese legend warmed people's hearts around the world with her sweet but strong ballads. She sang in six languages: Mandarin, Cantonese, Taiwanese, Hokkien, Japanese, Indonesian and English. Her most famous song, "The Moon Represents My Heart," (月亮代表我的心) remains one of the best-known songs in China to this day.

In Hong Kong, Roman Tam also had a heavy hand in the development of Cantopop. He formed his first band in 1967, and shortly thereafter went solo and dominated the scene, becoming known far and wide as "the Godfather of Cantopop." The genre was further developed throughout the 1970s when TV dramas began airing in Hong Kong and lending their theme songs to the Cantopop theater. Other stars of that era included Sammy Hui, Alan Tam and Jenny Tseng, all of whom helped launch Hong Kong entertainment into its Golden Era. Perhaps the most representative of that era, however, are Anita Mui and Leslie Cheung, who were known and loved for their incredible life stories as much as their amazing singing and acting. They both left indelible impacts on Hong Kong society and culture.

Anita Mui (梅艷芳)

Anita was nervous as she sang "The Windy Season" at the 1982 New Talent Singing competition in Hong Kong.

Halfway through the song, she heard a bell signaling her to stop.

"How long have you been singing?" the judge asked.

"More than ten years," she said.

"And how old are you?"

"Nineteen," she responded.

There was a stunned gasp from the judges, who wondered how such a young talent could have been singing almost all her life. They gave her the highest score of the 3,000 contestants, starting her off on the career that would establish her as "the Madonna of Asia."

Anita Mui began singing for money when she

was about eight years old to help her family survive. The youngest of four children, her poor single mother worked while she and her sister Ann Mui sang around the city at places like the Li Yuan Amusement Park, clubs and restaurants, and on the street.

Anita eventually dropped out of school to support her family, which attracted derision from some during her early years. Many today feel that this helped prepare her to become one of the hardest workers in show-biz, a woman who would set records by performing concerts for over 30 consecutive nights on multiple occasions. Known as the "ever-changing Anita Mui" for the elaborate and gaudy dresses she characterictically wore on stage, Mui developed a sassy personality. She sold over 10 million records, including her 1985 album *Bad Girl*, which became 8X platinum certified (by Hong Kong standards, which means 400,000 copies sold). But she wasn't just known for her success in singing and acting, she was also applauded for her charity work and activism, particularly for her heavy donations to care centers for the elderly and her organization of a SARS relief concert in 2003. She died that same year of cervical cancer at the age of 40.

Leslie Cheung (張國榮)

Leslie Cheung was the youngest of ten children. Similar to Mui, his parents divorced when he was young and he lived through a very troubled childhood, making his pairing and friendship with Ms Mui particularly fitting. The two would co-star in four movies and countless concerts throughout their careers.

Unlike Mui, however, Cheung grew up in a middle class family and was educated in England from age 13. Working as a bartender during his 20s, he landed his first record deal in 1977 after placing second in a contest. But it wasn't until 1982, when he joined Capital Artists (the same year Mui joined), that his career really took off. By the time he was named Asia's Biggest Superstar at the 2000 CCTV-MTV Music Honors, he had already won eight Radio Television Hong Kong (RTHK) Top 10 song awards.

Anita and Leslie's careers seemed to mirror each other: besides all of the projects they did together both stars retired within one year of each other (both returning a year later), and both of them tragically perished in 2003. Within months of Anita's death, Leslie jumped from the 24th floor of the Mandarin Oriental Hotel after struggling with depression for years.

Three Decades of Cantopop

In the late 1980s and '90s, four big stars emerged in the Cantopop scene: Andy Lau, Aaron Kwok, Jacky Cheung and Leon Lai. Together, they are known as the "Four Heavenly Kings of Cantopop." Andy Lau, the biggest star of the four, got his start as a television drama actor after graduating from TVB's artist training school. From 1985 to 2005, he acted in over 100 films, which earned a total of over HK$1.7 billion, making him the most bankable box office star in Hong Kong history and leading many to brand him as representative of

Leslie Cheung and Anita Mui

what they feel is an overly-commercialized and prepackaged industry.

With the rise of Mainland China's economy, many Hong Kong stars have come to dominate the Mainland Chinese music market. Conversely, many stars from China and elsewhere in Asia have come to Hong Kong to launch their careers. The Beijing-born star Faye Wong got her start in Hong Kong, eventually becoming maniacally popular throughout China and winning the Asia Pacific Most Popular Hong Kong Artists award six times between 1993 and 2000.

Some of the most popular stars in the post-2000s include Kelly Chen, Leo Ku, Joey Yung, Miriam Yeung, and Eason Chen. Eason Chen is especially noted by his fans for his expertise in multiple instruments, including the piano, bass guitar, guitar and drums, and for writing a fair amount of his own songs (both of these qualities contrast with the majority of modern Cantopop stars).

Today, Cantopop concerts at big arenas like the Hong Kong Coliseum or the Star Hall are characterized by the swathes of rabid fans swaying glow sticks as much as by the artists and performances they host.

> Classic Anita Mui Songs: "Woman Flowers" (女人花), "Bad Girl" (坏女孩), "Song of Sunset" (夕阳之歌), "I'll Walk Alone" (孤身走我路)
> Classic Leslie Cheung Songs: "Monica, Past Love" (當年情), "Silence is Golden" (沉默是金), "Closer" (貼身)
> Classic Cheung Films: *A Better Tomorrow*, *Farewell My Concubine*, *Days of Being Wild*
> Classic Mui Films: *July Rhapsody*, *Eighteen Springs*
> Films Featuring Both: *Rouge*

Live Cantopop in Hong Kong

Cantopop idols these days perform in huge arenas on international tours. If you're interested in seeing a big concert in Hong Kong you can check out the websites for the Hong Kong Coliseum at **www.lcsd.gov.hk/CE/Entertainment/Stadia/HKC** and the Star Hall (aka KITEC) at **www.kitec.com.hk** to see what shows are coming up during your visit.

Cantopop in Hong Kong is not only limited to big artists in massive venues, however. Catching singers and aspiring stars singing old favorites at lounges and on the streets is one of the many joys of Cantopop in Hong Kong. It may be a bit more difficult than when Anita Mui was a youth, as these so-called "lunch singers" have become fewer and fewer since the 1980s and '90s, but there are still a few old style lounge bars on the street Anita once sang on where you can find the Cantopop hopeful and nostalgic.

One of the best options is the vibrant night market Temple Street (pg 71) in the working class neighborhood Yau Ma Tei. It was here that aspiring artists used to sing on makeshift stages and perform Cantonese Operas, and a few aging men and women still perform these street style Cantonese Operas outside the Yau Ma Tei post office most nights at 20:00. Along the side of the street there are outdoor karaoke bars set up under tents, and crowds gather here between 20:00 and 23:00 for cheap drinks and to sing HK$20 songs. The amiable owner Hao Hao at the southernmost karaoke bar loves to have foreigners sing at her place. She has a small selection of 1950s-'80s English songs (Sinatra, Beatles, John Denver, etc) and employs one English speaking man who can help you set up your songs. He and the guests are usually happy to sing along with you or help you sing a Chinese song if you can read characters.

Further up the street, north of the Tin Hau Temple, is a stretch of lounge bars strung with Christmas lights where women sing songs from a stage similar to the clubs of old. There is a cover charge of around HK$20 (drinks are also around HK$20) and you should be prepared to tip the singers you enjoy. Tips are how the singers earn most of their take, and average donations range from HK$20 if you really like a song to HK$50 if you have a request.

Rock & Indie

Few institutions have done as much to promote rock in Hong Kong as The Underground HK. The group hosts rocking local shows at various venues throughout the city each weekend. Some of the more frequent venues they have used include Backstage Live and The Live House, where you can keep an eye out for their CD compilations and newsletter.

The scene showcases a good variety of local music through bands like My Little Airport (indie pop), King Ly Chee (hardcore), Dear Jane (punk), DP (hard rock/stoner rock) and Laura Palmer (noise pop). See what shows are coming up online at The Underground's website (**www.undergroundhk.com**) or visit some of the venues in Lan Kwai Fong and the Wan Chai area. Among them, the Fringe Club, the Wanch, the Hard Rock Cafe and Sense 99 are known for hosting rock and indie shows. Check out our listings on page 218 for music venues.

One crazy band to check out is Lazy Mutha Fuka (aka LMF). Their music takes everything from punk and metal to hip hop (and more) and synthesizes it together into something uniquely awesome. If you're lucky enough to find one of their shows you won't be let down. Some of the original members are now performing in a hip hop group called 24Herbs.

Traditional Chinese Music

Traditional Chinese music, such as that played on the *er hu* and *gu qin*, doesn't have much of a presence in modern day Hong Kong. Your best bet is often to catch beggars playing Chinese zithers on the street, and if you catch one (they are often quite skilled) and stop for a listen you should drop them a HK buck or two. The Hong Kong Chinese Orchestra is the city's main traditional music troupe, and you can catch their performances at the Hong Kong Cultural Centre, the City Hall Theatre and other venues a few times a month.

Economy

Hong Kong's economy is one of the most dynamic out there. With low taxes and a low regulatory burden, Hong Kong has been rated as the freest economy in the world by the Heritage Institute's Index of Economic Freedom for 17 straight years.

With no import or capital gains taxes, Hong Kong's economy is driven by its trade and finance industries, which are enhanced by its relations with Mainland China.

Hong Kong is primarily a service-based economy, with services making up a whopping 93% of its GDP and 88% of its total employment. Only 1.6% of the city's GDP and 3% of employment are manufacturing based, a massive contrast with Mainland China. The so-called Four Key Industries – financial services, trading and logistics, tourism, and professional services – constitute more than half the GDP, with trade as the largest of the four, employing 774,400 people and contributing 25% of the city's total GDP.

Hong Kong practices an economic policy called "positive non-intervention" that was introduced by Finance Secretary John James Cowperthwaite in the 1960s and '70s. It is essentially a hands-off policy, somewhat similar to laissez-faire economics, but the government will intervene at times when it feels intervention will generate an advantage for the economy.

Cowperthwaite explained his policy thus:

"If we cannot rely on the judgment of individual businessmen, taking their own risks, we have no future anyway... I still believe that, in the long run, the aggregate of the decisions of individual businessmen, exercising individual judgment in a free economy, even if often mistaken, is likely to do less harm than the centralized decisions of a Government; and certainly the harm is likely to be counteracted faster."

In practice, this means that in addition to low taxes and limited regulation, Hong Kong also has low government spending, with limited social spending and no military. Government spending only makes up 21% of GDP, and the national debt is only 32% of GDP. To compare, in 2012 the United States debt was 106% of GDP and the European Union's was 87%.

Many of the drawbacks to Hong Kong's highly competitive market include rapid inflation, unsatisfactory secondary education institutions, a small market size and lagging innovation. Land prices are a huge driving force in causing inflation in Hong Kong, which doubled in only three years from 2008 to 2011. Although some of Hong Kong's universities, like Hong Kong University, are among the best in Asia, the city actually has a university shortage, and most high school graduates go abroad for college.

Trade

In 2012 trade income in Hong Kong totalled a massive US$947 billion, and only $7.5 billion of that came from locally-produced goods. An impressive US$435 billion came from re-exportation, which not only suggests the savvy of the city's export businesspeople, but gives a nod to the city's advantageous export policies, which particularly include little to no import tarrifs.

Re-exportation occurs when goods are imported to a port with favorable trade policies and then re-exported elsewhere to take advantage of those policies. Over half of Hong Kong's annual re-exports go to Mainland China, where there are high import tariffs. Machinery, appliances, telecommunications equipment and clothing make up the bulk of the re-exports. The Comprehensive Economic Partnership Agreement (CEPA) Hong Kong signed with China in 2003 has done a great deal to make trade less restrictive between the two partners.

Services were also exported for US$128 billion in 2011. Merchandising, transportation and travel each made up about one-fourth of the exported services that year as well.

Finance

Hong Kong had long been home to the fifth largest stock exchange in the world, although it is now ranked sixth or seventh after being overtaken by Shanghai's Stock Exchange. It has been one of the world leaders in terms of IPOs in recent years, in large part due to Mainland Chinese companies going public. In 2009, it was the top exchange for IPO fund raising, powered by the success of the Agricultural Bank of China's US$22 billion joint listing with the Hong Kong and Shanghai Stock Exchanges, then the largest IPO in the world. Hong Kong was also the number one exchange for IPO funds in 2011, if you include a major joint listing it did with the London Stock Exchange.

As with trade, Hong Kong's financial industry is also heavily reliant on Mainland China. About 66% of the IPOs in Hong Kong in the first half of 2012 were Mainland Chinese companies. Each of China's four major banks made IPOs on the Hong Kong Stock Exchange, three of which were joint affairs with the Shanghai Stock Exchange and were among the top ten largest IPOs in history.

> **Economic Info: GDP (PPP) per capita**: $51,946 (8th highest, 2012, World Bank). **Median income**: HK$20,700 per month (2012, Information Services Department of HK gov). **Unemployment rate**: 3.3% (2012, IMF). **Gini coefficient,** a measure of inequality: 0.53 (2007, World Bank).

Tourism

Tourism is the fastest-growing industry in Hong Kong. While employing 6% of Hong Kong's workers from 2000 to 2009, it accounted for 28% of all new jobs created in the city. Perhaps the largest driving factor is Mainland tourists, who still need to apply for a special permit to visit Hong Kong and come annually in great swarms and colored hat-clad tour groups. Restrictions have been greatly loosened since the signing of CEPA, which created the Individual Visit Scheme. Since then, Mainland tourism has shot up to over 20 million visitors a year and makes up a stunning 70% of all of Hong Kong tourism. Mainland Chinese love to go shopping in Hong Kong, where no import tax makes high end fashion and technology purchases much cheaper than in the Mainland.

The government continues to take actions to try to increase Hong Kong's tourism appeal. They are continuously redeveloping areas and turning historical buildings into preserved shopping centers. Currently, there is a large cruise ship port under construction near the airport, and it seems only a matter of time before Hong Kong becomes a major cruise destination.

Distress on the Horizon?

Concerns about Hong Kong's economic future have been sparked by a slowdown in GDP growth in recent years and a decline in certain standards of economic competitiveness. Recently, some investors have been moving capital away from the territory. One important example of this is Li Ka-shing (李 嘉 誠), the 85-year-old chairman of Cheung Kong Holdings and Hutchinson Whampoa, whose US$31 billion net worth makes him the richest man in Asia. His companies, which have controlled about 15% of the market cap of the Hong Kong Stock exchange, do business in plastics manufacturing, real estate, retail, assets trading, ports, electricity and internet. Cheung Kong Holdings has recently been hit hard by a slowdown in housing sales, which fell sharply in 2013 as prices hit record highs and a new tax was introduced on some home purchases.

In reaction to the soaring prices, Li Ka-shing has been investing huge sums outside of Hong Kong and selling some of his Hong Kong properties. Since 2010, Cheung Kong Holdings has invested more than HK$140 billion (US$18 billion) in Europe, which now accounts for more of the company's revenue than Hong Kong and China combined. Similarly, Hutchinson Whampoa invested HK$7.6 billion in Europe over the first half of 2013, compared to HK$1.4 billion in Hong Kong. Meanwhile, Li is trying to sell PARKnSHOP, Hong Kong's second largest grocery store.

Multiple factors are causing the investment slowdown in Hong Kong and Li Ka-shing's

Li Ka-shing (李 嘉 誠) is the richest man in Asia. The 85-year-old chairman of Cheung Kong Holdings and Hutchinson Whampoa has a US$31 billion net worth.

westward investment shift. While some are looking at Li's actions as a sign of changes in Hong Kong's economy, others caution against reading too much into investment strategies in the short term. Indeed, the move to Europe might reflect Europe's economic situation as much as it reflects Hong Kong's. As Phillip Securities director Louis Wong put it, "They've taken advantage of the downturn in Europe to invest in projects with good returns."

Expats in Hong Kong

They call it "Asia's World City," but while Hong Kong does indeed have much diversity among its residents, it is a rather segregated city. According to an informal survey by HSBC (Hong Kong and Shanghai Banking Corporation), 80% of expats in Hong Kong socialize almost entirely with other expats. On any given night at the bars in SoHo you often feel like you are in the United Kingdom.

Expats in Hong Kong come from many different countries and spend much of their time in communities with fellow expats of their own ethnicity or nationality. According to the HSBC ratings, Hong Kong is a great place for expats because of its relatively high salaries, widespread use of English and well-developed infrastructures. Only two of those benefits apply to travelers, however, who only get to see the high prices that come with high salaries.

In 2011, a record number of work visas were approved for foreign expats looking for opportunities in Hong Kong. 30,557 people were given work visas for white collar jobs based on having skills and a job offer that met minimum standards. In addition, some 280,000 people were allowed over as domestic workers, and there are even more who do business under other visa programs.

Filipinos and Indonesians make up the largest populations of expats. Citizens of both countries living and working in Hong Kong number over 130,000. Westerners comprise a minority of the expat population in Hong Kong at less than 30,000, and thousands of them have become Hong Kong citizens over the years. Brits make up the largest of the Western nationalities, with Americans coming in a close second.

The rest of the expat population comes from Africa, with around 20,000 coming from a scattering of African countries, though Ghana and Nigeria top the list. Many of them engage in trade, importing and exporting commodities between Hong Kong and their home countries, and some 5% of them are refugees.

European and American expats generally like to hang out in the bars in the Mid-Levels areas of Lan Kwai Fong and SoHo. Many venues are almost entirely filled with Westerners. SoHo means South of Hollywood Road, so if you follow the Mid-Levels Escalators up to Hollywood Road, you'll be in the "Gweilo Ghetto," as some have come to calling it – the "Foreigner Ghetto."

The bars along Shelley Street, which the escalator follows after passing Hollywood Road, and the bars just north of Hollywood Road in Lan Kwai Fong, are full of Central bankers and young tourists partying all night. SoHo, along with Lockhart Road in Wan Chai, is a good place to watch a cricket or rugby match in a British pub.

The Mid-Levels is also a haven for foreigner real estate. The expat-centered real estate company Square Foot estimated that 45% of the flats in SoHo are occupied by foreigners.

Hong Kong Island was where the British developed first, so it has remained more popular for expats than Kowloon. Central is the home of government and finance, while the south side of Hong Kong Island is also a popular place for expats, particularly the town of Stanley, which has an abundance of nice European restaurants that many have compared to the French Riviera. Stanley's beaches, and those to the north around Repulse Bay and to the east at Shek O, are natural habitats for expats on the weekend. Housing here is highly sought after, but only available for the rich or employees of the rich. Many high level executives with multinational firms are put up here among the beachfront properties.

Some expats tire of the crowded, noisy life in downtown and want to live away from the bustle, which has lead to the ballooning popularity of a few areas in the New Territories among expats. Among the biggest draws is Sai Kung, a former fishing town just south of the beautiful Sai Kung and Plover

Cove Country Parks. There you'll find some very nice seafood restaurants and great hiking trails, as well as beaches within easy access. It's good for a weekend trip, and housing is still cheaper than it is in Central.

Two of the most popular expat island destinations, Discovery Bay on Lantau and Yung Shue on Lamma Island, offer examples of the relative diversity of Hong Kong's island communities. While Discovery Bay is especially coveted by families with children for its resort-like feel – its suburban streets lined with expensive hotels, bayside shopping malls and plenty of palm trees – Lamma Island is for known for its hippie and bohemian populations. Far less developed than Hong Kong Island and lacking in Discovery Bay-style shopping malls, Lamma Island is only accessible by ferry and has some of the most stunningly beautiful beaches and landscapes in the city.

Though Discovery Bay has little to offer tourists, other places on Lantau Island are great for tourism and are popular with expats.

Religion

Religion has played a very significant role in shaping Hong Kong. The British first brought freedom of religion to the territory under their Basic Law, and through the melting pot of cultures and peoples that have come to Hong Kong, the city has seen a great variety of spiritualities come through its doors.

Though religion still plays a major role in the lives of many Hong Kongers – something evidenced by its hundreds of active temples and spiritual sites – strict adherence to specific faiths has declined in recent decades as the city has become one of the posterchildren of China's modern face. In fact, according to the US Department of State, 57% of Hong Kong's citizens do not follow any religion. The remaining 43% constitute believers from Taoism to Hinduism, with around 22% of the city's residents telling surveyors that religion was an important part of their daily lives.

Here are a few of the major religions you'll find in Hong Kong.

Taoism

Taoism, a one-time philosophy examining the Universe and humanity's relationship to nature, has seen a great deal of Buddhist influence over its history. What began as a contemplation method concerned simply with the "Tao," or the "Way," (i.e. the nature of the Universe) eventually evolved into a monastic system through a meld with certain aspects of Buddhist doctrine. The Taoism of yesteryear, marked by hermits and secretive wise men and women searching for enlightenment through thought, meditation and elixirs, is now seen mostly in the form of monk-filled temples chanting around statues of immortals.

Around one million Hong Kong residents consider themselves Taoist, and the city is full of temples dedicated to those who achieved enlightenment and became immortals, Taoism's version of Buddhas and bodhisattvas. Some major Taoist institutions to look out for are the Yuen Yuen Institute in Tsuen Wan and various Man Mo temples around the city. Taoist institutes in Hong Kong are well known for participating in or creating programs to assist the needy.

Buddhism

The largest religion in China, Buddhism is a direct import from India. Focused on reaching nirvana (or enlightenment), through meditation, and a strict lifestyle that avoids worldly vices and adamantly embraces respect for life, Buddhism is well known for its peaceful and compassionate image. Most believers practice vegetarianism, and the strongest practitioners focus their meditation on peace and compassion for all other life. Buddhism takes many forms and has many sects; in China the most prevalent is the Chan sect, which is known as Zen in Japan and the West.

More than one million Hong Kongers claimed to be Buddhist in 2010, a number that trumps the Taoist population by only a small margin. However, the presence of Buddhism does seem to take the day in Hong Kong, and it can be felt in nearly every corner of the city, from the beautiful Chi Lin Nunnery in Kowloon to the famous Tian Tan Buddha of the Po Lin Monastery on Lantau Island. Nearly all Buddhist organizations in Hong Kong have a strong devotion to social welfare programs and assistance.

Confucianism

Less of a religion than a philosophy, Confucianism developed as a moral code originally meant to curb the disgraces of government leaders and realign society with a reverence for elders and proper conduct. Its spiritual side came from the deep respect it pays to the dead and to the cosmos. The sage Confucius, born in the Shandong city of Qufu, began professing his lessons from under an apricot tree to a small number of students over 2,500 years ago, and today the social tenets of his philosophy have become the backbone to nearly all modern Chinese beliefs. Familial piety and an emphasis on being (at least on the surface) ethically upstanding – the foundation of modern Chinese culture – owe their strength to Confucius and his influence.

Though many Confucian buildings in Hong Kong and China are called "temples," their spiritual side usually consists of little more than a veneration of Confucius and Chinese ancestors. Confucian institutes in Hong Kong are more involved in education and upholding the ideals of the philosophy, which is why many Confucian institutes in Hong Kong are aimed at educating youth.

Islam

Islam is believed to have entered China as early as the 8th century via the Silk Road. While much of the Islamic influence found in the country can be seen in the north and the northwest, particularly around the area from Shaanxi to Xinjiang, it has had a strong presence in Hong Kong as well. The city's first mosque, Jamia Mosque, was built in 1840 and originally served Punjabi Muslims

who had been recruited as a police force. It is generally agreed that Islam became a part of Hong Kong culture around this time.

Today, the city is home to around 220,000 practicing Muslims, and the number is growing. Including the original Jamia Mosque, the city now boasts six mosques in total, as well as a number of Islamic organizations.

Christianity

The earliest records of Christianity in Hong Kong came with the British in 1841. That year, both Catholicism and Protestantism established congregations in the city, which have since grown moderately to 353,000 and 480,000, respectively. Both, like Buddhist and Taoist organizations, are deeply involved in community and social welfare programs throughout the city and have presences in government and education.

Mormonism also has a healthy following in Hong Kong, with around 22,500 registered members (though only 5,500 are estimated to be active practitioners).

Hong Kongers in Their Own Words

We asked a few Hong Kongers – some natives, some transplants – what it's like to live here and why you should come.

Jason
34
Hong Konger

Food represents Hong Kong culture because you can have Chinese food, Western food, Indian food or just about anything else to eat here. Hong Kong's great mix and cultures is well represented in our cuisine, but the city is still so much more than just food. It's energy and vitality, hospitality and flashiness.

My father opened this wine shop in the Chungking Mansions in 1961. It was a luxury housing complex back then. Now it has changed so much, filled with immigrants and migrant workers and cheap hostels. During the '80s the Indians and Pakistanis came, and they opened all these small food shops and restaurants serving halal food. This place seems to get more interesting and colorful by the day.

Chen Li,
49
Hong Konger

Sunny, 15, Hong Konger

Hong Kong is really exciting. Life is so fast-paced in this well-developed city: within this international shopping and eating paradise you can find just about anything you want.

Wu Sitong, 28, Mainland Chinese

I found a job and moved my family here a few years ago for a better life. We wanted to escape the pollution and food safety scandals of the Mainland and enjoy a more open system. I love all the cultural events we have access to here, whether it's some Western thing like horse racing and cricket or an open discussion in the media, and there is plenty of traditional Chinese culture here that helps us feel right at home. It will be a great place to raise my child – once she's born that is!

Andreas, 25, German

If you want to learn authentic kung fu, come to Hong Kong, the home of Bruce Lee, Jackie Chan and Yip Man. I began studying in Germany, but then I found out that my master was a fraud, like so many others who just study for a few months then go abroad to start up a school – it's not the real thing. Finally, I just went for it and came to Hong Kong where I found this school, and now I am taught by one of the legendary Yip Man's former students. Awesome!

Emma, 30, Australian

Hong Kong's political atmosphere is very exciting these days. There's always conflict, a protest, or some kind of march going on. So when I saw a job offer at an English-language Hong Kong newspaper, I jumped at the opportunity. For travellers here, all I can say is you never know what's going to happen – and that's not just in politics. Things are changing everyday.

Theophilus, 24, Ghanaian

I first came to Hong Kong for study, and now I'm looking for a job. I like the city's stable economy and internationalism, but it's not that easy for Africans to find jobs here, unless, of course, you know someone in the trading industry.

Margaret, 33, British

It's almost like I never left home. These bars in Lan Kwai Fong and SoHo are made up of almost all foreigners – most of them British – and they've always got cricket on the tube. There's a really exciting party scene here at night, and during the day, drinking afternoon tea makes me feel like I'm back in London.

Chris, 40, British

I was nervous about moving abroad at this stage in life, but the company I work for was expanding to Asia. They sent me over and gave me a great set up, so I figured, why not? It turned out to be a lot easier than I expected. There are plenty of English speakers here – something I was very worried about – and there are plenty foreign grocery stores to make the transition easier. At the same time, it's still easy to experience different cultures, especially in the Kowloon street markets.

Milton, 22, American

There's just something about Hong Kong culture that drew me in like a magnet. I watched so many Hong Kong movies growing up, and recently I've discovered Cantopop, one of the most enjoyable and fascinating types of music I've ever known. So, I came here right after graduating and just floated around the city for a while, immersing myself in this unique city. Hong Kong does have a special feel in the small shops, tea and food halls and karaoke bars, but I do wish I had been here 20 or 30 years ago during the Golden Era of Cantopop.

Getting Prepared

Climate

Hong Kong has a humid subtropical climate, making it hot and muggy in summer and mild in winter. During the summer there are occasional rains, and you should be aware of typhoons. The best times to visit are the fall months between October and November when the weather is mild, sunny and dry, and the spring months of March and April, which see mild temperatures and sporadic showers.

Spring

The weather in spring is cool, humid and somewhat unstable. Weather can change from day to day, and you'll get plenty of cloud cover. The average high temperature in

March starts at 21°C (70°F) and rises to 24°C (84°F) by May. The amount of rain gradually picks up as well, starting with a monthly average of 67 mm in March and then rising to 317 mm by May. By the time May comes around, the rainy season has hit full throttle.

Summer

Summer is hot and humid, with average highs of over 30°C (86°F) each month and average lows of 26°C (79°F) or above. The average rainfall each month is over 300 mm, meaning that summer is the full on rainy season. Typhoon season is also in full force. The torpor of summer, with its wet, suffocating heat, can make outside activities unbearable

Typhoon Season

Typhoon season starts in May and ends in November. If the warning reaches level 8, public buildings and public transit in affected areas might close, though, typhoons rarely cause major problems. Modern buildings can withstand typhoon winds, and the streets of downtown are shielded from winds by the buildings. Many people remain out and about when the level 3 typhoon signals are up, and sometimes scheduled protests are even held during the storms.

Typhoon Signal	Signal Name	Meaning
1	Stand-by (戒備)	A typhoon or high winds are blowing around the vicinity of Hong Kong
3	Strong winds (強風)	A typhoon or high winds are expected to affect the city and persist
8	Gale or storm force winds (烈風 或暴風)	Storm force winds are blowing. Signal 8 is accompanied by a direction indicting which quadrant of Hong Kong is primarily affected. Government buildings, public transit and most private businesses close.
9	Increasing gale- or storm-force winds (烈風或暴風風力增強)	The storm is getting stronger
10	Hurricane (颶風)	A typhoon directly descends on Hong Kong. This rarely happens, but it is very dangerous, and the damage can be serious

great time to hit the beach and cool off in the ocean, and you can find a lot of discounts around town.

Fall

Autumn has the best climate, particularly October and November. While it's still shorts-and-T-shirt weather, it rarely gets uncomfortably hot and stays relatively dry (rainfall is about half that of the summer). By October, the average high and low are 28°C (82°F) and 23°C (73°F), falling by about ten degrees in November.

Winter

Winters are dry and cool with volatile temperatures. It can fall to 0°C (32°F) when northern winds come in, but more often it stays above 20°C (68°F). The average winter low hovers around 15°C (59°F) from December through February, while the average high flirts at 20°C (68°F). Rainfall is the lowest of the year during this time.

FYI

What to Bring

What you need to bring ultimately depends on what you plan on doing. Usual travel items like cameras, books and e-book readers, water bottles and toiletries are important. If you plan to buy souvenirs, it's a good idea to bring an empty duffel bag to transport the loot home. An inflatable pillow is useful on a long flight, and earplugs and eyeshades could be lifesavers if you're staying in a noisy hostel or are a light sleeper. Lastly, throw in some cold/flu medicine, some pain medicine (e.g. aspirin) and something for an upset stomach, just in case you come down with something and you're not feeling well enough to navigate the Chinese pharmacy.

Customs

According to customs regulations, those 18 years or older are allowed to bring one litre of alcohol (the bottle must be unopened and the seal unbroken) that is 30% or more alcohol by volume, and either 19 cigarettes, one cigar or 25 grams of tobacco products. Prohibited items include (of course) narcotics and weapons, as well as plants and animals (you will need a permit if you plan to bring

a plant or your dog). Finish your fruit and veggies before you arrive, otherwise you will need to declare them at customs.

Vaccines

For your own safety, you should have all routine vaccinations up to date before traveling. Also, travelers to Hong Kong are recommended by the CDC to get Hepatitis A and Typhoid vaccinations. Such sicknesses can be transmitted through contaminated food and water.

Hepatitis B is recommended for people who might have sexual relations with a new partner, get a tattoo or have other kinds of medical procedures. Rabies is not a major problem in Hong Kong, but for people who are going to be spending a lot of time in rural areas, a rabies vaccine might not be a bad idea.

Smoking

Smoking is illegal in almost all public places, including privately-owned businesses and restaurants. People often smoke on the street, but there are heavy fines if you smoke in parks or outdoor places where smoking is explicitly banned.

Useful Smart-phone Apps

Here are a number of apps for smartphones that will come in handy during your Hong Kong trip:

MTR Mobile

Cost: FREE
This free app by the MTR Corporation has a map of the subway system and station information.

Hong Kong Taxi Translator

Cost: $0.99
This app translates street names into Chinese so that you can show your driver.

Dining Concepts

Cost: FREE
Dining Concepts allows you to find and make reservations at some of Hong Kong's nicer restaurants.

Open Rice

Cost: FREE
An app that includes a large directory of Hong Kong (and Mainland China) restaurants and reviews. The listings and reviews are in

English as well as Chinese.

Openbar HK

Cost: FREE
A great app that helps you find bars and lists promos and happy hour deals.

Momo (陌陌)

Cost: FREE
A fun app for meeting local people, Momo displays other users that are in your vicinity and lets you chat with them.

Cyberable

Cost: FREE
An app by Cyberable.net that can assist those with various disabilities.

Phones

If you want to use a phone in Hong Kong and avoid hefty overseas roaming charges, you can buy a local SIM card or rent a phone that can use international cards.

Rental Phones

For HK$68 (US$8.75) per day, you can rent an Android phone from Handy with unlimited local and international calls and have it delivered to your hotel. Reserve one today at **www.handy.travel/hk/en/**.

Of course, if you just need to call family and friends every once in a while, Skype is a free choice for voice and video chatting and also offers affordable rates for calling other people's phones.

Local SIM Cards

If you just want to make local calls you can purchase a local SIM card from some hostels and hotels or from the Chungking Mansions mall. Calling prices are very cheap, so if you charge it with HK$20 it should last you for a week. You can't make international calls on a typical local card.

Electrical Outlets

Electrical outlets in Hong Kong are not compatible with standard American, European or Chinese outlets. Converters are usually provided by hotels and hostels and are available for cheap in convenience stores, electronics stores and malls, such as the Chungking Mansions.

Money

Hong Kong uses the Hong Kong Dollar, written with either the HK$ or the $. It is issued by three different banks, two of them private, and each bank has somewhat different designs. Some of the currency is very colorful, especially the ten dollar note (pictured below).

$1, $2 and $5 currencies are only available as coins, and banknotes come in denominations of $10, $20, $50, $500 and $1,000. You can find $10s in both coins and bills. Hardly any stores or restaurants accept the Chinese *yuan*.

US$100 are worth about HK$775, while 100 Euros equal about HK$1,033. You can exchange money at booths all around the city. Exchanging at the HSBC bank costs a fee of HK$50, regardless of the amount exchanged.

Upscale restaurants take foreign credit cards, but smaller restaurants are cash only. It is easy to get cash from your debit card or credit card at ATMs at any of Hong Kong's major banks, and you should always carry enough cash on you for your day. Some international banks like Citi Bank have a big presence in Hong Kong, too.

Australia	A$1	HK$6.94
Canada	C$1	HK$7.39
China	¥1	HK$1.27
Euro Zone	€1	HK$10.34
New Zealand	NZ$1	HK$6.06
Singapore	S$1	HK$6.06
UK	£1	HK$12.04
USA	US$1	HK$7.75
Exchange rates at the time of research		

Festivals & Events

There are exciting festivals and events in Hong Kong year round. Check out some of the events occuring around the time of your visit to really spice up the adventure!

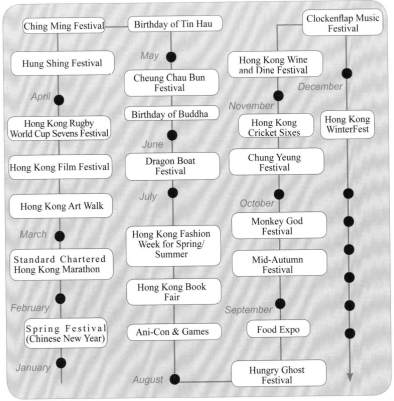

Hong Kong Festivals, Holidays & Events

January & February

Spring Festival (Chinese New Year)

Lunar calendar date: 1st month, 1st day to 1st month, 15th day
2014 date: January 31 – February 14
2015 date: February 19 – March 5
2016 date: February 8 – 22

Spring Festival is the most important festival on the Chinese calendar. It starts with the Chinese New Year celebration on the eve of the first day as families gather for a new year's dinner. At 20:00 in Tsim Sha Tsui (TST), there is a New Year's Eve parade that runs down the Golden Mile of Nathan Road and the TST waterfront area around the Cultural Centre. On night number two, you can catch a fireworks display over Victoria

Harbour starting at 20:00. The third day gets rowdy with horse races at the Sha Tin Racecourse, while the final day of Spring Festival is Lantern Festival when there are brightly lit displays made out of lanterns.

Hong Kong locals often buy flowers to give as gifts during this time, meaning the Flower Market is very crowded during the weeks leading up to Spring Festival. Many people go to temples as well. Of particular note is the Che Kung Temple in Tai Wai, which becomes crowded with about 100,000 people on the second day of Spring Festival (Che Kung's birthday).

Standard Chartered Hong Kong Marathon

Date: Late February
Website: www.hkmarathon.com

The Hong Kong Marathon takes place every year during the second half of February. Tens of thousands of people compete in multiple events, which include a full marathon (42.2 km; 26.2 mi), a half marathon (21.1 km; 13.1 mi), a 10k (6.2 mi), and a 3k wheelchair race. Participants in the full marathon must be 20 years old or above and must have completed a race of 10 km or longer in the past three years, while those participating in the other races must be 16 or above. The marathon entry fee is HK$300 (US$40). Participants can register on the website.

March

Hong Kong Art Walk

2015 date: see website
Website: www.hongkongartwalk.com

On the day of ArtWalk, 70 galleries on Hong Kong Island open their doors and allow participants to view art and eat appetizers provided by participating restaurants. This charity event raised HK$400,000 for the Society for Community Organizations in 2013. Adult tickets cost HK$450 (US$58) each.

Hong Kong Film Festival

Date: mid to late March, two weeks long
Website: www.hkiff.org.hk

At 12 venues across Hong Kong, the Hong Kong Film Festival showcases over 300 films from about 50 countries. It features films from established as well as up-and-coming independent directors. Tickets cost HK$65 (US$8.30) or HK$75 (US$9.70) for each

event and can be purchased at **www.hkiff. org.hk/en/booking_guide.php**.

Hong Kong Rugby World Cup Sevens

2015 date: see website
Website: www.hksevens.com

The Hong Kong Sevens is the 7th round of the HSBC Sevens World Series. 28 teams from different nations compete in the seven man game, which uses half the players of a typical rugby squad for a faster-paced match. A party atmosphere descends over the sporting community during the week of this competition, which is held at Hong Kong Stadium near Causeway Bay.

April & May

Hung Shing Festival

Lunar date: 2nd month, 13th day
2015 date: April 1

Hung Shing was a government official famed for promoting the study of science, astronomy, geography and mathematics during the Tang Dynasty. He is worshipped today, particularly by fisherman, as a protector against natural disasters. The most festive celebrations take place at the Hung Shing Temple in the village of Ho Sheung Heung in the New Territories

Ching Ming Festival

2015 date: April 5
2016 date: April 2

On Ching Ming Festival, also known as Tomb Sweeping Day, Chinese people pay respects to their ancestors by cleaning their graves and offering them faux money. This is also a popular time of year for an outdoor excursion as the plants and flowers are in spring bloom. Kite flying is another popular activity, and some people attach a lantern to their kite to send into the night sky.

Birthday of Tin Hau

Lunar date: 3rd month, 23rd day
2015 date: May 11

Tin Hau is the goddess of the sea, and her birthday is one of the most celebrated spiritual festivals in the city. You can see a great parade and lion dances at Shap Pat Heung village in Yuen Long, and Tin Hau boat parades at various Tin Hau temples. The Tin Hau Boat Parade at High Island in Sai Kung Country Park is a long running traditional boat parade, the culmination of a festival by the local Tanka and Hakka people that happens every two years. The next Tin Hau Boat Parade at High Island is on April 22, 2014. The Tin Hau Temple at Joss Bay hosts an annual Tin Hau boat parade, though it isn't quite as remote or traditional as the one at High Island. For more information about the goddess Tin Hau and the over 70 Tin Hau temples in Hong Kong, check out our section on Chinese temples on page 145.

Cheung Chau Bun Festival

Lunar date: 4th month, 5th to 9th day
2014 date: May 3 – 7
2015 date: May 22 – 26

Cheung Chau Bun Festival is a unique holiday celebrated on Cheung Chau Island. Observed since the Qing Dynasty, this bread-filled fiesta celebrates Pak Tai, a Taoist god who ended a famine with – you guessed it – buns. Good luck buns are affixed to shrines, and a giant bun tower is constructed. At midnight on the third night, contestants race to the top of the tower and collect buns in backpacks. The buns on the tower are plastic, but everyone eats actual lotus or red bean-filled buns the next day. For the first two days of the festival, there are lion dance performances outside the Pak Tai Temple, and there is a Piu Sik parade with "floating children" in procession down the street in the afternoon of the third day.

Buddha's Birthday

Lunar date: 4th month, 8th day
2014 date: May 6
2015 date: May 25

To celebrate the birthday of Siddhartha Gautama, the founder of Buddhism, Buddhists descend on temples throughout the city and bathe statues of the Buddha in bowls of water and eat bitter tasting cookies to represent the passing of hardship. The ceremonies at Po Lin Monastery are known for being especially magnificent.

June

Dragon Boat Festival

Lunar date: 5th month, 5th day
2014 date: June 2
2015 date: June 20
2016 date: June 9

The Dragon Boat Festival is a celebration of summer that rips through Asia with dragon boat races. At various fishing towns in Hong Kong there are races and boat parades. The biggest of the races takes place in Victoria Harbour, where race spectators can also join a beer fest on the shore, which is bursting with music and other activities. Stanley and Tai O Fishing Village are also among the best places to watch local races.

July

Hong Kong SAR Establishment Day

Date: July 1

SAR Establishment Day, the anniversary of Hong Kong's establishment as a Special Administrative Region in 1997, has two different kinds of events. There is the flag raising ceremony at Golden Bauhinia Square in Wan Chai with parades and helicopters flying over Victoria Harbour, complimented by an evening fireworks show over the harbour. Concurrently, protesters against the CCP march from Victoria Park to Central. In 2003, the Chief Executive stepped down shortly after 500,000 people marched, and the protesters have been striving to bring the same amount of energy every year since.

Hong Kong Fashion Week for Spring/ Summer

Date: July 7 to 10, annually
Venue: Hong Kong Convention and Exhibition Centre
Website: www.hktdc.com/fair/hkfashionweekss-en/

This fashion expo for the summer showcases all kinds of apparel from 1,268 exhibitors. Admission is free to those who apply online.

Hong Kong Book Fair

Date: July 16 to 22, 2014
Website: www.hkbookfair.hktdc.com/en/
Venue: Hong Kong Convention and Exhibition Centre

The Hong Kong Book Fair at the Hong Kong Convention and Exhibition Centre in Wan

Chai is held annually and hosts speakers and presentations, and has books for sale.

Date: late July
Website: www.ani-com.hk

Hong Kong's biggest comics festival, Ani-Con exhibits comic books and game related products, while also hosting cosplay competitions. (Cosplay is where fans dress up as their favorite anime characters, usually as part of a competition team.) There are also some performances by Japanese voice artists and a very entertaining dance competition.

August

Hungry Ghost Festival

Lunar date: 7th month, 15th day
2014 date: August 10
2015 date: August 28
2016 date: August 17

Da Shi Tai, King of Ghosts

In Chinese culture, when someone dies they are believed to go to an underground court to be judged, and many are thought to require tributes given on various dates throughout the year in order to keep the soul from suffering in the afterlife. During Ghost Festival neighborhood celebrations, Taoist priests perform rituals to feed the ghosts and send reformed ghosts to Kik Lok Sai Kai, "the extremely happy world."

The folk holiday of Ghost Festival is celebrated throughout Southern China and has grown from aspects of Buddhism, Taoism and Chinese folk traditions. The week-long festival starts on the 15th day of the 7th month in the lunar calendar, a time when when people burn joss paper and make food offerings to the hungry ghosts in the streets. Many neighborhoods in Hong Kong then host week-long celebrations that include makeshift temples and Cantonese opera stages. On display are paper mache statues of the gods, especially the god of ghosts, Da Shi Tai (大 士 台), and there is a large furnace where joss paper is torched. Some of the largest celebrations are those that take place in Ngau Tau Kok, Tsz Wan Shan and Kowloon City.

Food Expo

Date: mid August
Venue: Hong Kong Convention and Exhibition Centre
Website: www.hktdc.com/fair/hkfoodexpo-en/

Hundreds of exhibitors in the food and drink industry offer free food samples to public attendees at this delicious expo. The floor is divided into a trading section for business to business exchanges and a public section where brands promote themselves to consumers. There were over 1,000 exhibitors in 2013 and plenty of delicious eats to fill up on. Additionally, chefs put on cooking demonstrations. Public tickets are free, but you have to apply in advance on the website.

September

Mid-Autumn Festival

Lunar date: 8th month, 15th day
2014 date: September 8
2015 date: September 27
2016 date: September 15

Mid-Autumn Festival is one of the most important festivals in traditional Chinese culture. It's a time to be with family and, of course, eat moon cakes. Traditional moon cakes are round pastries about 10 cm wide and are filled with lotus paste and salted duck egg yolks or a flavored gelatin (kind of like gummy candies). Other fillings include sweet bean paste, date paste, red bean paste and five kernel nut paste. In Guangdong and Hong Kong, there are also moon cakes with ham, chicken, duck, pork, and even ice cream.

The legend behind Mid-Autumn Festival tells of an ancient person named Hou Yi – famed for his excellent archery – and his wife Chang'e. Hou Yi was given an elixir of immortality by an admiring god when he shot down nine of the ten suns plaguing Earth. He planned to share the elixer with his wife, but when he was out hunting on the 15th day of the 8th month his apprentice came to steal the potion. Chang'e swallowed it in defiance and, as she rose to immortality in the heavens, chose the moon as her home in order to stay close to Hou Yi. The grieving husband put Chang'e's favorite cakes and fruits on the grass every year as offerings to his wife, and soon inspired one of China's most important holidays.

Monkey God Festival

Lunar date: 8th month, 16th day
2014 date: September 9

The Monkey God, star of the Ming Dynasty era novel *Journey to the West*, is one of the most famous characters in Chinese literature. The mischievous deity is said to be able to possess humans and force them to perform unnatural acts. At the Monkey God Temple at Po Tat Estate in Kowloon's Sau Mau Ping, celebrations involve participants running barefoot over hot coals or climbing ladders of knives. The less courageous will burn paper and parade around with flags.

October

Chung Yeung Festival

Lunar date: 9th day, 9th month
2014 date: October 2

Like Ching Ming Festival, the Chung Yeung Festival is a day to worship ancestors and enjoy the outdoors. During this festival, people love to hike into the mountains to see and smell the chrysanthemum flowers, as well as indulge in chrysanthemum wine and tea. A special kind of rice cake is on sale in bakeries.

Hong Kong Cricket Sixes

Date: Late October
Venue: Kowloon Cricket Club
Website: www.cricket.com.hk

The Hong Kong Cricket Sixes tournament in Kowloon gathers eight international teams for fast-paced six-on-six cricket matches. Each match takes 45-minutes and is designed to be relatively high scoring. Tickets can be purchased at the website.

November

Hong Kong Wine & Dine Festival

2014 date: October 31 to November 3
Venue: The New Central Harbourfront
Website: www.discoverhongkong.com/eng/
see-do/events-festivals/highlight-events/
wine-dine-festival.jsp

A delicious festival of jazz, wine and offerings from 70 food booths, the Hong Kong Wine and Dine Festival will have your mouth in heaven. The Classic Wine Pass ticket for HK$200 (US$26) affords you eight tokens good for trying wines. The Grand Wine Pass for HK$480 (US$62) gives you an additional five tokens for premium wines in the Riedel Grand Tasting Pavilion. This festival marks the beginning of Hong Kong Wine and Dine Month, which runs throughout November and includes street carnivals and restaurant deals.

Clockenflap Music Festival

Date: Late November
2014 date: check website
Website: www.clockenflap.com

This annual festival is an attempt, as the organizers put it, "to give Hong Kong a festival worthy of our major metropolis." In 2013, headlining bands included Franz Ferdinand, Two Door Cinema Club and Chic. The festival has seven music stages, an art village, a film tent, a silent disco and other attractions. Tickets go for HK$480 (US$62) to HK$980 (US$126).

December

Hong Kong WinterFest

Date: December holiday time

WinterFest is a set of events and displays that celebrate the Christmas and New Year's season. Tiffany & Co puts up an 18 m-tall Christmas tree and festive decorations on Statue Square. On New Year's Eve, there is a fireworks show over Victoria Harbour.

Visa

Citizens of 165 countries do not require a visa to visit Hong Kong. There are just 57 countries whose citizens require a visa (some of which include Iran, Cuba and North Korea). Citizens of most countries, including the countries of North America and Europe, can stay in Hong Kong for 90 days per entry. British citizens can stay for 180 days per entry. For a full list of countries, visit **www.immd.gov.hk/en/services/hk-visas/visit-transit/visit-visa-entry-permit.html#general**.

Crime

Hong Kong is a very safe city. Its murder rate in 2011 was 0.2 per 100,000, and each year since then it has been below 1.0, according to its police statistics as cited by the United Nations Office on Drugs and Crime. In comparison, the United States' murder rate was 4.7 and the majority of European countries averaged around 1.0.

The only real crimes you need worry about in Hong Kong are pickpockets. The best way to avoid being a target of theft – besides always being aware of your surroundings, especially in crowded areas – is to keep your money and valuables inside your clothing, close to your body. Don't keep them in pockets, but instead consider a money belt to keep under your shirt.

Religious Services

Hong Kong has an atmosphere of religious freedom and has many active religious groups throughout the city. In the Yau Ma Tei Community Centre Rest Garden you can often see charitable religious groups passing out food or doing service projects. Every major religion is represented in this city, and if you're looking for a place to worship during your stay then you will likely have many options.

Christian

There are many Christian churches throughout Hong Kong. **The Vine Church** in Wan Chai is one that holds services in English. Services take place every Sunday at 9:15 and 11:30 and there is a musical service at 16:00. Additionally, they hold Flight Youth meetings every Friday night at 18:30.

St John's Cathedral in Central, which opened in 1849, is the oldest cathedral in East Asia and also holds English services. You can attend them on Sundays at 8:00, 9:00, 10:30, 11:45, 14:00 and 18:00, or Monday through Friday at 8:00.

The Vine

Address: 29 Burrows Street, Wan Chai
Website: www.thevine.org.hk

St Johns Cathedral

Address: 4-8 Garden Road, Central
Website: www.stjohnscathedral.org.hk

St Andrew's Church (Anglican)

Address: 138 Nathan Road, Tsim Sha Shui
Website: www.standrews.org.hk

Jewish

For Jews in Hong Kong, there are a number of synagogues and organizations where you can have a shabbat meal. The **Kehilat Zion-Hechal Ezra Synagogue** in Kowloon hosts free Shabbat meals (donations welcome, reserve by email) every Friday night after Shabbat services. Weekly times are listed on their website.

The **Ohel Leah Synagogue**, built in 1901, is another option. They host Morning Chabura services every day at 6:15 and services all day during High Holy Days. They also host Shabbat dinners in cooperation with the JCC (reserve a seat by email: info@JCC.org.hk).

Kehilat Zion-Hechal Ezra Synagogue

Address: 62 Mody Road, 1/F, Unit 105, Wing On Plaza, Tsim Sha Tsui
Website: www.kehilat-zion.org

Ohel Leah Synagogue

Address: 70 Robinson Road, Mid-Levels
Website: www.ohelleah.org

Chabad House of Hong Kong

Address: 7 Macdonnell Road, 1/F, Mid-Levels

St Andrew's Church (Anglican)

Website: www.chabadhongkong.org

Chabad House of Kowloon

Address: 11 Hart Avenue, 2/F, Tsim Sha Tsui
Website: www.chabadhongkong.org

Muslim

Hong Kong actually has five active mosques, though the main one is the **Kowloon Mosque and Islamic Centre** right outside Kowloon Park in Tsim Sha Tsui. It holds prayers ten times a day and can hold over 3,000 people. Daily prayer times are listed on their website.

The **Jamia Mosque** is the oldest in Hong Kong, built during the 1840s. It can hold around 400 worshipers and is located on Shelly Street near the top of the Mid-Levels Escalators.

Kowloon Mosque

Address: 105 Nathan Road, Tsim Sha Tsui
Website: www.kowloonmosque.com

Jamia Mosque

Address: 30 Shelly Street, Central

Mormon

There are a few Mormon churches around Hong Kong. The Church of Jesus Christ of Latter-day Saints in Kowloon Tong has endowment sessions Tuesday through Friday, six times a day. You can find their full schedule on their website.

Church of Jesus Christ of Latter-day Saints

Address: 2 Cornwall Street, Kowloon Tong
Website: www.lds.org/church/temples/hong-kong-china?

Buddhist, Taoist or Chinese Folk Religion

It's not hard to find a Buddhist or Taoist temple in Hong Kong! Check the Temples section on page 145 for in depth information.

Hong Kong
Reading & Film List

A great way to prepare for a trip to Hong Kong is to take in some literature on the city. Here are some of our favorites.

Magazines & Websites

HK Magazine – **www.hk-magazine.com** – A guide to Hong Kong cultural and nightlife events. This magazine is available for free at some restaurants and hotels in downtown.

Time Out Hong Kong – **www.timeout.com. hk** – Similar to HK Magazine, includes event listings and restaurant and bar listings.

Books

Marvels of a Floating City by Xi Xi – This collection of stories by Xi Xi presents a Hong Kong local's perspective on the city's identity and the challenges it faced during the 1980s as it floated between West and East.

Hong Kong: A Cultural History by Michael Ingham – The author of this book creates a vivid portrait of Hong Kong as viewed through literary and cinematic creations that apply through history to specific locations in Hong Kong.

Gweilo: Memories of a Hong Kong Childhood by Martin Booth – British author Martin Booth grew up in Hong Kong during the 1950s and produced one of the most celebrated memoirs on this period.

East and West by Chris Patten – The Last British Governor of Hong Kong reflects on the issues surrounding the transfer of Hong Kong during his governorship and the policies he established to expand democracy before the handover. Later in the book he considers the debate between Eastern and Western ideals of government.

Opium War, 1840-1842: Barbarians in the Celestial Empire in the Early Part of the Nineteenth Century and the War by Which They Forced Her Gates by Peter Ward Fay – This authoritative account on the First Opium War lays out in detail the story of how Hong Kong originally fell under British control.

Books into Film

Rouge, book by Lilian Lee, film by Stanley Kwan – This story presents a nostalgic view of 1930s Hong Kong opium dens through the ghost of the courtesan Fleur (Anita Mui), who returns from Hell to find her lover (Leslie Cheung). The poignant film version is a heart-wrenching tale of love and dishonesty, made more emotional by the performances of the late Leslie Cheung and Anita Mui.

Love In a Fallen City, book by Eileen Chang, film by Ann Hui – A love story presented over the backdrop of World War II Hong Kong.

Movies

Made in Hong Kong directed by Fruit Chan – On the surface this is a movie about a low-level Triad member struggling with his own lack of control over his meaningless life. But, when considered in its time period (published in 1997), the deeper questions it raises about Hong Kong's future become apparent.

Fist of Fury by Lo Wei – Bruce Lee enters a Japanese kung fu school carrying a sign that says "Sick man of Asia" that he was given as an insult, returns it and then proceeds to lay a serious smack down on the criminally-minded school. The film was one of the Hong Kong film industy's outlets regarding the struggles China faced against foreign aggression since the Opium Wars – a period (between 1839 and 1949) that is pounded in to the heads of Chinese school children as the "century of humiliation."

My Life as McDull by Toe Yuen – This 2002 animated film about a pig living in Kowloon City was praised for its absurdist and satirical portrayal of working class life in Hong Kong.

Transportation

Airport

Hong Kong International Airport (HKG) is located on Chek Lap Kok Island just off of Lantau Island. There is an Airport Express that runs directly from the airport to the city.

Airport Express Subway Line

The Airport Express MTR line is a direct and easy way to get downtown. It stops in western Kowloon (at Kowloon Station) and then Central (at Hong Kong Station) and costs HK$60-100 for the whole trip to Central. You can save money using the MTR by taking the Airport Express to Tsing Yi Station and switching to the Tung Chung Line or by taking the S1 bus to Tung Chung Station and switching to the Tung Chung Line

Bus

Buses A (HK$40) and E (HK$20) head to different areas of downtown, but bus E is cheaper because it's also used by airport workers.

To Central: Buses E11, E33
To Mong Kok: Bus E21
To Yau Ma Tei: Bus E23
To Causeway Bay: Bus E11
To Kowloon City: Buses E23, A22
Find more bus routes at:
www.hongkongairport.com/eng/transport/to-from-airport/bus_from_hkia.html

Taxi

A taxi from the Airport to Central costs about HK$220.

Getting Around Town

Octopus Card

The Octopus Card (八達通) allows for travel on all of Hong Kong's public transit services and can be used to purchase items at some stores. Pick one up at the airport or at a kiosk in the Airport Express stations for HK$150 (HK$70 for seniors and kids). This includes HK$100 worth of travel and a refundable HK$50 deposit. Even if you only stay in town for a week, picking one up will make traveling around the city far more convenient since you won't have to constantly wait in ticket lines.

Subway

The subway covers most places on the north side of Hong Kong Island and the urban areas of Yau Ma Tsim and Kowloon City, as well as some of the New Territories. There are 10 lines. A subway map application called **MTR Mobile** is available for free on smart-phones.

Island Line (blue)
Runs across the northern part of Hong Kong

Island
Central
Admiralty
Causeway Bay
Sheung Wan
Mid-Levels Escalators (Central)
Lower Terminus of the Peak Tram (Central)
Western Market (Sheung Wan)
Hong Kong-Macau Ferry Terminal (Sheung Wan)
Causeway Bay Shopping District (Causeway Bay)
Sunbeam Theatre (North Point)

Tsuen Wan Line (red)
Runs through the Yau Tsim Mong and western Kowloon and connects to Central on Hong Kong Island
Tsim Sha Tsui
Yau Ma Tei
Mong Kok
Central
Temple Street Market (Jordan and Yau Ma Tei)
Ladies Market (Mong Kok)
Sneaker Street (Mong Kok)

Kwun Tong Line (green)
Starts at Yau Ma Tei and goes through Kowloon City and eastern Kowloon.
Mong Kok
Kowloon Tong
Diamond Hill
Festival Walk (Kowloon Tong)
Wong Tai Sin Temple (Wong Tai Sin)

Tseung Kwan O Line (purple)
Connects eastern Kowloon to eastern Hong Kong Island at Quarry Bay and North Point
North Point
Clearwater Bay (via buses outside of Po Lam or LOHAS Park)

West Rail Line (magenta)
Runs from east Tsim Sha Tsui to the far northeastern area of Tuen Mun
East Tsim Sha Tsui
Hung Hom
Yuen Long
Tuen Mun

Tung Chung Line (orange)
Connects Hong Kong Island and Kowloon to Lantau Island
Hong Kong (near Central)
Nam Cheong
Tung Chung (the connection point to anywhere on Lantau)

East Rail Line (light blue)
Runs all the way to the Shenzhen border
Futian Checkpoint (Lok Ma Chau)
Luohu Checkpoint (Lo Wu)

Sha Tin
Kowloon Tong
Mong Kok East
Hung Hum

Ma On Shan Line (brownish)
Goes to Ma On Shan and other areas in the northeast of the New Territories
Che Kung Temple (Che Kung Temple Station)
Ma On Shan Country Park (Ma On Shan)

Disneyland Resort
Just two stops
Sunny Bay
Disneyland Resort

Airport Express

Runs between the airport, Western Kowloon and Central

2015 MTR Expansion

There are currently some new expansions underway to allow the MTR to service south Hong Kong Island. First, the Island Line is being expanded west via the West Island Line, which will go all the way to Hong Kong University and Kennedy Town. From University, the South Island Line (West Section) will be built to serve southern Hong Kong, with a stop at Aberdeen. The South Island Line (East Section) will connect from Admiralty to the South Island Line West and include a stop at Ocean Park. A new line will also run through the Harbour area of Kowloon City. This construction is expected to be completed in 2015.

Buses

Hong Kong's buses cover the city quite well. If you can prepare your route ahead of time then it's a great way to get around the city. Since most of northern Hong Kong Island and Kowloon are covered by the MTR, most people only use buses for the southern side of Hong Kong Island, the New Territories and Lantau Island.

Buses run from 5:30 or 6:00 to 00:00 or 00:30, but there are small numbers that will continue until 5:00 in the morning in certain areas. Bus fares can range from HK$2.50 to HK$52, depending on the destination, and you will need exact change or an Octopus Card.

On Hong Kong Island, the bus terminus below Exchange Square in Central and the one in Admiralty can get you to Aberdeen,

MTR System Map

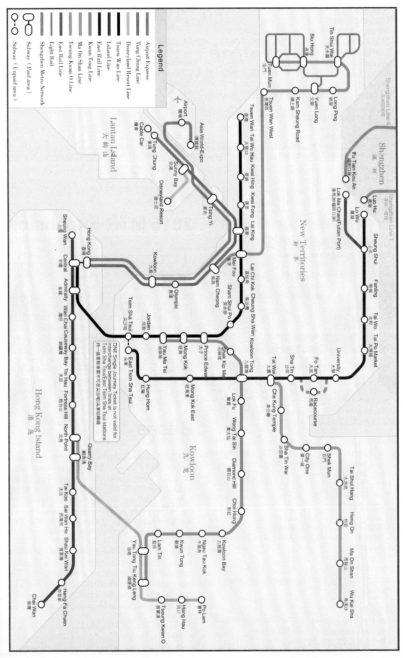

046

Repulse Bay and other destinations on southern Hong Kong Island. In Kowloon, you will want to head to the Star Ferry bus station for buses up Nathan Road.

Good user-friendly route finding tools can be found at First Bus (**www.nwstbus. hk**) and Kowloon Motor Bus (**www.kmb. hk**). Kowloon Motor Bus has a route app for smart-phones as well. Buses on Lantau Island operate under New Lantau Bus (www. newlantaubus.com).

Minibus

Vans with up to 16 seats are known as minibuses in Hong Kong. There are red and green minibuses. **Red minibuses** (HK$2 to HK$22) are actually cream-colored with a red stripe down the roof. They pick up passengers when they are hailed and drop off at requested destinations along designated routes. The routes are printed on the windows, but they are almost always in Chinese. Payment is given when departing and drivers can give change. You can also use your Octopus Card.

Green minibuses – also known as maxicabs – are cream-colored with a green stripe and they require exact change. They run along designated stops only. Two useful routes are the 6 (HK$4.70) from Hankow Road in Tsim Sha Tsui to Hung Hom Station in Kowloon and the 1 (HK$8.40) to Victoria Peak from outside Hong Kong Station.

Ferry

Hong Kong is loaded with ferries. Make sure to check individual transport info for a specific dock; you can find ferry schedules printed at their respective piers and company websites. The main ferry in Hong Kong is the renowned **Star Ferry**, an attraction in its own right and one of the cheapest transport options in the city.

Ferries to Lantau Island can be found in Central next to the Star Ferry. For more information on ferry routes visit the company websites. Hong Kong & Kowloon Ferry Co can be found at **www.hkkf.com.hk** and New World First Ferry is at **www.nwff.com.hk**.

Taxi

Taxis in Hong Kong are plentiful and convenient. There are three colors you should be aware of:

Blue taxis serve Lantau. Flag fall is HK$15 and then HK$1.30 for every 200 m after that.

Green taxis serve the New Territories. Flag fall is HK$16.50 and then HK$1.30 for every 200 m after that.

Red taxis serve Hong Kong Island and Kowloon. Flag fall is HK$20 for the first 2 km and then HK$1.50 for every 200 m after that.

Trams

The tram serves Hong Kong Island, going from Kennedy Town on the east to Shau Kei Wan on the east. It was the first mass transit system in Hong Kong. Now the Island Line of the MTR serves most of the areas the tram does, but there is still a sense of old Hong Kong nostalgia in riding the tram.

Single journey: Adult ticket HK$2.30, Child ticket (age 3-12) HK$1.20, Senior ticket HK$1.10. A four-day ticket costs HK$34 and a month-long ticket costs HK$200.

For more information on Hong Kong Trams, visit their website: **www.hktramways.com/ en/index.html**

Light Rail

The light rail line serves some of the suburbs in northwestern New Territories such as Yuen Long, Tin Shui Wai, Siu Hong and Tuen Mun. You'll need to take it for some of the sights in these areas.

Rides on the modern and comfortable Light Rail are quite pleasant, and some people find the rail to be part of the attraction of these areas. Air-conditioned and fast, they run from 5:30 in the morning to 00:30 and 1:30 the next day, with trips around every 12 minutes (depending on which line and which day).

Light rail fares run between HK$4 and HK$5.80 for adults and HK$2 and HK$2.90 for children and seniors over 65, depending on the distance traveled. You can use the Octopus card here, or if you don't have one just find one of the ticket vending machines on the train platforms. In a charming show of faith, there are no ticket checkers, and riders are trusted to charge their Octopus cards accordingly when they exit.

Top Attractions

pg 49

Victoria Peak

pg 52

The Mid-Levels Escalators

pg 55

Tsim Sha Tsui Waterfront & the Avenue of Stars

pg 59

Repulse Bay

pg 62

Stanley

pg 65

Po Lin Monastery

pg 68

Chi Lin Nunnery

pg 71

Temple Street Night Market

pg 74

Tai O Fishing Village

pg 77

Ping Shan Heritage Trail

pg 80

Ladies Street Market

pg 82

Star Ferry

Victoria Peak

English name: Victoria Peak
Chinese name: 太平山
Location: Western half of Hong Kong Island
Altitude: 552 m (1,811 ft)
Website: www.thepeak.com.hk

English name: The Peak Tower Viewing Platform
Chinese name: 凌霄閣觀景平檯
Address: 128 Peak Rd
Phone: 2849 0668

English name: The Peak Galleria Viewing Deck
Chinese name: 山頂廣場觀景檯
Hours: 10:00-22:00
Phone: 2849 4113
Address: 118 Peak Rd
Website: www.thepeakgalleria.com

English name: Victoria Peak Garden
Chinese name: 山頂公園

English name: Victoria Peak Tram
Chinese name: 山頂纜車
Phone: 2522 0922

The Peak opening hours:

The Peak Tram	7:00-24:00	Mon-Sun & Public Holidays
Peak Tram Historical Gallery	7:00-24:00	Mon-Sun & Public Holidays
The Peak Tower	10:00-23:00	Mon-Fri
	8:00-23:00	Sat, Sun & Public Holidays
Sky Terrace 428	10:00-23:00	Mon-Fri
	8:00-23:00	Sat, Sun & Public Holidays
The Sky Gallery	10:00-23:00	Mon-Fri
	8:00-23:00	Sat, Sun & Public Holidays

Peak Tram Tickets:

	Return	Single
Adult	HK$40	HK$28
Child (age 3-11) / Senior (age 65 above)	HK$18	HK$11

Peak Tram Sky Pass (The Peak Tram & Sky Terrace 428):

	Return	Single
Adult	HK$65	HK$53
Child (age 3-11) / Senior (age 65 above)	HK$31	HK$24

Transport:

The Peak Tram – The Peak Tram will take you from Garden Rd in Central to the top of Victoria Peak. Access The Garden Rd Tram Station from either the Central or the Admiralty MTR Station along the Island Line. From either station it's just a short walk to the Peak Tram Lower Terminus. You can also take buses 8, 3A, and 101 from outside of Hong Kong subway station or bus 22S from the Star Ferry pier to the Peak Tram terminal station.

Bus – 15 will take you all the way up Peak Rd to the top of the Peak. You can also hop off bus 15 one stop early at the bottom of the Peak (near the Botanical Gardens) for a hike up the Central Green Trail or Old Peak Rd to the top. Buses 22 and 1 can also take you here.

Taxi – Any taxi on Hong Kong Island will take you to the top of Victoria Peak, but it will easily be the priciest option. Show this sentence to your taxi driver: 中環花園道山頂纜車總站 (Garden Rd Peak Tram Lower Terminus).

Hiking – There are a number of paths to the top of the Peak from outside of the Hong Kong Botanical Gardens. The most popular path is Old Peak Rd, but other nice options include the Tramway Path, the Pinewood Battery or one of the country park trails. From the top of the Central and Mid-Level Escalators there are signs leading you towards the Botanical Gardens.

The view of downtown from the top of Victoria Peak

Easily one of Hong Kong's must-sees, Victoria Peak is the highest point on Hong Kong Island. It offers two large shopping malls – the Peak Tower and the Peak Galleria – which house viewing decks and a host of restaurants. If you can brave ultra-touristy establishments like Bubba Gump Shrimp (巴佈甘蝦业公司) and Madame Tussaud's (杜莎伕人蠟像館), you'll be treated to sweeping, 360 degree panoramas of the city from their excellent viewing decks. Victoria Peak also includes a garden and some easy but beautiful hiking trails, and is part of the Pok Fu Lam Country Park (薄扶林郊野公園).

Known locally as The Peak, the commercial and residential districts here are the "peak" of the Hong Kong real estate market. Prized as prime real-estate by Hong Kong's most affluent residents since the 1800s, the area is loaded with expensive homes.

Before You Go

When arriving at the top of the Peak, whether by tram, bus, or taxi, it is easy to get lost if you don't know where you're going. The majority of visitors arrive via the Peak Tram – an excellent and convenient mode of transport – and if you go this route keep in mind that the tram stations and the main bus stops are located at each of the malls, letting visitors off into a sea of people,

souvenir hawkers and a maze of shops. Make sure you have an idea of where you are going before you arrive.

Info & Cautions

The view from the Peak is especially breathtaking at night when the skyline is lit up, but be aware that the Peak Tram gets particularly crowded during this time. Things begin to mellow out again after 21:00, and there is almost no wait time at 22:00 and 23:00.

History

From 1806 to 1810, Victoria Peak was used as a lookout by the local pirate Chang Pao. In 1810, he was captured and forced to work for the Canton government, but his legacy still whispers rumors of vast fortunes hidden on various islands.

Victoria Peak was undeveloped until the 1860s, when Hong Kong Governor Sir Hercules Robinson began a development push and soon commissioned a path to facilitate sedan chair passage up the slopes. The path allowed wealthy residents the option of building a home at the top – so long as they could afford to be carted around in a sedan chair – and by 1863 between 20 and 30 families (including then-governor Sir Richard MacDonnell) called Victoria Peak home.

As the 1880s rolled in, word of Victoria Peak's cool air was enticing more visitors to escape the sweltering Hong Kong summers, and soon businessman Alexander Findlay Smith – certainly hearing the distant jingle of the tourist dollar – made a successful petition to the governor to open a tram to the top of Victoria Peak, where he owned land and planned to build a hotel. When the Victoria Peak Tram opened in 1888, its terminal station was built right outside his Peak Hotel. The savvy business move by Smith was a boon for the area as well; the tram became the first funicular cable car in Asia (an impressive feat considering it climbed up slopes as steep as 27 degrees) and brought unprecedented access to the mountain. By 1926 the original steam-powered tram was upgraded to an electric version. Smith's hotel, however, did not fare as well – after years of decline it finally burned to the ground in a fire in 1936, and today its former site is occupied by the Peak Tower.

From 1904 to 1947, residence on the Peak was restricted only to expatriates (although the Governor made exemptions for prominent Chinese, such as Madame Chiang Kai-shek, First Lady of the Republic of China), but these days the only barrier is the size of your bank account. In 2010 and 2011, *Financial News*'s real estate survey found the Peak's Severn Road to be the most expensive street in the world, with one square meter of property costing over US$78,000.

Layout

At an altitude of 552 m (1,811 ft), Victoria Peak is visible from anywhere on Hong Kong Island. The summit of the peak has a radio telecommunications facility up top but it's off limits to the public. The main tourist attractions on the Peak – the tower and the mall – sit at around 396 m (1,299 ft), and the tippy-top of the tower hits an elevation of 428 m (1404 ft). Follow the hiking trails to get up to the top.

To find the majority of the shopping and eating here, look no further than the **Peak Tower** and the **Peak Galleria**, both sitting at the end of Peak Road outside the tram terminus. If you're interested in seeing the fancy-pants Severn Road, just head east down Finlay Road.

Victoria Peak Garden is located to the east of the Peak Tower, down Mt Austin Road.

Stage 1 of the Hong Kong Trail, called the Pok Fu Lam Native Tree Walk, starts just to the north of the tram station, initially following Lugard Road. For an easy hike, follow the 3.5 km (2 mi) circle from here around the peak by linking up with the Harlech Road fitness trail back to the tram station. You could also start from the Harlech Road side and come out on Lugard. The brave and very fit can continue down the entirety of the Hong Kong Trail Stage 1 and end up at the Pok Fu Lam Reservoir 7 km (4 mi) on the other side of Victoria Peak.

One of the best ways to escape the crowds is to head up the 500 m (1,640 mi) of Mt Austin Road to the site of the old governor's mansion. It was burnt to cinders by the Japanese during WWII, but the beautiful gardens are still a fine sight.

Aside from the two malls, other popular viewing points include the **Lugard Road Lookout**, the **Lions View Point Pavilion**, and many others along the Hong Kong Trail.

The Peak Tower

Love it or hate it, the Peak Tower – which has been described as looking like an anvil – has a very distinct design. It has a big, moonlike half oval on top of a glass-encased building support. The design has gone through a number of changes, but it has always kept the concept of having a large structure resting on top of a tower-esque lower structure. Originally a much smaller building, it was redesigned in the 1990s to create the wide crescent moon you see today.

The **Sky Terrace 428** viewing platform at the Peak Tower is the highest viewing platform in Hong Kong and is where you will want to go for stupendous views of the city and the coastline below. It can be accessed with an independent ticket or a ticket purchased with your tram ticket.

The Peak Galleria

The one thing that sets the Peak Galleria apart is that it is the highest mall in Hong

Kong. Its viewing platform is lower than that of the Peak Tower, but it is free. You'll find plenty of shopping and restaurants, but if you're itching for something local, try the **Tsui Wah Restaurant**. This Hong Kong chain restaurant is set up in the "tea and food hall" (chaa can teng; 茶餐廳) tradition that takes Western dining-style food and adds a Chinese twist.

Hong Kong Trail

The Hong Kong Trail is a 50 km (31 mi) loop all around Hong Kong Island that starts at Victoria Peak. Above the towering skyscrapers of the city, it provides an excellent escape from the bustle and dust of downtown Hong Kong, and the average hiker can burn a good hour hiking the path around the peak. A good approach is to start at Lugard Road and then take the cutoff at the Harlech Road fitness trail. If you'd like a longer hike you also have the option of continuing all the way to the Pok Fu Lam Reservoir (about a two-hour hike). The Native Tree Walk at the beginning of the hike is well designed and shows off a great variety of local plant life. This part of the hike – along the beginning of Victoria Peak – is fairly easy, but prepare for some moderately difficult terrain once you move beyond Harlech Road (you can choose to

go back to the tram here instead) with some steeper paths as you head down towards the western side of Hong Kong Island. After descending through a shady forest, you'll arrive at the reservoir, which includes plenty of surrounding areas to explore. From there, transportation can be taken back to anywhere on the island.

Victoria Peak Garden

A ten to 20-minute walk along Mt Austin Road from the Peak Tower, Victoria Peak Garden offers up a serene area of blooming flowers and open space, and doubles as a small zoo. There are hundreds of different kinds of birds and dozens of mammals and reptiles on display in about 40 pens throughout the garden, as well as countless more plant species. If you come on a day when the crowds are mellow, it can be a wonderfully relaxing experience. Meander through the walkways and pavilions sprinkled around the grounds and keep an eye out for a hidden greenhouse and various relaxing places to sit.

The Mid-Levels Escalators

Chinese name: 中環至半山自動扶梯
Operating Hours:
Downhill direction (Mid-Levels – Central): 6:00-10:00
Uphill direction (Central – Mid-Levels): 10:00-00:00
Transport:
There are numerous entrances to the escalators throughout the Central and Western districts. This transport info is for the bottom entrance at 100 Queen's Rd Central, 400 m (1,312 ft) northwest of the Central MTR Station.
Subway – Island Line, Central Station, walk 400 m (1,312 ft) northwest on Queen's Rd Central
Bus – 3A, 4, 4X, 37A, 90B, 91, 94 to "The Center" bus stop then walk southeast to Queen's Rd Central; or 5, 10, 37A, 90B, 101, 104 to Queen Victoria St Stop and walk west to the entrance

What was created as a unique form of transportation has become something of a novelty tourist attraction. The Mid-Levels Escalators are the longest outdoor covered escalator system in the world: a series of 20 escalators and three moving

walkways stretching an eye-popping 800 m (2,625 ft) of total length and with a total vertical rise of 135 m (443 ft). Opened in 1993, the fascinating system was created to ease congestion between the Harbour level Central district and the Mid-Levels area at the base of Victoria Peak (aka Mount Austin). In recent decades, the escalators have piqued the interest of film makers, who have featured them in films such as *Chungking Express* (1994), *Chinese Box* (1997), and *The Dark Knight* (2008). With entrances and exits at many bustling streets (such as Des Voeux Road Central, Queen's Road Central, Cochrane Street, Wellington Street, and Hollywood Road) and bars and cafes up and down their routes, you can kill two birds with one stone by using this unique transportation system to cruise around the area's points of interest while gawking at one of the city's most intriguing tourist draws.

Before You Go

Riding the escalators from bottom to top only takes about 20 minutes if you don't walk. Take them to places all around the Mid-Levels area to explore, but keep in mind that they only run in one direction at a time (see the Vital Info).

Info & Cautions

As you're cruising around the Mid-Levels on their "only-in-China" escalator system, remember that they are primarily a means of transportation for Hong Kong locals. This means you'll need to show courtesy to those using them to move quickly: stay to the right if you are not walking so you don't block the left lane, which is for walkers. If you are walking and someone behind you would like to go faster, pull over for a second and let them pass. These courtesies are especially important during morning and evening rush hours.

History

Hong Kong's mountainous terrain has always posed a challenge for construction and transportation development. As the city's development hit a breakneck pace by the early 1990s, concern about increasing levels of congestion on the winding roads that rose up to the hilly Mid-Levels inspired one of the most creative transportation devices in the world.

The world record-holding transportation system was completed in 1993, and shortly after they were opened, the escalators were targeted by a scathing government report deriding them as "a costly white elephant." It accused the Highway Department's "poor handling of the project" as the main reason that the escalators not only virtually failed in their goal to reduce congestion, but also ran a whopping 153% over budget. With five revisions from its February 1991 ground-breaking, the initial estimated cost of HK$97 million had ballooned to HK$245 million by its October 1993 opening.

Since then, however, the escalators have become a beloved part of the cityscape. Newspapers have taken to calling them a "stairway to urban heaven" and they have often been lauded as providing a "slice of life to Hong Kong." They are no doubt appreciated – the old markets, delicious restaurants, and bustling housing units along their snaking path draw some 55,000 travelers to the escalators per day (the initial projected estimates were 27,000).

Despite their initial controversy, the escalators have surely shown their worth to the city. In fact, the government has recently changed its critical tune and the creation of a second Mid-Levels Escalator system has been thrown onto the docket, though few details on the project have been confirmed. If nothing else, the escalators – which were praised by the Danish Architecture Centre as a sustainable form of urban transportation – could possibly soon be seen as a landmark creation for a greener urban environment.

Layout

The Mid-Levels Escalators start at 100 Queen's Road Central, at the intersection of Queen's Road Central and Cochrane Street. Following the hillside, they meander south along Cochrane Street for nearly the first half of their length before moving onto Shelley Street and finally ending at Conduit Road. Along the way, they pass by excellent Hong Kong landmarks, such as the old Central Market, the old Central Street Market, Hollywood Road Antiques Street (pg 135), the colonial era Central Police Station (pg 91), the SoHo bar district, the Jamia Mosque (pg 154), and many high-rise apartment complexes.

Taking a ride on the escalators provides a sweeping panorama of Hong Kong daily life. Riders can catch a glimpse of the myriad environments where locals work, eat, live and play.

The Escalators' Starting Point

The Escalators begin on a raised walkway that can be accessed by an escalator (yes, another escalator) at 100 Queen's Road Central or from the stairs at Cochrane Street (about 50 m [164 ft] south). Across the street from the escalator entrance building you'll see the old **Central Market**, your first landmark. Opened in the 1850s, the Central Market was Hong Kong's first wet

market, but the current buildings were put up in 1939 in the German Bauhaus style. Unfortunately, the market was closed in 2003 and is currently being renovated to create a "Green Oasis," which apparently just means more shops and restaurants.

Lyndhurst Terrace

Around Wellington Street, the Escalators gain some altitude and cross over Gage Street and Lyndhurst Terrace via a footbridge. You can access them by the street-side stairs at Lyndhurst Terrace. Look to the right when ascending for a view of the Central Street Market on Graham Street, the oldest street market in Hong Kong still in operation.

Hollywood Road

After Lyndhurst Terrace, the Escalators will bring you to Hollywood Road (pg 135) – a stretch of famous antique shops – and then along a bridge on Hollywood Road for a short distance before moving to Shelley Street. At the corner of Cochrane Street and Hollywood Road, the old **Central Police Station** comes into view. Built in grand colonial style in 1864, the building is currently undergoing a redevelopment project that will turn it into a cultural and tourism center by 2014 while preserving its historical architecture. Consider hopping off at Hollywood Road to explore the antiques and art shops lining the road to the west.

SoHo Bar District

As the Mid-Levels Escalators ascend Shelley Street, they enter the SoHo (South of Hollywood Road) bar district. Stopping here for lunch and a coffee, or an evening of bar hopping, should no doubt be a part of your Mid-Levels Escalators itinerary. Most bars and restaurants begin to peter out as you approach Caine Road.

Mosque Street & Conduit Road

After Caine Road, escalator traffic decreases significantly. This is the final stretch of the Mid-Levels Escalators, and the surrounding scenery is mostly apartment complexes. The Jamia Mosque entrance is located right alongside the escalator on Shelley Street; you can get a look at its fine exterior, but if you're a non-Muslim you won't be able to go in. The escalators finally end at Conduit Road, where you can take green minibus 3 back to Central or continue to peruse the area around the Escalators (there are some stairs along the side that you can use to head back down to the Mid-Levels).

Tsim Sha Tsui Waterfront & the Avenue of Stars

English name: Tsim Sha Tsui Waterfront
Chinese name: 尖沙咀海濱

English name: Avenue of Stars
Chinese name: 星光大道

Transport: The Tsim Sha Tsui Waterfront is hard to miss. It's located right at the Tsim Sha Tsui MTR Station. The station has long underground tunnels with almost two dozen exits emptying out at all places of interest.
Subway – Tsuen Wan Line, Tsim Sha Tsui Station, follow signs to the right exit.
Avenue of Stars: Exit J or L6
Space and Art Museums: Exit J or L6
Cultural Centre: Exit L6
Ocean Terminal, Harbour City Malls: Exit L6 or L5
Peninsula Hotel: Exit L4 or L4 or F
Chungking Mansions: Exit H or D1
iSquare Mall: Exit H or C1
Ferry – *From Hong Kong Island*: Star Ferry from Central to Star Ferry pier in Tsim Sha Tsui, between Ocean Terminal mall and the Hong Kong Cultural Centre

The first thing that many tourists go to see once they settle into Hong Kong, Tsim Sha Tsui (TST) and its unbeatable waterfront views will knock your socks off – lucky for you there are places to dip your feet in the water. A great day can be spent at TST strolling the promenade in the sun and visiting museums, but it's worth it to stick around into the evening hours as well, when the brilliantly lit-up neon skyline is joined by a fantastic laser-light show over the water.

When you first emerge from the Tsim Sha Tsui MTR station you will know you are somewhere special, as Indian touts greet you with calls for tailored suits, a refreshing sea breeze cools your face, and a spectacular view of boats cruising the water under a forest of skyscrapers stops you in your tracks. But it's not just the amazing scenery that gets you, the Tsim Sha Tsui Waterfront is also plentiful in cultural and shopping destinations, much of which is centered on Hong Kong's tribute to its once-world class film industry, the Avenue of Stars. There is also the Hong Kong Cultural Centre and Concert Hall, the Hong Kong Museum of

Tsim Sha Tsui Waterfront

Art, and the Hong Kong Space Museum.

Before You Go

To maximize your enjoyment of the Avenue of Stars, it's a good idea to bone up on your Hong Kong movie lore before you go. Certain names will be obvious to any foreigner, such as Jackie Chan and Bruce Lee, but with 102 names on the walk, a little bit of prior research can really help enrich the experience.

Also, remember that the sun can get quite strong, especially as it reflects off the water and pavement around you. Sunscreen is more than a good idea; it's a great idea. Slather up if you expect a day out.

Info & Cautions

In Ocean City and the Tsim Sha Tsui shopping areas to the east, you are bound to be approached by touts offering tailoring or other services. It's possible to get very cheap tailoring done here, but you'll obviously need to bargain hard. If you're not in the market for a tailor, just ignore them and keep walking. Further from the waterfront, around the Chungking Mansions, you may be approached by people offering hash, cocaine or prostitutes. Don't let them freak you out – they are harmless – and just keep walking.

History

The Tsim Sha Tsui Waterfront tourism area we know today is only a relatively recent creation. In fact, the land on which it is built didn't even fully exist until the start of the 20th century. It was the wide-mouthed river that used to flow through TST that gave the area its name, which means "Tip Sand Mouth," but the 19th century saw that river wholly swallowed up by a great effort of land reclamation.

At the onset of colonialism, Tsim Sha Tsui was regarded as a garden city and was used as a place of transit and export between Kowloon and Hong Kong Island. Then known as Heung Po Tao (fragrant quay), TST was a major gathering point for incense trees that were to be shipped to Hong Kong Island and, from there, the world. Actually, it was the incense at Aberdeen on Hong Kong Island that gave the city its name, which means "Fragrant Bay" (香 港) in Chinese.

Soon, foreign expatriates began setting up homes in the area as residential and transportation development began to take off in the early 20th century. The legendary Star Ferry began operating in 1888, connecting Hong Kong Island to Kowloon, and a bustling Kowloon Station rose in 1915, bringing Canton (Guangdong) and Hong Kong together by train. Development skyrocketed by the 1980s as the city began catching a serious case of the tourism bug. Kowloon Station was demolished, save for the historic clocktower that still stands in its place.

Since the '80s, the area has seen more and more tourism and notoriety, greatly encouraged by the rabid construction of cultural institutions, museums and other commemorations of Hong Kong's fascinating culture.

Layout

The Tsim Sha Tsui Waterfront is spread out at the south edge of Kowloon with shopping on the west side and the Avenue of Stars cultural area on the east side. Along the whole waterfront, you can take in spectacular views of Hong Kong. The museums and the entrance to the Avenue of Stars are all situated along Salisbury Road at Salisbury Garden.

Avenue of Stars

At its peak, Hong Kong's powerful film industry dominated the Asian market and captured the imagination of the world. Scenes featuring Jackie Chan fighting on a rooftop or Chow Yun-fat firing a gun out the window of a swerving car have had a lasting influence on cinema around the world, and today they are a beloved part of the city's heritage.

The Avenue of Stars pays homage to this impressive legacy through a series of plaques and statues dedicated to Hong Kong's most celebrated stars. Some people actually feel

Statue of Bruce Lee on the Avenue of Stars

the short strip is a somewhat lackluster tribute, but for most film fanatics, cruising the walkway and searching for their favorite celebrities is a fun experience. Besides the well-known greats like Jackie Chan, Bruce Lee and Jet Li, acclaimed directors like John Wu and Wong Kar-wai are also engraved in stars along the 440 m (1,443 ft) stretch, as well as the celebrities' handprints, signatures and a series of columns inscribed with details on Hong Kong's hundred years of cinema magic. You can also catch statues of film industry luminaries, the most commanding of which is of course Bruce Lee in a fighting stance from his 1971 classic *Fists of Fury*.

A Symphony of Lights

Of all the spots along the Tsui Sha Tsim waterfront, the Avenue of Stars offers the best views of Hong Kong Island across the water. People gather here en masse every night at 20:00 to watch the Symphony of Lights, a 44-building (on both sides of the Harbour) light show that paints the sky with a dazzling display of search lights, colored lights and laser beams, all set to a rhapsody of music that includes lyrics broadcast in Cantonese, Mandarin or English (depending on the night). English lyrics are broadcast on Mondays, Wednesdays, and Fridays (tune your radio to station 103.4 FM). Besides the Avenue of Stars on the Kowloon side, you can also watch from the promenade at Golden Bauhinia Square in

Wan Chai on the Hong Kong side.

Hong Kong Philharmonic Orchestra at the Hong Kong Cultural Center

At the same time as the Symphony of Lights, there are regular orchestral performances going on at the nearby Hong Kong Cultural Centre. Euphonic sounds fill the Concert Hall from the orchestra and its 8,000-pipe organ, which is the largest in Asia. The Hong Kong Philharmonic Orchestra plays here at 20:00 most Friday and Saturday nights, with tickets prices ranging from HK$120 to HK$160 and up. Occasionally, they also play on weekdays and afternoons, giving over 100 performances a year. For their upcoming schedule, visit the website: **www.hkphil.org/eng/concerts_and_ticket/concerts/**

The Grand Theatre of the Hong Kong Cultural Centre hosts operas, plays, ballets, and other performances, too.

Hong Kong Museum of Art

Chinese name: 香港藝術館
Admission: HK$10, FREE (Wed)
Hours: 10:00-18:00 (Mon, Tue, Wed & Fri); 10:00-19:00 (Sat & Sun); closed Thu
Hours: 10 Salisbury Rd

Art enthusiasts can continue on to the Hong Kong Museum of Art (adjacent to Salisbury Garden on the west) and appreciate the

traveling exhibitions of Chinese and Western art. The museum is lauded for its exhibitions of Chinese calligraphy, porcelain, Chinese paintings, and other traditional arts. Its permanent collection is relatively small, and the amount of contemporary art on display is somewhat lacking, but for an entrance fee of HK$10 and free admission on Wednesdays, it's hard to beat for art lovers.

Hong Kong Space Museum

Chinese name: 香港太空館
Admission: HK$10, FREE (Wed)
Hours: 13:00-21:00 (Mon, Wed, Thu & Fri); 10:00-21:00 (Sat & Sun); closed Tue

The Space Museum in the egg-shaped building just north of the Museum of Art can be a good place for families with children. The planetarium and Omnimax shows, which offer free headphones for listening in multiple languages, are particularly interesting for kids, but the exhibits feel like they haven't changed since the place was opened in 1980. The "stand and read" displays also seem outdated, lacking in interactivity and boring most visitors to death. As with the Museum of Art and all government-managed museums in Hong Kong, the Space Museum is free on Wednesdays.

Shopping

Tsim Sha Tsui is one of the reasons Hong Kong earned its shopaholic reputation. Further inland from the habor, TST has some bargain-friendly malls where you can buy cheap tailored suits, souvenirs, wholesale apparel items, and electronics. Most are found at places like the **Chungking Mansions** and the surrounding buildings. Across the street from the Mansions you'll also find the relatively higher end but still affordable **iSquare Mall** (國際廣場 ; 63 Nathan Rd; www.isquare.hk).

As you get closer to the Harbour, the shopping becomes more expensive and luxurious. Even if you don't have a few thousand Hong Kong dollars to drop on a shirt, the ostentatious complexes housing these stores are quite the spectacle. The **1881 Heritage Podium at the Hullet House**, with its exquisite square of staircases, columns, well-manicured bushes, and Ermenegildo Zegna's (a fashion designer) portrait is the height of luxury. In the same neighborhood you'll also find the Langham, the Kowloon Hotel, and the Peninsula Hotel. Each one of these grand hotels is a charming place for English tea time as well as luxury shopping and lodging.

More affordable but still quality shopping can be found at the west end of the waterfront at the **Ocean Terminal** (海 運 大 廈) and **Harbour City** (海港城), and on the east side, in front of the Salisbury Garden, at the **Sogo Department Store** (崇光百貨), which houses a Japanese grocery store with international food.

Repulse Bay

Chinese name: 淺水灣
Transport:
Subway – No direct subway to Repulse Bay. Take the subway to Central or Causeway Bay MTR Station and transfer to a bus that goes to Repulse Bay.
Bus – *From Central*: 6 (MTR Exit A), 6X toward Stanley Prison
From Causeway Bay: Green Minibus 40 toward Stanley Village
Taxi – Taxi fare from Central to Repulse Bay is about HK$90

Just 20 to 40 minutes outside the heart of the city, Repulse Bay offers beautiful sea and hillside views and a lively beach atmosphere. The Repulse Bay beach, long having been a haven of the upper crest, is one of the most popular and nicest beaches in the city. It has been highly developed and now includes quality amenities like showers, changing rooms, a playground, barbecue grills, beach volleyball courts and a shark net, as well as on-duty lifeguards from March to November. There are also plenty of luxury houses in the area (just in case you're in the market). Heck, there's even a Ferrari and Maserati showroom on the road leading up to the beach! Celebrities like Jackie Chan and Stanley Ho (a Macau gambling magnate; see pg 249) have homes here, and Ernest Hemingway used to spend time at the old Repulse Bay Hotel. The shopping and restaurants are well regarded, but be aware that things get mighty crowded during the summer. Rounding out the beach's attractions are the brightly colored **Tin Hau Temple**, which honors the sea goddess, and several statues that are popular for photo ops.

There are a few other beaches near Repulse Bay – Deep Water Bay, Middle Bay, and South Bay – that are less crowded and favored by visitors who prefer a less commercialized feel. Deep Water Bay is particularly noted for its big waves, and there is a lovely boardwalk connecting it and the Repulse Bay beach. The most secluded beaches, however, are Middle Bay beach and South Bay beach to the south, the latter of which sometimes go days with only a few visitors.

Before You Go

Be ready for crowds if you come to Repulse Bay in the summer. This is one of the most popular beaches in Hong Kong, and is especially favored by Mainland Chinese tour groups that pour out of endless tour buses. They love to jam up the entrance taking photos, and it can get frustrating for many foreigners, who are put off by the fact that Mainland tourists will often snap photos of them and their children without asking. You'll need to be on your toes.

Bringing your own food can also be a good idea, otherwise you'll be forced to buy snacks at the expensive grocery store that sits under the nearby apartments.

History

Repulse Bay hasn't always been the carefree beach escape that it is today. Historically, the area has had more than its share of bloodshed and brutal battles. It was in the 1800s that Repulse Bay was the staging ground for vicious pirate attacks on merchant ships. The British military drove most of the pirates out with the HMS Repulse, christening the bay with its namesake. Early maps, including Sir Edward Belcher's 1841 map (the first British survey of Hong Kong) referred to the area around Repulse Bay as Chonghom Bay.

In the 1910s, Repulse Bay was developed for tourism, and the beach was expanded with imported sand. After the Repulse Bay Hotel was built in the 1920's, the area became a classy getaway for the wealthy.

Violence was to hit the bay again in 1941 with the onset of World War II. When the Japanese invaded Hong Kong in 1941,

many residents fled to the relatively isolated Repulse Bay in the south, some taking residence at the Repulse Bay Hotel. The Japanese advance occurred quickly: by December 20, they had descended on the bay as hundreds of soldiers filled the beach and surrounding mountains and fired on the hotel. The next day, Major Robert Templar brought reinforcements. Templar and his men "rolled grenades along the beautifully carpeted corridors, [as if they were in] a bowling alley," taking out Japanese machine gunners set up in the halls. Even some of the civilian guests joined the fighting as the Japanese continued shelling the hotel from the outside. Several days later, Templar evacuated the British military. Civilians were taken as prisoners of war and held at a paint factory in North Point. The siege of the hotel is depicted in Ann Hui's 1984 film *Love in a Fallen City*.

The Repulse Bay Hotel from the film Love in a Fallen City

In 1982, the Repulse Bay Hotel was torn down and a luxurious new apartment was built in its place, along with a replica of the hotel lobby. The Repulse Bay, as the apartments are called, were built in a modern art deco style with contours of the building curving in wave-like patterns, a perfect look for beach apartments. You'll notice that one of the apartments has an eight story-tall hole carved out of the tower. This *feng shui* design was inspired by the legend of a dragon who lives in the hills surrounding Repulse Bay and enjoys watching the sunset in the evenings. Because construction of the apartments would have blocked his access to the bay, a hole was conceived to keep his path open and prevent a *feng shui* debacle.

Layout

Repulse Bay is on the south side of Hong Kong Island, on the edge of Tai Tam Country Park (pg 102), northwest of the Stanley Peninsula. It is part of a series of

A Repulse Bay apartment complex

bays extending in a southward hump from the island that culminates at Stanley. From north to south, the beaches found here are Deep Water Bay, Repulse Bay, Middle Bay, and South Bay, all lying within 6 km (4 mi) of each other.

Repulse Bay Beach

On the west end of Repulse Bay Beach is **The Repulse Bay** (the aforementioned apartment complex), the old site of the historic Repulse Bay Hotel and the current site of high-end apartments, where you can find a shopping center and a replica of the hotel lobby that contains a historical gallery emphasizing the hotel's Jazz Age ambiance. For high-end dining, the Repulse Bay complex includes the restaurants **Verandah** (露 台 餐 廳 ; address: G/F, The Arcade, 109 Repulse Bay Rd; phone: 2292 2822; closed Mon & Tue) and **Spices** (香 辣 軒 ; address: G/F, The Arcade, 109 Repulse Bay Rd; phone: 2292 2821). The Verandah serves European cuisine inside a colonial-looking building and hosts English afternoon tea and a delightful sunday brunch. Spices serves stylish Asian dishes.

On the east end of the beach you can find a great collection of colorful statues of cultural icons. In particular, head over to find a **Tin Hau Temple**, honoring the Taoist goddess of the sea, and the mosaic **Kwun Yam Shrine**, built in homage to the goddess of mercy. From here, Longevity Bridge steers its way out to sea through a series of statues, including those of the Monkey God, rams, and a fish with an open mouth that you can throw money into. It all looks a bit tacky and the colors seem a little bit too vibrant (almost fluorescent), as most of it was built

in the 1970s with funding from business and cultural leaders.

Near the middle of the beach, towards the western half, there is a public parking area on the beach side and public restrooms sit across the street. At the western edge of the beach, a seaview promenade begins that shoulders the coast from Repulse Bay Beach to Deep Water Bay Beach.

Deep Water Bay Beach

Follow the seaview promenade from Repulse Bay Beach and you end up at Deep Water Bay Beach. Hidden behind a cover of trees, Deep Water Bay Beach has a more secluded feel to it than Repulse Bay. The Hong Kong Gold Club is just behind the beach on the other side of Island Road.

Middle Bay Beach & South Bay Beach

On the east side of Repulse Bay is Middle Bay, a 600 m (1,970 ft) walk from the eastern edge of Repulse Bay beach. There is no public transportation from Repulse Bay to Middle Bay or Southern Bay, so you have to walk down South Bay Road to reach them. South Bay beach is a further 700 m (2,296 ft) down th road from Middle Bay beach. Once the home of noisy expat-filled beach bars, these two beaches have quieted down since government regulations closed down some of the noisier bars. The remaining beach kiosks are smaller and much more low key.

Stanley

Chinese name: 赤柱
Transport: With no MTR station, Stanley is best accessed by bus.
Bus – 6, 6A, 6X, and 260 from Exchange Square Bus Terminus at Central MTR Station are the best options to get to Stanley. They take a scenic coastal road past Repulse Bay and can be boarded along Connaught Rd in the Central area as well. Bus 66 leaves from the same terminus and stops at Stanley Plaza, but it only operates on weekdays during peak hours.
From Causeway Bay: Green Minibus 40 (runs all-day and night)
From Tsim Sha Tsui: 973 can be caught on Jordan Rd and Salisbury Rd (goes to Stanley Market)

Don't get confused, Stanley is still Hong Kong, even though it may look like the French Riviera. Sure, there are plenty of tree-lined streets, ocean-side restaurants serving cassoulet and beaches with droves of tanning foreigners, but in the French Riviera, you can't find bamboo bird cage decorations or Chinese calligraphy.

Stanley isn't just a market or a waterfront; it's a tranquil beach town on the south coast of Hong Kong Island. Get started on Stanley Market Road, where the huge trees that shade the streets are anchored by long roots weaving their way up buildings in a tangle of directions. They are a fitting metaphor for the streets of this laidback area, which is best explored by just picking a road and seeing where it takes you. Eventually, you'll be led to something that pleases your tastes.

History

Before the British arrived in Stanley, it was known as Chuck Chu, meaning Robber's Lair, as a testament to the pirates who lurked in the waters back in the day. The long-time fishing village was Britain's temporary administrative center when they landed in Hong Kong in 1842.

Stanley was the point of the allied forces' last stand on Hong Kong Island when the Japanese invaded in World War II. Countless civilians were held at the Stanley Internment Camp that was located here, and those who died defending Hong Kong at the time are buried at the Stanley Military Cemetery.

After the war, Stanley quickly became a popular tourist destination because of its distance from the city. The area was soon listed in 1950s travel articles as a highlight of Hong Kong, and this popularity has only continued to increase. It remains a crowded tourist market today, aided by the opening of the Stanley Plaza in 2000 and the Murray House in 2002, a building that was originally built in Central in 1844 before it was moved here.

Layout

Stanley is located on a peninsula sticking out from the very south end of Hong Kong Island, south of Deep Water Bay and Repulse Bay, and along the same road. The Stanley Market in the center of the village sits at the top of the small peninsula and is bordered by Tai Tam Bay on the east and Stanley Bay on the west. While it may not be the largest area you've ever come across, it is most certainly packed to the gills with things to do. Take in your surroundings as you walk under the shaded cover of wide-trunked trees and you will find parks, beaches, markets and shops galore.

Stanley Market (赤柱市集)

When you get to Stanley you will probably

first arrive at or near the Stanley Market. Be warned that it has the same kind of tacky products as the far superior Temple Street Market (pg 71) and Ladies Street (pg 80), but with higher prices and without as lively of an atmosphere. There are calligraphy depictions of English names for sale, but many locals have scoffed at the quality of the calligraphy, and you're still probably better off saving your money. You'll also find some small bird cages, wooden frames, and Chinese-themed decorations that might actually work well as a souvenir (if that's what you need), but otherwise, this market really isn't worth your time.

Beaches

The real reason you come to Stanley is for the beaches, which are lined with restaurants and shops.

Stanley Main Beach (赤柱正灘) is on the east side of the peninsula just down Stanley New

Street from the market. This is where you'll find the largest crowds of people swimming in shark-netted water (to keep the sharks out) and grilling on the beach. Those looking for water sports can check out the Water Sports Centre, which has wind surfing and kayaking lessons and rentals.

On the west side of the peninsula is the much less crowded **St Stephen's Beach** (聖士提反灣泳灘), a 15-minute walk south from the market. It also has barbecue pits, changing rooms, showers and water-sport rentals. St Stephen's Beach is just down the road from the Military Cemetery, where casualties of World War II are buried.

Military Cemetery (軍人墳場)

The Military Cemetery is the final resting site of about 500 allied soldiers who lost their lives, some of them defending Hong Kong to the bitter end in World War II, as well as 96 civilians who died at the Stanley Internment Camp. British soldiers were buried here from 1841 to 1866, but the practice was halted for nearly 80 years until the end of World War II. Built on a hill with sharp, grassy slopes, a set of stairs leads up from the main entrance with the Cross of Sacrifice displayed prominently on top.

Teresa Teng's Mansion (鄧麗君故居)

Her songs were banned in China throughout the 1980s, but that didn't stop Taiwanese singer Teresa Teng from setting the stage for Mandopop in China. With her sweet voice and good-girl image, Teng was a sensation whose love ballads proliferated despite being labeled "bourgeois" by the CCP in the 1980s (see pg 24 in the Overview for more on Teng).

In 1986, she bought a place in Stanley at **18 Carmel Street** and lived in the greenish blue house every autumn when Hong Kong hairy crabs were in season. After her death in 1995, her personal assistant Cheong Kam-mei continued to live in the mansion, listening to her music and watching her videos for nearly

Dresses inside Teresa Teng's Mansion

a decade until the place was sold in 2004. When the house was opened to the public, hundreds of thousands of people showed up to visit, a great testament Teng's impact on the lives and consciousness of the people of China. Giddy visitors finally got to see the interior of her famous residence, including her elegant dresses and her famous all-pink bedroom.

Unfortunately the home is not open to the public anymore, but you can still stop by to admire it from the outside. Those who want to see Teresa Teng memorabilia can visit the Teresa Teng New Life Coffee Shop (甜蜜蜜 新生咖啡店 ; address: Shop 35, East Tsim Sha Tsui Station; phone: 2723 6634) in Tsim Sha Tsui.

Ma Hang Park (馬坑公園)

Perched on the edge of a cliff, Ma Hang Park offers an impeccable view of the South China Sea. Walk along the **Sea View Terrace**, the **Heritage Corner** and the **Bird Watching Corner** for some outstanding views and great vistas. Don't forget to check out the **Pak Thai Temple**, dedicated to a dynastic military leader.

Dining

Stanley Promenade (赤柱海濱長廊)

A nice place for an ocean-side stroll, the Stanley Promenade is also a nice place to catch a bite to eat at an outdoor café. The cafes along the Stanley Promenade are quite casual, but a little bit on the expensive side. If you're looking for a pint of beer instead, the promenade also has some very nice pubs.

Murray House (美利樓)

The Murray House is the perfect spot for diners who want to enjoy the European flare of Stanley. Like the majority of Stanley's

sites, this house isn't an original Stanley construction. The old British colonial-style was first built in Central in 1844 at the current site of the Bank of China building, but disassembled in 1982, only to be reassembled in Stanley in 2001 in almost the exact same form (besides a few extra columns that were put up in a row along the shoreline walk). The dining inside takes things to an even more foreign level with high end Spanish, German and Vietnamese restaurants serving up anything but local food.

Stanley Plaza (赤柱廣場)

As far as shopping goes, the Stanley Plaza isn't trying to trick you. It's clear about what it is: a trendy mall. You can find shops like G.O.D., furniture and clothing stores, Dogaroo (a dog training school that also runs a café and a pet hotel), and even Taste, a typical international supermarket that pretends it isn't a supermarket. Their tagline "It's More than Food" purports to"add excitement to your daily grocery shopping."

The restaurants follow in form. As with the Murray House, you can "pretend you're in Paris" at the Chez Patrick Deli, or enjoy the "European-style casual al fresco dining" at Classified, but you have a few Chinese choices as well, such as the Xia Fei Shanghainese Restaurant and Chung's Cuisine.

For sleeping see page 180, eating page 208, and drinking page 224.

Po Lin Monastery

Chinese name: 寶蓮禪寺
Admission: FREE
Hours: 7:30-18:00
Phone: 2985 5248
Website: www.plm.org.hk
Transport:
1. Tung Chung MTR Station, Exit B, take the Ngong Ping Cable Car (25 min) and walk 10 min to the Monastery
2. Tung Chung MTR Station, Exit B, take New Lantao Bus 23 (45 min) from Tung Chung Town Centre
3. Catch a ferry from Central Pier 6 to Mui Wo, take New Lantao Bus 2 (40 min) to Ngong Ping Village

When it comes time for a break from the steel jungle it may be time to escape to Lantau Island for the monastery atop its renowned Ngong Ping Plateau. Built by three monks from Jiangsu Province, the massive Po Lin Monastery complex occupies a staggering 2,239 sq m (24,100 sq ft) and is sprinkled with enough intricate monastic halls, tantric Big Buddha chambers and lush forests and trails to keep you spiritually satiated for weeks. The star attraction, however, is the Tian Tan bronze Buddha statue, the largest of its kind in the world and one of Hong Kong's most prized spiritual treasures.

The largest island in Hong Kong, Lantau has remained mostly undeveloped because of its superbly rugged mountainous terrain, and

Po Lin Monastery Main Gate

while that makes it difficult for the building of urban centers, it was apparently perfect for Hong Kong's largest Buddhist monastery (as well as several others). Besides a few areas of over-touristification, Lantau Island and its wonderful monasteries remain some of the city's most memorably serene retreats.

The bus to Po Lin goes over mountain roads with steep grades and turns jarring enough to make you lose your Po Lin Kitchen (a vegetarian restaurant next to the monastery) meal if you have a weak stomach. Out the window are views of jagged coastline and an island-filled ocean extending into the horizon. You can see why in 1906 the three monks from Jiangsu chose this splendid location as the site for an enormous monastery.

Before You Go

The Po Lin Monastery is just one of many worthwhile sights on Lantau Island, all of which are accessible via bus. A full-day bus pass for Lantau Island will allow you to get on any of the buses and also see places like Tai O Fishing Village (pg 74) and Long Beach. Po Lin is also accessible via a hiking trail that will take you over Lantau Peak and a cable car with bird's eye views. If you want to take the cable car, you can buy tickets online in advance to skip the long lines (see the Vital Info for the website).

Notes & Cautions

Watch out for the Ngong Ping Village "theme park." The faux village was built by the MTR company as nothing more than a tourist trap, and trap tourists does it ever! It's placed right at the top station of the Ngong Ping 360 Gondola and the alighting point of the bus stop, so you'll need to be on your toes when you get off your transport as local touts try to direct you in. Po Lin Monastery is down a path a little ways in the opposite direction, so for those who don't get really pumped on completely fake villages built like a theme park, it's best to pull a 180 as soon as you arrive and high-tail it to the monastery.

History

In 1906, the monks Da Yue, Dun Xiu, and Yun Ming of Buddhism's Chan School traveled from Jiangsu to Hong Kong and found the sublime scenery next to Lantau Peak moving enough to build a monastery. Initially known as Tai Mao Pung (大茅蓬), the "Big Thatched Hut," in 1924 it was renamed Po Lin Monastery, a name meaning "Precious Lotus." Many of the first major buildings were built in the 1920s and '30s. Specifically, the Hall of Great Perfection was built in 1928, while the Hall of Bodhisattva Skanda, the Hall of Bodhisattva Ksitigardbha, the

Ancestral Hall, the Abbot's Chamber, the Five Contemplations Dining Hall, the Pagoda of the Lotus Sutra, and the Pagoda of the Flower Ornament Sutra were all built in 1930.

Inspiration for the Tian Tan Buddha first came in 1973 when the Venerables Chi Wai, Yuen Wai, and other monks visited the Caodong School of Japan and the grand Buddha statues in Zhanghua, Taiwan. In 1974, the government granted 6,567 sq m (70,687 sq ft) of land in Mount Muk Yue on which to build the statue, but work didn't begin until April 1982. When the full-size statue was ready to be constructed, it was built in 202 separate pieces, which were individually shipped to Hong Kong in 1989. The final piece was laid on October 13 of that year. Interior design and road construction continued for four years, and the inaugural ceremony for the Big Buddha was held on December 29, 1993, 11 years after the project started.

Still, the Po Lin Monastery didn't take off as a tourist attraction until the government figured out how to make transportation to the island easier. In 1997, the Lantau Link was created, connecting Lantau Island to the rest of Hong Kong by road and subway. In 2006, the Ngong Ping Cable Car was opened.

Layout

The Po Lin Monastery sits at the base of Lantau Peak to the west. The main attraction, the Tian Tan Buddha, rests on a *tian tan*, meaning "altar of heaven," atop Mount Muk Yue as he watches over the monastery below. The complex has seen a few renovations in recent years and now has fresh buildings in front. One of the additions is the **Grand Hall of Ten Thousand Buddhas**, which contains thousands of statues of Buddhas and bodhisattvas, each with a unique expression.

The first thing you'll come across on the monastery grounds is the *di tan* – the "altar of earth" – at the base of the Big Buddha mountain. A staircase of 260 steps leads from the *di tan* to the *tian tan* on which the Buddha sits. The main entrance to the monastery itself is the **Hall of Bodhisattva Skanda**. The **Main Shrine Hall of Buddha** showcases three Buddhas of the past, the present, and the future.

Tian Tan Big Buddha

On a clear day you can see the Tian Tan Big Buddha from Macau, that's how big this 34 m- (112 ft)-tall effigy is. Unlike the contrived tourist town of Ngong Ping 360, it was not created for tourism. This Buddha is imbued with deep philosophical and spiritual meaning and has become an important pilgrimage site for many Chinese. From conception to opening, it took decades to create. Details like the **Dharmacakra** (wheel of the law) on each of the palms, and the left hand positioned in the mudra of "fulfilling wishes" (i.e. palm turned up and fingers pointed downward), were masterfully designed to convey a deep significance. It is surrounded by six statues of bodhisattvas giving offerings to the Lord Gautama, while a bell inside rings 108 times a day, intended to help cleanse visitors of the so-called "108 vexations of mankind." Check out the mausoleum and museum just inside, where many late Hong Kong Buddhists lay (or hope one day to lay) at rest. Some of Hong Kong's most famous are memorialized inside, including the legendary singer Anita Mui, whose commemorative plaque is on level with the monks of the monastery.

Constructing the Buddha was quite a challenge. The road up to the monastery is squeezed by tight curves in many places, making it very difficult to haul some of the statue's massive and awkward pieces. The Buddha was actually first built in Nanjing as 202 individual bronze pieces that were shipped to Hong Kong, where they were assembled onsite. Due to the complexities of creating, transporting, and constructing the effigy, the Tian Tan Buddha was elected as the fourth engineering wonder of Hong Kong in 2000.

Ngong Ping 360

You would think that at a monastery would avoid the tacky, thoughtless, anything-for-a-dollar attitude gratuitously displayed at Ngong Ping 360. Think again. The Ngong Ping 360 themed village is set up to look like it's really old, but the buildings were only recently set up by the MTR company to be a gold mine for local developers. Inside, you'll find shops, restaurants and themed attractions, like the Monkey's Tale Theatre video that supposedly shows a "Buddhist-themed video." It's tacky commercialism at it's best, and if you want to

avoid it just walk east to the actual monastery after you get off the bus or tram. Both forms of transportation "conveniently" let you off at Ngong Ping.

Lantau Peak

The top of Lantau Peak, the second-highest peak in Hong Kong at 934 m (3,064 ft), offers breathtaking views of the vast ocean and the islands that scatter the waves, including those of Macau, Hong Kong, and Lamma. It's part of the Lantau Trail that runs around the island. Stage 3 of the trail will take you from the Po Lin Monastery to the peak, and you can keep hiking down the other side to Tung Chung Rd, where you can grab a bus to the Tung Chung MTR station. Another option is to sleep at the **Ngong Ping SG Davis Hostel** (滙豐銀行慈善基金戴維斯旅舍 ; phone: 2985 5610) and wake up early the next morning to reach the summit in time for sunrise.

A few other trails exist to the east of the monastery. For more on the hike to Lantau Peak and other trails in the area, see the entry for Lantau Island Country Parks on page 110.

Chi Lin Nunnery

Chinese name: 志蓮淨苑
Admission: FREE
Hours: 9:00-16:30
Phone: 2354 1888
Website: www.chilin.org (in Cantonese)
Address: 5 Chi Lin Dr, Diamond Hill, Kowloon (九龍鑽石山志蓮道五號)
Transport: Subway – MTR Diamond Hill Station, Exit C2, follow the signs and walk east down Fung Tak Rd for around 5 min

Hidden on the lesser traveled eastern side of Kowloon is a Buddhist nunnery of extraordinary beauty. Even if you have already been in Asia for months and are sick of temples, the Chi Lin Nunnery's resplendence will steal your breath. The complex of temples is expertly crafted in a traditional Tang Dynasty style: made completely of wood with no nails (Tang Dynasty architecture of this kind used dowel and bracket work to fit beams together). Not only beautiful, the Chi Lin Nunnery is

peacefully free from the hordes of tourists snapping selfies in front of every piece of scenery, and nunnery rules call on visitors to be quiet and respectful. Come for the bonsai trees, lotus-speckled ponds, evocative eaved-roof buildings and colorful bridges; stay for the pleasant pitter-patter of nuns making offerings to Buddha deep in their calming incantations.

The more than 33,000 sq m (8 acres) of Chi Lin Nunnery are divided into two areas: the nunnery itself and the **Nan Lian Garden** (南蓮園池 ; phone: 2329 8811; hours: 10:00-18:00; website: www.nanliangarden.org). Though the complex is nearly a century old, it was rebuilt in its present style in the 1990s. That being said, this place is far from the faux ancient architecture you might find in other parts of newly-built China. The amount of intricacy and loving detail put in to this, the largest complex of hand-crafted timber buildings in the world, is on a level of its own.

Before You Go

As an active nunnery, be aware that the Chi Lin Nunnery expects a level of courtesy and etiquette from its guests. There are a number of rules that should be observed. Visitors are asked to dress appropriately, and this means minimizing the skin you show (no shorts and no bare shoulders) and being aware of places that may ask you to remove your shoes upon entry. In the Nan Lian Garden, visitors shouldn't take group photos or use a tripod, and there is no eating or drinking in the garden outside of the vegetarian restaurant.

While the nuns are aware that this is a tourist destination, and they will not be offended if you aren't perfectly dressed for a nunnery, doing your best to hold yourself appropriately will earn you the respect of those around you.

History

The Chi Lin Nunnery was founded in Diamond Hill in 1934 at the foot of Ma On Shan Country Park's hills and mountains. It has always been open to the public, but it wasn't until 2000 that it became a major

tourist attraction after it was redeveloped in the Tang style. The redevelopment effort started in 1990, reaching its completiong in 2000, and upon its reopening the nunnery pulled in 13,000 visitors the first day and 23,000 the next. A staggering US$90 million was poured into the project, which imported wood and 400,000 typhoon-resistant Tang roof tiles from Japan. The crowds have fortunately tamed since reopening day, but it is still a hugely popular attraction, with about five dozen nuns living and worshipping inside.

Layout

The Chi Lin Nunnery faces the sea, with its main gate facing south as in traditional Chinese *feng shui* design. It's flanked on both sides by towering mountains, and the layout is based around three courtyards (two are open to the public) which are set in the middle and framed by ornamental halls and rooms. Making excellent use of open space, the courtyards help *qi* (vital energy) to flow freely through the complex, and many are graced by lovely gardens. Enter into the first courtyard via Shanmen (Mountain Gate).

First Courtyard

The first courtyard is marked by an elegant garden dotted with four lotus ponds, statues, rockeries, bonsai tea trees and lovely peonies. Look for the beautiful dragon head spouts pouring water into the ponds, rippling the water just enough to gently bob the lily pads and their pretty lotus flowers (the lotus is a very important flower in Chinese Buddhism, look for lotus themes around the complex).

Hall of the Celestial Kings

At the end of the first courtyard is the Hall of the Celestial Kings, an imposingly gorgeous building perched on a terrace and shouldering two side towers. The double-eaved roofing of the central hall is stunning enough on its own, but in combination with similar complementary roofs on the side towers, this building is quite the eye-catcher. Notice the two horn-like gilded ornaments capping the central hall, and try to get in close for a look at the flower etchings along the edges of the rooftop corners. The whole scene is touched off by soothing wind chimes that hang from the eaves. Inside is a statue of the Maitreya Buddha.

Second Courtyard

After the Hall of Celestial Kings, you enter the second courtyard, which houses the **Drum Tower** and the **Bell Tower** surrounded by five halls, with the Main Hall on the north end.

The **Ksitigarbha Hall** and the **Hall of Bhaisajyaguru** are both located on the right side of the courtyard. You'll find the Bell Tower on the second floor of the Ksitigarbha Hall. On the first floor is the bald statue of the Bodhisattva Ksitigarbha, who vowed not to obtain Buddhahood until "all hells were emptied" and is considered the bodhisattva of all hell beings. The Hall of Bhaisajyaguru has a **statue of Bhaisajyaguru**, the Medicine

Buddha. Bhaisajyaguru is said to heal the sick and suffering and is depicted here holding a medicine bowl. Suryaprabha, the sunlight bodhisattva, and Candraprabha, the moonlight bodhisattva, sit on either side of Bhaisajyaguru.

Across from those two halls are the **Jai Lin Hall** and the **Hall of Avalokitesvara**. The Jai Lin Hall, which has its own drum tower, displays a statue of Jai Lin Bodhisattva. Pop in the Hall of Avalokitesvara for a lovely statue of Guanyin, the goddess of mercy.

Main Hall

At the north end of the Second Courtyard, the stunning **Main Hall** beckons with its grand roof, which is covered with 28,000 clay tiles, weighs over 159 tons, and is surrounded by gardens and outstanding woodwork. Get your pictures outside, because not only is this hall a powerful sight, but once you're inside you won't be able to take photos of the **five gilded Buddhas**, including the inspiring Sakyamuni in the center, and the bodhisattvas that flank him. The Bodhisattva Majusre and the Bodhisattva Samantabhandra sit on Buddha's left and right, respectively, and two disciples stand in between them.

Nan Lian Garden

The Nan Lian Garden blooms outside the gate of the Chi Lin Nunnery just on the south side. Brick trails lead around the garden, which is covered with trees, flowers, and bonsais. The trails fork off around a pond, and on an island in the middle of the pond is the **Perfection Pavilion**, a two-story hexagonal tower with squintingly shiny gold paint. The island is connected by two perfectly red bridges, but visitors unfortunately cannot cross the bridges to the pavilion. Another pond is at the other end of the garden, which is crossed by a covered wooden bridge. At the very far end of the garden behind the other pond is the **Chi Lin Vegetarian Restaurant** (志蓮素 齋; phone: 3658 9388;12:00-21:00; HK$101-150) and the lovely **Pavilion of Pine and Tea** (松 茶 榭 ; phone: 3658 9390; tea from HK$150; hours: noon-19:30). On the north side is a garden with miniature bonsai trees.

Temple Street Night Market

English name: Temple Street Night Market
Chinese name: 廟街夜市
Admission: FREE
Hours: 24 hours

English name: Tin Hau Temple
Chinese name: 天后廟
Admission: FREE
Hours: 8:00-17:00

Transport:
Subway – *South entrance*: Jordan MTR, Exit A, walk west down Jordan St, turn right on the third street
North entrance: Yau Ma Tei MTR, Exit C, walk west on Man Ming Ln, turn left at the second street

There's nowhere that brings to life the gritty and vibrant street culture of working class Kowloon quite like Temple Street. This night market has everything, from a huge selection of trinkets and clothing to singing, fortune telling and even black market operations.

Entering from the south at Jordan Street, the market leads you under a strip of banners and red lanterns. Soon you come upon a warren of bustling vendor stalls selling paintings, T-shirts, Chinese decorations, bags, fake watches, toys, and much more. Spread out between the stalls, the outdoor tables of restaurants quickly fill up with swarms of hungry, happy and rowdy folk. Called *dai pai dong*, these open-air food stalls are where you can kill your hunger and light a fire in your belly with spicy crab, barbecued meat, and delicious noodle and rice dishes. On the adjacent streets, there is a wide variety of international dining options as well, such as sushi, Indian curry, Hainan chicken, and traditional Cantonese fare. There are even a few shanty-town style open buildings covered with corrugated metal scraps and filled with tables.

But the real fun starts when you get away from the restaurants and the night market stalls. Walk north of Kansu Street, where the fortune tellers huddle in their tents across from outdoor karaoke bars. This is a great place to wander, stopping occasionally to watch an elderly couple belt acappella Cantonese Opera outside the post office as if they haven't aged a day since 20 (starting at 20:00 most nights), or cheer on the past-their-prime divas singing Cantonese classics in lounge bars north of Public Square Street. Don't forget to enjoy the Tin Hau Temple complex that splits Temple Street in two. If you're feeling lucky, try to talk your way into one of the mahjong parlors darkened with tinted windows and stationed with burly door guards and win (or lose) some money. Keep your head up; you might even meet some Triad gangsters!

Before You Go

The street market officially opens every afternoon at 14:00, but it doesn't really get bustling until the evening.

Info & Cautions

Temple Street doesn't offer the best deals in town, nor does it offer the worst. Most deals fall somewhere in the middle, and like all markets, haggling is essential. A good rule of thumb is to never pay more than 50% of the original quoted price.

Temple Street does have a reputation for being a Triad and prostitute haven, but they don't bother tourists, and you'd be hard pressed to find them anyway.

History

Like a Chinese temple fair, this market sprung up around an old holy site. At the center of Temple Street, just north of Kansu Street, is the **Yau Ma Tei Tin Hau Temple** complex. Built in the 1860s, it was here that vendors began selling food and religious items just outside the temple. As Kowloon began developing more quickly, sellers had to move away from the temple and down the road. In 1975, a system was created to organize the market into 600 spots for merchants.

The market became a destination not just for trade, but also for entertainment. In the latter half of the 1900s, singers and Cantonese opera troupes began making the street their home base of performances, and it was here that Anita Mui began singing as a child in the 1960s and '70s. The professional and semi-professional soloists singing to Casio keyboard music along the lounge bars on the Yau Ma Tei section of the street are some of the last of their kind remaining in Hong Kong.

The unique local color of Temple Street later lead a number of directors to choose the sight for filming. Some of these flicks include *Queen of Temple Street* (1990), a film portraying prostitution, as well as the Triad story *The Prince of Temple Street* (1992).

Layout

From the south end at Jordan Street to the north end at Man Ming Lane (文 明 里), including the temple in between, the market along Temple Street covers nearly one kilometer, and all of the roads around the sides of Temple Street are packed with restaurants. Most people enter from the south gate on Jordan Street, which is considered the main entrance. North of the temple, you'll find the quieter, less crowded vendors. If you're looking to have your fortune read, then head to the road directly south of the temple.

Southern Entrance to Temple Street

The main entrance to the Temple Street night market is the gate at the intersection of Temple Street and Jordan Street. As you walk under the gate, notice the banners strewn across the street above as you soon find yourself walking down a line of stalls and restaurant tables. Brick and mortar restaurants are splayed out all along Woosung Street and Shanghai Street to the east and west. Temple Street continues north until it hits a break at the Tin Hau Temple.

Tin Hau Temple

Temple Street's namesake, Tin Hau Temple, is among the most famous of the many Tin Hau temples in Hong Kong. Built in the 1860s to honor the goddess of the sea Tin Hau, it is one of only two Tin Hau temples to be ascribed Hong Kong's highest historical status. The complex consists of the **Shing Wong Temple**, **Fook Tak Temple** and **Shea Tan**, and is bordered on either side by a

Food stalls at Temple Street Night Market

park. The large **Yau Ma Tei Community Centre Rest Garden** to the west is often full of Hong Kong locals during the day relaxing on benches with a tree in the center, and sometimes charitable groups pass out fruit and sing to the elderly during the day. The smaller Public Square Street Children's Playground and Rest Garden to the west include a beautiful and intricate Nine-Dragon Wall.

At the Tin Hau Temple, Temple Street briefly disappears, but it continues on the other side of the Rest Garden.

Fortune Tellers

Just after Temple Street crosses Kansu Street and runs into the temple, the stalls of fortune tellers come into view. There are numerous ways to tell fortunes, including palm reading and card reading, but one of the more interesting ways involves a bird picking a card with its beak. Some fortune tellers are able to speak English, and they typically make note of that on their signs.

Outdoor Karaoke

Across the street from where the fortune teller stands begin are a few outdoor karaoke bars set up under tents. Filled with plastic tables, chairs, bound paper books and down-to-earth, friendly people, the set up has an old-fashioned community feel to it and anyone can sing with the keyboard for HK$20.

If you can't sing in Cantonese, don't worry, the locals here love to show their stuff singing classic English songs by Frank Sinatra, the Beatles, John Denver and others (most of their favorites come from the era between the '50s and the '70s). That being said, don't expect to come here and find any English song from the mid-20th century; English song selections are definitely limited.

Cantonese Opera

Between the Kowloon Government Offices – which includes a post office – and the Tin Hau Temple on the pedestrian stretch of Market Street, a few people still sing Cantonese Opera around 20:30 on most nights (except Wednesdays for some reason). Once a hallmark of the Hong Kong music scene, Cantonese Opera is on a major decline, and there are only a few places left to see it preformed outdoors. Shrill voices backed by cymbals and *gauhu*, a dragon-headed string instrument, punctuate the nighttime sounds as the gaudily-dressed singers pair off in a choral conversation. Their costumes, with bright colors and elaborate headwear, are as outstanding and crazy as the performance itself.

Lounge Bars

North of Tin Hau Temple on Temple Street, the lounge bars begin. With bright lights and photo displays of their featured singers hanging outside, they're a piece of cake to find. Inside, ladies take to a stage adorned with strings of lights and sing Chinese classics to crowds of mostly men. Singers actually used to be quite ubiquitous at fashionable Hong Kong restaurants in the 1980s and '90s, entertaining patrons at lunch, but these days that tradition has all but died out as the "lunch singer" has lost all places to sing outside of Temple Street.

The singers earn much of their money from tips: throw down HK$20 if you especially like a song and HK$50 if you order a song. Many of them will hang out at the tables of their favorite customers when they aren't singing, but if you want to talk to them you'll need to be ready to hand over some cash.

At Man Ming Lane, the market area ends, and there is an entrance to Yau Ma Tei MTR.

Temple Street snacks

Tai O Fishing Village

Chinese name: 大澳漁村
Transport:
There is no MTR to Tai O, but it is accessible via buses that service Lantau Island. The easiest way to get to Tai O is to go to Tung Chung MTR station and catch a bus from there. You can also catch a bus from any of the tourist destinations on Lantau Island.
Bus – You can buy a Lantau all-day pass (HK$35 from Mon-Sat and HK$55 on Sun and public holidays) for unlimited rides around the island.
From Tung Chung: 11
From Po Lin Monastery: 21 (one bus every hour from 10:30 to 15:15; last bus at 17:00)
From Mui Wo: 1

Way out on the west coast of Lantau Island, the small village of Tai O sits, still caught in the old air of its past as a small fishing village banking off its major exports of salt and fish. The intriguing *pang uk* houses you can find here are a charming sight, evocative of the simple trading and fishing lifestyle of the local Tanka people. The Tanka, or "on-water people," are one of Hong Kong's most intriguing minorities and have been in the area far longer than the Cantonese (a group of the Han Chinese). Their presence on the island is so old that a British publication once described their

tenure in the area as having been "since a time unknown." A fascinating sea-faring people, the Tanka are known especially for pearl diving and other maritime trades, in addition to fishing.

Today, the streets of Tai O are still lined with fish drying in the sun, duck farms and craft-making huts, and – if you're lucky – you might be able to find a few of the old salt pans that once helped produce Tai O's most prosperous export. Street vendors sell not only fish, but also local products like fish balls and shrimp paste, as well as cheap bracelets made out of shells and other local crafts.

From Tai O you can take part in one of several types of boat excursion, including pink dolphin-spotting tours.

Just 20 minutes away from the Po Lin Monastery (pg 65), Tai O should be a mandatory addition to any Lantau day trip.

History

Historical records of the Tanka go back as far as the 1100s, while records of civilization on Lantau Island go back as far as the Bronze Age. Some historians consider the Tanka to be either aboriginals to the area or direct descendents of them, but this claim is often disputed.

What historians do agree on is that the Tanka had inhabited Hong Kong long before the Han Chinese came. There is also evidence that the Tanka were originally heavily discriminated against by the Han Chinese settlers. An official Qing edict from 1729 stated that the Tanka were part of the "mean class" and forbade them from settling on the shore.

The Tanka had always been involved in fishing, but these discriminatory policies kept them bound to the the water and helped to reinforce their connection to the sea. They found work in all forms of nautical trade, predominately fishing, pearl diving, guiding sampan boat taxis, and piracy. When China closed its doors to the outside world, many Tanka became involved in smuggling banned products to the Guangdong shore, including televisions, radios, refrigerators and even illegal immigrants. Some Tanka women found limited prosperity in the prostitution business, serving Portuguese and British foreigners during a time when many Han Chinese sex workers were far less willing to serve foreigners.

The salt trade in Tai O began to decline in the 20th century and was virtually over by the 1960s. Even after discriminatory policies were scrapped, the Tanka endured many years as outcasts, but that trend has largely folded over the past 60 years. Today, they are largely regarded simply as "Chinese whose profession is fishery." The name "Tanka" is often used as identification in official texts, but they prefer to be called "on water people" (水 上 人) or "boat people." These days, as many of the Tanka youth move to the city looking for employment in virtually any modern industry, the future of Tai O and its traditional heritage becomes more and more uncertain.

Layout

Tai O is a small island off the northwest coast of Lantau Island. The village is built on both Lantau Island and Tai O Island with a short bridge connecting the two. With most of the village made up of narrow alleyways, there are few vehicles and plenty of outdoor vendors. The small island covers less than 700,000 sq m (0.3 sq mi) and has two main streets: Shek Tsai Po Street runs along the south coast and Kat Hing Back Street lies parallel to the west coast. Walk down one of these roads a short distance and you are out of the main village and away from the crowds with a clear view of the ocean. Check out the house along Shek Tsai Po Street and its display of religiously inspired figures, scholars, officials and gods.

Yeung Hau Temple (楊侯古廟)

After passing by several fine historical buildings on Kat Hing Back Street, you will arrive at a road leading to a small tombolo (a mound of dirt attaching an island) with a temple on it. This is the Yeung Hau Temple, built in 1699 to honor Hau Wong, a general of the Southern Song Dynasty. The temple is small, but it contains a brilliantly decorated shrine colored in vibrant shades of red, yellow, green, and purple fabric murals pulled into decorative knots. In the best traditions of Chinese temple design, the eaves are inscribed with flowers, dragons and scenes from ancient folklore.

Kwan Tai Temple (關帝古廟)

Tucked behind the crowded center of the village in an unassuming location on Kat Hing Back Street, the Kwan Tai Temple, established in 1488, is the oldest in Tai O. Kwan Tai, who was a general in the Han Dynasty, is honored with a red-faced statue in the main hall. Focusing on military gods, this temple also includes statues of Zhang Xian, Zhou Cang, Gwan Ping and Hwang Ling Gong. Throughout the temple, statues display military horses, and incense burns in coils hanging from the ceiling.

On the 24th day of the 6th month of the lunar calendar, there are ceremonies at the temple to celebrate Kwan Tai's birthday. This date will fall on July 20 in 2014 and August 8 in 2015.

Hung Shing Temple (洪聖廟)

Overlooking the sea on the south side of Tai O, the Hung Shing Temple is a shrine to one of the lesser known gods of the sea, Hung

Shing, who was a Tang Dynasty official whose advances in geography and astronomy lent greatly to local sea navigation. Look out for the temple's white exterior inside a white wall a little ways up a hill. Hung Shing's birthday, on the 13th day of the second lunar month, is celebrated on April 1 in 2015.

Behind the Hung Shing Temple further up the hill is the **Hong Kong Shaolin Wushu Culture Centre** (香港少林武術文化中心 ; phone: 2985 8898; website: www.shaolincc.org.hk). With an open field in the center, this venue periodically hosts kung fu performances and classes. It has a hostel that can accommodate 64 people for long-term study and a canteen that serves vegetarian meals.

Dolphin Tour Boats

Boat tours departing from around the footbridge will show you a closer view of the stilt houses on the water and take you out to sea to look for endangered pink dolphins. It's estimated that there are only about 100 dolphins living in Hong Kong, mostly around Lantau Island, so seeing a dolphin on a Tai

O boat trip is a very rare treat. The boat trips are often relatively short but you'll appreciate the beauty of the sea and the view of the islands. Make sure you pack a camera on the off chance that you catch a glimpse of one of the rarest animals in the world.

A trip with the **Hong Kong Dolphinwatch** tour company, which leaves from Tung Chung every Wednesday, Friday, and Sunday, will give you a better chance at seeing a dolphin for a higher price (HK$380 per adult) and a longer duration (5 hours). It is reommended to schedule in advance at **www. hkdolphinwatch.com**.

Dragon Boat Races

Tai O hosts dragon boat races during the Dragon Boat Festival, a traditional Chinese festival in early to mid summer. The Dragon Boat Festival falls on June 2, 2014 and June 20, 2015. Read more about the Dragon Boat Festival and other year-round events in the Hong Kong Festivals section (pg 38).

Top: A home inside Tai O Fishing Village

Right: Tai O stilt homes from outside

Ping Shan Heritage Trail

Chinese name: 屏山文物徑
Transport:
Subway – Tin Shui Wai MTR Station, Exit E
Light Rail – Yuen Long Light Rail, Lines 705, 706, 751, or 751P, Tin Shui Wai Terminus

The Ping Shan Heritage Trail showcases some fantastic relics of pre-colonial Hong Kong along a set of old-timey but bustling villages, one of which is the awesome Ping Shan Village. This one kilometer urban hike in the northeastern district of Yuen Long lets you see temples and buildings as old as 1273 and the original inhabitance of the great and powerful Tang clan. The Yuen Long suburbs in the New Territories is one of the first places the Tang settled and built ancestral halls, worship temples, shrines, and villages. Now housing complexes and malls have sprung up around the area, but many historical artifacts remain.

Before You Go

Located in the northeastern New Territories, the Ping Shan Heritage Trail is far from downtown. Factor in about an hour for subway travel time from Central MTR to the Tin Shui Wai MTR Station where the trail begins.

History

The Tang clan is the most famous of the Five Great Clans of Hong Kong. First settling in Kam Tin in the northern part of the New Territories in the 11th century, the Tang's earliest remaining buildings date back to the 13th century and are found in Yuen Long (Ping Shan), just to the west of Kam Tin. It was around this time that Song Dynasty royal lineage entered the family when the Song – who were fleeing Mongol

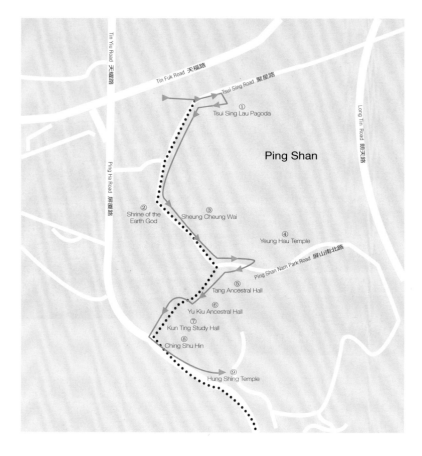

conquest in the north – came to the area and Emperor Gaozong married his daughter to a Tang clan member. The Tang clan prospered and spread into a distribution of "Five Wais and Six Tsuens" (Five Walled Villages and Six Villages). In 1899, the Tang of Ping Shan played a major role in fighting the British military, who had come to assert control over the New Territories, with Tang rebels holding the British off for six days. There are about 25,000 people of Tang ancestry living in the New Territories today.

Layout

The Ping Shan Trail winds through three Tang villages, including a walled village. It starts just outside the Tin Shui Wai MRT station. Leave Tin Shui Wai station through Exit E and cross Tsui Sing Road, and you will be greeted by the oldest pagoda in Hong Kong.

Tsui Sing Lau Pagoda (聚星樓 *)*

The Tsui Sing Lau Pagoda, literally "the Pagoda of Gathering Stars," was built in 1486. It's an eight-sided pagoda with three stories (13 m; 42 ft) made of faded green bricks. Inside there are stairs leading to the top where a Fui Shing shrine is housed, honoring the "Champion Star" deity who can bring success to students during exams.

Shrine of the Earth God (社壇)

Follow the Ping Shan Heritage Trail signs as you go past the Kwok Yat Wai College (郭一葦中學) and you will arrive at the next stop, the Shrine of the Earth God. This simple shrine to the Earth God "She Kung" protects villages and homes. The main feature is an incense burner made of red bricks, where villagers often burn joss paper and incense sticks.

Sheung Cheung Wai (上璋圍)

Just across from the Shrine of the Earth God, much of the wall protecting Sheung Cheung Wai village remains intact (you can enter through the gates). Like many walled villages, some modern style housing flats have been built, but some gatehouses, shrines, and a few old buildings still sit preserved in the traditional style.

Yeung Hau Temple (楊侯古廟)

The Yeung Hau Temple is dedicated to the deified military general Hau Wong and also contains other gods and goddesses. Hau Wong was a general who dedicated himself to protecting the Song Dynasty in Kowloon, and the three-sectioned temple is built with one part honoring Hau, while the other two areas house shrines for the Earth God and Kam Fa, the Patron Saint of Expectant Mothers. The temple's original date of construction is unknown, but it was renovated in 1963 and 1991.

Tang Ancestral Hall (鄧氏宗祠)

The Tang Ancestral Hall, down the road from the Yeung Hau Temple, is the main ancestral hall in Ping Shan and is often used for local celebrations. The three-hall, two-courtyard structure was built in 1273 and is hailed as one of the best examples of ancestral hall architecture in Hong Kong. Among the names inscribed in the hall, many were high-ranking officials of the Song Dynasty.

Yu Kiu Ancestral Hall (愈喬二公祠)

Right next to the Tang Ancestral Hall is the Yu Kiu Ancestral Hall. Built in the 1500s, it has the same layout as the Tang Ancestral Hall and was at one point used as a village school.

Kun Ting Study Hall (觀廷書室)

The Kun Ting Study Hall is a small building built by a 22nd generation Tang son in 1870 as a memorial to his father. The study hall was used to educate those preparing for the imperial civil service exams, as well as for ancestral worship. After the British took over, they briefly used it as a police station before it was returned to its educational purposes as a local study area. The design of the hall, with many designs and carvings, is one of the best of the Ping Shan area. It was restored in 1991.

Ching Shu Hin (清暑軒)

After the Kun Ting Study Hall, the rest of the

Kun Ting Study Hall

buildings are in very close proximity. The next one is the Ching Shu Hin, a guesthouse for distinguished visitors. Built in 1874, it is handsomely decorated with beautiful murals and moulded designs along the walls.

Hung Shing Temple (洪聖宮)

First built in 1767, the Hung Shing Temple you see today was actually rebuilt in 1866. It is a simple two-hall structure honoring Hung Shing, a government official in Guangzhou during the Tang Dynasty. Now you are near the end of the Heritage Trail and you can continue heading down the road a little ways into **Ping Shan town**. Inside Ping Shan, there is the **Ping Shan Tang Clan Gallery Heritage Trail Visitor Centre**, which contains more information about Ping Shan's history, and if you head west from Hung Shing Temple you can find Hang Mei Tsuen Park.

Ladies Street Market

Chinese name: 女人街
Transport:
Subway – Mong Kok MTR, Exit D3
Bus – Many buses stop on Argyle St near the entrance to Ladies St
To Tung Choi St/Argyle St station: bus 701, 701S, 796C, E21A
To Mong Kok station: bus 2A, 13D, 13P, 16, 18, 41, 44, 44P, 58X, 59X, 67X, 98C, 98S, 203E, E21

The streets of Mong Kok are sights to behold: walls of people crisscross the sidewalks in front of you, while the space above your head is cluttered with signs seemingly packed into every conceivable space. Many poles are crowded with more signs than they can hold, and strings of Chinese characters stretch halfway across the street as the smell of frying noodles and boiling dumplings spills out from restaurants all along the way. All the while, layers upon layers of neon LEDs are as numerous as the swathes of people underneath.

In the heart of it all is the Ladies Street Market. This chaotic section of Tung Choi Street is perhaps the most crowded street in the most crowded district on earth (see Info & Cautions). These days, the street that was once the notorious headquarters of the Triads boasts an essential Hong Kong vibe: a bustle of shouting salesmen and women and steaming food stalls that just screams, "this is the real Chinatown!" You'll be kicking yourself if you don't give this riotous street at least one walk through.

Most tourists and locals come here for the rock-bottom prices and the shopping experience. Though you'll find plenty of women's items like dresses, stockings, and cosmetics – hence the name "Ladies' Street" – there are more than enough Chinglish-stamped shirts, CDs, DVDs, electronics and whatever else to go around. Value can be hit or miss, with a few quality deals hidden in one of the many stalls where the vast majority of goods are knock-offs and often very low quality. You get what you pay for, and you'll need to bone up on your haggling skills to match the masters here. When you're not working out a deal for unparalleled savings, give some time to check out the performers, musicians, and promoters working just beyond the stalls.

Before You Go

Mong Kok is anything but relaxing. Between the huge crowds, aggressive shouting sales people and air conditioning water periodically dripping on you, you might find yourself pining for the peace and quiet of a downtown café if you stay in Mong Kok too long. Consider taking this area in slowly at first.

Info & Cautions

There's a phrase in China that means extremely crowded: 人山人海, literally "people, mountain; people, sea." While this phrase can apply to countless places throughout China, Hong Kong may take the cake, especially in Mong Kok. And this is not just a feeling; the Guinness Book of World Records has more than once ranked Mong Kok as the most crowded place in the world, with a population density of 130,000 people per sq km (340,000 per sq mi). Keep your wits about you and always be wary of pickpockets. It's a good idea to travel very light here and keep your valuables under your clothes (i.e. under your shirt in a money belt) or in a place where you can see them at all times. Sticking your wallet in your back pocket here is asking for trouble.

Sales people are sometimes very aggressive in the Ladies Street Market. Beyond being heavily pressured to buy, you might find yourself in an argument if you don't buy something. There are a few isolated stories of sales people grabbing customers who didn't buy anything, restraining them until they finally made a purchase. While this is very rare, a good rule of thumb is to not touch anything if you don't want it. Touching an item is often used as an excuse to say that you must buy it because it's no longer in its original condition.

History

Civilization in Mong Kok goes back as early as the Jin Dynasty (265-420 CE), evidenced by pieces of pottery and tools excavated in 2004 from Tung Choi Street, the present site of Ladies Market. Around that time, what is now the most crowded area in the world was – believe it or not – a simple range of farming villages for hundreds of years. In fact, Tung Choi Street got its name from the water spinach (tung choi; 通菜) that villagers grew alongside it in the 1920s.

Mong Kok was a coastal region until 1950, when reclamation west of the unbelievably creatively-named "Reclamation Street" greatly expanded the land area. The current English name of Mong Kok originates from pre-reclamation times when the shrubby coastal area was known in Cantonese as "fern corner" (望 角) and pronounced as "Mong Gawk" (Mong Kok is the English transliteration). Eventually the area was renamed 旺 角 , meaning "prosperous and crowded corner," but the new Cantonese

pronunciation of "Wong Gawk" did not make it into the English system, and today it is still known by its former name of Mong Kok.

During the early phases of Mong Kok's development, the area was actually an industrial center. It wasn't until the 1970s that Ladies Street was officially opened to create a number of uniform sanctioned spaces for the hawkers who had been haphazardly setting up along the streets.

Layout

Mong Kok is the northernmost area of the Yau Tsim Mong administrative district in Kowloon. Ladies Street runs along the southern part of Tung Choi Street from just south of Argyle Street four blocks south to Dundas Street. Besides the Ladies Street Market, the area has plenty of other markets, malls, and places of interest.

Ladies Street

South of Argyle Street, along Tung Choi Street, a tall and crowded line of stalls begins. This is the Ladies Street Market, and it extends to Shantung Street. Beyond the market area, however, if you move south to Soy Street you can find a gaggle of street performers. Bands play on the street, beggars paint calligraphy detailing their struggles, and one particularly notable performer kicks metal bowls into the air and catches them on his head. Besides the mountains of goods for sale, keep your eye out for the countless food stalls dotting the street corners and selling delicious snacks like fish balls or barbecue. The best selection of snack stalls can be found up and down Soy Street.

Shanghai Street

One of the oldest streets in Hong Kong, Shanghai Street was completed in 1887 and was the most prosperous street in Kowloon by the late 1880s. As such, it's here that you can find a host of historic shophouses and a cacophony of very cool store signs. Shophouses, called tong lau (唐 樓), are simply business spaces on the first floor with residential space on the upper floors. The section of shophouses from 600 to 626 Shanghai Street contains a scattering of 12 that are considered some of the city's most historic buildings.

Other Markets

There's something exciting on every corner of Mong Kok, so jump in and do some of your own exploration. Some of the other popular markets include the sneaker market on **Fa Yuen Street**, the **Flower Market** on Flower Market Road, the **Bird Market** on Yuen Po Street, and the **Goldfish Market** on northern Tung Choi Street.

Fa Yuen Street is a bit more like a local version of Ladies Street Market. One street to the east, Fa Yuen Street runs directly parallel to Ladies Street and is a little bit less crowded. It specializes in fashionable shoes from the street-side store fronts, which has earned it the nickname Sneaker Street. The stalls sell everything Ladies Street does, along with some produce and usually lower priced goods. As with Ladies Market, the Sneaker Street section is located only south of Argyle Street.

When you're no longer in the mood for the entertaining mess that prevails along Ladies Street, head to the Flower Market on Flower Market Road just north of Prince Edward Road in northern Mong Kok for a bit of floral color. The streets here are lined with blooming flowers and are a particularly pretty contrast to the neon-lit Tung Choi area. It gets particularly crowded around Spring Festival when it stays open past its usual closing time of 19:00 to accommodate the Hong Kong locals on the lookout for New Years orchids.

At the end of the Flower Market is the Yuen Po Street Bird Garden. Along a street with traditional Chinese garden design elements, older men congregate to show off their own caged song birds, and you can buy one for yourself from the local vendors.

North of Ladies Street on Tung Choi Street is the Goldfish Market. Check out the goldfish and aquariums out front, but step inside for some exoticism, where you can see spiders, snakes, and other creepy and interesting animals in the back of shops.

Star Ferry

Chinese name: 天星小輪
Website: www.starferry.com.hk
Transport:
Subway – *To Tsim Sha Tsui Star Ferry Pier*: Tsim Sha Tsui MTR Station, Exit L6, walk west one block down Salisbury Rd
To Central Pier 7: Central MTR Station, Exit A, follow the above-road walkways
To Wan Chai Ferry Pier: Wan Chai MTR Station, follow Flemming Rd north to Hung Hing Rd, which runs adjacent to the pier on the shore

The Star Ferry was ranked as one of the top ten city boat trips in an article by *National Geographic*, as well as the #1 most exciting ferry ride in a poll by the Society of American Travel Writers in 2009. We guarantee you'll be ranking the cheap ride as the best value cruise in the world!

Touts

There are a lot of touts promoting tailored suits and Harbour tours outside of the Star Ferry Pier in Tsim Sha Tsui. Unless you need a new seersucker suit for the horse races, just ignore them.

The Star Ferry is the iconic transportation method for getting across Victoria Harbour and provides stunning views of the skyline as it rises up along the water. Until 1972, there were no tunnels, and for some 100 years (since 1888) coal and diesel-powered ferries were used for crossing the Harbour. The fleet became somewhat of a legend, with boat names like Morning Star ringing as household names with many Hong Kongers. Today, there may be multiple cross-Harbour tunnels and subways lines linking Hong Kong Island with Kowloon, but the Star Ferry remains one of the city's most beloved traditions.

Choose a clear night and ride from Tsim Sha Tsui to Central if you want to see the buildings lit up in glorious bright lights and neon advertisements. At 20:00, Hong Kong has the nightly Symphony of Lights, a dazzling display of flashing lasers and dancing lights. The Star Ferry that leaves just before or at 20:00 will stop briefly in the middle of the Harbour for a view of the show.

Star Ferry in the early 20th century

History

In the early days of Hong Kong, the only way to get from the Kowloon Peninsula to Hong Kong Island was to hire a sampan, a small flat-bottomed wooden boat. Crossing in this manner took much longer in the 1840s and the passenger capacity was notably reduced. In the 1870s, coal-fired ferries began to pop up, ferrying a relatively small amount of people back then. Grant Smith was one of the first people to own a ferry in Hong Kong, and Doarbjee Naorojee Mithaiwala bought the ferry from him in 1880, starting what would become the Star Ferry.

Naorojee was a Hong Kong success story, moving to the city from India and working his way up from a simple cook to the owner of a popular hotel. He started using the ferry in 1880 for his friends and associates, and when he later acquired three more ferries he quickly opened the company up as a public business. In 1888, he established the Kowloon Ferry Company. Ten years later Naorojee sold the company, and in 1898 it became known as the Star Ferry.

Other ferry competitors sprouted up around this time, such as Yaumati Ferry, which was founded in 1897, but none could compete with the Star Ferry. Crossing the Harbour hundreds of times each day for decades on end, the Star became a symbol of Hong Kong. The producers of the 1960 film *The World of Suzie Wong* noted (and increased) its iconic status when they chose it as the meeting place of their male protagonist and Suzie in the film's opening scene.

During World War II, one of the ferry's most historic events occurred when then-governor Sir Mark Aitchinson crossed the Harbour on the ferry to surrender to the Japanese. The Japanese would later commandeer the Star Ferry, using its ships for their own purposes, including transporting POWs. Some of the ships were sunk by US bombing campaigns during the war, including the Golden Star, which was bombed in 1943 and resurrected after the war.

In 1966, the Star Ferry became the center of controversy when a fare increase sparked violent protests. After the colonial government approved fare increases of about 25% (HK5¢ at the time), a 27-year-old named So Sau Chung started a hunger strike at the Star Ferry Terminal in Central on April 4. The next day, Lo Kei joined him in the hunger strike, and they gained a public following. So was arrested that day, and 1,000 people assembled in Tsim Sha Tsui to protest his arrest. When So was sentenced to two months in prison on April 6 the subsequent night, protests quickly turned violent as protesters threw rocks at vehicles, looted stores, and attacked the Yau Ma Tei Police Station. In the ensuing police crackdown, which involved hundreds of rounds of tear gas and dozens of rounds of ammunition, at least one protester was killed and 258 were given prison sentences.

The Star Ferry riots are depicted in Gary Kawai Cheung's book *Hong Kong's Watershed: The 1967 Riots* as a prelude to the radical 1967 Maoist riots in Hong Kong. Although the Star Ferry protest didn't start out as a leftist political movement, the arrest of a peaceful protestor quickly brought the anti-colonial sentiment simmering under the surface of 1960s Hong Kong to a rapid boil.

In 1972, the Cross-Harbour Tunnel was opened, allowing for automobiles to cross the Harbour. The eastern and western Harbour crossings were opened in 1989 and 1997, respectively, and two subway line crossings were built, making the Star Ferry no longer the fastest and most convenient way to cross the Harbour. However, it certainly remains the most enjoyable.

Layout & Prices

The Star Ferry operates two transportation lines and a Harbour Tour. The transportation lines go back and forth between Tsim Sha Tsui in Kowloon and either Central or Wan Chai on Hong Kong Island. The most popular route is to go from Tsim Sha Tsui to Central, as you will be approaching the spectacular skyline of Hong Kong. Ticket prices are an affordable HK$2.5 on weekdays and HK$3.4 on weekends for upper deck tickets. Lower deck tickets are about HK$0.5 cheaper, but for many they aren't worth it because the lower deck has poor views. You can also use the Octopus Cards for the Star Ferry.

The Star Ferry today

Piers

The three piers from where Star Ferry operates are located at Tsim Sha Tsui on the Kowloon Peninsula, Central on Hong Kong Island, and Wan Chai on Hong Kong Island. The Tsim Sha Tsui pier is at the far west side of Tsim Sha Tsui, just west of the Hong Kong Cultural Center. In Central, Star Ferry arrives at and departs from Pier 7, almost directly north of the Central MTR Station. The Wan Chai Ferry Pier is just east of the Expo Promenade, where the large "turtle shaped" expo center sits. Piers are all well marked with English signs pointing to the entrances and exits.

Star Ferry top deck

Star Ferry Harbour Tour

The Star Ferry also operates a Harbour Tour, which takes riders aboard a replica 1920s ferry on a one-hour circular route of the whole Harbour. The tour costs HK$85 for a daytime trip, which runs every hour from 11:00 to 17:00. They leave Tsim Sha Tsui at 11:55, Central at 12:15 and Wan Chai at 12:30. Night trips cost HK$160 and leave Tsim Sha Tsui at 18:55 and 20:55 (as well as 17:55 from October 1 to January 31) and Central at 20:15. The Symphony of Lights Harbour Tour costs HK$180 and leaves Central at 19:15 and Tsim Sha Tsui at 19:55.

Star Ferry bottom deck

Other Attractions

Parks & Heritage Buildings (pg 86)
* Hong Kong Zoological & Botanical Gardens
* Hong Kong Park
* Hong Kong University Heritage Buildings
* The HSBC Building & the Bank of China Tower
* Wan Chai Historic Buildings
* Central Police Station
* Tsim Sha Tsui Clock Tower
* Lam Tsuen Wishing Tree
* Hong Kong Convention & Exhibition Centre
* Happy Valley Racecourse
* Mai Po Marshes
* Hong Kong Wetland Park
* Kadoorie Farm & Botanic Garden
* Sha Tin Racecourse

Country Parks (pg 99)
* Tai Mo Shan Country Park
* Tai Tam Country Park
* Sai Kung Country Park
* Plover Cove Country Park
* Shek O Country Park
* Lantau Island Country Parks
* Ma On Shan Country Park

Walled Villages (pg 114)
* Kat Hing Wai
* Fanling Wai
* King Yin Lei Mansion
* Tsang Tai Uk

Towns & Villages (pg 119)
* Pui O
* Aberdeen
* Mui Wo
* Sai Kung Town
* Lau Fau Shan & Pak Nai
* Sheung Shui
* Shui Tau Tsuen
* Tsuen Wan
* Tuen Mun
* Yuen Long
* Tai Po
* Sha Tin

Markets (pg 130)
* Western Market
* Cat Street
* Des Vouex Dried Seafood Street
* Yau Ma Tei Wholesale Fruit Market
* Hollywood Road
* Chun Yeung Street Wet Market
* Apliu Street Flea Market
* Other Markets

Museums (pg 138)
* Hong Kong Museum of Art
* Hong Kong Heritage Musuem
* Dialogue in the Dark
* Hong Kong Heritage Discovery Centre
* Hong Kong Museum of History
* Hong Kong Science Museum
* Sam Tung Uk Museum of Hakka Culture
* Police Museum
* Yuen Yuen Institue
* Chuk Lam Sim Monastery
* Tsing Shan Monastery
* Miu Fat Monastery
* Other Museums

Temples & Monasteries (pg 145)
* Joss House Bay Tin Hau Temple
* Lin Fa Kung Temple
* Ten Thousand Buddhas Monastery
* Sik Sik Yuen Wong Tai Sin Temple
* Hollywood Road Man Mo Temple
* Jamia Mosque

Beaches (pg 155)
* Big Wave Bay Beach
* Hap Mun Wan Beach
* Long Ke Wan Beach
* Turtle Cove Beach
* Cheung Sha Beach
* Silvermine Beach and Mui Wo

Islands (pg 159)
* Tung Ping Chau Island
* Po Tai Island
* Cheung Chau Island
* Lamma Island
* Other Islands

Amusement Parks (pg 165)
* Disneyland
* Ocean Park

Parks & Heritage Buildings

If there's one thing Hong Kong has by the bucketful, it's character. This city lives and breathes through its unique heritage, and though everything that's worth seeing in Asia's World City is technically part of this "heritage," there are a few particularly standout sights that ooze bonafide history and boom with Hong Kong's modern voice. For this reason, we've made a special section just to show them off, and you'd better not pass them up either, because these blooming parks, raucous horse derbies, battling bank buildings and parading colonial monuments are more than just a testament to Hong Kong's "then and now," they are part of the heart and soul of this city. So clap those hands and give a few whistles as we present some of Hong Kong's most special attractions.

Hong Kong Zoological & Botanical Gardens

Chinese name: 香港動植物公園
Admission: FREE
Hours:
Fountain Terrace Garden: 6:00–22:00
Greenhouse: 9:00–16:30
Others: 6:00–19:00
Phone: 2530 0154
Address: Albany Rd
Transport:
Subway – Island Line, Central MTR Station
Bus – 3B, 12, 12M, 23, 23A, 40 to Botanical Gardens Stop on Garden Rd

Hong Kong Zoological & Botanical Gardens in 1864

One of the earliest gardens in Hong Kong, the Victorian era Hong Kong Botanic Gardens were opened in 1871 and contain a large and beautiful variety of greenhouses, fountains, sculptures, playgrounds and even a zoo. The zoological area was only recently added in 1975.

The gorgeous and shady retreat is home to some 1,000 varieties of plants divided into a camellia garden, a magnolia garden, a greenhouse, a palm garden, a bauhinia garden, an azalea garden, a bamboo garden, and a herb garden. The zoo is surprisingly good looking and comprehensive, showing off about 700 animals in total (600 of them birds), including alligators, lemurs, turtles and giraffes.

Throughout the garden you can look for statues and memorials scattered about. At the southern entrance, there is a memorial to the Chinese who died in World War I and II, and you can keep an eye out for a statue of King George VI, erected here in 1941 to commemorate the 100th anniversary of his establishment of colonial rule in Hong Kong.

Hong Kong Zoo's statue of King George VI

Hong Kong Park

Chinese name: 香港公園
Admission: FREE
Hours:
Park (Outdoor Facilities): 6:00-23:00
Sports Centre: 7:00-23:00
Squash Centre: 7:00-23:00
Booking office for sports facilities: 7:00-22:00
Aviary: 9:00-17:00
Conservatory: 9:00-17:00
Park Restaurant: 11:00-22:30
Squash Centre & Light Refreshment Restaurant: 11:00-21:00
Phone: 2521 5041
Address: 19 Cotton Tree Dr, Central
Transport:
Subway – MTR Admiralty Station, Exit C1, follow the signs up the escalator to Hong Kong Park.

The dramatic scenery to be found at Central's Hong Kong park is punctuated by its stunning botanical landscaping, a sprinkling of historic buildings and even some animals. The design of the park has won a number of awards, including the 1998 Honour Award for Urban Design presented by the Hong Kong Chapter of the American Institute of Architects. Although the park is certainly gorgeous, you'll likely notice that its design is hardly natural, and lends much credence to the stereotype of Chinese gardens being a display of man's control over nature. Everything is clean-cut and orderly, exhibiting the intent of the designers rather than an innate course of nature. Set with mountains on one side and skyscrapers on the other, the park provides some of the most riveting scenery in the city.

The most popular part of the park is the Edward Youde Aviary in the middle, which includes 800 birds of 100 different species. Walkways lead through the aviary at different levels, going all the way up to the treetops, and allow visitors an excellent vantage point to view the birds. Check out the manmade lake that's bustling with waterfowl.

Hong Kong Park was part of Cantonment Hill and its military barracks in the 1800s, and today it retains many of those historic buildings. The old Wavell House, which housed British soldiers, is the site of the modern day **Aviary Education Centre**. The Office of the Park is located inside the **Rawlinson House**, the former house of the British Deputy General. It's also a good idea to give some time to the **Hong Kong Visual Arts Centre** – housed in an old barracks site – where local artists and staged exhibitions show their stuff. The Flagstaff House, built in 1846, houses the **Flagstaff House Museum of Teaware** (pg 144).

The park, which covers 80,000 sq m (861,112 sq ft), was opened to the public in May 1991.

Hong Kong University Heritage Buildings

Chinese name: 香港大學文物樓
Website: www.hku.hk
Transport:
Subway – Island Line, Sheung Wan MTR Station, walk west for around 15 min or take bus 101
Bus – 22, 101 or 90B to HKU

The University of Hong Kong (informally known as Hong Kong University or HKU) was founded in 1911 as Hong Kong's first local university at a time when foreign countries were opening universities in China. Now it is one of the top universities in Asia. Over its history, it has been influential in developing Hong Kong's education and culture, underscored by the fact that its current medical school is the alma matter of Dr Sun Yat-sen, revolutionary and first President of the Republic of China. In 1924, Sun gave a speech at HKU espousing his ideals for governance in China. There, he remarked, "Hong Kong and the University of Hong Kong are my intellectual birthplace." He is honored with a statue in the **Foyer of Cheung Kung Hai Conference Centre** (鍾 江海會議中心) at the medical campus and the Sun Yat-sen steps that lead up from **Sun Yat-sen Place** (中山廣場) outside the university library.

Hong Kong University's rich history includes four officially recognized Heritage Buildings on campus. The first structure was the prosaically-named **Main Building** (本部大樓). Completed in 1912, this building has a clock tower in the center and four turrets gracing the corners, as well as some nice courtyards outside. It was first used for just about everything on campus and currently contains offices, lecture rooms, the library, the clinic and a temporary hostel for students.

The oldest building at HKU, however, is **University Hall** (大學堂). Built as a private residence around 1860, it was acquired by the university in 1954 and became a male dormitory. Notice the striking colonial architecture and evocative gothic features. The exterior is lined with pointed arches, while the wall is topped with crocket ornamental designs. Check out the iron spiral staircase inside.

The **Hung Hing Ying Building** (孔慶熒樓), a small domed building at the entrance just behind the Main Hall, was built in 1919. As you glance around it keep an eye out for the towers and tufters of the Main Hall rising above the Hung Hing Ying Building's dome, appearing as an extension of the building from afar. It housed the Department of Music from 1996 until January 2013.

The **Tang Chi Ngong Building** (鄧志昂樓) is the newest and perhaps least interesting of the four heritage buildings. It is a flat three-story building that was opened in 1931 and is coated with Shanghai plaster.

Hung Hing Ying Building

University Hall

The HSBC Building & the Bank of China Tower

Chinese name: 滙豐總行大廈 / 中銀大廈
Transport:
Subway – Central MTR Station on the Island Line
Bus -
To HSBC Bldg: 6, 12, 12A, 12M, 13, 23A, 40M, 66, 88R, 930, and 962 stop outside on Queen's Rd Central
To BOC Tower: 1, 5, 5S, 10, 11, 15, 26, 75, 101, 104, 113, 690, 914, 960, and 961 stop outside the Tower

The grandest buildings in Hong Kong's skyline are those owned by financial institutions. Among them, the HSBC Building and the Bank of China Tower in Central are particular stand outs.

The Hong Kong and Shanghai Banking Corporation (HSBC) Building (180 m; 262.5 ft), located at 1 Queen's Road Central, is one of Hong Kong's modern masterpieces of design, engineering and innovation. Conceived by British architect Sir Norman Foster in 1978, the structure is framed by large steel modules on the outside, while the walls are made mostly of glass and aluminum. Its ingenious lighting scheme relies heavily on natural sunlight, and it even uses mirrors to reflect sunlight into the lobby, creating a natural power-saving system and

a warmly lit interior. From its inception in 1978 – when it was replacing a previous building from 1935 – to its completion in 1985, the HSBC Building was the most expensive building in the world at around US$668 million. Outside of the building are two bronze lions that were crafted in 1935 as part of the previous bank building on the site, and you can do like the locals and rub their paws for good luck. The building is the fourth Hong Kong and Shanghai Banking Corporation building to be built on that site since the first one in 1865.

Of course, when the Bank of China decided to move in years later, they unsurprisingly sought to outdo the HSBC (which is still considered the largest bank in the world by assets). The 315 m- (1,033 ft)-tall Bank of China Tower, built at 1 Garden Road one block away from the HSBC Building, was the tallest building in Asia when it was completed in 1989; its masts reach an additional 52 m (170.5 ft). Designed by the world-renowned architect I M Pei, the winner of the Pritzker Prize and designer of the Louvre Pyramid (among other honors), the BOC Tower is composed of interlocking three-dimensional triangular frameworks meant to evoke growing bamboo shoots. The triangular design causes the building to look very different from various angles. Additionally, the triangles also create a lot of sharp edges, giving the building its distinctive "knife" or "meat cleaver" look.

The haughty BOC building is considered to be bad for the *feng shui* of other buildings in the area because of the sharp edges that, according to *feng shui* theory, "could cut the other buildings." Since HSBC is a competitor with Bank of China and their buildings are next to each other, the HSBC building set up a sort of *feng shui* defense when they installed cannon-like structures on the top of their building aiming right at the BOC Tower.

In a final twist to the area's *feng shui* war, the Cheung Kong Center (長江集團中心), built in between both buildings in 1999, was built as a very simple, traditional "American black office block" style in order to absorb the negative energy of the clashing buildings on its flanks.

Wan Chai Historic Buildings

Chinese name: 灣仔歷史建築
Transport: Subway – Island Line, Wan Chai Station, Exit A3, walk south to Queens Rd East and find Stone Nullah Ln near Morrison Hill

One of the first Chinese neighborhoods to spring up on British-controlled Hong Kong Island, Wan Chai plays host to some of the earliest 20th century residential establishments of Chinese Hong Kongese citizens and is touched with some of Hong Kong's most unique history.

When the British established their center of government in Central (then called Victoria), Wan Chai was far enough out that it became a particularly cheap neighborhood, attracting a slew of coolies and Chinese workers. Today, Wan Chai may be best known for its girlie bars on Lockhart Street, near the Luk Kwok Hotel, where the area's so-called "yum-yum girls" became the topic and setting for the novel and film *The World of Suzie Wong.* But it's the historical buildings of the early working class laborers that lie to the south (past Queen's Road East) that have made Wan Chai historically special for better part of a century.

A good place to start is **Stone Nullah Lane**, where you can first check out the outstanding **Pak Tai Temple**, built by local residents in the late 1800s. Further along this street and the roads that intersect it, you can find some great 1920s *tong lau* buildings, which are easily identified by their bold paint jobs. The most famous sits from 72 to 74A Stone Nullah Road and is simply known as the **Blue House** (藍 屋). Originally the site of a 19th century hospital, the Blue House was built in the 1920s, and its pretty four-storied sky blue exterior is complimented by a set of white balconies whose style is quite rare in the city today (see pic). This kind of *tong lau* was built with shops on the first floor and high-ceilinged residences above.

Just down the road from the Blue House, the **canary yellow apartment** at 2 to 8 Hing Wan Street was built just a few years later. It's not actually called the yellow house (apparently only the Blue House has a name), but it's impossible to miss it with its bright exterior and laundry hanging outside.

On that same block, and just next to the yellow house, is a **pink house** and a narrow **tan building** stuck in between the two, while across the street sits an **orange house** at 8 King Sing Street. All built from the 1920s to the '50s, the orange house, Blue House, yellow house and pink house consitute the highlights of the Urban Renewal Authority's Wan Chai preservation project.

Past these bright and colorful buildings something darker lurks at the end of Ship Street, west along Queen's Road East. **Nam Koo Terrace** (南 固 臺) was built around the same time as the other residences but was used as a military brothel by the Japanese during World War II. Eventually, chilling stories of the ghosts inside began to spread, and by the late 20th century the building had become a novelty attraction for local youths to test their mettle. One November night in 2003, a group of middle school students posted up in Nam Koo for the night. As the night went on one of the girls began acting more and more erratic, terribly frightening her friends, who also began to hear "ghostly voices." The police soon came and were forced to use physical means to tear the unstable girl from the home. When the girls claimed to have been attacked by a ghost, they were all given psychological evaluations.

Soon after the story was published in the *Oriental Daily*, reprints in other publications sensationalized the event, and within days throngs of locals had come to see the newly branded "Wan Chai Haunted House." Since then, the house has seen several suicides and remains a source of urban legend. Now locked up, its stone walls and patios are becoming overgrown with plants, shrubs and trees.

Central Police Station

Chinese name: 中區警署
Admission: FREE
Hours: 10:00-18:00
Website: www.centralpolicestation.org.hk
Address: 10 Hollywood Rd (中環荷理活道 10 號中區警署建築群)
Transport:
Subway – Tsuen Wan Line, Central MTR Station
Escalators – The Mid-Levels Escalators outside Central MTR station lead to the Central Police Station on Hollywood Rd
Bus – 12A, 13, 23A, 26, 40M and H1 to Old Central Police Station

This compound in Central is one of the best preserved examples of colonial era architecture in Hong Kong and holds a particular claim to fame as one of the filming locations for John Woo's renowned film *A Better Tomorrow* (1986). It consists of Central Police Station, the Central Magistracy and the Victoria Prison Compound.

The **Victoria Prison** is the oldest of the three. Built in 1841 and only recently decommissioned in 2006, it was Hong Kong's first prison, and some of its most famous former inmates include left-wing authors Ai Wu and Dai Wangshu. The latter was imprisoned here by the Japanese during World War II while working as a newspaper editor in Hong Kong.

The most striking of the three buildings is the Central Police Station, whose impressive exterior projects a powerful aura over Hollywood Road (pg 135) down below. Note the gleaming white granite window arches and columns of the **Headquarters Block**, built in 1919, or the staunch power of the **Barrack Block**, which was built in 1864 and is the oldest of the seven blocks within the Police Station. The Barrack Block faces the prison and you'll have to move inside the complex away from the road for a decent view.

The entire complex has fallen under plans to transform it into a boutique shopping mall, art gallery, cinema, museum and heritage area with the intent of preserving its architectural heritage. Two new buildings are being built as additional art galleries, and they are said to be sticking with the historical theme.

Nearby Sights

Lan Kwai Fong bar district (pg 213)

Tsim Sha Tsui Clock Tower

Chinese name: 尖沙咀鐘樓
Recommended time for visit: 20-30 min
Transport:
Subway – Tsuen Wan Line, Tsim Sha Tsui Station, Exit E, walk towards Salisbury Rd, turn right and take the subway (pedestrian tunnel) to the Hong Kong Cultural Centre, turn right again and walk straight ahead towards the waterfront
Ferry – Star Ferry from Central or Wan Chai to Tsim Sha Tsui and follow the signs

Clock Tower and Tsim Shai Tsui Railroad Station in 1914. The tower does not yet have its big clock.

Any Chinese immigrant to Hong Kong from 1915 up to the mid-1970s can tell you about the Tsim Sha Tsui Clock Tower, or as it was previously known, the Kowloon-Canton Railway Clock Tower. As the terminus of the railway that linked Kowloon to Guangdong (Canton), this was the final stop for any emigrants entering Hong Kong and the transition point for the millions of Chinese boarding boats to begin new lives in places around the world. Today, its red brick and granite exterior is one of the coolest sights along the Tsim Sha Tsui waterfront, and the views of Victoria Harbour from its 44 m- (144 ft)-tall top are superb.

Harkening to the fascinating Age of Steam, the tower was put up in 1915, originally with only one small clock stolen from the long-vanished Pedder Street Clock Tower. The railway station itself was completed in 1910, and though the tower was determined to be an integral part of the complex, its construction did not begin until 1913 because materials were diverted towards fighting the First World War. It was finally completed in 1915 and worked nonstop until the 1970s when, despite protests from locals and the Heritage Society, the historic railway station was demolished in favor of a new location at present-day Hung Hom Station. A deal was struck, however, to allow the Clock Tower to remain, and in 1990 it was listed as one of the city's Declared Monuments.

For most people visiting the Tsim Sha Tsui waterfront, the Clock Tower is a must see, not least because it is an easy-to-reach and an excellent sight. If you want to head to the top of the tower (highly advised) you'd better save some breath for the climb up the wooden spiral staircase inside. Your reward at the top is an unbeatable view of the area.

Tsim Sha Tsui Clock Tower

Lam Tsuen Wishing Tree

Chinese name: 林村許願樹
Transport:
Subway & Bus – East Rail Line, Tai Po Market Station, take bus 64K or 64P to Fong Ma Po Stop

Just outside of Tai Po in the New Territories stands a Chinese banyan tree where for years people from all around would come to toss oranges with wishes written on paper streamers into the branches. If the wish stuck in the tree, that meant there was a chance it would come true, and the higher up, the more likely it was said to come true. But alas, after years of more and more orange-tethered wishes crashing into the branches, the tree finally succumbed to the added weight, and in 2005 a branch snapped off (along with it oh-so-many wishes). Now the original tree is held up with a network of beams, and people hang wishes elsewhere in the town using plastic fruit and a plastic tree. There are also some wooden wish racks on which you can hang a wish, and the most traditional time to hang a wish is on a Chinese festival like Spring Festival.

Lam Tsuen still has a festive atmosphere about it, even if some of the wish-hanging trees are plastic. In fact, the wish streamers actually make the plastic trees more colorful, as if the place were always decorated for a party.

With the tree at the center, Lam Tsuen in English means "Tree Village," but Lam Tsuen Valley actually consists of 23 villages in total. Fong Ma Po is the actual village near Tai Po where the trees are located, and Ngau Kwu Leng and She Shan Tsuen villages, which includes the Chan Ancestral Hall, are nearby. Search the area around the wishing trees for a **Tin Hau Temple**, a **lion dance theater** and the Lam Tsuen Country Park.

Hong Kong Convention & Exhibition Centre

Chinese name: 香港會議展覽中心
Recommended time for visit: 1 hour
Website: www.hkcec.com
Phone: 2582 8888
Address: 1 Expo Dr, Wan Chai, Hong Kong Island
Transport: Subway – Island Line, Wan Chai Station, Exit A5, walk across the footbridge, turn right and go through the lobby of Central Plaza, continue across the connecting overhead walkway, descend to the ground level, walk towards the waterfront ahead, the statue and monument will be on your left

Winning high accolades from around the globe for its top-down design and efficient use of limited space, the world class Hong Kong Convention & Exhibition Centre (HKCEC) is a masterpiece of modern construction and a gleaming testament to the development and wealth of the city. The enormous 40,000 sq m (430,556 sq ft) place is beautiful from the outside and is capped with a massive aluminum roof that was designed to resemble a seabird in flight.

The HKCEC's history is still young, but it's already marked by several noteworthy events, including one that changed history. In 1997, the handover of Hong Kong to China (after 150 years of British rule) was officially held here on June 30 in the pouring rain as millions of eyes around the world watched on television.

Jackie Chan fans will remember the HKCEC from the film *New Police Story* (2004) as the backdrop for the last fight and the grand finale.

Nearly every day you can find an exhibition inside the HKCEC.

Golden Bauhinia Square

Commemorating the event of the 1997 handover, Golden Bauhinia Square (金 紫 荊 廣 場) was gifted by the central government that same year and works as a pleasant – though crowded – promenade just outside the HKCEC. As the emblem of Hong Kong, the Bauhinia is represented in a blooming statue in the center of the promenade, and the area stands as a sort of Mecca for Chinese tourists who flock to take pictures in front of the historical monument.

Flag Raising Ceremony (7:50 – 8:03)

If you're interested in seeing the Hong Kong police elite raise the flag of the PRC against the backdrop of beautiful Victoria Harbour, you can swing down to Golden Bauhinia Square before 7:50 in the morning. Make sure you come early if you want a spot. On the first of each month there is an enhanced ceremony beginning at 7:45 that includes a rifle unit and a performance by the Police Pipe Band. The ceremony may be cancelled if there is inclement weather.

Happy Valley Racecourse

Chinese name: 跑馬地馬場 or 快活谷馬場
Admission: HK$10
Website: www.happyvalleyracecourse.com
Phone: 2895 1523
Address: 2 Sports Rd, Happy Valley, Hong Kong Island
Transport:
Subway – Island Line, Causeway Bay Station, follow the signs to the racecourse
Tram – Happy Valley tram to the end of the line and walk across the road to the track

If you've never been to a horse race then you should definitely honor Hong Kong's Happy Valley Racecourse with your maiden voyage. Even if you've seen your share, the fiery atmosphere of Happy Valley and its cheering crowd of good natured, downright rowdy folk is one thing in Hong Kong that is unmissable. Races are usually held from September to June on Wednesdays and weekends (first race 19:30). The best to hit up are the Wednesday evening races, when the thrilling ambiance is second to none. And hey, if you pick the right horse you could end up crossing over to Macau for a lavish weekend of spending and more gambling!

Happy Valley held its first races all the way back in 1846. These days, there is a sister course at Sha Tin Racecourse in the New Territories, but trust us, Happy Valley is the place you want to be for races. There is even a Hong Kong Racing Museum located here. It's all too much fun to pass by.

Hong Kong Racing Museum

Chinese name: 香港賽馬博物館
Address: 2/F, Happy Valley Stand, Happy Valley, Hong Kong Island
Phone: 2966 8065
Website: entertainment.hkjc.com
Transport:
Subway – Causeway Bay Station, Exit A, walk along Matheson St to Wong Nai Chung Rd, continue to walk for approximately 15 min
Bus – 75, 90 or 97 to the museum

Mai Po Marshes

Chinese name: 米埔濕地
Admission: HK$70 (tour); HK$100 (solo)
Hours: 9:00-17:00
Tour times: 9:30, 10:00, 14:00, 14:30 (Sat, Sun & public holidays)
Recommended time for visit: 3 hours
Phone: 2471 3480
Address: Mai Po, Sin Tin, Yuen Long
Transport: Bus – 76K from Yuen Long MTR Station (West Rail Line) or Sheung Shui MTR Station (East Rail Line) to Mai Po Lo Wai village, walk 20 min west to the WWFHK car park

Easily Hong Kong's most stunning ecological masterpiece, the 1,500 hectares (3,706 acres) of Mai Po Nature Reserve bear witness to a year-round habitat for more than 380 species of resident and migratory waterfowl, many of whom make a stop over here on an enormous annual winter migration from Siberia to Australasia. The park is counted as one of the most important wetlands in the world, and whether you are a nature lover or a city slicker, coming to see the sheer beauty of Mother Nature at work in this spectacular biome should be a top priority.

But it's not just birds you'll find at this hotbed of biodiversity. With a huge cluster of mudflats, reed beds, intertidal mangrove trees and the delightful *gei wai* (shrimp ponds), this protected area adjoining Deep Bay is swarming with life, including mammals, reptiles and some very large insects. The best season to come is during the winter months, when the rarest and most stunning birds – such as the Dalmatian pelican, spotted and imperial eagle, Saunder's Gull and a quarter of the global black-faced spoonbill population – pass through. It's during this time that an estimated 55,000 birds come through the area, but if you are in Hong Kong during another season, the park is still out-of-this-world. Among the mangrove-filled trails and floating boardwalks, countless blinds are placed for you to observe the birds at close range without them knowing you're there.

Jointly managed by the city's Agriculture, Fisheries & Conservation Department and the World Wide Fund for Nature Hong Kong (WWFHK), the park is pinned at the northeast end by the **Mai Po Visitor Centre** (phone: 2471 8272) and the **Mai Po Education Centre** (phone: 2482 0369) on the south end. At the former you'll need to register for free to enter the park, and at the Education Centre you can find information and displays on the history and ecology of the wetlands and Deep Bay.

Guided tours are almost essential at the Mai Po Marshes, particularly because without them there are almost no time slots for solo travelers. You can make tour reservations through the **WWFHK** (世界自然基金會香港分會; address: 1 Tramway Path, Central; 24-hour hotline: 2526 1011; website: www.wwwf.org.hk), but you'll need to make them very early, especially if you plan to come during the winter months. If you have binoculars you should bring them; if not you can rent them at the visitor center for HK$70. Wear comfortable clothes, but refrain from bright colors that could scare away the birds, and definitely don't forget that camera.

If you can't make a tour or are set on going by yourself, you'll be forking over HK$100 and a HK$200 refundable deposit. Book well in advance, as time slots for solo visitors are highly limited.

Hong Kong Wetland Park

Chinese name: 香港濕地公園
Admission: HK$30 (adult); HK$15 (child)
Hours: 10:00-17:00 (Wed-Mon); closed Tue
Recommended time for visit: 2 hours
Phone: 2708 8885
Address: Wetland Park Rd, Tin Shui Wai
Transport:
Subway – West Rail Line, Tin Shui Wai MTR Station, then get on the Light Rail
Light Rail – Line 705 or 706 to Wetland Park Stop

Hong Kong Wetland Park was created in 1998 to protect Deep Day's delicate ecosystem. Within this 60 hectare (148 acre) park you can find an enthralling range of biodiversity, including rare waterfowl, waddling crabs, various fish and a handful of reptiles. Though it's not quite as big as the nearby Mai Po Nature Reserve, this park still packs an ecological punch, and it can be a great alternative if you don't manage to book a tour or get a time slot for Mai Po.

Besides the nature trails, boardwalks, bird hides (for inconspicuously viewing animals) and viewing platforms that make nature-watching a breeze, the park also features a large 10,000 sq m (110,000 sq ft) grass-covered visitor center complete with a film theater, several interesting galleries on the wetland wildlife, a play center for kids and indoor aquariums.

If you have binoculars definitely bring them, otherwise you'll have wait in line for the public fixed-point binoculars around the park. If you don't have any you could consider picking up an inexpensive pair while you're in town. Head to Apliu Street in Sham Shui Po (MTR Exit A), there is a cluster of camera and other shops selling fairly cheap binoculars.

Kadoorie Farm & Botanic Garden

Chinese name: 嘉道理農場暨植物園
Admission: FREE
Hours: 9:30-17:00
Recommended time for visit: 1 hour
Website: www.kfbg.org
Phone: 2483 7200
Address: Lam Kam Rd, Tai Po
Transport: Bus – 64K

Originally set up in 1956 as an aide to poor farmers in the New Territories, the Kadoorie Farm and Botanical Garden (KFBG) has since become a beacon of biodiversity conservation and sustainable living development. Sitting just south of Ng Tung Chai and north of the waterfall, the farm sits snugly in a valley and is a beautiful scene of gardens, terraces, streams and greenhouses. It makes for a wonderful visit for anyone planning a hike to Ng Tung Chai Waterfall in Tai Mo Shan Country Park.

Founded by English brothers Lord Lawrence Kadoorie and Sir Horace Kadoorie, the main aim of the farm and gardens, which are run by the Kadoorie Agricultural Aid Association (KAAA), has long been to educate farmers on conservation of local ecological life and to promote environmental awareness through mindfulness and sustainable practices. The original programs sought to revitalize the rural economy through interest-free loans, holistic practices and rehabilitation programs for native animals. It proved a huge success, transforming the lives of local agriculturalists and farmers, and in 1995 the city passed an ordinance to establish the Kadoorie Farm and Botanic Garden Corporation, which further expanded programs on flora and fauna conservation and the transformation to sustainable living in and around Hong Kong.

Since then, the organization has continued to expand its practices, focusing particularly on encouraging farmers to have a creative approach to their relationship with nature. In 1998 the KFBG launched its Ecological Advisory Programme, which now advises environmental NGOs, the government, academics, villagers, ecological consultants, and private developers on conservation practices.

Other Attractions

097

Sha Tin Racecourse

Chinese name: 沙田賽馬場
Admission: HK$10 (public stands); HK$100-150 (members area)
Hours: Open on race days, check website or call for schedule
Recommended time for visit: 1-3 hours
Website: www.hkjc.com
Address: Penfold Park
Transport: Subway – East Rail Line, Racecourse MTR Station

With some 474 races per season, the racecourse at Sha Tin gets roaring on Sunday afternoons – as well as some Saturdays and public holidays – and is one of Hong Kong's more unique experiences. Though it doesn't quite live up to the fire of Happy Valley, it still comes in a very close second.

The original design of the stands could accommodate 35,000 punters when it was commissioned in 1978 by Sir David Akers-Jones, then-Secretary for the New Territories, but today the track can hold a whopping 85,000 boisterous fans, and the 20 stables have capacity for 1,260 horses. On the opening day of its 2007 season, the track set a single-day attendance record with over 60,000 punters and the Hong Kong Jockey Club raked in over US$106 million in bets.

A great Sunday in Sha Tin can be hitting up either the Ten Thousand Buddhas Monastery or the Hong Kong Heritage Museum by morning, having lunch in town at some of the great restaurants and then having an afternoon at the races.

Country Parks

It might be hard to believe when looking at the shining towers in the middle of Central, but 40% percent of Hong Kong is nature reserves and country parks, making the city a great place for hiking and outdoor exploration. The vast majority of Hong Kong – 952 sq km (368 sq mi) – consists of little-developed areas of the New Territories, and most of these places have been set up as country parks, replete with hiking, biking, swimming and more. The largest island in Hong Kong, Lantau Island, has only sparsely developed mountain terrain. With so many bays and coves, there's no lack of excellent views, sunshine and fresh-air to fulfill that outdoorsy hunger.

Tai Mo Shan Country Park

Chinese name: 大帽山郊野公園
Transport:
Subway – Tseun Wan Line, Tsuen Wan Station, then take bus 51 from the Tsuen Wan West Railway Station Bus Terminus
Bus – *From Tai Wo MTR Station*: 64K goes to Ng Tung Chai Rd, near the Tai Mo Shan trail and the waterfall trail on the north end of the park
From Tsuen Wan West Railway Station Bus Terminus: 51 goes to the visitor center

When Song Dynasty Emperor Bing noted the eight mountains that gave Kowloon its name, he surprisingly did not include Mt Tai Mo Shan, even though it's on this peak that you can really feel the dragon in the mountain breathing.

Tai Mo Shan is an extinct volcano, but on Kwun Yum Shan, a hill in the same range, there are little cracks in the rock called "hot pots" where warm air seeps up from deep within – the locals have come to call this "dragon breath." Composed of volcanic rock, the grass-covered mountain rises epically into the clouds on an overcast day, and at 975 m (3,140 ft), it is the tallest mountain in

Hong Kong. In fact, Tai Mo Shan Country Park contains five of the ten tallest peaks in Hong Kong: Tai Mo Shan, Sze Fong Shan, Wo Yang Shan, Miu Gou Toi and Wo Tong Gong.

Wetter and colder than elsewhere in the city, Tai Mo Shan Country Park is known for an abundance of streams that run down the lower altitudes of the park. A series of waterfalls are on display alongside the Ng Tung Waterfall Path, which connects to the MacLehose Trail. It gets so cold here in the winter (relative to the rest of the city, that is) that Hong Kongers like to come to see frost – a rare sight in Hong Kong – on the coldest days of the year. The frozen shrubs and glistening white grass were so interesting to the Hong Kong weather service that they sent out a press release about it in 2010.

Tai Mo Shan Peak Hike

Heading to the peak of Tai Mo Shan is a relatively straightforward hike that follows a paved road. Take bus 64K to Ng Tung Chai Road and hike south along the Ng Tung Waterfall Path to Section 8 of the MacLehose Trail, then turn right and follow the trail to the mountain summit as you pass by Sze Fong Shan (785 m; 2,575 ft) to the east.

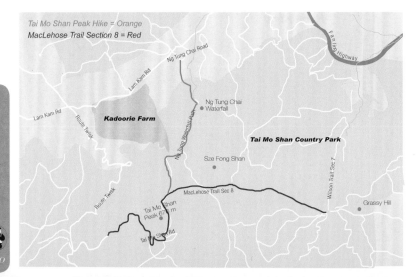

Tai Mo Shan

Mt Tai Mo Shan in the clouds

Trails

MacLehose Trail Section 8: Summits Tai Mo Shan and begins in the east of the park, starting from the Wilson Trail Section 7. Since the summit trail is on a road, you can also bike it. The trail up the mountain isn't too steep, but to get to it you will need to hike into the park from where you arrive, and you should be prepared to climb 400 m (1,312 ft) to the peak over moderate grade. Distance: 9.7 km (6 mi); Time: 4 hours; Difficulty: Moderate.

Ng Tung Waterfall Path: A trail to four waterfalls: Middle Fall, Bottom Fall, Main Fall and Scatter Fall (off a forbidden trail). It's a good trail to reach the middle of MacLehose Trail Section 8. Distance: About 4 km (2.5 mi) for the full trail; Difficulty: Easy.

Lodging

Sze Lok Yuen Hostel: A good hostel off Tai Mo Shan Road at 600 m (1,968 ft). Along with 84 dormitory beds, it also has campsites for up to 50 people.

Address: Tai Mo Shan, Tsuen Wan, NT
Phone: 2488 8188

Rotary Park Campsite: This campsite near the visitor center has 24 spaces.

Address: Rotary Park, Tai Mo Shan Country Park

Tai Tam Country Park

Chinese name: 大潭郊野公園
Transport:
Subway – The MTR stations north of Tai Tam Country Park are Quarry Bay, Tai Koo, Sai Wan Ho, and Shau Kei Wan, all on the Island Line and all of which require some walking to the north entrance of the park. The Hong Kong Country Trail and the Quarry Bay Jogging Trail can be used to enter the park from these locations.
Bus –
To the start of Hong Kong Trail Sec 5: 6, 41A, 76
To the start of Wilson Trail Sec 1: 6
To the eastern entrance of the park: 14 from Tai Tam Rd in Shau Kei Wan

Hong Kong street signs can give a lesson in British imperial history. It's interesting to note how many places here are still named after generals, diplomats, officials and other high profile colonizers. One of the names most often adorning locations in the city is Jardine, which ironically refers to William Jardine, one of the leading opium traders who was instrumental in igniting the Opium Wars with China (you'd think they'd be ready to forget this guy). Take a look at the heights he once occupied from the peak of Jardine's Lookout in Tai Tam Country Park.

Tai Tam Country Park is a 1,315 hectare area of rolling hills, mountains, and valleys in southeastern Hong Kong Island. From the 433 m- (1,421 ft)-high Jardine's Lookout and three other mountains, traders could (and still can) watch the ships coming in and out of the Harbour ports. The tallest of the mountains here is **Mount Parker** (柏 架 山), which at 507 m (1,663 ft) is the second tallest point on Hong Kong Island. To catch the truly remarkable views at the top you can use two trails that run through the mountains. Hong Kong Trail Section 5 and Wilson Trail Section 2 both scale Jardine's Lookout and Mount Butler, then head east to the peak of Mount Parker.

These heights create a valley in the middle of the park with four water reservoirs, which Hong Kong Trail Section 6 goes through. Sprinkled throughout are forts, some of which were used in World War II, as well as a variety of plant life that caused this park to be named a Site of Special Scientific Interest (SSSI). Among the colonial artifacts are the ruins of an old bungalow on top of Jardine's Lookout that were said to have been a home to his business partner, James Matheson.

Mount Parker Hike

You can start from Wilson Trail Section 1, which comes up from Stanley in the south and heads north over **Violet Hill** (紫羅蘭山). From here you will pass through the **Hong Kong Parkview Mansions**, after which the path turns into Wilson Trail Section 2 and veers right to take you east over **Mount Bulter**. Mount Parker is about 2 km (1 mi) further down and sits just outside the north east boundary of the park at the end of Mount Parker Road.

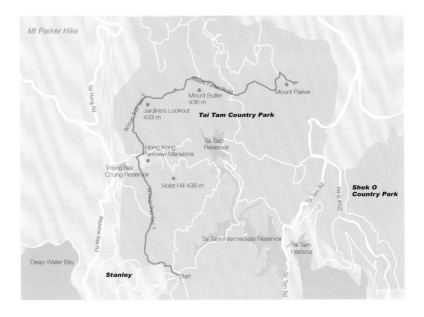

Trails

Hong Kong Trail Section 5: Starts at Wong Nai Chung Gap, ends at Mount Parker, summits Jardine's Lookout. Length: 4 km (2.5 mi); Time: 1.5 hours; Difficulty: Difficult, steep climbs.

Hong Kong Trail Section 6: Starts at Mount Parker, ends at Tai Tam Road, goes through Tai Tam Valley. Length: 4.5 km (2.8 mi); Time: 1.5 hours; Difficulty: Easy, flat paved walk.

Wilson Trail Section 1: Starts at Stanley Gap Road, ends at Parkview Mansions, covers western Tai Tam Country Park from south to north and over Violet Hill. Length: 4.8 km (3 mi); Time: 2 hours; Difficulty: Difficult.

Wilson Trail Section 2: Starts at Parkview Mansions, ends at Quary Bay, covers Jardine's Lookout and Mt Butler. Length: 6.6 km (4.1 mi); Time: 2.5 hours; Difficulty: Above Average.

Sai Kung Country Park

Chinese name: 西貢郊野公園

Transport: You first need to get to Sai Kung Town and then take a bus into the park.

Subway – Ma On Shan Line, Wu Kai Sha Station, take bus 299 to Sai Kung Town; or Kwun Tong Line, Diamond Hill MTR Station, take bus 92 to Sai Kung Town

Bus – *From Sai Kung Town*: 7, 9, 94, 96R and 698R go to the Sai Kung Country Park Visitors Centre; 94 and 7 go along Pak Tam Rd where there are trail heads for MacLehose Trail Sections 2 and 3

Ferry – Charter boats and boat taxis regularly leave from Sai Kung Town to Sai Wan beach; a ferry from Ko Tong Hau Pier goes to Ko Lau Wan Pier for access to the northern end of the Sharp Peak Hiking trail

While Hong Kong Island's iconic view is a soaring-tower cityscape as you gaze down from the top of Victoria Peak, the New Territories takes the scene in the opposite direction with a serene four-directional view of secluded bays and beaches from the top of the 468 m (1,353 ft) **Sharp Peak** (蚺蛇尖) in Sai Kung Country Park.

For oceanside hiking, this is your place. Sai Kung is divided into two sections – Sai Kung East Country Park and Sai Kung West Country Park – and boasts the most bays and coves of any country park in Hong Kong, as well as a solid sprinkling of campgrounds. From the top of Sharp Peak, you can see some of Hong Kong's most pristine beaches: to the west is Chek Keng Hau, while out east is Nam She Wan Beach, and to the south are those of the Deserted Beaches Hike.

Deserted Beaches Hike

The beaches of Tai Long Bay (Tai Wan, Ham Tin Wan and Sai Wan) and are the highlights of the Deserted Beaches Hike, which – as the name suggests – brings you past reclusive beaches with few visitors. Start the hike from Pak Tam Au on Pak Tam Road and head east on MacLehose Trail Section 2 for around 6 km (4 mi) or so until you reach the Sharp Peak Path, where you'll veer right towards beautiful **Tai Wan** (大灣) Beach.

When you've had your fill of Tai Wan, head south into the trees for just about 2 km (1 mi) until the jungle gives way to a wooden plank bridge that spans a small river. This will take you onto the light sands of the immaculate **Ham Tin Wan** (鹹 田 灣) Beach. You can stop for a snack at one of the restaurant shacks here, then it's over a ridge where the spectacular view of **Sai Wan** (西 灣) Beach greets you. There are several hostels and a campsite here, as well as a few restaurants. This is a good spot to take a break and sip a beer on the sand.

From Sai Wan, hike south to Chui Tung Au and then go north to Sai Kung Sai Wan Road

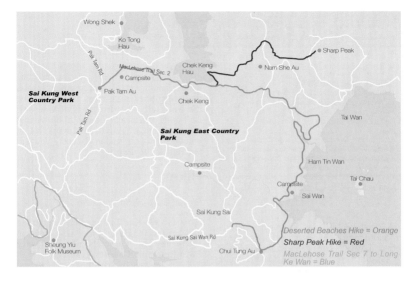

Deserted Beaches Hike = Orange
Sharp Peak Hike = Red
MacLehose Trail Sec 7 to Long
Ke Wan = Blue

to head back. It's also an option to start from Sai Kung Sai Wan Road and do the hike in reverse order, heading back the way you came from Tai Wan.

Villages

Tai Long Bay, like many of the highlights of Sai Kung Country Park, is located in Sai Kung East Country Park, which fills 4,477 hectares. Next door, Sai Kung West Country Park is attached, covering its own 3,000 hectares. In each section, there are plenty of abandoned villages to explore and numerous coves throughout the undulating coastline. One village, Sheung Yiu, near the entrance to Sai Kung East, has been turned into the **Sheung Yiu Folk Museum** (上 窰 民 俗 文 物 館 ; 9:00-16:00; Wed-Sun), which recreates a traditional Hakka village.

An even better idea than the Sheung Yiu Folk Museum may be to head to **High Island** (or Leung Shuen Wan; 糧船灣洲), an area south of High Island Reservoir (and no longer an island, due to the reservoir), where traditional village life is still fairly strong. There are still several dozen Tanka and Hakka locals living here in the Pok A, Tung A, Sha Kiu Tan and Pak Lap villages. Every two years, they hold a weeklong festival to celebrate the birthday of the goddess of the sea, Tin Hau. The highlight is the Boat Parade on the eve of her birthday where Tin Hau's statue is carried onto a boat and paraded out into the ocean as Cantonese Opera troupes perform on shore.

Trails

Maclehose Trail Section 1: This trail goes to North Island. Length: 10.6 km (6.6 mi); Time: 3 hours; Difficulty: Easy, flat.

Maclehose Trail Section 2: This trail covers the Deserted Beaches Hike that visits the amazing Tai Long Bay beaches. Length: 13.5 km (8.4 mi); Time: 5 hours; Difficulty: Moderate, some steep areas.

Maclehose Trail Section 3: At the end of Section 2 at Pak Tam Road, Section 3 begins on the other side of the road and goes through hilly areas of Sai Kung West. Length: 10.2 km (6.3 mi); Time: 4 hours; Difficulty: Difficult.

Sharp Peak Trail: Access the Sharp Peak summit trail either from Maclehouse Trail Section 2 or from Ko Wan Pier. The trail gets pretty steep. Check the weather conditions before hiking and never hike this one in inclement weather. It would be a bad place to get stuck in a storm.

Pak Tam Chung Nature Trail: A short and easy trail from the Sai Kung East Country Park Visitor Centre (phone: 2792 7365) with views of mangroves and bamboo gardens. Length: 1 km (0.6 mi); Difficulty: Very Easy.

Plover Cove Country Park

Chinese name: 船灣郊野公園
Transport: The best option is to first take the subway to Tai Po village and then bus into the park.
Subway – East Rail Line, Tai Wo Station, take a bus from the Tai Po Market terminus in Tai Po village
Bus –
From Tai Po Market terminus: Green Minibus 20C goes straight to Wu Kau Tang, a parking area from which multiple trails can be accessed; bus 75K goes to Tai Mei Tuk, a recreational and picnic area at the edge of the Plover Cove Reservoir where you can access the Pat Sing Leng Nature Trail

Abandoned villages, mythical waterfalls, and oddly eroded rock formations cover 4,594 hectares (11,352 acres) of little-inhabited forest in Plover Cove Country Park. Set amongst the most northwestern waters of Hong Kong, just across the water from Shenzhen at its northernmost tip, Plover Cove's coastlines have secluded rocky beaches and some of the most dramatic scenery in the New Territories. All around this riveting land, hiking trails meander past old villages, making Plover Cove far away from any thoughts of Hong Kong's modern lifestyle.

At the end of an easy, less-than-1 km path, the **Bride's Pool Waterfall** (新 娘 潭 瀑 布) is the main tourist attraction near the entrance to the park at the Wu Kau Tang (烏蛟騰) parking area. Walk through moss covered trees and you'll soon arrive at a horsetail waterfall splashing down a rock bed. Like so many others in China, the name of the waterfall has a legend of a woman behind it. Supposedly, a woman fell out of her sedan chair when her servants were passing by a slippery rock edge on the way to her wedding and she tragically drowned in the pool. Some say the souls of the woman and her grief-stricken groom inhabit the two intertwining trees you see above the waterfall. The Bride's Pool Waterfall isn't quite spectacular enough to do without a legend, but it is pretty and works as an introduction to the stunning scenery you will find further into the park.

Hikes

Plover Cove Reservoir Hike

From the Wu Kau Tang parking area at the trail head of the Bride's Pool Trail, you can choose any one of several trails. The **Plover Cove Reservoir Country Trail** (船 灣 淡 水 湖郊遊徑) passes by several old villages and travels along the southern peninsula, where there are striking views of the **Plover Cove Reservoir** (船灣淡水湖) to the west and the Tolo Channel to the east. The peninsula, which extends almost 5.5 km (3.5 mi), gets so narrow by the end that you can easily see both bodies of water on either side of the ridge trail. At the very end, the trail brings you to the dam of the Plover Cove Reservoir, from where you can walk over to the barbecue pits at Tai Mei Tuk. The total length of the trail is 15.5 km (9.5 mi).

Tiu Tang Lung Trail to Yan Chau Tong Marine Park

Another notable trail that starts at Wu Kao Tang is the Tiu Tang Lung (吊 燈 籠) Path, which has a northern and a southern route, both of which head out to the coast of the **Yan Chau Tong Marine Park** (印 洲 唐 海 岸 公 園). At the park, the trail goes through mangrove and sea-grass forests with a view

Left: Bride's Pool Waterfall
Top: Yan Chau Tong Marine Park

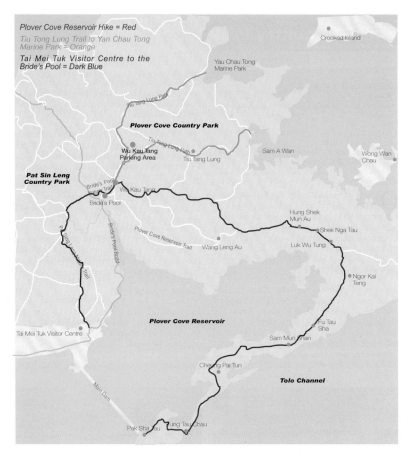

Plover Cove Reservoir Hike = Red

Tiu Tong Lung Trail to Yan Chau Tong Marine Park = Orange

Tai Mei Tuk Visitor Centre to the Bride's Pool = Dark Blue

Crooked Island

Yau Chau Tong Marine Park

Plover Cove Country Park

Tiu Tang Lung Path

Wu Kau Tang Parking Area

Tiu Tang Lung

Sam A Wan

Wong Wan Chau

Pat Sin Leng Country Park

Bride's Pool Nature Trail

Wu Kau Tang

Bride's Pool

Bride's Pool Road

Plover Cove Reservoir Trail

Wang Leng Au

Hung Shek Mun Au

Shek Nga Tau

Luk Wu Tung

Ngor Kai Teng

Pat Sin Leng Nature Trail

Plover Cove Reservoir

Tai Mei Tuk Visitor Centre

Tiu Tau Sha

Sam Mun Shan

Cheung Pai Tun

Tolo Channel

Main Dam

Pak Sha Tau

Tung Tau Chau

out into the fishing waters and islands. The two largest of the islands, **Crooked Island** (吉澳) and **Double Island** (Wong Wan Chau; 往 灣 洲), are still inhabited by the Hakka. Boats can be taken to Crooked Island where there are cannons, Qing Dynasty monuments and a sea cave, as well as some Hakka villages. Away from the eastern coast, Tiu Tang Lung Path loops back inland and splits into multiple paths, one of which ends up following the northern coastline, where Mainland China is in sight.

Tai Mei Tuk Visitor Centre to the Bride's Pool

A shorter hike begins at the **Tai Mei Tuk Visitor Centre**, where you can grab the **Pat Sin Leng Nature Trail** (八仙嶺自然教育徑), a 4.4 km- (2.7 mi)-long stretch that heads up to the Bride's Pool. The hike takes about two hours, and from Bride's Pool you can grab

minibus 20C to head back to Tai Mei Tuk if you'd like. You can also start from Bride's Pool and do the trail in reverse.

There's plenty more to explore in Plover Cove Country Park. It's the largest park in the New Territories, so feel free run wild and find your own great spots. Ask at the Visitor's Centre about the campgrounds where you can stay the night.

Bike Rentals & Trails

Renting a bike in Plover Cove is a great idea. Check out **Lung Kee Bikes** (phone: 2662 5266; HK$30 per day; 9:30-18:00) for good deals and info. There are several more locations from where you can rent as well, and you can find a good bike trail starting from Tai Mei Tuk that runs to the University at Ma Liu Shui.

Shek O Country Park

Chinese name: 石澳郊野公園
Transport:
Subway – Island Line, Chai Wan Station (the easternmost station)
Bus –
To Hong Kong Trail Sec 7: 14, 314 and 16M
To Hong Kong Trail Sec 8: 9
To Pottinger Peak Country Trail: Minibus 16A, 16M, 16X and 18M to Holy Cross Catholic Cemetery stop

On top of the hills on the far southeast peninsula of Hong Kong, Shek O Country Park is home to serene vantage points of clear-sea coastlines and the Tathong Channel islands. Around 3 km (1.9 mi) north of Stanley, the Shek O Village on the park's eastern coast is one of the most charming old-timey spots in the city.

Three popular hiking trails run through Shek O Country Park: Hong Kong Trail Stages 7 and 8 and Pottinger Peak Country Trail. The Dragon's Back Hike, part of Hong Kong Trail Stage 8 and situated on the spine of the Shek O Peak hill range, was named by *Time Magazine Asia* as the best urban hike in Asia. A view of the Stanley peninsula

across the Tai Tam Harbour appears to the west, and the Big Wave Bay and Shek O Wan Beaches (waiting at the end of the trail) appear to the east.

Hong Kong Trail Stage 7 is lower in altitude and follows the western shoreline a little ways inland. It starts at the edge of Tai Tam Country Park and then turns into Stage 8 towards the southern end of the park. From To Tei Wan Village, Stage 8 runs back north again and into the hills. An easy hike, it has ordinary views of the less interesting western seaside.

Pottinger Peak Country Trail at the north end of the park is a good morning walk trail. An easy hike close to the city, it still offers great highland views of the shoreline.

Dragon's Back Hike

From MTR Shau Kei Wan Station, go through Exit A3 and take bus 9 from Shau Kei Wan bus terminus to To Tei Wan Village on Shek O Road. The entrance to the hike is on Shek O Road near To Tei Wan Village (just look for the sign). Starting from here,

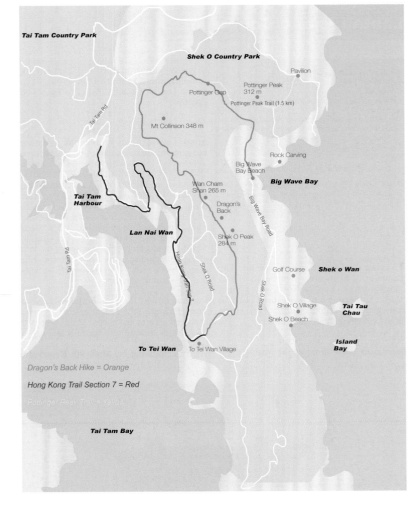

Tai Tam Country Park

Shek O Country Park

Pavilion

Pottinger Gap

Pottinger Peak 312 m

Pottinger Peak Trail (1.5 km)

Mt Collinson 348 m

Tai Tam Rd

Rock Carving

Big Wave Bay Beach

Big Wave Bay

Wan Cham Shan 265 m

Tai Tam Harbour

Dragon's Back

Lan Nai Wan

Shek O Peak 284 m

Big Wave Bay Road

Golf Course

Shek o Wan

Pak Tam Rd

Hong Kong Trail

Shek O Road

Shek O Road

Shek O Village

Tai Tau Chau

Shek O Beach

To Tei Wan

To Tei Wan Village

Island Bay

Dragon's Back Hike = Orange

Hong Kong Trail Section 7 = Red

Pottinger Peak Trail = Yellow

Tai Tam Bay

the Dragon's Back hike will take you over Shek O Peak, Wan Cham Shan and Mount Collinson, and then around Pottinger Gap and down to Big Wave Bay Beach. Keep an eye out for paragliders jumping off the Dragon's Back ridge.

Trails

Hong Kong Trail Section 7: A walk down the western side of the park that isn't extremely notable. Length: 7.5 km (4.7 mi); Time: 2 hours; Difficulty: Easy.

Hong Kong Trail Section 8: Including the famous Dragon's Back Hike, this trail offers

excellent ocean views. Length: 8.5 km (5.3 mi); Time: 3 hours; Difficulty: Moderate to Difficult.

Pottinger Peak Country Trail: A short trail with good views close to the city. Length: 1.9 km (1.2 mi); Time: 1.5 hours; Difficulty: Easy.

Beaches

Big Wave Bay and **Shek O**: Some of Hong Kong Island's best beaches, Big Wave (2 km north of Shek O Beach) and Shek O have fine sand and relatively big waves (by Hong Kong standards). Read more about them in the beaches section on pg 155.

Lantau Island Country Parks

Lantau is a nature-lover's island. The majority of its area is made up of two country parks: Lantau North and Lantau South. Covering 5,640 hectares (13,936 acres), Lantau South Country Park is the largest country park in Hong Kong.

Whether you're into hiking, climbing mountains, swimming at the beach, clam digging, mountain biking or visiting temples, there is more than enough fun in the Lantau Country Parks to keep you satisfied.

South Lantau Road

South Lantau Road follows the southern coastline of the island (providing excellent access for the North and South Lantau Country Parks and their various trails) and has a scattering of top notch beaches. Heading southwest from **Mui Wo,** after about 5 km (3 mi), you will find **Pui O** beach and its villages. Further down is **Cheung Sha**, which includes a village and a beach that extends over 3 km (2 mi). Upper Cheung Sha Beach is a bit prettier and sports modern changing facilities, while Lower Cheung Sha Beach plays host to beachfront restaurants and excellent windsurfing.

Further down, the beach and village at **Tong Fuk** are still decent and have some apartments, cafes and shops. At this point the road begins to head into the hills and off to the North Country Park. It's around here that you can check out the **Shek Pik Reservoir,**

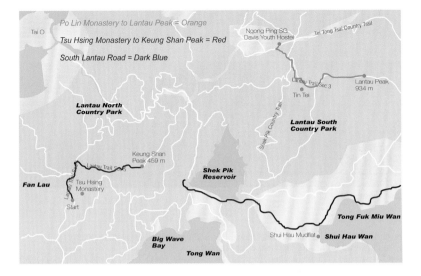

Po Lin Monastery to Lantau Peak = Orange

Tsu Hsing Monastery to Keung Shan Peak = Red

South Lantau Road = Dark Blue

Tai O

Ngong Ping SG Davis Youth Hostel

Tei Tong Tsai Country Trail

Lantau Trail Sec 3

Lantau Peak 934 m

Tin Tei

Lantau North Country Park

Shek Pik Country Trail

Lantau South Country Park

Keung Shan Peak 459 m

Lantau Trail Sec 5

Shek Pik Reservoir

Fan Lau

Tsu Hsing Monastery

Start

Tong Fuk Miu Wan

Shui Hau Mudflat   Shui Hau Wan

Big Wave Bay

Shui Hau Mudflat

Tong Wan

which was completed in 1963 to provide Lantau, Cheung Chau and Hong Kong Island with drinking water. From the reservoir you can head north to find an old **Bronze Age Rock Carving** (銅石器時代石刻) and either head northwest on the road to **Tai O**, hop on Lantau Trail Section 8 to find the campsites at **Fan Lau**, or hike into the mountains to discover the **Tsu Hsing Monastery** and the **Man Cheung Po Campsite** (see below).

Fan Lau

South of Tai O in the southwestern end of Lantau North Country Park is a beautiful lesser-developed area called Fan Lau. On a point extruding into the South China Sea you can find the **Fan Lau Fort** (分流炮台), which was built by the Portuguese in 1729. After the British took Hong Kong, the Portuguese abandoned the fort, and even though it underwent some restoration work back in 1985, today it's little more than a few crumbling, overgrown walls. It actually seems to fit with the surrounding scenery this way; certainly more than if it had been fully restored and overrun by tourists. It is only accessible via Lantau Trail Sections 7 and 8. There are no villages around Fan Lau, just the fort, and opposite it a **Tin Hau Temple** (天后廟) faces directly into the ocean. The quiet scenery is absolutely wonderful here.

The beaches along the Lantau Trail here are also quite tranquil. Bereft of lifeguards, shark netting, restaurants, and dotted here and there with a few small local boats, they are some of the best places in Hong Kong to get away from it all. **Tsin Yue Wan Beach** (煎魚灣), on

the shore north of Fan Lau Fort, looks out on Peaked Hill, an island with a precipitous rise from the sea.

Campsites

East of Fan Lau, the **Kau Ling Chung Campsite** (狗嶺涌營地), with 34 camping areas, is located near a beach and a gurgling stream. North of Fan Lau Fort and just south of Tsuen Yue Wan Beach, you can find the **Tsuen Yue Wan Campsite** (煎魚灣營地), where taking in surreal views of the sunset over Lantau Channel is all part of the experience. The Buddhist **Tsu Hsing Monastery** is located adjacent to the **Man Cheung Po Campsite** (萬丈布營地) and boasts a very cool statue of a flying dragon.

Hikes

Lantau's two tallest mountains are the second and third tallest mountains in Hong Kong. **Lantau Peak** (鳳凰山 ; 934 m; 3,064 ft) and **Sunset Peak** (大東山 ; 869 m; 2,851 ft) tower above the middle of the island and provide some top-notch hikes and world-class views.

Po Lin Monastery/Ngong Ping SG Davis Hostel to Lantau Peak

The Po Lin Monastery is built in the shadow of Lantau Peak, and it's around here on the Ngong Ping Plateau that you'll want to begin your climb on Section 3 of the Lantau Trail. Your best bet is to head to (or stay at) the **Ngong Ping SG Davis Hostel** (near the Big Buddha; see pg 179) and start from the sign-

Lantau Peak

posted trail at the hostel. An excellent plan is to either set off at 4:00 and make it to the top for sunrise or leave around 16:00 to be there to catch sunset. Both are spectacular experiences with utterly stunning panoramas, but just make sure you bring warm clothes and flashlights; high-altitude air can get quite chilly when the sun is not out, even during the summer. On especially clear days you can see Macau (65 km; 40 mi east) from the top. More details about Lantau Peak are included on page 65 in the Po Lin Monastery section.

As the name suggests, **Sunset Peak** is also an excellent place to catch the sunrise or sunset. It's not as well known as Lantau Peak – which is more rugged than most mountains on Hong Kong – but the hike is a little less taxing.

Tsu Hsing Monastery to Keung Shan Peak

Towards the southwest of the island is **Mount Keung Shan** (羌山 ; 459 m; 1,506 ft). The hike to the top is fairly easy along the old paved trail that winds through the sparse but calming forest. A good hike to the top of Keung Shan if you stay at the Man Cheung Po Campsite near Tsu Hsing Monastery is to hop on Lantau Trail Section 5 and follow it to the peak of Keung Shan (about 2.5 km; 1.5 mi).

Shui Hau Mud Flat: Clam Digging

The tide at **Shui Hau** (水口) **Beach** goes out in the afternoon, and you can walk right out onto the formerly-submerged area, where sea creatures like oysters, crabs and a whole lot of clams are exposed. You can rent clam digging equipment from stores in Shui Hau town (they have bag storage) and rake through the mud searching for tasty treasures.

Chi Ma Wan: Mountain Biking

Chi Ma Wan (芝麻灣), near Pui O, is known for its Chi Ma Wan Correctional Institute (芝 麻灣懲教所), as well as some good looking rock formations, but what you might be particularly interested in is the area's solid mountain biking. An 11 km (7 mi) track along the peninsula is one of the best mountain biking spots in Hong Kong. The trail gets challenging, with rock drop offs, and is best for more experienced riders. Check with the **Hong Kong Mountain Bike Association** (香港爬山單車協會) for detailed directions of how to get to the trail at the website: **www. hkmba.org/index.php/trail/lantau-island/ chi-ma-wan**

Wandering the Lantau Trail

The Lantau Trail does a circuit of the whole island over a division of 12 stages. While there are those who choose to hike the whole trail, this will take several days, and there are plenty of stages you can do in just an hour or a day. Following any of these trails from their posted areas is a great way to find your own hidden gems on this mountainous island, or you can jump on a bus and get off when you see something interesting. Besides what we have covered here, there are still monasteries, vistas and gardens just waiting to be discovered.

For more on some of the attractions on Lantau Island, see the Po Lin Monastery (pg 65), Tai O Fishing Village (pg 74), Pui O (pg 119), Cheung Sha Beach (pg 158) and Mui Wo/Silvermine Beach (pg 121).

Ma On Shan Country Park

Chinese name: 馬鞍山郊野公園
Admission: FREE
Transport:
Subway – The Ma On Shan Line follows the park most of the way to the north and there are several stations servicing the park. The station with access to Mt Ma On Shan is Ma On Shan Station. The mountains to the south like Kowloon Peak and Tate's Cairn are closest to Shek Mun Station.
Bus – Minibuses 26, 803, 803A, 805S, 807A, 807K, 808, 810 and 811S can take you to Sunshine City, a mall outside Ma On Shan Station. Village bus NR84 runs from Sunshine City to Ma On Shan Village and leaves at 8:00, 9:30, 10:30, 13:00, 16:00, 16:40, 17:30.

Mountaineers, head to Ma On Shan Country Park. Anchored by mighty Mount Ma On Shan (which at 702 m [2,303 ft] is the fifth tallest in Hong Kong), this park is where you can find the trailheads for the two main paths up the mountain. The demanding **western path** follows a steep ridge with a rope anchored into the trail that you can hold on to for dear life. A sign alongside the trail warns that the route is "very difficult and suitable only for experienced and well-equipped hikers." Believe it, this trail is no joke. Experienced hikers equipped with suitable shoes, water and snacks will earn magnificent views of the Tolo Harbour, Port Shelter and Sai Kung's protruding land from the peak of the Hung Backs (Ngau Kgak Shan) at 677 m (2,221 ft). Take a rest here before continuing to the summit, which takes about three to five hours to reach from the bottom.

The easier route is to follow Section 4 of the MacLehose Trail. As far as public park trails go, it is still more difficult than most stretches of the MacLehose, but it's still not as steep as the other Ma On Shan trails. Winding through the trees on the north side of the peak, the trail runs east, bypassing the summit of Ma On Shan, so you'll need to watch for the small path that branches off near the top and goes to the summit. If you continue following the MacLehose trail it will later take you by Pyramid Hill (Tam Kam Chung) and towards the park's southern peaks.

Kowloon Peak (飛 鵝 山) and Tate's Cairn (大 老 山) are among the eight mountains that the young Emperor Bing of the Song Dynasty counted when he named Kowloon (meaning "Nine Dragons"). His courier quickly corrected him, saying it was nine dragons, noting – with a good deal of brown on his nose – that the emperor is also a dragon. From the summit, sweeping views of Kowloon City and Victoria Bay will fill your eyes, giving you an idea of how the emperor must have felt when he looked out over his land. **Kowloon Peak** also has some bolted rock faces for climbers, as does **Beacon Hill** (畢架山).

Trails

MacLehose Trail Section 4: Running from north to south through the entirety of the park, MacLehose Trail Section 4 goes up and around the major hills and mountains. Length: 12.7 km (7.9 mi); Time: 5 hours; Difficulty: Difficult.

Campsites

Ma On Shan has a number of campsites in the mountains, notably **Ngong Ping Campsite** (昂 坪 營 地) on the MacLehose Trail/Ma On Shan Country Trail south from Pyramid Hill, and **Shui Long Wo Campsite** (水浪窩營地) in an area at the south end of the park along Section 3 of the MacLehose Trail, near the boundary between Ma On Shan and Sai Kung West country parks.

Other Attractions

Walled Villages

Early settlers to Hong Kong usually found that they were fending for themselves. Pirates ravaged the land, and the government was so ineffective in defending the people that the Qing Dynasty (1644-1912) in its early years actually gave up and evacuated Hong Kong, leaving the territory at the mercy of the pirate Koxinga. Between the years 1661 and 1662 there was an exodus of some 16,000 people, and those who stayed behind – or those who moved to Hong Kong after the Qing departure – lived in walled villages (圍村) in order to defend their homes and their lives.

It wasn't just pirates they were concerned with, either. Tigers roamed Hong Kong at the time, and the Hakka people were engaged in centuries of conflict with the Punti. These two groups built the majority of the walled villages in Hong Kong; among their most prominent families were the "Five Great Clans" of the New Territories: the Tang, Man, Hau, Pang and Liu clans. Rich and influential families, these clans carved out great influence during their long histories in the New Territories, and the walled villages here were each built by one of the Five Great Clans. This makes these villages some of the most fascinating pieces in Hong Kong's epic tale, and many of them remain populated today (though the traditional homes are slowly becoming more modernized in new Western European villa styles). You'd better get out and see them while their fascinating history is still around to experience.

Kat Hing Wai

Chinese name: 吉慶圍
Address: Kam Tin, Yuen Long, New Territories
Transport:
Subway – West Rail Line, Kam Sheung Rd Station, Exit B, walk over a footbridge to Kam Po Rd, then turn to Kam Sheung Rd (it takes about 20 min to walk from Kam Po Rd to Kat Hing Wai)

In addition to pirates and tigers, the walls around Kat Hing Wai village are famous for their defense against another invasive enemy: the British. Kat Hing Wai was one of the last villages in the New Territories to surrender to the British in 1898, and to this day it remains one of the most populated walled villages with about 400 current residents.

The walls of this 100 m (328 ft) by 90 m (295 ft) village guard the clan and are marked by sturdy iron gates. Still, new buildings are easy to see from the outside, towering above the wall with multiple stories and television antennas. Most buildings are organized in charming narrow alleyways and still have traditional decorations on their first floors. Many of the residences inside are new, attesting to the notable prosperity of Hong Kong's New Territories, though you can still find some older buildings, particularly the wonderful ancestral halls and family shrines. The lovable villagers meander through their laid-back days wearing their characteristic wide brimmed black hats.

The Tang clan that built this village in the 1600s is one of the most famous in the New Territories. Among the "Great Five Clans" of Hong Kong, they claim royal lineage dating back to the Song Dynasty. When the Jurchens defeated the Northern Song, Emperor Gaozeng fled south and established the Southern Song Dynasty while his daughter headed to the Kam Tin area of the New Territories and married Tang Wai-kap (circa 1100 CE). Together they founded the Tang clan, which prospered greatly and soon established more villages in the Kam Tin area. Their villages are collectively known as the "Five Wais and Six Tsuengs": Lo Wai, Ma Wat Wai, Wing Ning Wai, Tung Kok Wai, San Wai, Ma Wat Tsuen, Wing Ning Tsuen, Tsz Tong Tsuen, Siu Hang Tsuen, Kun Lung Tsueng and San Uk Tsuen.

Fanling Wai

Chinese name: 粉嶺圍
Transport: Subway – East Rail Line, Fanling Station, Exit C

The historic village of Fanling Wai, built by the Pang clan during the late 16th or early 17th century, is actually a walled village, and many of the buildings are considered top notch historical sites. The legend of the village's founding sounds off about the inhabitants' fears of disturbing an eagle in a nearby town and dragons in the hills behind Fanling Wai. Worried that the creatures would bring up more than just mischief in the village, they built three decorative mountain peaks to ward off the eagle, as well as lychee trees to neutralize the dragon's energy in a classic adherence to Chinese *feng shui* design.

The clan's founder, Pang Kwai Gon, moved to the area in 1190. A simple farmer at the time, he eked out a living with his son Dik Yin, at one point giving refuge to a *feng shui* master who, in gratitude, advised them of a burial site capable of bestowing particular fortune on the clan. Since their burial at Wong Hau San, to the east of Fanling Wai, Kwai Gon and his Pang descendants have been known as one of the Five Great Clans of the New Territories.

As the clan prospered over the centuries (perhaps due to that one-in-a-million burial site) they later set up the walled town at Fanling Wai. Don't miss the **Pang Clan Ancestral Hall** (彭 氏 宗 祠), built in 1846, the **Tsz Tak Study Hall** (思 德 書 室) of the same year, or the 42 original homes from the village's founding. They are all outstandingly preserved. The somewhat unremarkable pond was dug out and filled with fish in order to pacify a phoenix. On the bank of the pond outside the village entrance, cannons and watch towers guard the front. The inscription by the door reads: "In front lies the phoenix water! Behind, rest the dragon hills!"

The Pang Family keeps meticulous records of their family history, which you can view at **www.pangsfamily.com**. They make a trip back to Fanling Wai every ten years.

King Yin Lei Mansion

Chinese name: 景賢里
Admission: FREE (call 2848 6230 for tickets)
Address: 45 Stubbs Rd
Transport:
Bus –
From Lee Garden Rd at Causeway Bay: Minibus 26 goes
to the mansion
From Central: 15 (Central–The Peak), get off at Bradbury
School, walk east and cross the road to the north side at
the first signal-controlled pedestrian crossing, continue
east and turn left at the first intersection

Layout Plan of King Yin Lei

Only a few buildings still exist in Hong Kong from the Chinese Renaissance, a style of architecture that was popular in the 1920s and '30s. Easily visible from the bus 15 stop outside, this three-sided courtyard house, built with red bricks and green-tiled classical Chinese pyramidal hip-and-gable roofs, is known as the King Yin Lei Mansion and is a stunning sight in the midst of the city.

The three-story house was built by Shum Yatchor, a merchant from Guangdong, and his wife Shum Li Po-lun in 1937. Standing on the hillside of Victoria Peak, which was once restricted to foreigners only, it represented an early example of the rise of the wealthy Chinese merchant class during the 1930s. In 1978, Yeo Chei Man purchased the house and renamed it from its original name of Hei Lo to King Yin Lei. It was sold again in 2007 and declared a monument in 2008 to prevent the owners from tearing it down (they were given compensation land nearby), at which point the government took control and restored the

demolished area of this palace-within-the-city.

The decorations inside and outside of the house are simply gorgeous, particularly the resplendent gardens that overlook the city out back. Make sure to give them some time and note their dazzling complement to the green gabled roof. Inside, the rooms are ornately decorated and luxurious, especially the dining room, which features a high-carved ceiling and marble tiles. Every so often, the government hosts open days for which free tickets are distributed for public tours.

Standing amid modern residential skyscrapers, King Yin Lei and its rare red brick façade harken to the days when newly arrived Chinese transplants came to Hong Kong with the dream of striking it rich. This dream house became the models of their desires, further enhanced when it became the main location for the famous 1980s TVB drama series *Yesterday's Glitter* (京華春夢), starring Liza Wang (汪明荃) and Damian Lau Chung-yan (劉松仁).

Tsang Tai Uk

Chinese name: 曾大屋
Transport:
Subway – Ma On Shan Line, Che Kung Temple Station, Exit D, walk east to Lion Rock Tunnel Rd and turn right
Bus – 61S, 74A, 82M, 82S, 85A, 249X, 803, 803A, 804 and N281 to Tsang Tai Uk Stop

The small walled village of Tsang Tai Uk still retains its traditional architecture, which is more than can be said for a good many other villages around Hong Kong, where tall villas and fancy cars are spreading like wildfire. This hamlet of just three rows of houses wasn't built until after the British arrived, but that may be why it still sports its original gray-brick tiled roof and Hakka architecture.

Tsang Tai Uk, or Shan Hai Wai (meaning "Walled Village at the Mountain's Foot"), as it's also known, is a rustic walled fortress

pinned by watch towers on all four corners. It was built by the Hakka merchant Tsang Kook-man in 1848 to house the Tsang clan. A few people still live here, so the residences in the back are normally closed off to visitors, but the front courtyard and the **ancestral hall** are open and worth a visit.

The one- or two-storied houses of this hamlet are what many travelers have in mind when they think of a "traditional" Hong Kong village. You can see the faded, darkening colors of the bricks, chipped white paint on the corners and wooden carvings and character decorations lining the sides of the doors. They may have air conditioning units hanging out the side of the windows – something they certainly didn't have in the 19th century – but hey, villagers need to survive the sweltering Hong Kong summer heat too!

Towns & Villages

What's the difference between "Walled Villages" and "Towns & Villages"? Besides the obvious answer of "walls," the places in this section are a bit more dynamic than those you'll find in the "Walled" chapter. While walled villages have their share of mystique, intrigue and culture, and certainly shouldn't be passed by, what you'll find in the following pages are towns and villages that range from modern beachside boutique havens and chic foodie paradises to ancient ritual-filled wonders and easygoing seafaring hamlets. The last five towns in this section, starting with Tsuen Wan, make up the New Towns of the New Territories, nature- and temple-filled modern towns that flank Country Parks and rural villages.

Pui O

Chinese name: 貝澳
Transport:
Subway – Tung Chung Line, Tung Chung Station, take bus 3M (Mui Wo) to Pui O
Bus –
From Tung Chung: 3M
From Mui Wo: 1 or 2
Ferry – A ferry from Central goes to Mui Wo throughout the day

It's actually quite easy to miss this village when driving on the road to the Po Lin Monastery. It's a pity when that happens because what you're missing out on are quiet villages, wild buffalo and a gorgeous beach. You won't miss out on a McDonalds or a line of skyscrapers, however, because this dreamy little area of hamlets has none.

The four villages Lo Wai, San Wai, Lo Uk and Ham Tin of the Pui O area are spread out among lovely, bucolic scenery at the foot of some fine rugged mountains. Wild buffalo graze in the open fields, and there is a simple paved walk connecting some of the areas. In years past these fields were cultivated for rice, but the farms here were abandoned long ago, and today you're more likely to see students from an international school cruising around this lovely area than you are to see a farmer. When you need an even more relaxing environment, head over to the immaculate beach, whose sparkling sand seems to reflect colors from across the spectrum. For how beautiful this beach is, it's surprisingly lacking in people.

There are campsites at Pui O as well, including one near the beach (surf the website **www.lcsd.gov.hk/camp/en/p_ng_po.php**), and houses in the village are available for rent.

Aberdeen

Chinese name: 香港仔
Transport:
Subway – Island Line, Central or Causeway Bay Station, then take a bus
Bus -
From Central: 70 from Exchange Square Station
From Causeway Bay: 72 or 76 from Moreton Terrace
From North Point: 38, 42, 41A
From Tsim Sha Tsui: 973 from Mody Rd
Ferry – If you are on the Outlying Islands, there are ferries from Pak Kok Tsuen and Sok Kwu Wan to Aberdeen

Those who are familiar with Hong Kong's English translation of "Fragrant Bay" might be wondering which of Hong Kong's many bays is so fragrant. We'll tell you the answer (it's Aberdeen), but you'd better head down there and smell it for yourself.

When British boats first landed in southern China it was at the town of Aberdeen, which was called Hong Kong (香 港) by the Cantonese because of the wooden incense that was collected and exported from the bay. The British soon began referring to the whole island as Hong Kong, and by the time they realized their mistake, the name had become commonplace. Aberdeen itself was named after then British Foreign Secretary and later Prime Minister George Hamilton-Gordon, the 4th Earl of Aberdeen. Nowadays, this area of Hong Kong is packed with sights and great activities. Besides sampan boat cruises and floating restaurants, Hong Kong's best amusement park and some of the city's best seafood can be found here.

This one-time fishing village on the south side of Hong Kong is the traditional home to the Tanka seafaring people. Today, most of the Tanka live on the waters of Aberdeen Bay, where you can still see quite a few people residing in boats (look for the vessels with laundry out drying). This whole area of the Harbour is actually known as the **Aberdeen Floating Village** (香 港 仔 水 上 人 家). If you'd like to take a tour of the bay, sightseeing sampan boats can give you a ride around the Harbour to see the Tanka villages and boats. Look for the signs down by the waterfront labeled "Sightseeing Sampan."

The biggest boat in the Harbour is by far the **Jumbo Floating Restaurant** (also called the Jumbo Kingdom). They don't call it jumbo for nothing; like an enormous floating temple, the complex was designed after traditional imperial palace architecture, and inside the huge restaurant you'll find a veritable theme park complete with more restaurants, a cooking academy, shopping plazas, a wine garden and a bronzework exhibition hall. The grand Cantonese dining room inside and the al fresco Western restaurant and bar on the top floor can hold over 2,000 people combined. The Jumbo Kingdom becomes a particularly splendid sight at night when its city of lights become illuminated. The restaurant has been visited by countless international celebrities and its exterior has appeared in films like *Infernal Affairs 2* (2003) and *The God of Cookery* (1996).

At the west end of the Aberdeen Promenade is the **Aberdeen Fish Market Canteen** (香 港仔魚市場海鮮餐廳), where fishermen bring in their catch at the end of a long night. The market operates early in the morning and closes around noon. In this area you can find some exceptional seafood. The canteen mainly serves workers, but outsiders can come in at around noon and dine on market fresh seafood. Expect to pay anywhere from HK$200 to HK$400 a person (depending on how nicely you want to dine). Make a reservation by calling 2552 7555 in advance. It is open from 5:00 to 14:00 daily.

Other points of interest in Aberdeen include the **Tin Hau Temple** (天 后 廟), **Chinese Permanent Cemetery** (香港仔華人永遠墳場), and the fun and hugely popular **Ocean Park** (海洋公園 ; pg 166).

For sleeping see page 178, eating page 202, and drinking page 222.

Mui Wo

Chinese name: 梅窩
Transport:
Ferry – *From Central Pier 6*: A ferry runs to Mui Wo from 6:00 until 1:30 in the morning, leaving twice an hour (on the 10 and 50 min marks) for most of the day
Subway – Tung Chung Line, Tung Chung Station, then take bus 3M to Mui Wo

Like Stanley, Mui Wo is something of a refuge for expats. A third of the population of Lantau Island lives in the drowsy town of Mui Wo and the surrounding hamlets. The town is full of quaint foreigner-seducing shops, such as an English-language bookstore, a spa, antique shops and a British pub. Expat magazine *Timeout Hong Kong* described the area as a "dreamy little island corner."

Feeling the white sand on your feet and looking at the clear water of Silvermine Beach (on the northwest corner of Mui Wo) is one of Lantau's more popular relaxing experiences, and there are showers, changing rooms and toilets to make things convenient. **The Silvermine Resort** tries to give it a "resorty" feel with their hotel and restaurants right on the beach, which include a high-dining restaurant, a bar and lounge, and the outdoor Blue Horizon Café (海天一色 ; phone: 2984 6863). The hotel receives mixed reviews, with some people saying the rooms are derelict and dirty, especially for prices of between HK$1,200 and HK$1,800 a night, and their bar isn't much better. A better-received choice among expats is the **China Bear** (中國熊 ; phone: 2984 9720), a bar in town which offers standard pub fare and beers.

From Silvermine Beach you can take a hike to the **Silvermine Waterfall** (銀鑛瀑布) by the **Silvermine Cave** (銀礦洞). The waterfall is excellent when it really gets roaring in the rainy season, and the cave was mined for silver in the 19th century. On the way to the cave you'll pass a small Man Mo Temple (文武廟), which was originally built in the 16th century and has undergone several recent renovations. To find the hiking trail from Mui Wo follow Mui Wo Rural Committee Road West and you will see the marked path heading north.

Silvermine Beach is a very good place to experience expat life, and it's quite convenient to find, located right next to the ferry pier. But if you have a lot of time to spend in Lantau, make sure you don't just stay in the confines of Mui Wo; there are far too many cool places on Lantaua to become addicted only to Mui Wo.

For eating see page 206 and drinking page 224.

Upper stream of the Silver Mine Waterfall, Mui Wo, Lantau Island

Sai Kung Town

Chinese name: 西貢市
Transport:
Subway & Bus – Ma On Shan Line, Wu Kai Sha Station, take bus 299 to Sai Kung Town; or Kwun Tong Line, Diamond Hill MTR Station, take bus 92 to Sai Kung Town

Often lauded as "Hong Kong's Backyard Garden," Sai Kung Town is home to excellent eating and drinking and is a gateway to beautiful country parks. It's located to the east of Ma On Shan and the southwest end of Sai Kung Country Parks on the coast of the New Territories, and it's the perfect place to post up before or after a great hike or island-boating excursion. Come for the town's vibrant seafood market and awesome restaurants, stay for some drinks in one of the solid pubs.

Running down the coast is a sidewalk and a pier into the Harbour packed with fishing and recreational boats, and it's from here that you can hire a boat to go to one of the Outlying Islands. Along the main restaurant stretch, the rich variety of fish and sea creatures accentuate Prince Phillip's not-so-well-thought-out description that Hong Kongers eat everything with four legs except the tables and chairs.

Don't expect a quaint little village, though. This is a bustling place where waitresses standing outside some of the main restaurants thrust laminated English menus at you, advertising set meals at a few hundred dollars and crab around HK$180, while doormen try to seduce you into their bars. Every night, the place is lit up as much by the lights as it is by the party-going crowds.

Sai Kung is also a top spot for windsurfing. Equipment can be rented at the **Wind Surfing Centre** (2792 5605; 9:30-18:00, Sat & Sun; call ahead on weekdays) on Sha Ha, just north of town. It's a 15-minute walk from town, or bus 94 can take you here.

From Sai Kung Town, there are some lovely nature areas to explore.

Sai Kung Country Park – This is the country park with the most bays, coves and secluded beaches. If Corona wanted to film a commercial in Hong Kong, they might film it here. Read more on page 104.

Mount Ma On Shan – Ma On Shan peak towers in the background of Sai Kung Town at 702 m (2,303 ft). Read about it and the Ma On Shan Country Park on page 113.

Kau Sai Chau (滘西洲) – An island close to Sai Kung Town with a public golf course on the northern end and an undeveloped natural area in the south; eagles, herons and other birds and animals can be seen here. The Jockey Club Golf Course ferry goes from the pier to the island.

Charter a Boat – Private drivers and companies offer all kinds of rides, boat taxis, fishing, snorkeling trips and more.

For sleeping see page 180, eating page 206, and drinking page 224.

Lau Fau Shan & Pak Nai

Chinese name: 流浮山 ; 白泥
Transport: Green Minibus –
To Lau Fau Shan: 35 from Tai Fung St in Yuen Long
To Pak Nai: 33 from Tai Fung St in Yuen Long

An exceptional place for lunch and wandering when spending a day in Yuen Long, the fishing village of Lau Fau Shan, just outside of town, holds the territory's only oyster farm and a mighty cluster of seafood restaurants ready to shuck them up.

A good plan for Lau Fau Shan (if you're into seafood) is to stumble in just a little bit before lunch. The village has long been an oyster fishing haven, and though some of that culture is slowly disappearing, there's still enough going on to make a walk along the shoreline areas worthwhile. Around the oyster market you can have a laugh with the chatting farmers shucking away at oysters while sparkling Deep Bay and Shenzhen sit in the background. If you want to head to the shore, just find the restaurant-lined, paved path that sits next to the public toilet.

Just 4 km (2 mi) to the southwest of Lau Fau Shan is the quiet rural setting of Pak Nai, a place where locals and domestic tourists love to drop their jaws and click their cameras at the village's glorious sunsets over Deep Bay. The coastline here – running along Deep Bay Road – runs for 6 km (4.5 mi), and pretty much anywhere you choose along the seaside will deliver what many consider to be the best sunsets in the city. Along Deep Bay Road (which becomes Nim Wan Road after Upper Pak Nai) you'll find a delightfully bucolic landscape of fish ponds, farms, mangroves and beaches that become iridescent with oyster and clam shells at sunset. When you come here on green minibus 33 you can just call the driver to let you off at any spot that looks tempting.

Sheung Shui

Chinese name: 上水
Transport: Subway – East Rail Line, Sheung Shui Station

Sheung Shui is an area of nine villages settled by the Liu clan. All the villages are packed together in this tight corner one subway stop away from Shenzhen.

The original village, Wai Loi Tsuen, was built in 1584. The name means "On Water," and it's one of the only villages with an intact moat, making up for a wall that is somewhat less impressive (more like nonexistent) than other villages. The moat goes around the back, circling the space of buildings, which are surrounded by a metal fence. A raised plot of land gives the idea that a grander stone wall was once in its place. Like Kat Hing Wai, there are mostly modern buildings here today, and most are arranged in rows alongside a main road that runs down the middle.

The **Liu Man Shek Tong Ancestral Hall** (廖萬石堂), located across the street from Wai Loi Tsuen, is the ancestral hall for Shueng Shui's villages. With two halls and three courtyards, it's pretty and worth a visit.

Shui Tau Tsuen

Chinese name: 水頭村

Hours: All halls, temples and historic buildings here are open 9:00-13:00 & 14:00-17:00 Sun, Sat & public holidays

Transport: Bus – 64K to Kam Tin Rd, walk north through the pedestrian underpass below Kam Tin Bypass, pass Kam Tin Rd and cross the river to Chi Ho Rd, cross the bridge that spans a small stream then turn right and then left to enter the village

The traditional village of Shui Tau Tsuen, located on the peripheries of Yuen Long New Town, is slowly losing its old-timey charm, but there are enough preserved buildings with eaved roofs adorned with fish and dragons to warrant a jaunt out to this cool piece of Hong Kong's long heritage.

It's the traditional architecture that Shui Tau Tsuen is famous for, especially its special roofs. The new buildings that are rearing their heads around here more and more feel oddly juxtaposed with the old structures, but alas, that is the modern character of Hong Kong. Two of the most prominent examples of the impressive architecture can be seen at the **Tang Kwong U Ancestral Hall** (9:00-13:00 & 14:00-17:00 Sun, Sat & public holidays) and the **Tang Ching Ancestral Hall** (9:00-13:00 & 14:00-17:00 Sun, Sat & public holidays). Both were built during the early 1800s as areas of ancestral worship and today they are part of the village's protected sites. Check out the **Hung Shing Temple** sandwiched in the middle of the two halls, as well as the **Yi Tai Study Hall** to their south. The latter was built for the gods of war and literature and it has the most powerful presence in town. Near the edge of town you can find a **Tin Hau Temple** (天 後 廟) from 1722 with a 106 kg iron bell inside.

Tsuen Wan

Chinese name: 荃灣

Transport: Tsuen Wan MTR Station lets out on Sai Lau Kok Rd, and the bus station is just opposite on Castle Peak Rd (take Exit A2 from the subway). Green minibuses and regular buses run around town from here. You can take a bus to Tsuen Wan from towns around the New Territories, but if you are coming from Kowloon or Hong Kong Island, subway is the best choice.

Subway – Tsuen Wan Line, Tsuen Wan MTR Station; or West Rail Line, Tsuen Wan West MTR Station
To Sam Tung Uk Museum: Tsuen Wan MTR Station, Exit E, walk southeast along Sai Lau Kok Rd for 5 min until Lau Kok Rd

Bus –
From Tuen Mun: 60M
From Yuen Long: 68M
From Tai Mo Shan: 51 to Tai Ho Rd
To Yuen Yuen Institute: Green Minibus 81 from Shiu Wo St, two blocks south of Tsuen Wan MTR Station, Exit B1
To Western Monastery: Same as Yuen Yuen Institute
To Chuk Lam Sim Monastery: Green Minibus 85 from Shiu Wo St

Despite the fact that most of its makeup is unremarkable residential and industrial buildings, the New Territories New Town of Tsuen Wan has enough to do in its peripheries to warrant a day if you're looking to get out of the city. Early risers can be especially rewarded by the morning *yum cha* sessions in Chuen Lung Village, and just about any busybody can find something breathtaking in nearby **Tai Mo Shan Country Park** (pg 100). What probably makes Tsuen Wan standout most, however, is the small collection of tranquil monasteries and holy places adorning the outskirts.

In hills to the northeast of town sits the Taoist complex of the **Yuen Yuen Institute** (pg 150), a beautiful spiritual station that combines reverence of Taoist, Buddhist and Confucian tenets into a fascinating swirl of incense, statues and pavilions. The institute is one of Tsuen Wan's best sights, and if you come to this area you'd better plan an hour or so to see its lovely grounds.

If you're still in the mood for some far eastern wisdom after the Yuen Yuen Institute, take a pleasant walk (or ride on green minibus 81) down the hill to the excellent **Western Monastery** (西 方 寺 ; address: Lo Wai Rd; hours: 8:30-17:30; phone: 2411 511), for a look at something wholly Buddhist. The complex is peaceful, and the architecture of the main building – modeled after traditional Chinese palace designs – is a

pleasure to make a leisurely cruise through. Check out the Hall of the Maitreya and the Great Buddha's Hall before moving on to the building behind, which is topped with an awesome nine-story pagoda and is often overrun with mantra-chanting monks.

Another option from Tsuen Wan includes a trip to the fantastic **Chuk Lam Sim Monastery** (pg 151) in a wonderfully idyllic setting. Relegating a few hours to this monastery is a superb alternative or addition to either of the other holy sites around town.

When you're feeling a bit too enlightened for your own good, consider grabbing a taste of traditional Hakka village life at the **Sam Tung Uk Musuem** (三棟屋博物館 ; address: 2 Kwu Uk Lane; hours: 9:00-17:00 Wed-Mon; phone: 2411 2001). A well conceptualized and maintained museum, it sits on the former site of a Hakka walled village (the Chan Clan was resettled elsewhere in 1980) and looks to recreate the life of its former townsfolk through a series of some 12 traditional three-beamed houses, all replete with genuine furniture, kitchenware, agricultural tools and even wedding clothes and items. Most of these fascinating cultural items came from Hakka villages in Guangdong, and behind them you can find the village's old school, housing interactive and media displays on all topics Hakka.

For sleeping see page 180, eating page 209, and drinking page 225.

Tuen Mun

Chinese name: 屯門

Transport: The easiest way to get to Tuen Mun is the subway. Alternatives include taking ferries from Lantau Island, the Light Rail or buses from other towns in the New Territories. Most sights around town are best reached by the Light Rail.

Subway – West Rail Line, Tuen Mun MTR Station

Ferry – From Tung Chung, Sha Lo Wan or Tai O on Lantau Island to the Tuen Mun ferry pier

Light Rail – Tuen Mun Light Rail Station is near the southern end of the network and is linked to the MTR station

To Tsing Shan Monastery: Line 610, 615 or 615P to Tsing Shan Tsuen, follow the signs to the monastery from the west of the station (about a 30 min uphill walk)

To Miu Fat Monastery: Line 751 to Lam Tei Station, cross the walkway over Castle Peak Rd and then walk north 150 m (492 ft)

To Ching Chung Temple: Line 505 to Ching Ching Station

Bus –

From Tsuen Wan: 60M runs from Tsuen Wan MTR Station, Exit A3 to Tuen Mun

To Miu Fat Monastery: 63X from Mong Kok MTR Station stops out front of the monastery

Like most of the New Towns in the New Territories, the center of Tuen Mun has little to see as far as attractions, but the settings around the outside are stocked with a set of charming temples and delightful monasteries. When you're ready to close the day out there are good eats and drinks to be found back in town.

One of the most mesmerizing structures in town, especially when viewed from afar, is the huge **Miu Fat Monastery** (pg 153), north of Tuen Mun town center. The Ten Thousand Buddhas Hall on the top of this Thai-influenced monolith is built to resemble a blossoming crystal lotus and gives the building a spectacular presence when illuminated at night. It's easily accessible by Light Rail.

If you're up for some exercise and something a bit more isolated, consider the steep, 30-minute hike to **Tsing Shan Monastery** (pg 152) from the Light Rail station below. This funky complex is technically considered Hong Kong's oldest temple since its founding dates back some 1,500 years, but the buildings you see here now were all rebuilt in 1926. It's worth a visit not only for its yesteryear charms, but also for the fact that scenes from Bruce Lee's 1973 classic *Enter the Dragon* were filmed here.

The last of the worthwhile sights in the area is the **Ching Chung Temple** (青 松 觀 ; address: Tsing Lung Rd; hours: 7:00-18:00; phone: 2370 8870), a shady Taoist retreat that means "Green Pine Temple" in English. You can find some pines here, but more than anything we're sure you'll be swooned by the lovely bamboo, bonsai trees and tranquil ponds that adorn the grounds. Just a short walk through the scenery reveals the temple's main building, dedicated to Lu Sun Young, one of the Eight Immortals of Taoist lore (a group which inspired the martial arts forms of the Eight Drunken Immortals style).

For eating see page 209 and drinking page 225.

Yuen Long

Chinese name: 元朗
Transport: The best way to get to Yuen Long is by subway/MTR. Accessing the small villages around Yuen Long requires taking minibuses from Yuen Long MTR Station, but other sights around town can be accessed via subway or light rail from other parts of Hong Kong (i.e. without needing to come to Yuen Long Town first).
Subway –
To Yuen Long: West Rail Line, Yuen Long Station
To Mai Po Marshes: West Rail Line, Yuen Long MTR Station; or East Rail Line, Sheung Shui Station, then take bus 76K from either station
To Ping Shan Heritage Trail: West Rail Line, Tin Shui Wai Station
To Hong Kong Wetland Park: West Rail Line, Tin Shui Wai Station, then take the Light Rail
Bus – *To Mai Po Marshes:* 76K from Yuen Long MTR Station or Sheung Shui MTR Station
Green Minibus –
To Lau Fau Shan: 35 from Tai Fung St
To Pak Nai: 33 from Tai Fung St

day is needed to catch both the **Ping Shan Heritage Trail** (pg 77) and the **Mai Po Marshes** (pg 96) before lunch in Yuen Long and a visit to a rural village or two in the afternoon. The best villages to visit are **Lau Fau Shan & Pak Nai** (pg 123), **Kat Hing Wai** (pg 115) and **Shui Tau Tsuen** (pg 124); you might want to consider saving lunch time for one of the many seafood restaurants lining the shores of Lau Fau Shan before watching the sunset from Pak Nai.

Seeing the Mai Po Marshes is a great experience, but it's almost impossible to do without a guided tour. If you don't manage to sign on with one (they require fairly advanced booking) then your next best option is to check out **Hong Kong Wetland Park** (pg 97).

Last, but certainly not least, the town of Yuen Long has a formidable cluster of great restaurants featuring tasty seafood and good dim sum. There are enough delicious places here to make you happy for all three meals. Even if you don't make it early enough for morning dim sum, you can at least make this town your lunch and dinner home base.

For eating see page 210 and drinking page 225.

Yuen Long is less of an attraction itself and more of a jumping off point for some fantastic sights in the area. Essentially a transportation hub, you'll first need to connect here in order to reach the walled villages and outstanding wildlife reserves of the area.

Planning a full day for Yuen Long and its greater neighborhood is a good idea, especially when you consider that a full

Other Attractions

Tai Po

Chinese name: 大埔
Transport: Take the subway to Tai Po village. From here you can use buses to the surrounding attractions.
Subway – East Rail Line, Tai Po Market or Ta Wo East Rail Stations
To Hong Kong Railway Museum: From Tai Wo East Rail Station walk south through the Tai Wo Shopping Centre and cross the Lam Tsuen River via Tai Wo Bridge, find the museum to the southeast
To the farmer's market: From Tai Wo East Railway Station take Exit B and walk through Tai Wo Plaza, then follow the signs to Oi Wo House; the market will be next to the power substation
Bus – You can take bus 71K between the two subway stations
To Lam Tsuen Wishing Tree: 64K from Tai Po Market Station and get off at Fong Ma Po
To Kadoorie Farm & Botanic Garden: 64K to the farm
Green Minibus –
To Fung Yuen Butterfly Reserve: 20A from from Tai Po Market East Rail Station and tell the driver to let you off at Fung Yuen Chun King Sor (鳳園村公所)
To Ng Tung Chai Waterfall and Tai Mo Shan Country Park: 25K from Tsing Yuen St

With the most diverse selection of sights and attractions of any of the New Towns, beautiful Tai Po and its collection of charming markets, nature reserves, temples, a cool museum and its proximity to excellent Country Parks, easily make it the number one day destination in the New Territories.

A great way to start your day at Tai Po is to first take a perusal through the **Tai Po Street Market** (大埔街市 ; address: Fu Shin St; 6:00-20:00) to see one of the most intriguing and energetic wet markets in the New Territories. On the northern end of Fu Shin Street, where the market is located, you can find a nice little **Man Mo Temple** (文武廟 ; 8:00-18:00) to pass a tranquil 20 minutes or so. From there it's an easy several-minute walk to the **Hong Kong Railway Museum** (香港鐵路博物館 ; address: 13 Shung Tak St; admission: FREE; hours: 9:00-17:00 Wed-Mon; phone: 2653 3455), which is inside the former Tai Po market train station. Here, you can follow the development of railroads in the area and check out a 1911 narrow-gauge steam locomotive.

Right in the center of town and to the north of the Tai Po Market and Man Mo Temple, an excellent **farmer's market** (大埔農墟 ; Tai Wo St; hours: 9:00-17:00 Sun) can be found on Sundays. There are plenty of interesting things on sale, and the energy is vibrant,

especially if you show up just after it opens.

The best time to hit up the markets is in the early morning, though they are open all day. If you're not into the market scene then another superb option is to make a jaunt out to the wonderful **Fung Yuen Butterfly Reserve** (鳳園蝴蝶保育區 ; address: 150 Fung Yuen Rd; admission: HK$20; hours: 9:00-17:00; phone: 3111 7344), a special site of scientific interest ablaze with more than 180 species of colorful butterflies. Over one third of the lovely insects here are rare or endangered, and the best time to catch a glimpse of the greatest variety of them is in the morning hours before 10:00, but any time of day will still bring great rewards at this unique place.

If you saved either the markets or butterflies for morning, then after lunch could be a good time to head for the **Lam Tsuen Wishing Tree** (pg 93) and toss one of your own wishes into the plastic recreated tree (the real one lost a branch and is recovering nearby). A smattering of great hikes are also available in the area, one of the best being a hike to beautiful **Ng Tung Chai Waterfall** (pg 100) in Tai Mo Shan Country park – you can continue following the trail to the top of Mount Tai Mo Shan – after a visit to the lovely **Kadoorie Farm & Botanical Garden**

For eating see page 208.

Sha Tin

Chinese name: 沙田
Transport: Though there are buses that can reach Sha Tin from various parts of Hong Kong, subway is by far the most convenient way to get to the town and all of its attractions. However, reaching nearby Sai Kung Town is best done by bus.
Subway – East Rail Line, Sha Tin Station
To Che Kung Temple: Ma On Shan Line, Che Kung Temple MTR Station
To Hong Kong Heritage Museum: Ma On Shan Line, Che Kung Temple MTR Station, walk east along Che Kung Miu Rd, go through the subway underpass and cross the footbridge over the channel
To Ten Thousand Buddhas Monastery: Ma On Shan Line, Sha Tin MTR Station, Exit B, walk down through the traditional homes at Pai Tau Village, turn left at Pai Tau St and then right at Sheung Wo St where you will follow the signs to the monastery
To Sha Tin Racecourse: East Rail Line, Racecourse Station
Bus – 299 to and from Sai Kung Town

Exploring the New Towns of the New Territories wouldn't be complete without stumbling upon a few of their fascinating surprises. And while Sha Tin runs with the pack in terms of offering a set of pretty religious complexes – one nestled a good hike up a mountain – Sha Tin marches to the beat of a different drum, particularly on Sundays when gamblers and jockeys stampede the thunderous **Sha Tin Racecourse** (pg 98). As the town's main draw, the rip-roaring, horserace-of-a-good-time you can have here against the backdrop of Mount Ma On Shan means you'd better time your trip to Sha Tin to fall on a race day.

Transport to Sha Tin will probably spit you out at **New Town Plaza**, a crowded shopping mall with a decent conglomeration of chain restaurants. You can get your grub on here, but other than that this place works somewhat as your transport hub to the other sights in the area. A great place to spend a morning before the races is the glittering **Ten Thousand Buddhas Monastery** (pg 147), tucked with its 400 steps just half a kilometer north of New Town Plaza and Sha Tin Station. The monastery is loaded with eaved-roof buildings among its relaxingly shrubby grounds. There are a ton of Buddha statues here too; the actual count is something around 12,800.

If your spiritual bone is not tickled quite enough by those thousands of Buddha statues, then hop on over to the **Che Kung Temple** (車公廟; address: Che Kong Miu Rd; admission: FREE; hours: 7:00-18:00; phone: 2691 1733), a large Taoist complex dedicated to the Song Dynasty general Che Kung, a man recognized for dispelling Sha Tin of a plague. On the 3rd day of the Chinese New Year the temple is overrun with worshippers coming to spin the sails of the copper windmill inside.

Sha Tin is also home to one of the best museums in the city: the **Hong Kong Heritage Museum** (pg 139). With thoughtful and superbly executed exhibits in a dozen galleries, the edification here is wrapped in fun and entertainment, and the outstanding children's areas on the ground floor can help you give your little ones a learning experience they won't forget.

For sleeping see page 180, eating page 207, and drinking page 224.

Markets

You may have heard that Hong Kong is a shopping paradise, but this usually takes different forms for different travelers. While it is famous internationally for the fashionable and luxury goods that are generally cheaper than other places in the world, this is certainly not the only – nor the most interesting – shopping Hong Kong has to offer. Famous top-end brands may line streets around Tsim Sha Tsui and Central, but that's not what shopping looks like for many local Hong Kongers.

Much of Hong Kong still makes their purchases in traditional markets, those where vendors set up stalls hawking a great cacophony of varied items. Many of these street markets have grown famous for certain products, which you can hear in their names: Fa Yuen Street became referred to as Sneakers Street (pg 232), Tung Choi Street North is known as the Goldfish Market (pg 233), Flower Market Road was given the official moniker… well, Flower Market Road (pg 233).

Sometimes entire streets become famous tourist attractions, such as the case with Ladies Street (pg 80), but many more retain their local charms, staying off the radar of foreigners who aren't as interested in visiting wet markets selling vegetables (Chun Yeung Street Wet Market) or hardware and electronics markets (Apliu Street Fleat Market). Those who skip these places, however, miss out on some of the most colorful local character in the city.

Every neighborhood in Hong Kong has a small local meat, fruit and vegetable market. Known as "wet markets" (named so because they contrast with dry markets that sell dry items like clothing, electronics, dried food, etc), these are where Hong Kongers have traditionally purchased fresh food to take home and cook. Some wet markets fill just one corner of the street, while others take up many blocks; some even have their own multi-story complexes that include cooked food stalls where multiple restaurants serve full meals out front.

No matter how much time you spend in Hong Kong, you'll miss out on an important vision of what Hong Kong is and where it has come from if you don't include at least one market on your itinerary. We're not talking about a department store, either. Take our advice: flip through the next section, choose a market (or three) that looks right for you, and give it some of your time. You won't regret it.

Western Market

Chinese name: 西港城
Admission: FREE
Phone: 6029 2675
Address: The Western Market is located at 323 Des Voeux Rd Central (德輔道中 323 號), less than 200 m (656 ft) from Sheung Wan MTR Station
Transport:
Subway – Island Line, Sheung Wan Station, Exit C, walk west on Connaught Rd Central (幹諾道中) for two blocks
Tram – The Hong Kong Tramways tram stops just outside of the Western Market at the Macau Ferry Terminal Station on Connaught Rd; a single adult ticket costs HK$2.30

The oldest market building standing on Hong Kong Island, the Western Market was originally built in the mid-19th century in the classical Edwardian style and is a handsome and imposing sight. Its reddish brown bricks make a bold contrast to the white arches and pillars framing the front windows, as well as the powerful gray-brick arched entrance. At each of the four corners of the three-story building there are window-lined towers surrounded by polychromatic brickwork, while inside the narrow aisles are interspersed with columns.

At one time it was a roaring food market, but these days the Western Market mostly functions as a textile and tailor market, housing an auxiliary of shops, restaurants and a grand dining hall. The building was set up as a protected historical site in 1990, making a trip here worthwhile as both a heritage site and an interesting place for some unique shopping. On the first floor you'll find bakeries, cafes, and a few cutesy art shops, while those looking for fabric will want to make for the second floor, where rolls of every color and pattern overflow out onto the walkways. The top floor holds a banquet hall that serves up some outstanding (but pricey) Cantonese fine dining and often hosts wedding banquets.

The Western Market is a relaxing place to wander around while enjoying the sights of the architecture and boutique art shops. This western section of Hong Kong surrounding the market is one of the oldest sections on the island, and there is a score of interesting historical buildings in close vicinity. A great afternoon can be spent meandering around nearby sights like the **Man Mo Temple** (pg 149), **Cat Street** (see next page), **Ladder Street**, and the **dried seafood market on Des Voeux Road West** (pg133).

Cat Street

Chinese name: 摩羅上街
Admission: FREE
Address: Lascar Row
Transport: Subway – Island Line, Sheung Wan Station, Exit C, walk south down Cleverly St, turn left on Queen's Rd Central to Lok Ku Rd, follow the road to Lascar Row Centre and head to the other side of the building to find the road

Cat Street on Upper Lascar Row is a trinket market just off the Hollywood Street Antique Street. The street market here is loaded with interesting and random curiosities: old watches, broken watches, faded publications, Mao's Little Red Book, stamps, matchboxes, jewelry, coins, and more. The few items of interest are likely to be reproductions (many of the old-looking coins were minted recently), but you can still find some things here – like old or throwback propaganda posters – that might look good on your wall. Check out nearby Hollywood Street for some really beautiful antiques in the street-side stores.

Though you may not be terribly interested in some of the memorabilia here (much of which is straight up mass produced) it's probably a good idea to give some time to this street while you can. It was recently announced that this little swath of Upper Lascar Road was on the docket for demolition in favor of a new high-rise apartment complex that is set to take up the most worthy plot of land on the block – it's already going through the planning stages. It won't be long until this little part of Hong Kong's character becomes all but a fading memory. If you're interested in coming by but the thought of browsing reproductions is holding you back, there are some authentic shops set on the three floors of one particular shop: the **Cat Street Galleries** (Casey Bldg, 14/F 38 Lok Ku Rd; 11:00-19:00 Mon-Sat). This small set of shops is an excellent destination for browsing or legitimate shopping alike, and it is unfortunately the spot that will be most affected by the new apartment buildings. Get here while you can!

Des Voeux Dried Seafood Street

Chinese name: 海味街
Transport:
Subway – Island Line, Sheung Wan Station, Exit C, near the Western Market
Bus – 1, 5B, 5S, 18, 26, 71, 113, 905, H1 and M47 to the market
Tram – Hong Kong Tramways, Macau Ferry Terminal

If you're looking for something you can really raise some eyebrows at, check out the Dried Seafood and Tonic Food section of Des Voeux Road West (德辅道西), one of the strangest markets (to Western tastes) in town. The wide and utterly bizarre variety of dried carbon-based life forms will largely be unrecognizable to you (which is why this place is so fun), and though you'll be able to identify them as seafood, we bet dollars to clams that this is all you'll be able to say for many of them. If you have a Chinese dictionary look up the characters and see which ones you've heard of, or which ones your dictionary has heard of!

Most of the fascinating items here are used in Traditional Chinese Medicine, and most are simply unknown in the West. In the philosophy of the complimentary forces of *yin* and *yang* – cornerstones of Chinese medicine – tonics (herbs with special qualities) are thought to regulate the body's heating *yang* energy and to aid digestion.

Besides the unrecognizable items and the stiff-as-a-stick snakes and the dried alligators, perhaps the most peculiar items in this market are the bird's nests. Used in bird's nest soup, they are some of the most expensive delicacies in Hong Kong and are made from swiftlet saliva and cooked up in a broth. One kilogram of bird's nest costs HK$50,000 (US$6,449.80). Hong Kong natives consume more than half of all the bird's nests in the world.

Yau Ma Tei Wholesale Fruit Market

Chinese name: 油麻地果欄
Transport:
Subway – Kwun Tong Line, Yau Ma Tei Station, Exit C, walk south down Shanghai St past Gascoinge St, the Fruit Market is at the corner of Reclamation St and Kansu St (it's also a short walk north from the north end of the Temple Street Night Market [pg 71])

Do you think Hong Kong people bargain hard at consumer markets? You haven't seen anything until you see a wholesale market. The Yau Ma Tei Wholesale Fruit Market is sort of an offbeat novelty experience, replete with plucky shop owners, aggressive banter, and liberal use of both abacuses and calculators. This behind the scenes look at how distribution takes place for all that fruit you see in store fronts during the daytime is a worthy spectacle if you're up late and need some adventure.

Quite tame by day, it's during the wee hours of the morning between 00:00 and 6:00, that the streets are covered with fruits from all over the world as tattooed laborers unload semi-trailor trucks and pile boxes up and down the street, shouting, whistling, sweating and hustling as they load them onto local trucks for delivery to buyers.

The market was opened in 1913, and the building it is housed in is considered an important historical site. If you're only down to come by day you can still wander through the corridors to find around 200 stores selling produce from more than two dozen countries.

Few tourists actually come here during the midnight working hours. It's almost all workers, buyers and sellers, and if you swing by at this time it's highly suggested that you leave the unloading laborers to their work; don't try to talk with them unless you want to annoy some very tough men. They are friendly as long as you don't disturb their work, and if you hang around long enough the shop owners might even offer you a fresh, pre-retail slice of watermelon. If you do need to buy fruit in bulk, you can get it a lot cheaper here than at the store. By the time 7:00 rolls around the market streets that were once piled with boxes of fruit clears and morning traffic starts down the streets.

Some may tell you that the Yau Ma Tei Fruit Market is full of violence. It's really not these days and is watched over by guards and CCTV cameras, though things were bit dicier in the 1970s when Triads colluded with corrupt police officers to run a scene of drugs and rackets. Those underworld activities that were foiled by an investigation in 1976 and '77 were preserved in pop culture through films like *The Prince of Temple Street* (1992), in which the final scene involving a fight between warring Triad members was filmed at this fruit market.

Hollywood Road

Chinese name: 荷李活道
Transport:
Subway – Island Line, Sheung Wan Station, walk north to the road
Escalator – The Mid-Levels Escalators have a stop on Hollywood Rd
Bus – 26 runs along Hollywood Rd; minibus 55 runs across Queens Rd just to the north

The trinket and antique shops up and down Hollywood Road are overflowing with Tibetan rugs, Chinese porcelain, Ming and Qing Dynasty sculptures, furniture and a myriad of fascinating old items. They can certainly be pricey, but if you don't have the money to buy, it's still free to browse the unique and beautiful items on display.

The eastern end of the street starts at the old Central Police Station, an antique in its own right, and extends quite a ways west to Queen's Road West. The street itself was the second street built by the British in 1844 when they began their colony here, and it soon became a place where foreign traders sold the relics and artifacts they had "collected" during their travels around China. The antique shops, concentrated towards the western half of the street, have developed since that time, and their antique inventories grew notably after the fall of the Qing Dynasty in 1912 and the chaos of the early years of the People's Republic of China. Now there are stores filled with collections of sculptures, rugs, ceramics and antique furniture more rich in history than those found in some museums.

Most of the stuff you'll find here is the real deal, although there are certainly some reproductions in the mix that you'll need to watch out for. It's a good idea to check with your hostel or hotel which shops are reputable before heading over (they change frequently). Ceramics can be particularly difficult to date and even professionals appraisers can be fooled. A "Ming Dynasty" ceramic can often just as likely be a Qing Dynasty one or even a modern ceramic produced last week.

Just past the Man Mo Temple on Upper Lascar Row, there are outdoor stalls selling what can generously be described as trinkets. Here, you can be sure almost everything you see of interest is fake. There are reprints of Mao's Little Red Book and replicas of Ming Dynasty coins (with their characteristic square holes), as well as paper currency helpfully labeled "dollar." There is junk of all sorts, some of which is genuine, but much of which is not.

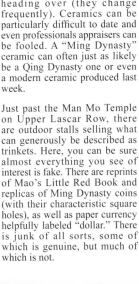

Chun Yeung Street Wet Market

Chinese name: 春秧街街市
Transport:
Subway – North Point MTR station, Exit A2, walk west one block
Bus – 2, 2A, 8X, 10, 18, 19, 23, 27, 38, 42, 42C, 63, 65, 77, 81 to the market
Tram – North Point Tram

The wet market is just about two blocks long, but it has an incredible ambience with a tram track running right down the middle and all the daily necessities a North Point resident needs splayed out along the street. An intimate market like this one is a neighborhood affair.

It's not just food that can be found at this particular wet market either. The south side of the street is mostly apparel shops, and the north side of the street has produce as well as fresh meat and flopping fish. Some of the wet markets in crowded areas like Central are being gentrified and shut down, but that's not going to happen in North Point anytime soon, evidenced by the sheet metal awnings over the merchants businesses, which make a bold statement of permanence and contrast to the put-em-up, take-em-down wood structures of other fading markets.

Tong Shui Road on the east end of Chun Yeung Street even has its own street level Buddhist worship activities. Some people set up makeshift shrines under the elevated highway, placing bronze or wooden statues in red boxes alongside incense, oranges, and plastic chairs for observers on special occasions.

Apliu Street Flea Market

Chinese name: 鴨寮街跳蚤市場
Transport:
Subway – Sham Shui Po MTR Station, Exit C2

The Apliu Street Flea Market – unlike many of the other atmospheric markets of Hong Kong – hasn't been swamped by tourists yet. Perhaps this is because it doesn't focus on souvenir products like the ubiquitous "I (heart) HK" T-shirts. The focus of this market is hardware and electronic appliances, and you can find a treasure trove of goods here, including clocks, laptops, camera cases, and mobile accessories, as well as used appliances like typewriters, vacuum cleaners, fans and cookware. You probably won't be bringing any iron woks home to give to your family or friends, but if you want to skip the tourists outlets for a day and see how a more local market looks and feels, a visit to the Apliu Street Flea Market can be a very rewarding trek.

Unlike, say, the Temple Street Night Market, Apliu Street Flea Market is open all day, and it usually starts to die down after 22:00. It's really quite fascinating to see the variety of shops stuck next to each other as you first walk by a remote control shop, followed by an LED light shop, then a magnet shop, and finally a camera lens shop. When you get hungry you can always take the adventure up a notch with some fried noodles with goose intestines. Street food stalls and restaurants around here serve real, non-Westernized local food, and there's plenty that may make you raise an eyebrow. It's all part of the adventure, so grab those chopsticks and dig in!

The Golden Computer Shopping Arcade, two blocks up at the corner of Yen Chow Street and Fuk Wa Street, has a few floors of deals on computer and digital devices and hardware if you're in need of something like a new flash drive.

Other Markets

Hong Kong includes far too many markets to count. There certainly isn't enough room to include every worthwhile wet market, as almost every neighborhood has their own, each with their own unique charm. Those mentioned here are the most deserving of a shout out.

Kowloon City Wet Market

The Kowloon City wet market, located in a Municipal Services building, is – to say the least – big. It roars with 566 stalls and is known for having high quality produce and meat. About two floors of the building are filled with stalls and another section even sells clothing. The third floor has other services: an athletic facility, a public library and cooked food stalls.

Kowloon City is one of Hong Kong's most traditional and vibrant neighborhoods. It was once the site of the Kowloon Walled City, a crazy, crowded living space that was for a time controlled by the Triads and ungovernable by the British. In 1994, the Kowloon Walled City was demolished, and it's just south of these arboreal remains that you can find the Kowloon City Wet Market, one street over from Nam Kok Dao (南 角 道 ; a Thai restaurant street). There are also Vietnamese restaurants nearby, as well as small grocery shops on Hau Wong Road that sell quality wines and imported food.

Location: Kowloon City Municipal Services Bldg at 48 Hau Wong Rd, Kowloon City (Lok

Fu MTR Station or bus 2, 2A, 11K, 12A, 75X, 85, 85A, 85B or 85C to Fuk Lo Tsun Rd Stop).

Fa Yuen Street Market & Cooked Food Stalls

The market section of the Fa Yuen Street Municipal Services building isn't as big as the one in Kowloon City, but the cooked food hall takes up the whole top floor, making it a great place for a meal. The 15 stalls serve a variety of food, including Thai and Chinese, as well as congee from a well regarded stall called **Mui Kee Porridge**. There is an open dining area outside the main room as well.

Location: Fa Yuen St Municipal Services Bldg at 123A Fa Yuen St, Mong Kok (Mong Kok MTR Station).

Queen's Road Ladder Street Markets

On the small Ladder Street stair alleyways that rise from Queen's Road to streets higher in the hills, you will find many lined with stalls selling various products. Because the streets here are so crowded with people just trying to get up the hillside, the products tend to feel much more packed-in than they actually are. You'll note how the shop owners have found innovative ways to hang products from just about everywhere and have piled their bags and baskets up towards the clouds.

Location: Various ladder streets connect to Queen's Rd in Central

Other Attractions

Museums

In a city seemingly overwhelmed with culture, it's no surprise that Hong Kong is jam-packed with a grab-bag of worthy museums. Whether you're in the mood for a tour-de-space in the Hong Kong Space Museum, a joyful and brainy childhood romp through the Museum of Science, a hipster patter through the Museum of Art, or a ride through time at the Hong Kong Museum of History, this city has you and your present disposition covered. There are more than those mentioned here as well, so adjust your glasses and get ready to see the nerdier side of Hong Kong.

Hong Kong Museum of Art

Chinese name: 香港藝術館
Admission: HK$10
Hours: 10:00-18:00 (Mon-Fri); 10:00-17:00 (Sat & Sun)
Phone: 2721 0116
Website: hk.art.museum
Address: 10 Salisbury Rd
Transport:
Subway – Tsuen Wan Line, Tsim Sha Tsui Station, Exit L6; or East Tsim Sha Tsui MTR Station, Exit J
Bus – 1, 1A, 2, 6, 7, 8A, 8P or 9 to Hong Kong Cultural Centre

The Hong Kong Museum of Art has quality collections of Shang Dynasty and later era antiques, thousand-year-old scrolls, Qing Dynasty ceramics and local paintings of Hong Kong and Guangdong scenery. While it may not be the Met in New York – a tall order to live up to – the seven galleries spread over six floors give a solid tour of China's art history, one that can be comfortably tackled in a few hours.

Don't miss the superb ceramics in the **Chinese Antiques Gallery**, the 18th and 19th century paintings of Guangzhou, Hong Kong and Macau in the **Historical Pictures Gallery**, or the fine painting and calligraphy of the **seventh gallery**. The **Gallery of Chinese Fine Art** has a combination of modern art and 20th century paintings, but those looking for a good taste of contemporary Hong Kong art will certainly be disappointed with the fairly lackluster showing.

Much of the quality of the museum relies on its temporary exhibitions, which at times can be quite large, as when the Andy Warhol exhibition "15 Minutes Eternal" came through in 2012.

The actual building, which looks like three big boxes laid out on the promenade, is always plastered head to toe with promotional posters and is one of the most derided architectural entities in the city. Some have scathed that "putting an art museum inside those blocks reflects a lack of aesthetic sensibilities," while others cry for a larger museum on the scale of the Tate Modern in London or the Louvre in Paris.

The Hong Kong Art Museum is in close proximity to other museums and places of interest along the Tsim Sha Tsui waterfront.

Hong Kong Heritage Museum

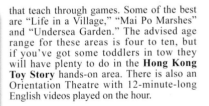

Chinese name: 香港文化博物館
Admission: HK$10 (adult); HK$5 (concession); FREE (Wed)
Hours: 10:00-18:00 (Mon & Wed-Sat); 10:00-19:00 (Sun); closed Tue
Recommended time for visit: 1-2 hours
Phone: 2180 8188
Website: www.heritagemuseum.gov.hk
Address: 1 Man Lam Rd, Sha Tin
Transport: Subway – Ma On Shan Line, Che Kung Temple MTR Station, walk east down Che Kung Miu Rd, go through the subway channel, cross the pedestrian bridge and the museum will be 200 m (656 ft) to the east

This standout museum in Sha Tin has a great series of thoughtful and inventive temporary exhibits and some superb permanent exhibits in 12 galleries. The richness of the museum's features make this place a great destination for adults and kids alike, and if you're a family traveling in Hong Kong it's probably worth it to have a day in Sha Tin just for this museum.

Starting with the ground floor, besides the book shop, you'll find a world of fun for the little ones in the **Children's Discovery Gallery**, which is replete with eight galleries that teach through games. Some of the best are "Life in a Village," "Mai Po Marshes" and "Undersea Garden." The advised age range for these areas is four to ten, but if you've got some toddlers in tow they will have plenty to do in the **Hong Kong Toy Story** hands-on area. There is also an Orientation Theatre with 12-minute-long English videos played on the hour.

Moving on to the first floor, the most impressive of the museum's permanent exhibits include the fun **Cantonese Opera Heritage Hall**, where you can use a computer simulation to virtually dress and make up in opera garb and watch videos of old operas (with English subtitles); the **Chao Shao-an Gallery**, featuring the works of brilliant Lingnan watercolorist Chao Shao-an; and the **New Territories Heritage Hall**, boasting scenes from traditional life in the New Territories, mostly through a mock Hakka village.

Don't forget to save some time for the second floor, especially its **TT Tsui Gallery of Chinese Art**, where you can catch some beautiful ceramics, jade and lacquer pieces, bronze, furniture stone carvings and more.

Hong Kong Heritage Museum side entrance

HKHM Cantonese Opera Heritage Hall

HKHM New Territories Heritage Hall

Bruce Lee Kung Fu Art Life Exhibition at the Hong Kong Heritage Museum

Other Attractions

139

Dialogue in the Dark

Chinese name: 黑暗中對話
Admission: HK$150 (Tue-Fri); HK$180 (Sat & Sun); closed Mon
Hours: 10:00-19:30
Phone: 2310 0833
Website: www.dialogue-in-the-dark.hk (English available)
Address: Shop 215, 2/F The Household Centre, 8 King Lai Path, Mei Foo, Kowloon
Transport:
Subway – Tsuen Wan Line or West Rail Line, Mei Foo Station, Exit G, walk a block north to Nob Hill Square
Bus – 171, 6, 171A, 171P, 904, or 905 to Lai Chi Kok Bus Terminus, walk to the museum

What is it like to be blind? Dialogue in the Dark tries to create an atmosphere that helps the non-blind better understand the world that the blind live in and to help raise awareness. At Dialogue in the Dark you are given a cane and led with a blind guide into a darkened room. During the one hour experience, you will walk through areas set up to represent a city street, a food market, a boat and a café, where you'll maneuver your way through various obstacles. In groups of about ten people, visitors move within an area and try to discern their surroundings through touch, hearing and smell. The goal is to "facilitate social inclusion of marginalized people," according to one version of the organization's mission statement. Each journey concludes with a group discussion with the guides.

Many visitors have been highly moved by the experience. Common reactions include people paying more attention to their listening and communicating skills, learning not to take their eyesight for granted and having greater respect for the blind. Corporations have scheduled Dialogue in the Dark training sessions in order to try to enhance teamwork, communications and leadership skills.

This unique experience, with 20 venues throughout the world (none in North America), is something that can't be seen – nor smelled, touched or heard – just anywhere.

Hong Kong Heritage Discovery Centre

Chinese name: 香港文物探知館
Admission: FREE
Hours: 10:00-18:00 (Mon-Wed & Fri-Sat); 10:00-19:00 (Sun & holidays)
Phone: 2208 4400
Address: Kowloon Park, Haiphong Rd, Tsim Sha Tsui, Kowloon
Transport:
Subway – Kwun Tong Line, Tsim Sha Tsui Station, Exit A1, walk along Haiphong Rd and into Kowloon Park; the center is next to Bird Lake

Explore the unique culture that makes Hong Kong a one-of-a-kind international city at the Hong Kong Heritage Discovery Centre. This museum, opened in 2005 in Kowloon Park inside the old British barracks, has immersive exhibits on countless aspects of Chinese art, lifestyles and culture, both traditional and contemporary.

Exhibits during the time of research included those on Bruce Lee (Kung Fu Art Life), Chinese woodblock printing, and the Fashion of Eddie Lau. Lau was most famously known as Anita Mui's fashion designer and close friend, and some of the dresses that made Anita the "Ever Changing Anita Mui" are on display here. The Hong Kong Heritage Discovery Centre feels less like it's lecturing you about a long distant past through its information boards and more like it's putting the past out there for you to explore. Permanent exhibitions on topics like Chinese art, Cantonese opera and the New Territories strike the same tone.

Hong Kong Museum of History

Chinese name: 香港歷史博物館
Admission: HK$10
Hours: 10:00-18:00 (Mon, Wed, Thu & Fri); 10:00-19:00 (Sat & Sun); closed Tue
Phone: 2724 9042
Website: hk.history.museum
Address: 100 Chatham Rd South, Tsim Sha Tsui East, Kowloon
Transport:
Subway – The Hong Kong Museum of History is located in the middle of a triangle of MTR stations – Jordan, Tsim Sha Tsui, & Hung Hom (it is somewhat closer to Hung Hom, just south of Hong Kong Polytechnic University)
Bus – 5, 28, 110, 203, 796X, 973, 973P, A21, E21X and N271 to the Hong Kong Science Museum Stop (see next page; the two museums are side by side)

"6,000 years of Chinese history; 150 years of Hong Kong." The opening words of the Hong Kong Museum of History's video on the handover of Hong Kong to China set the tone for the rest of the museum and suggest that, in the long span of Chinese history, Hong Kong is but a blip on the radar. The film covers only up to 1997 (when the city was handed back to China), and that's also about as far as the exhibits within the museum dare to go. The title "A Better Hong Kong" is displayed at the end of the film, sending you off to "The Hong Kong Story," a collection of eight galleries promising to represent 400 million years of local history.

Though it head-scratchingly ends 17 years prior to 2014, the historical frame covered by the museum does highlight the uniqueness of the territory. The natural environment hundreds of millions of years ago is described in the first gallery through fossils, topography and flora and fauna. Expounding how there were people living here some 6,000 years ago, the **Prehistoric Hong Kong** gallery puts on a very interesting show through dioramas of the ancient Hakka people and some very cool replicas of ancient junks, but it is the later four galleries on the **Opium War**, **Colonization**, **Birth and Early Growth of the City**, the **Japanese Occupation** and the **Modern City** that encapsulate the bulk of the history that made Hong Kong what it is today.

In these galleries, the museum attempts to bring history to life by setting up exhibits inside mock-up historical settings. The Japanese Occupation room is designed to look like an air-raid shelter, while the **Folk Culture in Hong Kong** gallery shows off replica houses of the local people, and the mock-markets and tea houses give nice color to the 1930s and 1960s sections.

The broad scope of time represented, from prehuman to 1997, makes any individual time period somewhat scant on extensive details, but it is still an excellent museum for someone less familiar with Hong Kong's long history.

The Hong Kong Story takes up the main two floors of the museum, and there are some other spaces for temporary exhibits.

Hong Kong Science Museum

Chinese name: 香港科學館
Admission: HK$25
Hours: 10:00-19:00 (Mon, Tue, Wed & Fri); 10:00-21:00 (Sat & Sun); closed Thu
Phone: 2732 3232
Address: 2 Science Museum Rd, Tsimshatsui East, Kowloon
Transport:
Subway – The Hong Kong Science Museum is located in the middle of a triangle of MTR stations – Jordan, Tsim Sha Tsui, & Hung Hom (it is somewhat closer to Hung Hom, just south of Hong Kong Polytechnic University)
Bus – 5, 28, 110, 203, 796X, 973, 973P, A21, E21X and N271 to the Hong Kong Science Museum Stop

Kids will have a blast playing with the hundreds of interactive exhibits at the Hong Kong Science Museum. With three floors of displays, this museum has galleries about all kinds of topics in science. It is divided into sections that are built around themes like motion, sound, food, home sciences, telecommunications and more. The concept here is to learn by doing, whether that means yanking on the pulleys that teach about motion laws, playing with the refrigerator and air conditioning displays in the **Home Sciences** gallery, or getting lost in the **World of Mirrors**.

The museum is designed for kids, and though it might not do a whole lot for most single adults (some will like it though), parents can easily be entertained if they bring the family. Don't expect anything specific about Hong Kong, however; it's a shame, considering they surely could have included something about local land reclamation or the city's engineering marvels.

The Hong Kong Science Museum is right next to the Hong Kong Museum of History (pg 141) if you want to make it a museum day.

Sam Tung Uk Museum of Hakka Culture

Chinese name: 三棟屋客家文化博物館
Admission: FREE
Hours: 10:00-18:00 closed Tue
Phone: 2411 2001
Address: 2 Kwu Uk Lane
Transport:
Subway – Tsuen Wan Line, Tsuen Wan Station
Bus – 40, 43X, 48X, 49X, 52M, 57M, 58M, 59A, 60, 63M, 66, 67M, 68A, 69M, 73X, 278P, or A31

The Hakka people are famous for their walled villages that were built by ancestral clans for community and defense. The Sam Tung Uk Museum of Hakka Culture is an 18th century walled village that has been preserved and turned into a very well-done museum on 18th century rural life.

Inside this "three beam dwelling" there are homes and store rooms set up in three main rows along a central path, including the **Entrance Hall**, **Assembly Hall** and **Ancestral Hall**. The Ancestral Hall contains a shrine to the clan's ancestors and family historical documents. Visitors can walk around the halls and see traditional farm tools before entering the exhibition room in the back for more details on Hakka culture.

The Hakka are a group among the Han Chinese that moved south, largely to Guangdong and Fujian, and many of them settled in Hong Kong. They have traditionally been distinguished from the Punti people of Southern China and the non-Hakka Han because of their distinct language and culture, and the fact that they were more migratory than many of their Han brethren. The name Hakka means "guest people" in Chinese, while Punti means "local,"which is ironic since the Hakka were settled in Hong Kong long before the Punti.

The Sam Tung Uk walled village was built by the Chan clan in 1786, and the last resident vacated the town only fairly recently in 1980, at which time the village fell under government protection.

Police Museum

Chinese name: 警隊博物館
Admission: FREE
Hours: 14:00-17:00 (Tue); 9:00-17:00 (Wed-Sun);
closed Mon
Phone: 2849 7019
Website: www.police.gov.hk
Address: 27 Coombe Rd, The Peak, Hong Kong Island
Transport:
Subway & Bus – Tsuen Wan Line, Central MTR Station,
take bus 15 from Exchange Square to Wan Chai Gap Rd
Stop; or Island Line, Admiralty Station, take bus 15 to
Wan Chai Gap Rd Stop

You may know a little bit about Hong Kong's law and order system from relentlessly watching Hong Kong crime movies. Maybe you've even taken your movie knowledge further and looked up some articles on the Triads. If so, it's time to take it up a notch at the Hong Kong Police Museum, a place sure to dazzle laymen "cops and robbers" enthusiasts of all sorts.

The Hong Kong Police Museum includes galleries dedicated to the history and activities of Triad societies and the police responses to their crimes. Although relatively small, it makes good use of its space and includes plenty of interesting memorabilia. On display in the **Orientation Gallery** you'll find firearms, historical photos and the head of a tiger that was shot in 1915. The **Triad Societies and Narcotics Gallery** displays photographs and information about the rituals of Triads and includes some heroin manufacturing equipment from a factory busted by the police in the 1980s. Another gallery covers 160 years of local police history and gives an interesting perspective on how it has changed. Don't forget the creatively named **Thematic Exhibition Gallery**, which puts up different displays every few months (which tend to run on "themes").

It doesn't take long to go through this 570 sq m (6,135 sq ft) museum, but it is definitely worth some of your time if you're into crime-busting. It's not quite as exciting as a Simon Yam or Chow Yun-fat film, but it's definitely more informative.

Sam Tung Uk Museum of Hakka Culture

Police Museum

Other Museums

Here are some other museums that we did not include in our detailed descriptions but nonetheless might be worthwhile, depending on your personal interests.

Hong Kong Maritime Museum

Chinese name: 香港海事博物館
Admission: HK$30
Hours: 9:30-17:30 (Mon-Fri); 10:00-19:00 (Sat & Sun)
Phone: 3713 2500
Website: www.hkmaritimemuseum.org
Address: Central Pier 8
Transport:
Subway – Tsuen Wan Line, Central Station, Exit A, take the skywalk 10 min towards Central Ferry Piers to Outlying Islands; or Tung Chung Line, Hong Kong Station, Exit A2, take the skywalk towards Central Ferry Piers

Tracking the development of boating and shipping in Hong Kong and Macau, this relatively small museum has some relics of Hong Kong navigational culture and history, instruments, information on the seafaring Hakka people, and some paintings and maritime charts.

Dr Sun Yat-sen Museum

Chinese name: 孫中山紀念館
Admission: HK$10
Hours: 10:00-18:00 (Mon, Tue, Wed & Fri); 10:00-19:00 (Sat & Sun); closed Thu
Website: hk.drsunyatsen.museum/en
Address: 7 Castle Rd, Mid-Levels, Central
Transport:
Subway – Tsuen Wan Line, Central Station, Exit D1 or D2, walk to the Mid-Levels Escalators and then walk west for around 5 min

Dr Sun Yat-sen was the revolutionary founding father of the Republic of China, he served as the country's first president for less than one year after being educated in Hong Kong. The two permanent exhibits in this museum track his life, history and accomplishments. The museum is built in an old Moorish-style house that Dr Sun's son constructed around 1901. It was the residence of Sun's first wife, Lu Muzhen, until her death in 1952. Ironically, Sun himself never lived here.

Museum of Coastal Defence

Chinese name: 香港海防博物館
Admission: FREE
Hours: 10:00-17:00; closed Thu
Phone: 2569 1500
Address: 175 Tung Hei Rd, Shau Kei Wan, Hong Kong Island
Transport: **Subway** – Island Line, Shau Kei Wan Station, Exit B2, walk east for about 15 minutes

Occupying a powerfully cool location in an old British fort (Lei Yue Mun Fort, 1887), this museum cannonballs you through the challenges of defending Hong Kong over the six centuries since the Ming Dynasty.

The Flagstaff House Museum of Teaware

Chinese name: 茶具文物館
Admission: FREE
Hours: 10:00-17:00; closed Tue
Phone: 2869 0690
Address: 10 Cotton Tree Dr (inside Hong Kong Park), Central
Transport: **Subway** – Tsuen Wan Line or Island Line, Admiralty Station, Exit C1, follow the signs up the escalator to Hong Kong Park

Tea has always been enjoyed by the Chinese, and it has also been enjoyed by the British, so Hong Kong is a great place for a tea museum. This small museum displays delicate antique ceramics that seem too beautiful to even drink tea from. There is an attached café where you can enjoy dim sum and actual tea from stylish tea cups.

Temples & Monasteries

Temples have held an important place in the lives of the Hong Kongese for centuries. Besides offering blessings and fortune to those going through hardships or those approaching a major life decision, temples have been places for locals to give offerings to their ancestors and to honor various gods and goddesses. The three major religions in China are Buddhism, Taoism and Confucianism, and most Chinese gods are humans that were deified long ago because of their legendary deeds and accomplishments. In Buddhism, these are usually either bodhisattvas or Buddhas, mortals who achieved enlightenment. Taoism reveres immortals, humans who came to embody the Tao – or the Way of the universe – and through this became deified. Confucianism is more concerned with the order of the cosmos and humanity within the universe, and, as more of a philosophy than a religion, it focuses far less on the idea of gods or afterlife.

Throughout Hong Kong a number of gods and goddesses will come up over and over again at temples around the city. Here are some of the most common deities honored in temples:

Tin Hau (also known as Matzu; 媽祖)

Tin Hau (天 后) is the goddess of the sea and is mostly worshipped in southern Asian countries with fishing and seafaring traditions. Because Hong Kong is a coastal land salted with hundreds of islands, Tin Hau is unsurprisingly very popular. There are over 70 Tin Hau temples in Hong Kong, with one on almost every populated island and near coastal areas. You will notice as well that some Tin Hau temples in Hong Kong – such as the one on Temple Street (pg 71) – are located inland. These temples actually once sat on the coast, but have since moved inland after great areas of land were reclaimed from the ocean over the years.

Tin Hau was originally a young lady named Lin Moniang (林默娘) born in Putian County in Fujian. She was an excellent swimmer, and it is said that she guided fishing boats to shore during frightening weather while wearing a red dress. Legend has it that she once saved her father, a fisherman, from drowning simply by dreaming about him after he was thrown overboard during a storm. She became deified shortly after her death in 987 CE as more and more people began to attribute their safety at sea to her benevolence. Her earliest temple in the city – the Tin Hau Temple at Joss House Bay (pg 146) – was built in 1266.

Kwan Yu (also known as Kwan Tai)

More than just a god of war, Kwan Yu (關 羽) represents integrity, honor and righteousness in the Chinese pantheon. He is often depicted in Man Mo temples together with Man Cheong (also known as Man Tai), the literary god. This pairing is meant to symbolize how good generals in Chinese culture ought to be cultured, well read and intelligent, in addition to being strong fighters. You can find a Kwan Yu shrine gracing the halls of many police stations as well as – believe it or not – Triad strongholds (the Triads actually started as a righteous resistance to Manchurian Qing rule).

Kwan Yu statues usually depict the immortal with a red face, a long beard and holding a long polearm with a crescent blade, known as a *guan dao*. According to myth, Kuan Yu's particular *guan dao* was called Green Dragon Crescent Blade and weighed around 18 kg (40 lbs). It was so heavy and difficult to wield that most accomplished soldiers could hardly swing it with two hands. Kuan Yu, of course, could swing it with great agility using only one hand.

A general of the Eastern Han Dynasty, Kuan Yu served under the warlord Liu Bei and helped establish the Shu Han state, one of the Three Kingdoms. By the end of the second century, the Han Dynasty had collapsed, and warlords such as Liu Bei took over governing the lands. Cao Cao, king of Wei, tried to reunify the Han Dynasty, but Liu Bei and Sun Quan of the Wu state united to defeat him at the Battle of Red Cliffs, a battle in which Kwan Yu played a key role. Kwan Yu's life story has been dramatized in the novel *Romance of the Three Kingdoms*, and he was deified during the Sui Dynasty (581-618).

Guanyin (also known as Kwun Yam)

Guanyin is a Buddhist bodhisattva known as the goddess of mercy. She is revered by multiple cultures and her legend has changed notably over its long history. Early depictions (prior to the Song Dynasty of 960-1279) show Guanyin as a male with a mustache, but by the 12th century, most depictions began showing her as a female, embodying the feminine traits of compassion and maternal kindness. According to most interpretations of the Lotus Sutra (one of the earliest and most influential writings in Mahayana Buddhism), Guanyin embodies both male and female and is not of a fixed gender. The ethnic Bai people of Dali in Yunnan Province, China have legends about Guanyin as a fierce warrior who saved the Dali people from multiple demons. In Hong Kong, you can find Guanyin statues at most Buddhist temples.

Joss House Bay Tin Hau Temple

Chinese name: 大廟灣天后古廟
Admission: FREE
Hours: 8:00-17:00
Transport:
Subway & Bus – Tseung Kwan O Line, Po Lam Station, Exit A, take green minibus 16 (Po Lam to Po Toi O) to the Clearwater Bay Golf & Country Club and then walk for about 10 min down the steps nearby
Ferry – During the Tin Hau Festival, there is special ferry service between North Point and Joss House Bay

The oldest temple in Hong Kong, the Tin Hau Temple at Joss House Bay was built nearly 800 years ago in 1266, and though it has gone through numerous restorations, renovations and a few reconstructions, it is still a very impressive old piece of Hong Kong history.

In 1266, two brothers were swept from their boat near Joss House Bay and when they drifted safely to the shore Tin Hau was thought to be their savior, prompting them to build the temple here in her honor.

Consisting of five rooms, the temple's main chamber is a beautiful shrine, marked by red, green and gold tapestries, and centered on three female statues with candles in lotus-shaped holders. A big metal pot sits in front to hold burning incense; get up close for a look at the ship etched into one side.

Take a walk outside the temple and enjoy the fresh air blowing off the fine bay, and consider packing a swim suit for a dip at the quality beaches here, or bring your clubs for a round at the nearby golf course. Every year on Tin Hau's Festival (pg 38), the temple hosts a boat parade. During this festival, the temple is mobbed by thousands of fishermen and worshippers. Many of them go to the side hall to search under a quilt on the Dragon Bed for lucky articles, such as lotus seeds, which are believed to increase the chances of conception.

Lin Fa Kung Temple

Chinese name: 莲花宫
Admission: FREE
Hours: 7:30-17:00
Transport:
Subway – Island Line, Tin Hau Station, Exit B, walk along Tung Lo Wan Rd for 5 min, continue onto Lin Fa Kung St West

A golden glow emanates from within this historical temple, built in 1863 to worship Kwun Yam (the goddess of mercy) and decorated in resplendent bright gold and red colors. To add to the temple's great luster, hundreds of lotus flower lamps have been gathered on the platform in the back, lighting the place up in spectacular fashion.

Within the glowing light of the temple's interior, check out the beautiful statue of Kwun Yam, as well as a massive holy stone and the 60 deities of time. A large dragon is depicted on the ceiling of the temple, marking Lin Fa as one of the main temples to host dragon dances during the Mid-Autumn Festival.

Dragon dances, marked by the serpentine movements of the large dragon costumes, are seen by many as an icon of China, but they are actually more prevalent in the south than in the north. Making it out to see them in all their glory – particularly the Tai Hang Dragon Dance – is one of China's best intangible cultural heritage experiences.

Kwun Yum Festival

There are four festivals in the lunar year to honor Kwun Yum. They fall on the 19th day of the second, sixth, ninth and 11th lunar months, and these days correspond respectively to her birth, ordination and deification. Apart from these festive days, the temple is particularly busy during the Kwun Yum Open Treasury on the 26th day of the first lunar month.

Ten Thousand Buddhas Monastery

Chinese name: 萬佛寺
Admission: FREE
Hours: 9:00-17:00
Phone: 2691 1067
Address: Tai Po Road, Sha Tin
Transport: Subway – East Rail Line, Sha Tin Station, Exit B

The Ten Thousand Buddhas Monastery is famous for – what else – its 10,000 Buddhas. Actually, it's over 12,000, and the Buddhas that cover entire walls at this monastery took over ten years to build and are bafflingly impressive. The place is even more stunning when you consider that Venerable Yuet Kai – a devout layman Buddhist – and his followers carried the wood and materials for the monastery up from the foot of the mountain on which the complex sits. The monastery is now accessible by about 500 steps, which themselves are lined with countless Buddhist statues, each with distinct bodies and facial impressions.

Technically, because the complex has no monks, it is now considered just a temple. This also means that the "monks" at the bottom of the hill asking for money are not actually monks, but are instead what we call "scam artists." Ignore them and keep your cash in your pocket; you can't buy karma from these guys.

The aptly named Ten Thousand Buddhas Hall is naturally the main attraction and obviously has a lot of Buddhas. But the 8 hectare (20 acre) monastery has a few other buildings as well. There is a nine-story pagoda that once had the honor of being on a HK$100 banknote, as well as a few statues of Kwun Yam, the goddess of mercy. One is in front of the Ten Thousand Buddhas Hall, and another is in front of a waterfall on the upper level of the temple complex (with yet more statues sitting on the surrounding rocks). The **Ten Thousand Buddhas Hall** holds Yuet Kai's preserved body in a case in the main hall.

Sik Sik Yuen Wong Tai Sin Temple

Chinese name: 黃大仙祠
Admission: FREE
Hours: 7:00-17:30
Phone: 2327 8141
Website: www.siksikyuen.org.hk (English available)
Address: 2 Chuk Yuen Village, Wong Tai Sin, Kowloon
Transport:
Subway – Kwun Tong Line, Wong Tai Sin Station, Exit B2

Small temples are sprinkled throughout every neighborhood in Hong Kong, but few of them have a temple as large and crowded as the Sik Sik Yuen Wong Tai Sin Temple. The multiple halls in this 18,000 sq m (193,750 sq ft) complex are grand and beautiful, so much that some actually require their own paid admission.

The temple actually started out fairly small, growing to its immense size over the course of several years. It began when a man named Leung Renyan opened an herbal medicine shop in 1915 and put a Wong Tai Sin altar in the back of his shop, as many Chinese do in hopes of bringing good luck and economic stability to their businesses. This particular shrine in Leung's medicine shop proved to be more profitable than most others as people would first come in to pray for advice from Wong Tai Sin and then conveniently find the medicine recommended by the deity to be on the shelf in front of them.

In 1918, Leung's shop was destroyed by a fire, and soon Wong's spirit instructed Leung to construct a new shrine. After divining the proper place to found the temple, Leung and other followers began construction. Today, the temple contains more spiritual entities than just Wong, including Lu Dongbin, Guanyin and Lord Guan, all inside the **Three-Saint Hall** (三 聖 堂). In here you can also find a portrait of Confucius and a collection of Confucian, Taoist and Buddhist literature.

Keep an eye out for the beautiful **Nine-Dragon Wall** (九 龍 壁), meant to protect against evil and invasive spirits, as well as intricate memorial archways and the Good Wish Garden (從心苑 ; 9:00-17:00), scattered with zigzagging bridges over a rocky, verdant pond.

This handsome temple is a popular one to say the least, and if you go on a weekend you might not be able to get into the main hall.

Hollywood Road Man Mo Temple

Chinese name: 文武廟
Admission: FREE
Hours: 8:00-18:00
Phone: 2540 0350
Address: 124-126 Hollywood Rd, Sheung Wan, Hong Kong Island
Transport:
Subway – Island Line, Sheung Wan Station, Exit A2, walk along Hillier St to Queen's Rd Central, proceed up Ladder St (next to Lok Ku Rd) to Hollywood Rd and the Man Mo Temple
Escalator – Get off the escalators at Hollywood Rd and then walk west a short way

The Chinese say burning incense feeds the ghosts of the departed. If that's true, all ghosts around the Hollywood Road Man Mo Temple are obese. Once inside, you will see (and smell) long coils of burning incense hanging from beams above your head. About nine rows by nine rows of incense coils fill a bottom level of beams, and if you look further above you'll see a second level sporting notably larger coils. At the front of the room are statues of Man Cheung, the god of literature, who was a 3rd century BCE statesman, and Kwan Tai (known in Mandarin as Guan Yu), who is worshipped as the god of war. This Man Mo Temple is the largest in Hong Kong, and it bears two side halls – a Lit Shing Kung and a Kung Sor – within its complex.

Built between 1847 and 1862, the complex is housed within a vibrant white and green wall and has been honored as a recognized historical building. In the old days, Hong Kongers used to go to the Kung Sor to settle disputes. The two parties would write promises on paper and run chicken blood over the document before burning it. Violation of that written, bloodied and burnt promise meant you would have to answer to the gods.

Kwan Tai was a general who helped establish the state of Shu Han during the Three Kingdoms period in the early 200s CE. His exploits were dramatized through legend and folklore to the point where he gained deific status during the Sui Dynasty (581-618). Fans of John Woo's action films might recognize Kwan Tai in films like *A Better Tomorrow*, where Chow Yun-fat's character is seen in contemplation at a Man Mo temple before the final fight scene. Similarly, Kwan Tai shrines can be seen displayed throughout the police departments in Woo's films *The Killer* (1989) and *Hard Boiled* (1992), attesting to the god's status in both the mafia and the police alike.

The other hall of Man Mo Temple, the **Lit Shing Kung** (meaning "saints' place") is an area of worship dedicated to a range of gods of the Buddhist and Taoist pantheons.

It doesn't require a lot of time to look around Man Mo Temple. A visit of 15-30 minutes will probably do the trick for most people, after which you can cruise down the antique shops along Hollywood Street.

Yuen Yuen Institue

Chinese name: 圓玄學院
Admission: FREE (donation)
Hours: 8:30-17:00
Recommended time for visit: 1 hour
Phone: 2492 2220
Website: www.yuenyuen.org.hk
Address: Lo Wai Rd, Tsuen Wan
Transport: Green minibus – 81 from Shiu Wo St, 2 blocks south of Tsuen Wan MTR Station, Exit B1

In hills to the northeast of Tsuen Wan you can find the spiritual stronghold of the Yuen Yuen Institute, a place where Taoist immortals, Buddhist bodhisattvas and Confucian saints all come together to wow both visitors and the reverential with their fierce visages. Just as impressive is the main building of the complex, which is actually a replica of Beijing's spectacular Temple of Heaven. Take in the calm of the three statues of Taoist immortals in the quiet first hall of the upper ground floor before continuing on to see 60 more of them in the lower level. This is an active spiritual center and you'll see plenty of the faithful bowing to these statues with incense in their hands and wishes in their hearts.

The institute was founded in 1950 by a group of monks from Sanyuan Gong in Guangzhou, which is part of the influential Longmen – or Dragon Gate – sect of the Quanzhen (Complete Reality) school of Taoism. Seeking to incorporate the wisdom of China's three most prominent spiritual philosophies and religions, the characters for the institute actually allude to the teachings of Taoism, Confucianism and Buddhism. The beautiful grounds – filled with monastic buildings, pavilions and quiet paths – are superb for spending an enlightening afternoon strolling around and smelling the swirl of incense and flowers before heading back to Tsuen Wan for dinner and drinks. That being said, vegetarians in the group may want to stick around for the institute's onsite vegetarian restaurant.

Festivals

The Lantern Festival that takes place every year on the 15th day of the first month of the lunar calendar makes a good showing at the Yuen Yuen Institute. Donations may be exchanged for your own lanterns – which are meant to bring luck and good fortune – for you to set off into the air with the legions from around the city.

There are also large celebrations here during the Chinese New Year.

Chuk Lam Sim Monastery

Chinese name: 竹林禪院
Admission: FREE (donation)
Hours: 8:00-16:30
Recommended time for visit: 1 hour
Phone: 2490 3392
Address: Fu Yung Shan Rd, Tsuen Wan
Transport: Green minibus – 85 from Shui Wo St, 2 blocks south of Tsuen Wan MTR Station Exit B1

One of the best and least touristy monasteries in the whole city, the stunning rural retreat of Chuk Lam Sim Monastery, off in the hills surrounding Tsuen Wan New Town, singlehandedly makes a trip to this distant New Territories village worth it.

Chuk Lam Sim means "Bamboo Forest" in English, and though little remains of any bamboo, the bucolic scenery here is still impressive. Out front of the steps leading up you'll find an incense urn and probably very few worshippers, while at the top of the steps the first temple building is graced by four complacent palm trees that seem to wave and bow to visitors as they approach. Behind it, the second temple structure contains three of the largest golden Buddha statues in the New Territories, and they are guarded by a contingent of 12 bodhisattvas. The scene is inspiring to say the least, especially in this relatively isolated area that sees surprisingly few visitors.

The temple complex was conceived in 1927 by an aged monk who supposedly was contacted by the Earth god Tou Tei and told to build on this holy site. It was completed five years later in 1932.

Tsing Shan Monastery

Chinese name: 青山禪院
Admission: FREE (donation)
Hours: 24 hours
Recommended time for visit: 1 hour
Phone: 2461 8050
Website: www.tsingshanmonastery.org.hk
Address: Tsing Shan Monastery Path, Tuen Mun
Transport: Light Rail – Line 610, 615 or 615P from Tuen Mun Station to Tsing Shan Tsuen, then follow the signs to the west of the station that lead to the monastery (about a 30 min uphill walk)

Though most of the beautiful complex you'll find at Tsing Shan – which means Clear Mountain – was reconstructed in 1926, the monastery is technically the oldest in Hong Kong, having been founded around 1,500 years ago by Reverend Pui To. Pui To was said to be an Indian monk who traveled with a wooden cup (his name translates as "wooden cup") and, upon taking up lodging in the serene area that is now Tsing Shan, decided to found a monastery here. The ultra relaxing grounds are verdant and shady and largely bereft of tourists. Among the collection of shrines and temples dedicated to various bodhisattvas, one stands as a grotto to the temple's founding father. Most of them are in various states of repair, but the ones that have slid ever so slightly into ruin still ooze their own special allure.

Tsing Shan Monastery itself has another special claim to fame for being the backdrop for scenes from the 1973 Bruce Lee masterpiece *Enter the Dragon*.

Nestled at the foot of Castle Peak, just outside of Tuen Mun in the New Territories, the cool Buddhist refuge at Tsing Shan Monastery (aka Castle Rock Monastery) is a lovely and tranquil place for an afternoon in the New Territories.

Miu Fat Monastery

Chinese name: 妙法寺
Admission: FREE (donation)
Hours: 9:00-17:00
Recommended time for visit: 1 hour
Phone: 2461 8567
Address: 18 Castle Peak Rd, Tuen Mun
Transport: Light Rail is the easiest way to get to the monastery, but you can also take a bus from nearby Mong Kok MTR Station
Bus – 63X from Mong Kok MTR Station stops out front of the monastery
Light Rail – Light Rail Line 751 from Tuen Mun Station to Lam Tei Station, cross the walkway over Castle Peak Rd and then walk north 150 m (492 ft)

Built with an enormous, three-story top hall that was made to resemble an opening crystal lotus flower, the Miu Fat Monastery, outside the New Town of Tuen Mun, is one of the most arresting structures in the New Territories. Altogether, the massive complex comprises a striking ten stories, and if you have a chance to come by at night you will see an even more eye-catching scene when the complex is brilliantly illuminated.

The monastery was built in 1950 with somewhat of a fusion of Thai and Chinese influences, noticeable not only in the crystal lotus shaped tower on top, but also in some of the Buddha statues and reliefs inside that take on a visible Southeast Asian feel. As you come upon the main entrance you'll first be greeted by some pleasant gardens and two sets of stone lions and elephants before reaching the two 19 m- (65 ft)-tall pillars adorned with beautiful golden-scaled dragons. Step inside and move through the building to explore the golden Buddha statue and three bigger effigies of the Lord Guatama, as well as a library and cultural welfare rooms.

The best part of the temple is the Ten Thousand Buddhas Hall. Head to the top floor for the cavernous **Mahavira Hall** where inside you'll find a spectacular scene: thousands of Buddha reliefs and a swath of Sino-Thai wall murals depicting scenes from Buddhist lore.

While you visit Miu Fat Monastery, remember that it is an active spiritual center whirring with dozens of brown-robed nuns. A respectful demeanor and proper dress (no bare shoulders, long pants) are essential.

Jamia Mosque

Chinese name: 些利街清真寺
Admission: FREE
Hours: 10:00-20:00 for Muslims only; it is not open to the public
Phone: 2523 7743
Address: 30 Shelley St, Central
Transport:
Subway – Tsuen Wan Line, Central Station, take the Mid-Levels escalators up past Caine Rd, you will see the mosque on the left

Follow the Central-Mid Levels Escalators all the way up past Caine Road and you will arrive at the first mosque ever constructed in Hong Kong. Built in 1849, Jamia Mosque (also called Lascar Mosque) served a congregation consisting of many Punjabi Muslims who had been recruited to serve in the police force. The architecture is fantastic. Inside the wrought iron gate, the mosque has a green exterior with arched windows and columns. It was expanded and partially rebuilt in 1915, fortunately retaining the original minaret. Outside of the mosque you'll see three large garden plots and some living spaces for worshippers. The Yatim Khana here is a home for widows and orphans.

Unfortunately for some, the inner mosque is only open to worshipping Muslims, meaning that many non-Muslims will miss out on its beautiful interior. But visitors can still admire the superior exterior of the handsome mosque, the curved designs etched into its outer gate, and the beautiful minaret. Prayer music can often be heard from as far away as the Mid-Levels Escalators.

The Jamia Mosque hosts sermons and religious classes delivered in English and Urdu, and visiting Muslims are encouraged to come to Jamia for worship.

Beaches

Since Hong Kong is made up of mostly islands and coastal land, it has a huge amount of recreational coastline. In fact, *The World Factbook* states that Hong Kong has 733 km (455.5 mi) of coastline for a land area of 1,054 sq km (407 sq mi). Its beaches are absolutely gorgeous, particularly as you get further from the city and explore some of the those that frame the islands or bask on the edges of country parks.

There are a total of 41 beaches administered by the Government's Leisure and Cultural Services Department. We have chosen six of the best to highlight in addition to a number of beaches that have been covered in other sections. We made our determinations based on natural beauty, convenience, amenities and recreational options, attempting to choose those that will most likely satisfy the greatest diversity of travelers. Whether you're into a bustling party beach or one of hidden tranquility, or if you're looking for a good hike to a remote beach out of the government's administrative reach, we've got you covered.

Generally, Hong Kong Leisure Services-administered beaches have shark nets, lifeguard duty during the summer, changing rooms and showers, and many often have water sports centers. Because of its many bays and islands, Hong Kong is not known for big waves, which tend to get muffled by the land formations. But it does have some beaches that can be suitable for surfing, particularly Big Wave Bay Beach, Cheung Sha Beach and the beaches of Tai Long Wan in Sai Kung Country Park (pg 104).

If you'd like to check out some beaches besides what we've reviewed here, you can view those in our sections on Lamma Island (pg 162), Cheung Chau Island (pg 161), Pui O Village (pg 119), Mui Wo (see pg 121 for Mui Wo and Silvermine Bay Beach) and in the far flung country park of Sai Kung. These all require a hike or a boat ride to get to.

Big Wave Bay Beach

Chinese name: 大浪灣泳灘
Transport:
Subway – Island Line, Shau Kei Wan Station, Exit A3, take bus 9 to Big Wave Bay Beach
Bus – 9 to Big Wave Bay Beach (also goes to Shek O Beach and Tei Wan on Shek O Rd, where you can start the Dragon's Back Hike)

When it comes to surfing, Hong Kong isn't Hawaii. There are a few places where you can find some surfing, but nothing that will blow you away. If you want to suit up and see what Hong Kong's surf has to offer, then the bay at the east end of Hong Kong Island has some of the biggest waves around, which is why they have so creatively named it Big Wave Bay (the beach is equipped with outdoor-seating restaurants and showers).

Some of the Outlying Islands actually have better surfing than here, but the breaks at this cozy beach can put on a reasonable show, and it is often filled with surfers snugly paddling out between two rocky headlands. Waves can rise as high as 2 to 3 m (9 ft or so) on a good day. Otherwise, this spot is particularly popular with local windsurfers.

One of the protected Declared Monuments of Hong Kong resides on one of the rock faces here: a **bronze age rock carving** discovered in the 1970s depicting geometric shapes and animals. Just south of Big Bay Beach and past a golf course, Shek O Beach also has some good surfing.

Hap Mun Wan Beach

Chinese name: 廈門灣泳灘
Transport:
Sampan – Sampans (HK$40) from Sai Kung Town are the only way to get to Hap Mun Wan Beach.
Getting to Sai Kung Town:
Subway & Bus – Ma On Shan Line, Wu Kai Sha Station, take bus 299 to Sai Kung Town; or Kwun Tong Line, Diamond Hill MTR Station, take bus 92 to Sai Kung Town

If you're worried about the water quality of Hong Kong's beaches but you're aching for a swim then Hap Mun Wan Beach is for you. Hap Mun Wan has received top rankings for water quality every year since the government began tracking it in 1986, and it's your best bet for a day of guaranteed pollution-free beach time fun.

Despite being on Kiu Tsui Chau Island across from Sai Kung Town, the beach is still quite popular and is packed with already-set-up umbrellas. Getting to the beach takes about half an hour from Sai Kung Town on HK$40 (or less) sampans, which is quite cheap when you consider the HK$1,000 you might have to shell out to go to Long Ke Wan Beach by boat.

Because the Cantonese pronunciation of Hap Mun sounds quite similar to "half moon" in English, some people have taken to calling it Half Moon Bay Beach. When you consider that the shape of Hap Mun Bay looks noticeably like a crescent moon, it makes the appellation Half Moon feel a bit more appropriate. Hap Mun (廈門) is actually pronounced as "Xiamen" in Mandarin, a name given to one of China's most famous beach cities in Fujian Province, further increasing the popularity of Hap Mun.

The beach sits on a narrow portion of the bottom of the island, and you can easily walk across to the opposite shore of mostly medium sized rocks, which doesn't make for much of a recreational area but has some pretty scenery. On the north part of the island is Ku Tsui Country Park, a treed area that no one seems to visit.

Long Ke Wan Beach

Chinese name: 浪茄沙灘

Transport: To reach this secluded beach you first need to get to Sai Kung Town. From there you will have to take a taxi to the beach trailhead or a ferry to the beach. Make sure you arrange return plans with your driver ahead of time.

Subway – Ma On Shan Line, Wu Kai Sha Station, take bus 299 to Sai Kung Town; or Kwun Tong Line, Diamond Hill MTR Station, take bus 92 to Sai Kung Town

Taxi – A taxi will take you straight from Sai Kung Town to the Long Ke Wan beach trail for about HK$100

Ferry – Junks will take you to Long Ke Wan Beach for about HK$900 (it might be more expensive or harder to find a junk willing to go on a weekday)

The clear shallow water of Long Ke Wan is set between two rock peninsulas and a reservoir. It is what you could call secluded while still being easily accessible. Fine sand and rock pools define the picturesque beach, while weekend junks docked in the water define how easy it is to get back to Sai Kung.

Long Ke Wan is one of the many amazing beaches in Sai Kung East Country Park (on the eastern coast to the north, Tai Long Bay offers three more stunning beaches). Spending some time at the serenity of Long Ke Wan is a splendid treat at the end of a hike through Sai Kung's nature trails. Starting from the beginning of **MacLehouse Trail Section 7** (see map, pg 105) in the park, it is about a two or three hour hike to Long Ke Wan. The closest you can get if you take a taxi all the way down the road is around a 15-minute walk from the beach. You could also take a junk from Sai Kung Town or a ferry from Sai Kung Town to other piers in the country park.

Once you arrive at the beach it's time to enjoy clear water, run silky sand through your toes and monkey around on the rocks cropped on the western corner. Scale all of the rocks and you'll find a small section of beach on the other side. Be prepared to possibly be lulled into staying some extra time on this super-relaxing beach, and consider bringing a tent to stay the night at the campground here.

Turtle Cove Beach

Chinese name: 龜背灣泳灘
Transport:
Subway – Island Line, Chai Wan Station, take minibus 16A to Turtle Cove; or Sai Wan Ho Station and then take bus 14
Bus – Minibuses 16A, 16M and 16X stop at Turtle Cove after leaving from Chai Wan

Less than ten minutes from Stanley, this small beach is nowhere near as crowded as the beach town. It's just 70 m (230 ft) wide, and it has no restaurants or shops. It can even be a bit difficult to find from the entrance in the trees. Look for it at the bottom of a steep hill at the end of a wooded walkway coming from the road where the bus lets you off.

The seclusion and lack of amenities makes Turtle Cove Beach quiet and very relaxing. The water is shimmering and clear, the waves aren't too big and the breeze is gentle. It's a great place to pack a lunch and some beers (there are barbecue pits you can cook at), wade out into the water and watch the world do its thing. The beach has changing rooms, showers and a lifeguard from April to October.

Cheung Sha Beach

Chinese name: 長沙海灘
Transport: Cheung Sha Beach is located on Lantau Island. You can take the subway to Tung Chung or a ferry to Mui Wo, at which point you'll need to take a bus.
Subway – Tung Chung Line, Tung Chung Station, then take a bus to the beach
Ferry – A ferry runs from Central Pier 6 to Mui Wo on Lantau Island. After arriving at Mui Wo you need to take take a bus to Cheung Sha Beach. The ferry leaves twice an hour from 6:00-1:30 in the morning. View the schedule at www.nwff.com.hk/eng/fare_table/central-mui_wo/
Bus -
From Tung Chung: 23 (toward Ngong Ping) and 11 (toward Tai O) both go by Cheung Sha Beach
From Mui Wo: 1 (to Tai O) and 2 (to Ngong Ping) go by Cheung Sha Beach
Get off at Cheung Sha beach stop shortly after the bus goes around a traffic circle onto South Lantau Rd (Lantau buses have an all-day bus pass option)

This is one of the longest beaches in Hong Kong, and while it's conveniently just down the road from a major bus stop, it somehow remains relatively secluded. Located on the south side of Lantau Island on a section flanked by two points of land and hidden from the road by a line of trees, the peaceful beach here offers up an exceptional view of the wide open ocean. When the crowds do come, it's not hard to find a spot away from them all and lose yourself along the 3 km (2 mi) stretch of beach.

The wind conditions at Cheung Sha Beach make it one of the better destinations for windsurfing. On any given day at Cheung Sha you can see dozens of windsurfers carving their way in between regular surfers while paragliders descend from Lantau Peak. The Long Coast Seasport shop (**www. longcoast.hk**) offers equipment rentals for windsurfing, sailing, sea kayaking, surfing, bodyboarding, and skimboarding, and they also host lessons and camps. The winter months between November and March are the best for windsurfing.

Cheung Sha is divided into upper and lower beaches, which are connected by a short path through the trees. The upper beach on the eastern side, with its showers, changing room, shops and restaurants, sees much larger crowds. The lower beach to the west is longer and far less densely packed.

After a swim in the ocean, you can enjoy a bite and a brew at one of a few nice restaurants along the beach. It's one of the best places to watch the sun set, and sometimes wild cows come down in the evenings. Because the beach is on Lantau Island it's highly recommended to include it as part of a day trip to Tai O Fishing Village (pg 74) or the Po Lin Monastery (pg 65).

Islands

With over 263 islands throughout Hong Kong and its Outlying Islands district, you could fill a book bigger than this just trying to talk about them all. Many are inhabited by humans, some with just birds, and plenty of them are laden with immaculate beaches, stunning sunsets, and hidden temples. To expedite the process of choosing which ones you should visit, we've laid out our favorites in the following pages, and you can be sure that your Hong Kong trip will not be complete unless you visit at least one.

Tung Ping Chau Island

Chinese name: 東平洲
Transport:
Ferry – The ferry leaves from Ma Liu Shui Pier (which is near University Station on the MTR East Rail) at 9:00 and 15:30 on Sat and only at 9:00 on Sun. It takes 1 hour 40 min and costs HK$90. On Sat and Sun it returns from Tung Ping Chau at 17:15. It also runs the Sun schedule on public holiday.

If you were a person in Southern China during the 1960s who, for whatever reason (Cultural Revolution, perhaps?) wanted to leave China, Tung Ping Chau would have been one of your options. The easternmost island of Hong Kong, Tung Ping Chau is just 4 km (2.5 mi) away from Guangdong and is one of the best spots around the city for diving.

Though the island had a large Chinese transplant population a century ago, the small 1.1 sq km island is mostly abandoned now, but its rock formations and coral reef make it a natural wonder. Tung Ping Chau is one of two marine parks in Hong Kong primarily designated for the protection of coral communities, making it a favorite spot for divers and snorkelers.

The shore of Tung Ping Chau has been battered by wave erosion for generations, creating interesting cliffs, stacks, stumps and platforms to walk and climb on. You can walk out on the side of the **Tau Am** (頭岩) cliff on the south side of the island and head along its small steps for some nice scenery. Further along, there are some platforms jetting out into some shallow water from a rock beach at **Yi Am** (二岩). There is also a sea cave at **Hoi Lo Tung** (海螺穴).

As far as secluded islands go, Tung Ping Chau has a lot going for it: reefs, rocks, and the first place to catch the sunrise in Hong Kong, as well as a smutty history of opium smuggling. There are only two ferries that run here on Saturday and Sunday (see Transport in the vital info box), and the ride is a long one. There's not much on the island as far as amenities, so pack a bag with what you need for a day out, and consider the possibility of camping on the island.

Po Toi Island

Chinese name: 蒲台島
Transport: The ferry to Po Toi leaves from Aberdeen on Tue, Thu, Sat & Sun. It also goes from Stanley to Po Tai on Sat & Sun.
Ferry -
Tue & Thu: Leaves Aberdeen at 10:00; returns at 14:00
Sat: leaves Aberdeen at 10:00 and 15:00; returns at 14:00 and 16:00. Leaves Stanley at 13:20
Sun: Leaves Aberdeen at 8:15, returns at 18:00; leaves Stanley at 10:00, 11:30, 15:30 & 17:00, returns at 9:15, 10:45, 15:00 and 16:30
On public holidays, the ferry runs on the Sunday schedule. The full schedule is at **www.traway.com.hk/ferry.html#Potoi**. Tickets cost HK$20 each way and are free for children under age 3.

Po Toi Island is one of the most popular islands for birds traveling through the area. It should be an interesting island for you, too, if you like birds, wildlife, rocks and fried calamari.

Every year, tens of thousands of birds pass through Po Toi Island on migratory routes. Over 300 bird species have been recorded here, 60% of all the species ever seen in Hong Kong, including some rare species which have only been recorded once in the past 30 years. The periods of spring migration from March to May, and fall migration from September to November, are the best times to come for birdwatching, when you can see flocks (sometimes numbering in the hundreds) pass by. Keep an eye out for certain birds with brilliant yellow, blue and red plumage. The best place to view bird migration is on the rocky Nam Kok Tsui (南角咀) point at the south end of the island.

Other interesting animals have been spotted here, such as the endangered Romer's tree frog, finless porpoises and humpback whales. However, you'll need to watch out for those that you wouldn't want to stumble on blindly, such as Burmese pythons.

Along the island trails, there is a scattering of rocks that have acquired nicknames inspired by their unique shapes. Some of the most famous include Turtle Rock, Monk Rock, Buddha's Palm, Kissing Rock and Coffin Rock. You can find **Coffin Rock** behind the deserted **Mansion of Family Mo**, one of a number of deserted homes on the island overgrown with weeds. Family Mo's house is said to be haunted (hence the name of Coffin Rock).

On the beach near the pier, there is one major restaurant, **Ming Kee Restaurant** (明 記 海 鮮 酒家 ; phone: 2849 7038), which has received rave reviews for years. Its Deep Fried Black Pepper and Chili Squid is highly recommended. The unpretentious open air restaurant under a yellow roof on a platform on the beach fits the vibe of the bucolic island perfectly. It isn't worth it to go just for the restaurant, but if the nature and wildlife of the island sounds appealing then Ming Kee is the place to eat.

Cheung Chau Island

Chinese name: 長洲島
Transport:
Ferry – Ferries run from Central Pier 5 to Cheung Chau all day, usually every half hour. The ordinary ferry takes about an hour, and a fast ferry takes just over half an hour. Once on the island, there is no motorized transport. It's small enough to walk anywhere, and bikes can be rented.

Western view of Cheung Chau

Known as the "dumbbell island" for its particularly...well, dumbbell shape, Cheung Chau Island stretches 10 km (6 mi) off the southwest coast of Hong Kong Island and is one of the oldest inhabited parts of the city. With a splattering of temples and good beaches, a cozy village, a prehistoric rock carving and a 19th century pirate cave, this retreat in the city's Island District makes for an excellent one- or two-day trip.

The two beaches **Tung Wan** (東 灣) and **Kwun Yam Wan** (觀音灣) are quite scenic, and it's at the edge of Tung Wan that you can check out the 3,000 year old rock carving. The two beaches are spread side by side on the east edge of the island with Tung Wan wandering alongside the village area. The village of about 20,000 people is on a narrow area in the middle "handle" area of the dumb bell-shaped island.

Tung Wan

The "Mini Great Wall" hiking trail begins near Kwun Yam Wan, south of the village, and gives great views of the windswept rocks along the coast. Check out the **Cheung Po Tsai Cave** (張 保 仔 洞), which is said to have held some of Pirate Cheung Po Tsai's booty in the early 19th century. Now – unfortunately – it's empty.

Most of the year, Cheung Chau is occupied by windsurfers and sunbathing daytrippers, but for a few days in spring, it becomes much more – an island obsessed with buns. Observed since the Qing Dynasty, the **Cheung Chau Bun Festival** (包 山 節) celebrates Pak Tai, a Taoist god who ended a famine. Good luck buns are affixed to shrines, and a giant bun tower is constructed. At midnight on the third night, contestants race to the top of the tower and collect buns in backpacks. The buns on the tower may be plastic, but over the next few days real lotus- and red bean-filled buns are consumed, and they are delicious. For the first two days of the festival there are lion dance performances outside the **Pak Tai Temple** (北帝廟), and on the third day a Piu Sik parade with "floating children" trundles down the streets of Cheung Chau village. The Cheung Chau Bun Festival takes place every year on the fourth lunar month from the 5th day until the 9th day (with the bun competition and parade on the 8th day). In 2014, those days will be from May 3-7; and in 2015, May 22-26.

If you don't visit while bun mania is sweeping the island, Cheung Chau still has enough nice beaches and scenery to keep it one of Hong Kong's best islands all year long. The other temples on Cheung Chau Island are **Pak Tai Temple**, a Taoist temple and one of the oldest in Hong Kong until it was rebuilt in 1989; four temples dedicated to Tin Hau, and Kwan Kung Chung Yi Ting, a traditional temple built in 1973 dedicated to Kwan Tai, the god of war.

Another good time to come to Cheung Chau is in May when the **Kwan Kung Pavilion** (關 公忠義亭) is surrounded by blooming cherry blossoms.

Lamma Island

Chinese name: 南丫島
Transport: You can only take the subway as far as the ferry pier in Central, from where you'll need to take a boat to Lamma Island.
Subway – Tsuen Wan Line, Central Station, walk to Central Ferry Pier 4
Ferry – From Central Ferry Pier 4, there are separate ferries to both Yung Shue and Sok Kwu on Lamma. The ferry to Yung Shue is the more popular route. It runs at least once an hour from 6:30 until 1:30 in the morning, and twice an hour for most of the day. The ferry to Sok Kwu runs from 7:20 until 23:30. The full schedule can be viewed at **www.hkkf.com.hk**.

The view of the power plant with three big smokestacks off to the right side of Hung **Shing Ye Beach** (洪聖爺泳灘) is a strange sight on what is considered to be Hong Kong's alternative free-spirited island.. No worries, as the locals would say, because the plant does little to take away from the relaxing vibes of Hong Kong's most bohemian beach. Tourists here just take in the view along with that of the fine sand, clear water and rolling hills. The barbecue area with tables is great for a party, and its proximity to the Yung Shue Wan Ferry Pier makes it the most popular beach on Lamma Island. It's really not hard to find a secluded beach, a laid back village or a great hike on this little-populated, care-free island.

Local weekenders like to walk across the island on the 6 km (4 mi) **Lamma Island Family Walk** boardwalk that connects the main western village **Yung Shue** (榕樹灣) with **Sok Kwu** (索罟灣) in the west, but off that trail, there are dirt paths through forests, over ridges and off to beaches on all corners. One of the beaches you can have mostly to yourself is **Lo So Shing Beach** (蘆鬚城海灘). Even though its just a short eastwardly hike from the Family Walk at Lo So Shing Village, few weekenders seem to go there. And even more beaches are yours to find if you venture on the lesser marked trails in the south of the island where no one lives. Just make sure to stay away from the Sham Wan (深灣) Beach between the months of June and October, a time when protected sea turtles breed on the beach, as you can incur some hefty fines if you go near them.

The Family Walk ends on the east side at Sok Kwu, one of the best places in Hong Kong to eat fresh seafood. The road becomes a long strip of restaurants at the edge of the sea. **Rainbow Seafood Restaurant** (天虹海鮮酒家 ; address: Sok Kwu Wan First St; phone: 2982 8100; website: www.rainbowrest.com.hk) is particularly noted for its quality, and diners can also enjoy a free ferry ride back to Hong Kong Island (that makes up just a little bit for its prices).

The tranquility and nature of Lamma Island have lead many expats to buy homes here. Like any hippie-ish trend once popularized, the prices have increased, bringing one thing from Hong Kong to the island: inflation. Most of the shops and restaurants in the charming village of Yung Shue that you walk through after getting off the ferry station are owned by long-time local residents, and it's a fantastically relaxing place to browse beach-themed gifts and eat and drink.

Other Islands

Hong Kong has over 200 islands. Most of them aren't considered tourist attractions and aren't easily accessible, but for the adventurous, we have put together a brief list of some of the more distant islands around Hong Kong.

Tap Mun Chau (Grass Island) – Off the northwest of Sai Kung West Country Park, Tap Mun Chau is mostly undeveloped, save for the 100-some people who mostly live in the fishing village near the pier in the south. The quality seafood restaurants here were frequented by Hong Kong's last British governor, Chris Patten.

To find the **Tin Hau Temple**, which puts on a great festival in April or early May, head northeast of where the boat lets you off. On the way is **New Hon Kee**, the island's most famous restaurant with meals from HK$100. There is an interesting rock formation called Balanced Rock 200 m (656 ft) south of the pebble beach on the southeastern shore. Bring a tent if you intend to stay the night on the island.

> Highlights: Seafood, Balanced Rock, Tin Hau Temple
> Transport: Water taxis run from Wong Shek Pier for HK$20 per person (subject to bargain), and ferries run from Ma Liu Shui pier (near University MTR station) at 8:30 and 15:15 every day and return at 13:45 and 17:20 daily (90 min).

Ninepin Islands (Kwo Chau Islands) – This group of 29 islands far to the southeast of Shek O has undergone massive erosion from tides, and thus has interesting rock shores with corroded holes, flats, arches and rock stumps.

Highlights: Rocks, Volcanic Columns, Lighthouse (on North Ninepin Island), Tin Hau Temple
Transport: Cruises operated by the Hong Kong Catamaran Club leave from Central Pier 9 and the Golden Bauhinia Pier. A half day cruise costs HK$590. For information, visit their website at **www.cata.hk/eng/cruises/ninepin. htm**. Sampans from Sai Kung Town will take you for cheaper, but such a small boat going a few kilometers over the open sea may not be as much fun... or perhaps even more fun!

Tung Lung Chau – To the south of Shek O, this island has rock cliffs on the east coast – some of the best climbing spots in the city – prehistoric stone carvings, and the ruins of the 300-year-old **Tung Lung Fort**. The fort was set up around the turn of the 18th century, and after being raided one too many times, it was abandoned in 1810. Now, there's little more than crumbling walls and an information center (9:00-16:00, Wed-Mon), the latter of which has an illustrated history of the fort. The 2.5 m (8 ft) by 2 m (6.5 ft) dragon rock carving lies on the northern shore and is one of the biggest rocks around.

Highlights: Cliffs, Stone Carvings, Tung Lung Fort ruins, rock climbing
Transport: Small boats known as *kai-to* offer ferry services on the weekends from Sam Ka Tsuen on the Kowloon side (from nearby Yau Tong MTR Station) and Sai Wan Ho on the Hong Kong side (from Sai Wan Ho MTR Station). The Sam Ka Tsuen ferry costs HK$36 round trip.

Soko Islands – This set of seven islands south of Lantau contains nine coral reefs.

Highlights: Reefs
Transport: No ferry; you'll need to hire a boat. The most cost-effective is to take the ferry to nearby Cheung Chau Island (pg 161) and hire a sampan from there. Price varies.

Sunshine Island – This green, plant-covered island south of Lantau was the old site of a drug rehabilitation center of the 1950s catering to China's endemic opium addiction. Today it is home to an abandoned farming community, as well as to the white-bellied sea eagle, Bogadek's legless lizard, and other animals.

Highlights: Wildlife
Transport: Hire a sampan from Cheung Chau Island.

Lung Kwu Chau – A marine park to the west of the New Territories, Lung Wu Chau is considered a site of interest for its dolphins. It's a good place to head if you'd like to try catching a view of the dolphins without hopping on a viewing boat.

Highlights: Dolphin viewing
Transport: The nearest pier where you might be able to hire a junk is at Tuen Mun. It is also in the vicinity of Tai O (pg 74).

Sha Chau – Just south of Lung Kwu Chau, this island also falls in the same marine park. There are sand bars connecting the islands.

Highlights: Dolphin watching
Transport: Tuen Mun or Tai O hired boats

Sunshine Island

Amusement Parks

If your Hong Kong trip leaves you hankering for a roller coaster, if you have kids, or if the thrill of the Dragon's Back Hike (pg 108) just doesn't get your heart beating fast enough, there is a plan B: amusement parks. In case you didn't know, Hong Kong has a Disneyland, and it's almost exactly the same as every other Disney park except with more signage in Chinese. If that's what you're here for, then knock yourself out. Just remember that the city also has its own Ocean Park, filled with mountaintop coasters, riveting island and ocean scenery, and enough animals to make up a zooquarium (it has a zoo and an aquarium).

Disneyland

Chinese name: 香港迪士尼樂園
Admission: HK$450 (one-day ticket); HK$585 (two-day ticket)
Hours: 10:00-21:00 (weekends); 10:30-21:00 (weekdays)
Website: www.hongkongdisneyland.com (English available)
Transport: Subway – Hong Kong MTR network, change to Disney Resort Line at Sunny Bay Station

Most people don't need much of an introduction to Disneyland. It's an amusement park divided into themed lands representing Disney movies and Disney's vision of fantasy. You'll also find plenty of Disney's vision of a fairly-priced meal, which shows more than ever how the park is one big fantasy land.

If you're intent on coming to Hong Kong for a visit to Disneyland, then remember that besides the high prices you're almost certainly going to have to deal with crowds

– massive crowds. Rudeness is an issue as well, so put on your thickest skin to deal with things like line-cutting, pushing and other inconsiderate behavior, much of which comes from Mainlanders who visit the city for this park. Your best bet is to make your visit on a weekday and hope that your chosen day is a mellow one.

Disneyland is divided into seven lands: Main Street USA, Tomorrowland, Fantasyland, Adventureland, Toy Story Land, Mystic Point, and Grizzly Gulch. Built on a plot of land reclaimed from Penny's Bay, the park is relatively small, the smallest of all the Disney parks in the world. It is laid out and designed just like the original Anaheim Disneyland, and the location of each themed area within the park is organized in the same way. Main Street USA and Sleeping Beauty's Castle are almost exact replicas.

All signs within the park are in English, Cantonese, Mandarin, Japanese and French.

Ocean Park

Chinese name: 海洋公園
Admission: HK $320
Hours: 10:00-22:00
Phone: 3923 2323
Website: www.oceanpark.com.hk
Transport: Bus – 629 from Central Pier 7 or from MTR Admiralty Station, Exit B, get off at the park

Located on a point on the south end of Hong Kong Island, Ocean Park combines amazing views with thrill rides, zoo areas and some excellent scenery. Often lauded as Hong Kong's best amusement park, this place is a truly worthwhile alternative for those thrill-addicts and animal lovers who just can't find within themselves any appreciation for Walt Disney or his many "lands." In fact, the park has recently seen a huge turnaround from some initially dismal visitor numbers – much to the credit of some giant and red pandas that were gifted from the Mainland – as well as near constant expansions and additions of new rides and scenic areas.

The park is cleaved in two by a verdant mountain. Visitors first enter through the huge and well put-together Waterfront side where the all-popular **Amazing Asian Animals** is located. This area features some impressive and educational animal setups and shows, including giant salamanders, awesome raptors, endangered Chinese alligators and a very interesting goldfish display. It's also where you'll want to head to for pandas. Don't leave the waterfront side without giving some time to **Aqua City**, which boasts an interesting replica of the old buildings that were once a part of Wan Chai in Old Hong Kong, as well as the very impressive Grand Aquarium. If you've got kids in tow, stop off for some animal shows over in **Whiskers Harbour**.

The other side of the mountain – accessed by either cable car or funicular train – is known as the Summit and is where the dragon's share of the thrill rides and smaller section of animals are located. Adrenaline-junkies will surely love rides like the Flash, the Whirly Bird or the all-popular Hair Raiser atop **Thrill Mountain**. The latter ride is the most exciting of any coaster in the park, but most of the rides here offer superb views of the sea and the islands below. For the best views of any ride, hop on the Mine Train, which is not the most thrilling of the Summit's attractions, but certainly boasts the most breathtaking views. Animal areas include the thorough dolphin shows of **Marine World**, as well as the bizarre creatures of **Rainforest** and the barking sea lions of **Polar Adventure**.

From the top of the lift hill on the **Dragon Roller Coaster**, you can see Lamma Island and other outlying islands in the China Sea. Enjoy the view! Then it's down a hill and through three upside down loops before arriving back at the station two minutes later.

New animals come frequently: the giant pandas arrived in 1999, two new pandas joined in 2007, and several baby penguins were born last year. In 2014, Ocean Park is expecting the arrival of eight koalas from Australia.

Cable Car & Ocean Express Funicular Train

There are two ways to get from the Watefront to the Summit: the cable car or the Ocean Express funicular train. The **cable car** brings you up high on the side of a hill overlooking the South China Sea. While it offers great views, it is also slow and you'll have to wait through some long lines. The **Ocean Express** train is faster, taking just four minutes, and moves 5,000 people an hour, but you will have to trade the mountaintop views for submarine scenery as you pass underwater.

Sleeping

In a city like Hong Kong, it's all about location, location, location. Sure, you may live in a nice, comfortable flat that actually has S P A C E, but what good does that do you when you're tollways, bridges and many MTR stations away from where the real action is? It's hip to be square in Hong Kong – as in square meters – to a point, but not at the sacrifice of living in Guam.

This lack of space in the most happening areas naturally affects the hotel industry and the hostel scene. With soaring rent, much of the city's lodging prices are sky high, and since rent is so expensive, it can be difficult to establish any grungy budget hostels reserved for those with backpacks super glued to their spine. In other words, whether you're coming into town for a visa run, sightseeing or a rugby game, save a bit of cash beforehand so you can actually stay in a decent place.

Luckily, though, there is a light at the end of Hong Kong's grim budget lodging tunnel. It's called the Chungking Mansions (along with its neighboring side kick the Mirador Mansions), and it's the most (in)famous budget joint in town. If you're looking to be centrally located and are not willing to spend an arm and a leg, this is basically the only place in town. See Budget under Kowloon for the low down.

So which neighborhood do you plan on staying in while in Hong Kong? If you answered "No idea." keep reading. Kowloon and northern Hong Kong Island are the two most popular places to stay, and like the *yin* and the *yang*, they both have their pros and cons. Kowloon is often cheaper, more historical and more accesible since you don't have to traverse the water. Hong Kong Island, on the other hand, is where the action

is: it's very well organized, has a fantastic transportation system to get you anywhere in town, and is home to some of the best nightlife and shopping. Another option is the New Territories, which is cheaper, more down to earth and quieter, but far away from most of the city's cool stuff.

Remember that Hong Kong also has numerous villages and beach towns to choose from too, and it's an archipelago with many islands. Places like Aberdeen and Stanley (on South Hong Kong Island), Lamma Island, Sha Tin, Repulse Bay, Tsuen Wan, Lantau and others offer some lovely accomodations away from the downtown area, and if you're looking for luxury at a discount, these places are worth a look.

Kowloon

Budget

Chungking Mansions (重慶大廈)

▶ PANDA PICK ◀

Located at 40 Nathan Rd (right next to Tsim Sha Tsui MTR) and built in 1961, this longstanding Hong Kong landmark is the place to be for budget accomodation. Standing at 17 stories and divided into A, B, C, D and E blocks, the massive complex has a multifunctional setting:

1) The Chungking Mansions actually have residential apartments. Today, it is estimated that 4,000 people live here.

2) It's a business center. There are tons of shops, knock off merchandise and kitsch

souvenirs for the buying, along with internet cafes and money exchange houses. See shopping on page 226 for more.

3) It also hosts a wide range of small eateries. They're all budget-friendly, and most specialize in South Asian food from India and Pakistan – all of which is delicious! See page 194 for more on eating in the big Chungking.

4) Actually, the Chungking Mansions should be an attraction all in themselves. There are Africans loading up boxes of clothes, sneakers and baseball caps to be sent back to their home countries, backpackers from Austria to Australia roaming the blocks, Nepalese cooking up a fresh batch of *dhal*, and Chinese pedaling anything and everything. In fact, this place is so popular and full of life that it was the theme of the 1994 movie *Chungking Express*. *Time Magazine* even called it the "Best Example of Globalization in Action" for the 120 different nationalities that passed through its doors in 2007, and it's estimated that 20% of cell phones used in Sub-Saharan Africa have been in the Chungking Mansions at some point.

5) Now onto the budget lodges. There are nearly 2,000 cookie cutter rooms to choose from, and many of them change names and management so often, so it's hard to pinpoint an exact "hostel" here. The good news is they really are more or less the same in size, and most offer singles and doubles, and AC, TVs, wifi, and private showers/toilets. The bad news is that they're not the nicest places to stay at – it's not uncommon to find a tiny cockroach running around – but a lot of them have been renovated and are in a lot better shape than they were a decade or two ago.

To find a room, simply walk up to the front entrance of the Chungking Mansions and you'll be approached by one of the sales representatives (who are usually from India) asking you if you need a room. Next they'll hand you a business card and tell you the price. Most of these guys are legit and

trustworthy, but you should never have to pay more than HK$250 for a single on weekdays (the price will inflate a bit on weekends and national holidays). Follow them up the elevator to the room (the entire journey will take much longer than you expect because of possibly the world's slowest elevators) and check out what they're offering. If you aren't satisfied with what they have, just give a firm "No," head back downstairs to the sea of salesmen, and start the process all over again. They won't get mad at your decision, they get turned down all the time, and if you turn your back they may even go down on the price a bit.

On a cautionary note, racial tension in the Chungking Mansions sometimes boils over and conflict errupts. It's poor and outdated wires and zero fire escapes have caused deadly fires in the past, and the area is also known as a center for drugs, prostitution, violent attacks, murders and illegal immigration. Recently, the government has installed new cameras and beefed up security to reduce the mayhem.

Now that you're horrified, don't be; the Chungking Mansions really aren't as bad as they sound, and the chances of anything disagreeable happening to you are slim to none. But, if you don't feel like haggling and following strangers up those painfully slow elevators, here are three of our recommendations out of the 50 or so businesses you could pick from within the Mansions:

New Peking Guest House (新北京賓館)

This hostel is very clean and one might even say pretty. The staff is inviting and the price depends on the size of the room you want. The one down side is that extra amenities like AC and heat will cost you a bit extra. Internet is provided. Privates from K$330.

Address: A1, 12/F Block A, Chungking Mansions, 40 Nathan Rd (Tsim Sha Tsui MTR) Phone: 2723 8320

Welcome Guesthouse (惠康招待所)

Welcome Guesthouse is set up in an old style building that is managed by a friendly old man. The rooms are quite small, but decent. Bathrooms and AC are optional. Doubles are HK$260 – HK$300.

Address: A5, 7/F, Chungking Mansions, 40 Nathan Rd (Tsim Sha Tsui MTR) Phone: 27217793 Website: www.guesthousehk.net

Chung King House (重慶招待所)

Located on the 4th and 5th floors, Chung King house is the only place in the mansions that operates like a small hotel. The rooms are renovated and reasonably sized with white wood furniture, TV, AC and bathrooms, so you can feel free to haggle on the rates. Singles from HK$250.

> Address: Suite A, 4-5/F, Chungking Mansions, 40 Nathan Rd, Kowloon
> Phone: 2739 1600
> Email: info@chungkinghouse.com
> Website: www.chungkinghouse.com

Mirador Mansions (美麗都大廈)

Everything we just said about the Chungking Mansions is almost exactly the same for the Mirador Mansions. Located directly north of big bad Chungking (or to the left when facing the entrance of the Chungking Mansions), Mirador has a gazillion rooms, eateries and shops to choose from. If you want the more adventurous experience, stay in Chungking. If you want something just a wee bit more civilized (emphasis on the "wee"), come on down to Mirador. Our favorite establishment in the complex is the...

Traveler's Friendship Hostel (友誼賓館)

The doubles are cheap and they have internet. There is a kitchen and a small library, but don't expect bag storage because there isn't any (not a square foot to spare). The staff is welcoming, but the hostel is not the cleanest. Singles from HK$220.

> Address: C1, 13/F, Mirador Mansions, 58-62 Nathan Rd, Kowloon, Yau Tsim Mong
> Phone: 2311 2520

Other places in Kowloon not in the Chungking or Mirador Mansions:

City Econo Guesthouse (城市客棧)

This small, discreet guesthouse is centrally located and near a lot of the places you may want to visit during your stay. Don't be fooled by the very banal exterior, the rooms are small but impeccably clean and comfortable, with AC, flat screen TVs and well-kept bathrooms. Singles from HK$250.

> Address: 5-6/F, Cumberland House, 227 Nathan Rd, Kowloon (Jordan MTR)
> Phone: 2730 0212
> Website: www.cityecono.com

Rooms for Tourist (逸園旅舍)

The rooms at Rooms for Tourist are roomy, particularly compared to most other hostels in Hong Kong, though they are a bit boring and underwhelming. They come equipped with AC, bathrooms, and TVs and the staff is extremely friendly. Singles from HK$300.

> Address: 6/F, 42 Mody Rd, Kowloon
> Phone: 9083 3300
> Website: www.room4touristhk.com

Rent-a-Room

Large and well decorated rooms are the highlights at Rent-a-Room, and they are spotless and well-equipped with TVs, showers, AC, and bathrooms. Free internet and wifi are provided, and it's conveniently

located next to Tsim Sha Tsui's well known shopping area. Starting at HK$209.

> Address: 2/F, Knight Garden Flat A, 7-8 Tak Hing St, Kowloon
> Phone: 2366 3011
> Website: rentaroomhk.com

Mid-range

Holiday Inn Golden Mile Long

PANDA PICK

Located close to the Chungking and Mirador Mansions, this is a good option if you want all the action and excitement of the Tsim Sha Tsui area but don't want any of the extra baggage of sleeping in crazy Chungking. The rooms serve as the perfect definition for a "mid-range" hotel, and they're a decent place for families as well. The swimming pool is a bonus. Rooms start around HK$1,000.

> Address: 50 Nathan Rd, Kowloon (Tsim Sha Tsui MTR)
> Phone: 2369 3111

Shamrock Hotel (新樂酒店)

The Shamrock offers an elaborate breakfast buffet featuring a wide variety of food as part of their standard room price. There are frequent special promotions as well, and good restaurants are available on the ground floor. Rooms are comfortable and clean, service is high quality and the hotel is ideally situated only a few steps away from the Jordan MTR Station. Singles from HK$1,500.

> Address: 223 Nathan Rd, Kowloo
> Phone: 2735 2271
> Website: www.shamrockhotel.com.hk

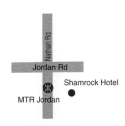

Star Guesthouse (星華賓館)

With a welcoming staff, very clean amenities and well equipped rooms, this small guesthouse is a solid option if you're looking to stay in Kowloon. Singles from HK$500.

> Address: 6/F, 21 Cameron Rd, Kowloon
> Phone: 2723 8951
> Website: www.starguesthouse.com.hk

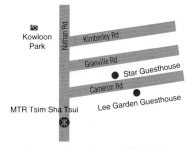

Lee Garden Guesthouse (利園賓館)

Picked up as an overflow backup by Star Guesthouse, this little hostel can take care of you for a good price (which includes AC), but the smaller rooms do not have bathrooms. Singles from HK$480.

> Address: Block A, 8/F, 34-36 Cameron Rd, Kowloon (Tsim Sha Tsui MTR)
> Phone: 2367 2284

Kum Loong Guesthouse (鑫鑨酒店)

Renovated only a couple of years ago, Kum Loong Guesthouse is centrally located close to major tourist spots like the Jade Market, Langham Place and Temple Street. Internet is provided, the rooms are comfortable, and there's a supermarket and several bars nearby. Rooms can also be rented by the month.

> Address: 10/F, May Ming Bldg, Flat B, 312 Nathan Rd, Kowloon
> Phone: 2970 1777

Citadines Ashley Hong Kong (香港馨乐庭亚士厘服务公寓)

If you plan an extended stay in Hong Kong, the Citadines may be the place for you. It's actually a residential building that offers a host of studio and one-bedroom apartments for visiting tourists. They feature spacious rooms and high-speed internet, and some may even up the ante with a kitchen. It has an excellent location in Tsim Sha Tsui. Daily rates start from HK$1,350.

Address: 18 Ashley Rd, Tsim Sha Tsui
Phone: 2262 3062
Email: enquiry.hongkong@the-ascott.com

Evergreen Hotel Hong Kong (萬年青酒店)

Clean rooms, nice staff and a solid location near the Jordan MTR station and Temple Street Night Market. Ask about discounts on rooms and internet. Rooms from HK$850.

Address: 48 Woo Sung St, Jordan, Kowloon
Phone: 2780 4222
Website: www.evergreenhotel.com
Email: info@evergreenhotel.com

Hotel Benito Hong Kong (華國酒店)

The doors at this one flung themselves open seven years ago in 2007, and with a spot just in the middle of Tsim Sha Tsui and a two-minute walk from the MTR station – why not

take them up on their HK$800 rooms?

Address: 7-7B Cameron Rd, Tsim Sha Tsui, Kowloon
Phone: 3653 0388
Website: www.hotelbenito.com
Email: info@hotelbenito.com

YMCA Salisbury (香港基督教青年會賓館)

Located a five-minute walk from the Star Ferry port and with astounding views of the bay, YMCA Salisbury is a great option that surprises many with its strong quality to price ratio. It's a good idea to reserve in advance to ensure you get a good deal, and be aware that prices change with the seasons. On the ground floor, there's a large, great-looking stone and wood lobby that is almost too comfortable. The rooms are sparkling clean, reasonably sized and well equipped, and guests can use the Y's pool, gym, sauna, self-service laundry room, hairdresser, restaurant and chapel. Rooms from HK$1,400.

Address: 41 Salisbury Rd, Kowloon
Phone: 2268 7000
Website: hongkongymca.onetime.com

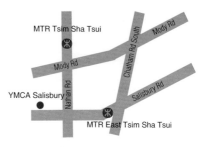

Caritas Bianchi Lodge (明愛白英奇賓館)

Located in Yau Mai Tei next to the MTR on a small street away from Nathan Road, Caritas Bianchi Lodge is excellent, with high quality and well-equipped rooms offering AC, TVs, and clean bathrooms, as well as nice views of King's Park. The lodge is a ten second walk from the night market and breakfast is included in the price. Frequent promotions are

offered so check beforehand for availability. There is an onsite restaurant. Rooms starting at HK$1,200.

Address: 4 Cliff Rd, Kowloon
Phone: 2388 1111
Website: www.caritas-chs.org.hk

Harbour Grand Kowloon (九龍海逸君綽酒店)

You're way too good looking to close yourself off to the world in an indoor swimming pool when the summer months roll around. That's why if you come by Hong Kong during the steamy season the Harbour Grand Kowloon and its outdoor swimming pool should have the honor of your consideration. When you've gotten enough pool-side sun, hop on the hotel's free shuttle bus to Tsim Sha Tsui. Rooms from HK$1,320. (Note: They also have another hotel at 23 Oil St, North Point on Hong Kong Island near the Fortress Hill MTR [Exit A] & the causeway.)

Address: 20 Tak Fung St, Whampoa Garden
Phone: 2621 3188
Website: www.harbourgrand.com/kowloon

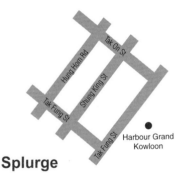
Harbour Grand Kowloon

Splurge

Stanford Hillview Hotel (仕德福山景酒店)

Centrally located in Tsim Sha Tsui, the Stanford's clean and comfortable rooms are nicely set up with clean bathrooms, carpeting, flat-screen TVs, comfy bed linens, safes, internet and wifi; all the comfort necessary for a pleasant stay. No breakfast is included, but there is a restaurant available on the ground floor featuring a buffet. You have to walk up a big hill to reach this hotel. Rooms from HK$3,000. See map for Hotel Benito.

Address: 13-17 Observatory Rd, Kowloon
Phone: 2722 7822
Website: www.stanfordhillview.com

Hyatt Regency Hong Kong, Tsim Sha Tsui (尖沙咀凱悅酒店)

The Kowloon skyline is a mighty fine sight, and you can grab plenty of it from the windows of the Hyatt Regency, whose 381 rooms are bedecked in pleasure. Check out their Sky Garden and outdoor pool, or unwind in your room's marble bathtub. Business and secretarial services are available in the Regency Club Lounge. Rooms from HK$2,000.

Address: 18 Hanoi Rd, Tsim Sha Tsui, Kowloon
Phone: 2311 1234
Email: hongkong.tsimshatsui@hyatt.com

Peninsula Hong Kong (香港半島酒店)

PANDA PICK

The Japanese ran this old spot as a military headquarters during WWII. When you've got the power in your hands, why not post up in the city's biggest, best and most decadently luxurious hotel? The Peninsula features some of the city's best restaurants, bars and luxury boutiques. And if you just eloped (or are considering it), pick up the HK$50,000 honeymoon suite package that includes a helicopter tour of the city! Rooms from HK$2,000.

Address: Salisbury Rd, Tsim Sha Tsui, Kowloon
Phone: 2920 2888

Regal Kowloon Hotel (富豪九龍酒店)

The Regal Kowloon has all the luxurious amenities you need. It's also just down from the Temple Street Night Market and the break-the-bank shopping spots over on Nathan Road. HK$1,100 to HK$2,300.

Address: 71 Mody Rd, Tsim Sha Tsui (MTR Tsim Sha Tsui Station Exit D2)
Phone: 2722 1818

North Hong Kong Island

Budget

Alisan Guesthouse (阿裡山賓館)

> PANDA PICK

You will immediately notice how welcoming the staff is here. Internet, wifi, TVs, showers, AC and colored bed sheets add character and comfort to the rooms, and they can be all yours for very reasonable prices. If you are not very sensitive to noise or have a good pair of earplugs, choose a room next to the street for a good view of the port. For breakfast, there is a little cafe located on the ground floor. Singles from HK$355.

Address: Flat A, 5/F Hoito Court, 275 Gloucester Rd
Phone: 2574 8068

Check Inn Hostel (卓軒旅舍)

Family owned and operated, this is easily one of the best budget hostels in Hong Kong, possibly the best. From the very attentive and knowledge staff to the exceptional cleanliness, you will definitely feel at home here and more than likely return whenever you come to Hong Kong (as do most who stay at Check Inn). Centrally located, this hostel is ideal for reaching nearly any area of Hong Kong by ferry, MTR, or taxi. Dorms from HK$160, singles from HK$300.

Address: 3/F, Kwong Wah Mansion, 269-273 Hennessy Rd, Wan Chai
Phone: 2955 0175
Website: www.checkinnhk.com

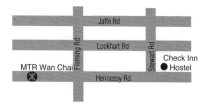

Jockey Club Mount Davis Youth Hostel (賽馬會摩星嶺青年旅舍)

Located at the peak of Mount Davis on the northwest side of the island, this is the perfect location for those looking to get away from the hustle and bustle of the city. The surrounding vegetation is the perfect complement to the superb panoramic views of the bay and the city. Dormitories are bunk-bed style and separated by gender. You can bring your own food for meals as they have a common room and a kitchen, and there is a washing machine available. They have regular free shuttles from Sheung Wan MTR to the hostel, with the last one leaving at 00:30. The 5A goes from Admiralty MTR to the bottom of the hill and then it takes about 30 minutes by foot (or three minutes by car) following the Mount Davis path. Dorms from HK$135.

Address: 123 Mount Davis Path, Western District
Phone: 2817 5715

Backpacker Hostel HK (香港旅館)

Backpacker Hostel HK's doesn't have the most spacious rooms, but they are well equipped, newly renovated and still a sound choice. Internet is provided as are free local calls, AC, laundry service, in-room bathrooms and a friendly staff. Bus A11 from the airport stops on nearby Gloucester Road. Privates from HK$160.

Address: Room C1, 2/F, 37 Paterson St
Phone: 2392 6868
Website: www.hostel.hk

Perch Studio

If you want a bit more privacy, the owners of the excellent Check Inn have another affordable option that is smack dab in the center of one of the busiest areas of the city. Once you walk out of the building, you are in the thick of the hustle and bustle that Hong Kong is famous for. Times Square is right at your fingertips, as well as shopping, dining, and more. Spacious by Hong Kong standards and recently renovated, this one is perfect for a weekend in the city. Singles from HK$160.

Address: 3/F, 531 Lockhart Rd
Phone: 2955 0175

Mid-range

Ibis North Point (宜必思北角酒店)

The rooms in this branch of the Ibis are not what you would call large. In fact, they are definitely what you'd call small because they are pretty freaking tiny. Though they are clean and comfortable enough, the real

advantage here is that you get great views of the Harbour and the hotel's location is hard to beat. Rates starting around HK$400.

Address: 138 Java Rd, North Point
Phone: 2588 1111

Walden Hotel (華登酒店)

The well-equipped rooms of this three-star business and leisure hotel are stacked up with desks, coffee and tea making equipment, satellite LCD TVs, mini bars and internet service. Talk about a mid-range hotel heaven! Rooms from HK$1,100.

Address: 353 Hennessy Rd, Wan Chai
Phone: 8200 3308
Website: www.walden-hotel.com
Email: rsvn@walden-hotel.com

Mingle Place By The Park (名樂居)

Piercing the heart of Wan Chai and within striking distance of nearby parks, shopping centers, historical attractions and the bustling Hong Kong Convention and Exhibition Centre, you're not doing too bad dropping HK$600 a night here.

Address: 143 Wan Chai Rd, Wan Chai
Phone: 2838 1109
Website: www.mingleplace.com/park
Email: park@mingleplace.com

Mingle Place By The Park

Island Pacific Hotel (港島太平洋酒店)

Business and fitness centers, room service, an outdoor swimming pool, a Western restaurant and an ever-important bar all make the Island Pacific a very acceptable choice. Large discounts are available. Listed rates from HK$2,147, discounted to HK$600, breakfast HK$141.

Address: 152 Connaught Rd West, Sai Ying Pun
Phone: 2131 1188
Website: www.islandpacifichotel.com.hk
Email: info@islandpacifichotel.com.hk

Lan Kwai Fong Hotel (蘭桂坊酒店)

You might be surprised how rare it can be to find Asian styling within the hotels of Hong Kong. At Lan Kwai Fong (two minutes' walk from Sheung Wan MTR) they've put a nice touch of Asian décor into their ornamentations, furniture and other auxiliaries. If that's not enough charm to seduce you, then consider that this hotel was named "Asia's Leading Boutique Hotel" by the 2009 World Travel Awards. Rooms from HK$1,620.

Address: 3 Kau U Fong, Central
Phone: 3650 0000
Website: www.lankwaifonghotel.com.hk
Email: enquiry@lankwaifonghotel.com.hk

Traders Hotel (formerly Hotel Jen) (盛貿飯店)

Nice views of Victoria Harbour and the nearby mountains, and excellent amenities (including a business center, restaurants, a bar and an outdoor swimming pool) make this one a solid choice, especially if you remember to ask about discounts. Rooms from HK$1,243 (discounts available), breakfast HK$152 (included with more expensive rooms).

Address: 508 Queens Rd West, Kennedy Town

Phone: 2974 1234
Website: www.tradershotels.com

Metropark Hotel Wan Chai (灣仔維景酒店)

Sitting in the center of the city and just coming off a massive HK$1 billion renovation, it's hard to believe that the LCD TVs and broadband-equipped rooms of this four-star can go for as low as they do. Better grab one now while the rates are still low. From HK$1,250.

Address: 41-49 Hennessy Rd, Wan Chai
Phone: 2861 1166
Website: hongkong.metroparkhotelwanchai.com
Email: rsvn.hkwh@metroparkhotels.com

Splurge

Lanson Place Hotel (逸蘭精品酒店)

Just a five minute's walk from Victoria Park, this beautiful option comes with fancy LCD flat-screen TVs, wireless internet and a host of other arousing treats. It's a bit further from Central (20 minutes by taxi), but the MTR station is less than a ten-minute walk away, and for the price this one stands as a very clear competitor. Listed rates from

HK$2,700.

> Address: 133 Leighton Rd, Causeway Bay
> Phone: 3477 6886
> Website: hongkong.lansonplace.com
> Email: enquiry.lphk@lansonplace.com

Grand Hyatt Hong Kong (香港君悅酒店)

With a name like the Grand Hyatt Hong Kong and leg-weakeningly sweet views of Victoria Harbour, it's hard to imagine not enjoying your stay here. But if you're still too uptight to enjoy this sparkling hotel, take a few hours in their renowned Plateau Spa to ease your bones. Rooms from HK$3,500-HK$4,600.

> Address: 1 Harbour Rd, Wan Chai
> Phone: 2588 1234
> Website: hongkong.grand.hyatt.com
> Email: hongkong.grand@hyatt.com

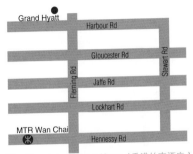

The Excelsior, Hong Kong (香港怡東酒店)

More are found at this splendid four-star; while shopping and entertainment galore is just around the corner. Nerds take note: staying at a hotel named The Excelsior might get you promoted to starship captain. From HK$2,180.

> Address: 281 Gloucester Rd, Causeway Bay
> Phone: 2894 8888
> Website: www.mandarinoriental.com/excelsior
> Email: exhkg-info@mohg.com

Conrad Hotel (港麗酒店)

Four-star hotels just not your cup of tea? Then cash in those poker chips and pull up a luxurious leather seat at the Conrad, where the five-star's venues and amenities include a swimming pool, a health club and five premium restaurants. From HK$4,000.

> Address: One Pacific Place, 88 Queensway, Central
> Phone: 2521 3838

Four Seasons Hotel Hong Kong (香港四季酒店)

PANDA PICK

What season would you like to experience at one of Hong Kong's most luxurious five-stars? It's not a winter vs summer choice, but what the Four Seasons offers up is even more compelling: rooms with wall-to-wall-window views of Victoria Harbour (or Victoria Peak), two outdoor infinity pools and an enormous 22,000 sq ft spa and a fitness center. Did we mention that this is the only hotel in the world to feature two three-star rated Michelin restaurants? If you can't afford this place consider robbing a bank (just kidding, don't do that). From HK$4,200.

> Address: 8 Finance St, Central
> Phone: 3196 8888
> Website: www.fourseasons.com/hongkong

Mandarin Oriental (文華東方酒店)

The original Mandarin Oriental, the flagship of one of Hong Kong's most prestigious hotel families, was reborn in 2006 after extensive renovations. Now, this awe-inspiring accommodation is back and most definitely in black, and if you think its rockin' attitude only includes an indoor swimming pool and a fitness center, you'd be mistaken. Au contraire, this gem also features the high-flying Michelin three-star restaurant Pierre, named for chef Pierre Gagnaire. From HK$4,000.

Address: 5 Connaught Rd, Central
Phone: 2522 0111
Website: www.mandarinoriental.com.cn/hongkong
Email: mohkg-reservations@mohg.com

Aberdeen

Bridal Tea House Hotel (红茶馆酒店)

A nice, (really) small and cozy hotel, Bridal Tea may be a bit hard to find and a bit far from Hong Kong Island's action, but the friendly staff, quiet locale and good little eateries nearby make it a great inexpensive choice. From HK$455.

Address: 150 Aberdeen Main Rd
Phone: 2780 6113
Website: www.bthhotel.com/BTH/en/Home
Email: enquiries@bthhotel.com

Ovolo Hotel

▶ PANDA PICK

One word with one punctuation mark desribes the Ovolo – Superb! This internationally renowned upper mid-range chain has several branches in Hong Kong, but we'd have to say that the one in Aberdeen is the best. Mixing elements from Aberdeen's old fishing village history and modern technology and comfort, the Ovolo satisfies all. The rooms with a stunning panoramic view of the ocean are the cherry on top. From HK$900.

Address: 100 Shek Pai Wan Rd (Near the intersection of Aberdeen Praya Rd)
Phone: 2165 1000
Website: www.ovolohotels.com/hotels/100SPW/en

Cheung Chau Island

Occasionally and especially during peak season, kiosks around the ferry dock on Cheung Chau offer studio apartments for short term rent. Other than that your options are pretty limited to just a few places.

Warwick Hotel

It's a little rough around the edges, but this big hotel has recently gone through some renovations, and the rooms with a sea view are wonderful. Rooms start at HK$1,000.

Address: Cheung Chau Sports Rd, Tung Wan Beach
Phone: 2981 0081
Website: www.warwickhotel.com.hk

Cheung Chau B&B

The rooms here vary greatly in size, so definitely check before making a deal. It's located near the Pak Tai Temple, and the rooftop terrace alone is worth a stay here and provides a great place to watch sunrises and sunsets. Rooms from HK$500.

Address: 12-14 Tung Wan Rd
Phone: 2986 9990
Website: www.bbcheungchau.com.hk

Lamma Island

Jackson Property Agency

Cheap studios and apartments can be rented through Jackson. All come equipped with a TV, private bathroom, microwave and fridge. Rooms start at HK$380 during the week but can hit HK$880 on weekends.

Address: 15 Main St, Yung Shue Wan
Phone: 2982 0606

Man Lai Wah Hotel

Some of the small but cozy double-beds here have balconies, and all are immaculate. Find it just ahead from the pier. From HK$350, up to HK$800 on weekends.

www.pandaguides.com

Address: 2 Po Wah Garden, Yung Shue Wan
Phone: 2982 0220
Email: manlaiwahhotel@yahoo.com

Concerto Inn

This little beachside boutique hotel is lovely, but it's a bit far removed, so we suggest staying here only if you need to get away from the city. They have a nice afternoon tea service. Rooms HK$800-1,280.

Address: 28 Hung Shing Yeh Beach, Yung Shue Wan
Phone: 2982 1668
Website: www.concertoinn.com

Sunrise Holiday Resort

A down to earth hotel with reasonable prices and a so-quiet-you-could-hear-a-pin-drop atmosphere. Rooms come equppied with TVs, comfortable beds and the basics; be sure to request one with the view of the ocean. Rooms from HK$500.

Address: Ground Floor, 15A Main St
Yung Shue Wan. Just a few minutes' walk from the ferry dock.
Phone: 2982 0606, 2982 2626
Website: www.lammaresort.com
Email: info@lammaresort.com

Lantau Island

There are many places by the pier that offer apartments for rent, especially during the busy tourist season. Lantau also includes the towns of Mui O, Ngong Ping and Tai O, so if you're looking to dive into one of these places, the below options have your name written all over them.

Also remember that Hong Kong International Airport is situated on Lantau Island. If you're popping in town for a short trip, there are numerous hotels to choose from around the airport. Three of the many convenient hotels with shuttle buses to the airport are the **Novotel Citygate Hong Kong**, the **Regal Airport Hotel** and the **Hong Kong Sky City Marriott Hotel**.

Other good options on the island include the following:

Ngong Ping SG Davis Hostel

On the west end of the kitschy Ngong Ping village, this hostel sits within earshot of the Tian Tan Big Buddha and is the best place on the island to stay if you want to get up and catch the sunrise from Lantau Peak. You need to be a HKYHA/HI cardholder (or be a guest

of one) to stay here, and the place is only open Friday to Monday. Around HK$110.

Address: Follow the signs from the paved road to the left of the Ngong Ping bus terminus
Phone: 2985 5610
Website: www.yha.org.hk

Espace Elastique

A small B&B with a fantastic breakfast and – get this – a rooftop jacuzzi! Book well in advanced because the rooms fill up faster than the speed of light. Rooms start at HK$600.

Address: 57 Kat Hing St, Tai O
Phone: 2985 7002
Website: www.espaceelastique.com

Tai O Heritage Hotel

Housed in an old police station and just a ten-minute walk from the old town, this new hotel passes all the requirements needed for a fine and comfortable stay. There's only nine rooms, so book ahead. Rooms start at HK$1,300

Address: Shek Tsai Po St. Tai O
Website: www.taioheritagehotel.com

Silvermine Beach Resort

If you don't judge a book by its cover then you shouldn't judge the Silvermine by its appearance. The rooms are surprisingly tidy for what you may expect, and the ones with views of the ocean always keep it fresh with a salty sea breeze. Rooms start at HK$1,100.

Address: Silvermine Bay Beach, Mui Wo
Phone: 2810 0111
Website: www.silvermineresort.com

Mui Wo

see Lantau Island

Ngong Ping

see Lantau Island

Repulse Bay

De Ricou Apartments

There aren't many options in exclusive Repulse Bay, but this one is right on the beach, lavishly decorated, clean and has tremendous views of the ocean. With these luxury apartments you get what you pay for, however, so expect to pay more than HK$2,000 per night. As the name suggests, they are actual apartments, so you'll find a a kitchen in case you don't want to dine at the two luxurious onsite restaurants. The minimum stay is two months.

Address: 109 Repulse Bay Rd
Phone: 2292 2879
Website: www.therepulsebay.com/en/apartment_2.asp

Sai Kung Town

Ling & Don's Guesthouse

Lovely Sai Kung Town is all about guesthouses; don't expect Holiday Inns or big international chains here. Ling & Don's cozy guestroom sleeps up to three, and though it's a bit hard to find, they'll happily pick you up at the bus terminal. Definitely call and book your room in advance. Rooms start at HK$500.

Phone: 6501 0119

Sha Tin

Hyatt Regency Sha Tin (沙田凱悅酒店)

My, oh my, is the Hyatt Regency Sha Tin a good looking hotel. And if you'd like to stay for the night and find out what it's like inside do we have some good news for you! This hotel, as far as amenities go, would easily rank among the Splurge options in Kowloon (there's a spa, heated pool, restaurant and even long-stay apartments available), but because of the location 20 minutes from the city and with few services in the area, you don't have to "splurge" to charm this classy hotel. Rooms start at HK$1,000.

Address: 18 Chak Cheung St, Sha Tin (next to University MTR Exit B)
Phone: 3723 1234

Website: www.hongkong.shatin.hyatt.com
Email: hongkong.shatin@hyatt.com

Stanely

Stanely Oriental Hotel

A little on the steep side with rooms starting at HK$15,000 (per week), this new boutique hotel is right on the beach and very modern. It's very nice and well managed, and the staff is delightful, but it's only good for travelers spending at least a week here.

Address: 90B Stanely Main St
Phone: 2899 1688
Website: www.stanleyorientalhotel.com.hk

Tai O

see Lantau Island

Tsuen Wan

Panda Hotel

Though it has no affiliation with this guidebook, Panda Hotel is one of the most comfortable places to stay in Tsuen Wan. It's close to the Tsuen Wan Metro Station, and there are regular shuttle buses heading towards Tsim Sha Tsui. All the rooms are tidy and clean, and the fitness center, pool and care are all far above average. The sea food buffet is a "reel" catch too. Rooms start at HK$2,500.

Address: 3 Tsuen Wah St
Phone: 2409 1111
Website: www.pandahotel.com.hk/en/
Email: enquiry@pandahotel.com.hk

Silka Far East Hotel

Just a few steps away from the Tsuen Wan Metro Station, this upper mid-range hotel is perhaps best reserved for the shopaholic since it's close to an array of shopping plazas. There is also a shuttle bus that transports guests to the city center. Rooms start at HK$700.

Address: 135-143 Castle Peak Rd
Phone: 2406 9090
Website: www.silkahotels.com/fareast

The Dorsett

A great outdoor swimming pool, gym and spa make the Dorsett a real hit. It's aimed more towards the business crowds, and the stylish lobby bar is an excellent place to grab a drink and a bite. Rooms from HK$880.

Address: 659 Castle Peak Rd
Phone: 3996 6666
Website: www.dorsetthotels.com/hongkong/tsuenwan
Email: info.tsuenwan@dorsetthotels.com

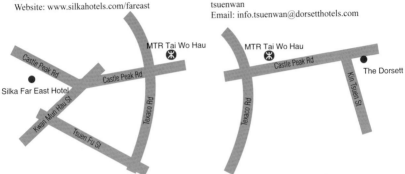

Eating

Foodies take heart: Hong Kong is serious about good food and great ambiance, and there is a broad spectrum of culinary treasures just waiting to be explored.

Hong Kong may be one of the most expensive cities in the world, but when it comes to eating, there are infinite options no matter your budget. From local Hong Kongese cuisine to international fare, nearly every country and continent is represented here. So whether you want to try out native dishes or expand your palate, there is something in Hong Kong for you and your taste buds.

Restaurants in Hong Kong compete in a "here today, gone today" atmosphere, meaning that some places recommended to you by a friend – or even what we have listed here – could very well be gone by the time you arrive in the city. For a restaurant to remain open, it must offer something noteworthy while also staying ahead of the pack, which makes the choices in Hong Kong range from time-perfected traditional dishes to cutting edge fusions and world-class culinary trend setters. For a visitor, this is one of the greatest benefits to the city as every taste is catered to with dazzling gusto. So, enough talk – dive right in and devour it all if you can!

Eating in Hong Kong can truly go from bargain basement to astronomical prices with the turn of a street corner, but be aware that the majority of restaurants will be a bit on the pricier side. If you're looking for more budget eating besides what we have mentioned in this chapter, head to markets like Temple Street (pg 71) or Ladies' Street

(pg 80) and grab some grub from the street stalls.

Cantonese Cuisine

Hong Kong is brimming with food from all corners of the world, but if you want to eat locally you are in for an ocean full of goodness. Cantonese cuisine – also known as Guangdong cuisine – is the dominant cooking style in Hong Kong and is considered local fare, and in Western eyes food does not get more quintessentially Chinese than this. It was Guangdong natives who catapulted Chinese food onto the radar of the world, following their adventurous maritime tendencies to establish a galaxy of Chinatowns in major cities around the globe. Because many Chinese expats in places like New York, San Francisco, Toronto, London and Paris are Cantonese, it is their fantastic cooking that has become globally synonymous with Chinese food.

Guangdong cuisine, known as *Yue Cai* in Mandarin, is one of the most popular of China's Eight Culinary Traditions, and it is as impressively popular around China as it is around the rest of the world. An especially popular Chinese saying goes, "Be born in Suzhou, live in Hangzhou, eat in Guangzhou, and die in Liuzhou." It's said that Suzhou people are especially good looking, Hangzhou is one of the most livable cities in China, Guangzhou cooking is unmatched, and Liuzhou wood is the best to build a coffin from. You will certainly be doing plenty of eating while in the area, and now you know how lucky you are to be able to chow down in one of the country's most renowned foodie destinations.

So what makes Cantonese cuisine so much better than the rest, anyway?

Fresh is better

While the opinions on why Cantonese dishes are so good will vary depending on who you ask, one huge reason everyone can agree on is the cuisine's characteristic obsession with freshness. Restaurants lined with tanks of live fish, mollusks and shrimp certainly attest to this fact, and any seafood fan will be in heaven picking and choosing their meals straight out of the water. But it's the other half of the story that really makes all Cantonese cuisine the talk of the Chinese culinary world, and that is cooking style.

Mainland China has a staggering amount of delicious food, but certainly the biggest complaint dished out to Mainland fare is that it is "too heavy." Whether it's too salty, swimming in oil or drowning in sauce, the greatest shortcoming of many Mainland dishes is the heavy hand dealt in the cooking, and the sluggish feeling diners get after big meals. It's no surprise, then, that Cantonese chefs and their steaming, quick-frying attitudes are looked highly upon. One of the greatest marks of Guangdong dishes is their light use of oil, restrained use of seasoning, and utmost effort to create delicate and balanced flavors that enhance the natural aroma and taste of the foods they cook, rather than "reflavor" them with sauces and salt. Flash and stir-frying carry the day, as does steaming, and deep-fried foods are a rare sight. The result is a style of cooking that brings out the best flavors of any ingredient through a subtle but perfectly coaxed harmony, leaving the diner with a feeling of energy and deep satisfaction, instead of needing a three-hour nap.

A tradition of top chefs

The tragic Cultural Revolution that drove so many from Mainland China during the turbulent 1960s ironically gave Hong Kong many cultural gifts, and among the martial artists, poets, philosophers and painters who found refuge in Hong Kong at the time, many of China's best culinary masters also came to escape the chaos. While Cantonese cuisine has a history longer than the CCP, the influx of chefs seeking to escape the tyrannical regime took Hong Kong's local dishes up several notches, and now, a new generation has grown up under the watchful eye of these masters to once again take their teachers' creations to the next level. With so many world class chefs in one place, it's only natural that the local culinary tradition continues to get better with age.

Catch of the day

If variety is the spice of life then life in the world of Cantonese food is hot as fire; just about anything is fair game for food in this neck of the woods. Guangdong cuisine draws greatly from its coastal waters, making good use of seafood and sea veggies, and just about anything else that moves through the water of its own volition has found its way onto a dinner plate at some point. From delicacies like abalone to endless varieties of fish and creatures with more legs than eyes, Guangdong's rich waters make eating all the better.

The strange creatures of Yue Cai do not only come from the ocean either. Be ready for some very bizarre non-marine dishes, such as those made from gizzards, fungus (truffles are big in Hong Kong) and certain insects. As Prince Philip not-so-eloquently put it in 1986, "If it has four legs and is not a chair, if it has two wings and flies but is not an airplane, and if it swims and is not a submarine, the Cantonese will eat it." While his somewhat tasteless words seriously lacked in the cultural awareness and sensitivity departments, they do show how shocking some of the creations can be to outsiders. So pick up those chopsticks and make sure you have a bit more perspective on new things than the prince.

Finally, remember that great chefs stress a dish's presentation as much as anything. Hong Kong chefs certainly know this, and their superb skills in combination with the magnificent assortment of creatures and veggies means that your eyes will have as much of a feast as your stomach (and that's half of what makes a good dish great).

Below are a few Hong Kong specialties you might want to try out. Most of the ones listed better suit the Western palate, but hey, even the most adventurous eaters will enjoy them.

Black Sesame Tong Yuen (黑芝麻湯圓)

Filled with either red bean paste or sweet black sesame, these rice balls are topped off with chopped nuts and are great for breakfast or a dessert. Two thumbs up!

Milk Tea (奶茶)

You can find milk tea anywhere in Hong Kong, from the local 7-11 to the more pricey restaurants in the city. This delicious treat is

Black Sesame Tong Yuen

Milk Tea

Sweet Rolls

Pineapple Bun

Portuguese Egg Tarts

essentially brewed black tea with condensed milk added. It definitely beats Starbucks.

Sweet Rolls (甜甜圈)

Sliced, toasted, buttered bread served hot? Sign us up! This is probably the best bargain around Hong Kong and one of the reasons they have remained so popular among locals and foreigners alike.

Pineapple Bun (菠蘿包)

Known by the locals as "*bor lor bao*," the hard, flaky outside looks something like a pineapple, while the inside is something else entirely. They can be filled with barbecued meat, slices of fruit, or even custard, so pick accordingly, and remember that the sweet ones are tasty, but are basically diabetes in a bun. Find them in local bakeries.

Meat Kebabs (肉串)

When it comes to street meat in Hong Kong, you simply pick your poison as there's something for everyone (except vegetarians). BBQ pork, roasted duck, and marinated chicken are just some of the options that can be found at vendors all over the city. Perfect for snacking on the go, this is your go to food when in a pinch.

Portuguese Egg Tarts (葡式蛋撻)

Known locally as *dan tat*, these baked shells of egg custard richness are simple and popular, and we dare you not to buy them by the half dozen (or dozen). They're good hot or at room temperature and can be found at bakeries all over the city, as well as in restaurants.

Potato Chips (薯片)

There are many varieties available in Hong Kong. From firecracker lobster flavored chips to Mong Kok sausage and roast ox. The bags are all very interesting as well, so you might want to pick some up and keep the bag as a souvenir.

Dim Sum (點心)

Canton's signature dish is dim sum; no doubt you've heard of it. Mandarin speakers call it *dian xin*, literally meaning "to touch the heart," and the Cantonese equally refer to dim sum time as *yum cha*, which means "drink tea." If you haven't had dim sum before, you're in for a treat. Carted around on cute little trolleys, the dishes, which range from spring rolls to pork-filled buns and *guotie* fried dumplings (and about a thousand others), are usually kept in steamers, and patrons are encouraged to pluck them up and devour them when they like what they see.

NORTHERN HONG KONG ISLAND & KOWLOON

The northern side of Hong Kong Island (HKI) and Kowloon have the largest variety of food, cooking and regional styles of anywhere in the Hong Kong area. Plus they're both connected to each other by metro, so skipping back and forth between the two is easy. With so many establishments from all over the world, it can sometimes be surprisingly tricky to find a restaurant of a particular regional style, including something authentically Hong Kongese. That's why, for

our restaurant listings of these two downtown areas, we have organized everything based on regional cuisine, making it a breeze to find your best options on a day when you're dying for dim sum or that romantic night that is just screaming Italian.

When you find yourself somewhere outside of North HKI or Kowloon in one of the city's outskirts like Aberdeen on South HKI, a town in the New Territories, or a fishing village, just zip on past these listings to pages 202 – 211 for our favorites.

Local Cantonese

Budget

Hing Kee Restaurant (興記菜館)

The Yau Ma Tei area is known for its traditional look and feel, and nowhere is that more apparent than in the cuisine. At Hing Kee, you will have far more options to choose from since the food is so affordable. Eat like the locals and people watch as you chow down on their stir-fries or one of their clay pot dishes. It's gonna be crowded, so be prepared to wait a while.

Address: 15-19 Temple St, Yau Ma Tei, Kowloon
Phone: 2384 3647

Tsim Chai Kee Noodle (沾仔記)

Known for their wonton noodles, this HK tradition has now expanded to include two restaurants in Central. You won't be waiting long before you have a table, and once you order their noodles you will know why they have remained a popular fixture among the locals for over a decade. Note: their second location is at 153 Queen's Road in Central.

Address: 98 Wellington St, Central, HKI
Phone: 2850 6471

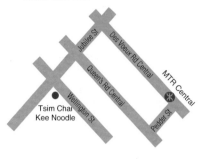

Luk Yu Tea House (陸羽茶室)

If you want Hong Kong at its most traditional, then Luk Yu Tea House is just the spot to go for early evening dim sum or the BBQ pork bun. Running strong for 80 years, Luk Yu Tea House is begging you to come take in the décor and then take out the taro cake for dessert.

Address: 24-26 Stanley St, Central, HKI
Phone: 2523 5464

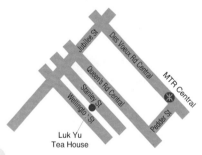

Bo Innovation (魔廚)

Interested in the traditional with a twist? Then Bo Innovation is for you, home to original dishes injected with a culinary fusion that keeps foodies coming back again and again. And then…there are the prawn

dumplings. Oh my, those magnificent prawn dumplings…

Address: Shop 13, 2/F, J. Residence, 60 Johnston Rd, Wan Chai, HKI
Phone: 2850 8371
Website: www.boinnovation.com

Lin Heung Tea House (蓮香樓)

If you're the shy type, then Lin Heung may not be for you, since you will more than likely have to share your table with a complete stranger. That's how packed this 80-year old restaurant usually gets, and for good reason, too. They make some of the best Cantonese dinner in the area, so good in fact it made Anthony Bourdain's top eats list. Great for dim sum.

Address: 160-164 Wellington St, Central, HKI
Phone: 2544 2556

Mid-range

Maxim's Palace (美心皇宮)

People start lining up for this place early because you've got to queue up to get to their dim sum – it's that popular. City Hall Maxim's is loud, with the food pushed around in traditional trolleys, and we're sure you'll love the experience.

Address: 3/F, Hong Kong City Hall (Lower Block), 1 Edinburgh Place, Central, HKI
Phone: 2521 1303

Din Tai Fung (鼎泰豐)

Dumplings, dumplings, dumplings! This is the place for dumplings and *xiaolongbao,* and it's well worth the line that you'll more than likely have to wait in. Din Tai Fung comes highly recommended, we're sure you'll return if you stay in Hong Kong longer than a week. Be sure to try the fried spinach as well!

Address: Shop 130, 3/F, Silvercord, 30 Canton Rd, Tsim Sha Tsui, Kowloon
Phone: 2730 6928
Website: www.dintaifung.com.hk

Victoria City (女皇城)

If you come to Hong Kong during the right months (Jun-Aug), then you may be able to taste one of the region's delicacies – *wong yau hai,* or yellow oil crabs. The rice rolls with XO sauce are also worth gnoshing on.

Address: 2/F, Sun Hung Kai Centre, 30 Harbour Rd, Wan Chai, HKI
Phone: 2827 9938

Yung Kee Restaurant (鏞記酒家)

Situated right near the area's most popular destinations for tourists and foreigners, Yung Kee doesn't just assume that you'll stop in and try their 1,000-year-old eggs, roast goose, or smoked pork, they'll seduce you in and keep you coming back with excellent service and succulent dishes that have been a staple in Hong Kong for over 70 years.

Address: 32-40 Wellington St, Central, HKI
Phone: 2522 1624
Website: www.yungkee.com.hk

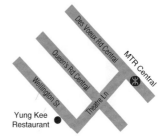

Fung Shing Restaurant (鳳城酒家)

This little "restaurant that could" is known for its traditional Shundé District cuisine, offering fried prawn and lettuce wraps stuffed with minced quail meat. Come early and stay late, because this North Point staple is one that's here to stay.

Address: 62-68 Java Rd, North Point, HKI
Phone: 2578 4898

Dong (東宮)

You should come to Dong's just for the bragging right of having had their so-called "forest of fungus." There are also other traditional dishes on the menu, as well as seafood soups for the less adventurous.

Address: Arcade Level 2, Miramar Hotel, 118-130 Nathan Rd, Yau Ma Tei, Kowloon
Phone: 2315 5166

Kin's Kitchen (留家廚房)

Classic Cantonese cuisine with a modern face is the best way to describe this restaurant, which offers delicious smoked chicken, arguably their most popular dish. Open for lunch and dinner.

Address: 9 Tsing Fung St, HKI
Phone: 2571 0913

Vbest Tea House (致好茶館)

Family owned and operated, Vbest is known for its MSG-free food, which is a welcome change of pace for this region of the world. The walk up the steep hill to reach this restaurant is the perfect way to work up an appetite for the awesome rewards you will eat inside.

Address: 17 Elgin St, SoHo, HKI
Phone: 3104 0890

Splurge

Lung King Heen (龍景軒)

The Cantonese food here is great, equal in both taste and presentation. And while it may not be the best in the city, it was still the first Chinese restaurant in Hong Kong to receive three Michelin stars, so that alone should be enough for you to swing down and try their signature steamed lobster and scallop dumplings. Better get here early.

Address: Four Seasons Hotel, 8 Finance St, Central, HKI

Phone: 3196 8888
Website: www.fourseasons.com/hongkong

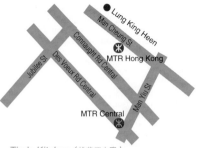

Tim's Kitchen (桃花源小廚)

You might want to make a reservation here before you come, because Tim's Kitchen's popularity has spread like wildfire. Their crab claws, king prawns, and Yunnan ham should not be missed. If you prefer something more exotic, expect some higher prices, but there are plenty of affordable options on the menu.

Address: Shop A & 1/F, 84-90, Bonham Strand, Sheung Wan, HKI
Phone: 2543 5919
Website: www.timskitchen.com.hk

Yin Yang (鴛鴦飯店)

Self-taught head chef Margaret Xu describes her food as "New Hong Kong," creating culinary symbiosis with organic vegetables and old-style cooking tools. How popular is Xu's take on traditional Hong Kong cuisine? You'll need to make reservations days in advance or call in for take-away.

Address: 18 Ship St, Wan Chai, HKI
Phone: 2866 0688
Website: www.yinyang.hk

China Regional

Budget

Crystal Jade La Mian Xiaolongbao (翡翠拉麵小籠包)

Get stuffed full of meat dumplings and other dishes in a rapid-fire style service that will have your head spinning. There will be a line, but you won't be in it long before you're devouring some of the best snacks in town.

Address: Shop 2018-2020, 2/F, IFC Mall 2, 8 Finance St, Central, HKI
Phone: 2295 3811

Sing Heung Yuen (勝香園)

Revered for their *dai pai dong* (outside food stall) and their tomato broths, Sing Heung Yuen has quite a following and is one of the most popular restaurants near Sheung Wan station. If you're in the mood for some fast food like quick noodles in beef and tomato, sandwiches or coffee and soft drinks, this is the place to go when you're out in Sheung Wan.

Address: 2 Shop Mee Lun St, Central, HKI (Sheung Wan MTR)
Phone: 2544 8368

Spring Deer Restaurant (鹿鳴春飯店)

You will feel like you've been time-warped back to the '70s when you step into Spring Deer, but this old style look comes with a history of great food that is well known in Hong Kong. Their Peking Roast Duck is one of their more famous dishes, and the time it takes to cook is more than worth the wait. The service is just as impeccable as the menu offered.

Address: 42 Mody Rd, Tsim Sha Tsui, Kowloon
Phone: 2366 4201

Ho Hung Kee Congee and Noodle Wonton Shop (何洪記粥麵專家)

If you're in Hong Kong, then it is an unwritten edict that you must experience congee (a type of rice porridge) at least once. There are so many varieties here to try out you may find that you can't get enough of it. And with prices this cheap, who could?

Address: 2 Sharp St East, Causeway Bay, HKI
Phone: 2577 6558

Mak's Noodle (麥奀雲吞麵世家)

Sometimes the key to good food lies in its simplicity. And this family-owned restaurant is well known throughout the city for their standout wontons and noodles. If you happen to be around Central, it is one of the best places to stop in for a quick bite.

Address: 77 Wellington St, Central, HKI
Phone: 2854 3810

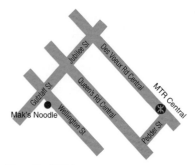

Wang Fu (王府)

Another restaurant of many that line Wellington Street, Wang Fu sells handmade dumplings that are an absolute must if you're in the area. You'll be back for their dishes, including their handmade noodles.

Address: 98-102 Wellington St, Central, HKI
Phone: 2121 8006

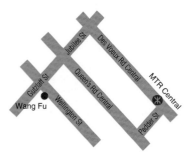

Po Lin Yuen Vegetarian Restaurant (寶蓮 苑素食)

Vegetarians, take heart: Po Lin Yuen serves up everything you could dream of and more (think radish pudding and mushroom dumplings). It won't set you back much in the way of dollars to find out if you have a new favorite dish.

Address: G/F 308 Queen's Rd West, Western District, HKI
Phone: 2517 1178

Tak Cheong Noodle (德昌魚蛋粉)

Tak Cheong's specializes in fish balls and flat rice noodles soaking in a tasty broth. It's one of the Tin Hau area's most popular lower-priced spots.

Address: 75 Electric Rd, Tin Hau, HKI
Phone: 2510 8783

Mid-range

Golden Valley (駿景軒)

Owned by local celebrity Albert Yeung, Golden Valley is known for having the best Sichuanese hot pot in town. You may be dining alongside some of the biggest pop stars on the scene, so keep your eyes peeled.

Address: 1/F, Emperor Hotel, 1A Wang Tak St, HKI
Phone: 2961 3330

Peking Garden (北京樓)

Come to Peking Garden for their Pekingese noodles or Hunan ham served in honey sauce. If you come in the evening, you might catch their nightly handmade noodles presentation. Bring your camera!

Address: 16-20 Chater Rd, Central, HKI
Phone: 2526 6456

Wu Kong Shanghai (滬江大飯店)

Good Shanghai and Chinese regional cuisine at bargain prices brings the locals back again and again. Wu Kong's Peking Duck, braised shredded eels, and pigeon in wine sauce are also big hits.

Address: 27 Nathan Rd, Kowloon
Phone: 2366 7244
Website: www.wukong.com.hk

Tim Ho Wan

Two words: pork buns. This is what Tim Ho Wan is most known for. Well, that and the quick service, which is a good thing because this place never slows down. We must say that the dim sum is pretty darn good too!

Address: Shop 72, G/F, Olympian City 2, 18 Hoi Ting Rd, Tai Kok Tsui, Kowloon
Phone: 2332 2896

Ser Wong Fun (蛇王芬飯店)

For those with a taste for the exotic, Ser Wong Fun has something on their menu for you…like snake meat! This is the dish Ser Wong is famous for, so even if you don't want to eat it, you might as well order it and take a photo or two to impress (or disgust) your mother back home.

Address: 30 Cochrane St, Central, HKI
Phone: 2543 1032

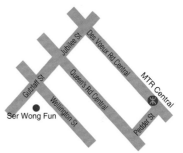

Tai Ping Koon (太平館餐廳)

It's said that this restaurant has been around since the 1930s, and you'll tast the tradition when you try the souffle and the chicken wings cooked in soy sauce. Their rice noodles cooked with beef are fantastic, but steer clear of the US pork chop (there are better items to be had). Service is generally a cut above and you'll probably need reservations.

Address: 40 Granville Rd, Tsim Sha Tsui, Kowloon
Phone: 2721 3559

Hunan Garden (洞庭樓)

Spicy! Get your extra shot of spice right here! Hunan food is known for its liberal use of peppers, so if you come here be prepared for a fire in your mouth. Hunan Garden goes the extra mile, serving up dishes like their shredded pork and chili, braised bean curd, and Hunan ham with pancakes. Your belly is going to love you.

Address: Shop 1302, 13/F, Times Square Food Forum, Causeway Bay, HKI
Phone: 2506 9288

Kau Kee Restaurant (九記牛腩)

A little Westernized but still very Chinese, Kau Kee serves up its classic smoked pomfret and roast pigeon for crowds of diners and has been doing so for decades. Try their famous and mouthwatering souffles. Locals rave about the beef brisket, which is the reason most people come to Kau Kee. Well, that and the ambience. Also suggested is the curry with red noodle. They stay open late and are the perfect option after a night out on the town.

Address: 21 Gough St, Central, HKI
Phone: 2815 0123; 2850 5967

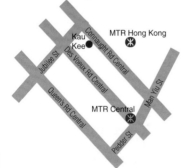

Chuen Cheung Kui (泉章居)

Chuen Cheung Kui boasts dishes that need an extra dose of bravery to try (like gizzard soup and stomach tidbit). You may find yourself

staying clear of these delicacies and trying their pulled chicken instead.

Address: 489 Hennessy Rd, Causeway Bay, HKI
Phone: 2577 3833

Ba Yi Restaurant (巴依餐廳)

Braised, boiled, fried, grilled and "other" is how Ba Yi serves up their mutton, complete with herbs that bring out the flavor. Open for lunch and dinner, this is one of the best places to eat on the northwest side of the island for Chinese food.

Address: 43 Water St, Sai Ying Pun, Central, HKI
Phone: 2484 9981

Mun Nam Restaurant (閩南小食館)

Jelly sandworm terrine anyone? If you're up for it, it's here. This place serves up dishes not found in most places in Hong Kong, like their Fujianese noodles. Dig in to their authenticity and seriously try to build up the courage to try the terrine.

Address: 25 Kam Ping St, North Point, HKI
Phone: 2807 2168

One Harbour Road (港灣壹號)

Beautiful in design, impeccable in menu, and with service that cannot be found anywhere else on the island, One Harbour Road is an option that is hard to beat. The pork belly is an excellent choice, as is the bean curd (tofu) and the Peking Duck. Be careful of the fish, however, which is sold by the pound and can surprise folks by its price in the end. For those on a budget, set lunches are available at a decent price.

Address: 7-8/F, Grand Hyatt Hong Kong, 1 Harbour Rd, Wan Chai, HKI
Phone: 2588 1234; 2584 7722

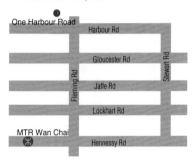

Chiu Chow Garden (潮庭)

They are known at Chiu Chow for their seafood dishes and their selection of sole fish. Try the pie stuffed with shredded chicken and/or pork sauce and the foie gras. Along with northern Guangdong dishes, this one also has good dim sum.

Address: Shop 202, 2/F, Hutchison House, 10 Harcourt Rd, Central, HKI
Phone: 2536 0833

Wing Lai Yuen (詠藜園)

Well known among Hong Kong locals, Wing Lai Yuen serves up great wonton chicken in a traditional clay pot of great chili broth, as well as other Sichuan dishes. You'll also have a chance to try out your Cantonese because no one speaks English.

Address: 15-17 Fung Tak Rd, Wong Tai Sin, Kowloon

Phone: 2726 3818
Website: www.winglaiyuen.com.hk

San Xi Lou (三希樓)

One of Hong Kong's best Sichuanese restaurants, San Xi Lou will tingle all your senses with its excellent range of spices and flavors. It's the favorite of the local Sichuan expat crowd, and that's more than enough to tell you it's legit.

Address: 7/F, Coda Plaza, 51 Garden Rd, Wan Chai, HKI
Phone: 2838 8811

Splurge

Yi Jiang Nan (憶江南)

Yi specializes in Shanghainese cuisine

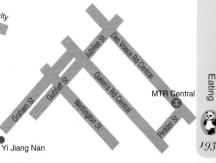

presented in stellar fashion. With fresh ingredients, excellent veggie and meat dishes, and a hip Asian interior, this place is the perfect marriage of good food, great décor, and unmatched ambiance.

Address: 33-35 Staunton Rd, Soho, Central, HKI
Phone: 2136 0886

Hong Zhou Restaurant (杭州酒家)

Zhejiang cooking is considered a rarified delicacy that few restaurants can undertake to brilliance, but Hong Zhou is an exception! They serve up a select menu that is one of the critical darlings of the Hong Kong culinary scene. Depending on your hunger, your bill could be reasonable or astronomical.

Address: 1/F, Chinachem Johnston Plaza, 178-188 Johnston Rd, Wan Chai, HKI
Phone: 2591 1898

Western & International

If you find yourself craving some food from back home, you have plenty of options in Hong Kong. But you will also more than likely have to pay more for that privilege. That being said, your options are varied and the restaurants are all top quality.

Budget

Chungking & Mirador Mansions

The adventure of staying at the Chungking and Mirador Mansions goes far beyond a place to lay your head at the end of the day. Besides bargain shopping and the general adventure of life, you can also scare up some delicious budget fare here, most of which comes from the Indian subcontinent, including Indian and Pakistani food. Unlike almost every other eatery in town, bargaining can be done at the plethora of holes-in-the-wall and small restaurants. Prices are already

cheap – a combo platter of rice or bread, meat or veggies and a drink should run around HK$80 – but if you have a good attitude and ask nicely, it's possible to knock five to ten bucks off the quoted price. The food here is as authentic as it gets, and these places can be great spots to chill with some chai tea and chat with the affable owners.

Address: 36-44 Nathan Rd (Chungking), 58-62 Nathan Rd (Mirador), Tsim Sha Tsui, Kowloon

Mid-range

Café Causette

One of the great things about Causette is their lunch specials available during the week. Make a reservation to avoid the crowds and you too will be able to boast about their great food. One of the go-to places for lunch (or even breakfast for their omelets) in Central.

Address: Mandarin Oriental Hotel, 5 Connuaght Rd, Central, HKI
Phone: 2825 4005

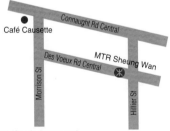

Goldfinch (金雀餐廳)

Sometimes change is not a good thing. Case in point: Goldfinch has been a fundamental part of Hong Kong Island since the '60s and not much has changed, which includes the great food and service. Maybe they should change the mediocre steaks though...

Address: 13-15 Lan Fong Rd, Causeway Bay, HKI
Phone: 2577 7981

Hennessy Rd
Yee Wo St
Percival St
Lee Garden Rd
Pak Sha Road
Goldfinch

Café Renaissance (萬麗咖啡室)

If you're a fan of seafood, this is the right place for you as they offer one of the freshest selections around, from crab legs to whelk, oysters and lobster. Everything is served fresh daily, and you're going to learn a lot about dipping sauces (they have a ton of them and they're all delicious). The downside to Café Renaissance is its lack of windows, ruining what could be excellent views of the Harbour.

Address: M/F, Renaissance Harbour View Hotel, 1 Harbour Rd, Wan Chai, HKI
Phone: 2584 6970

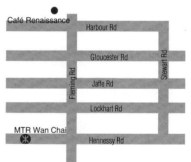

Café Renaissance
Harbour Rd
Gloucester Rd
Stewart Rd
Fleming Rd
Jaffe Rd
Lockhart Rd
MTR Wan Chai
Hennessy Rd

Harbourside Restaurant (港畔餐廳)

When it comes to the Harbourside, it's all about the location and that amazing buffet. Also of note are the ginger skewered chicken and the wide selection of breads to choose

MTR Tsim Sha Tsui
Mody Rd
Chatham Rd South
Mody Rd
Nathan Rd
Salisbury Rd
Salisbury Rd
MTR East Tsim Sha Tsui
Harbourside Restaurant

from. Get a great view of the city and a great bite all rolled up in one. Make reservations to ensure yourself a primo view.

Address: LG/F, InterContinental Hong Kong, 18 Salisbury Rd, Tsim Sha Tsui, Kowloon (Tsim Sha Tsui MTR)
Phone: 2313 2323

Stone's

Sometimes, there's nothing like a good old-fashioned burger stacked with all the fixings. At Stone's, that's exactly what you'll get: real burgers with bacon slices, assorted cheeses, and various sauces to your specifications. And what else? Beer, of course. American and European brews on tap, cold, foaming and waiting to be guzzled. We know you just got hungry!

Address: G/F, China Tower, 1-9 Lin Fa Kung St, West Tai Hang, HKI
Phone: 2570 6858

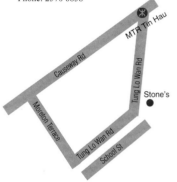

MTR Tin Hau
Causeway Rd
Tung Lo Wan Rd
Stone's
Moreton Terrace
Tung Lo Wan Rd
School St

Three on Canton

For the ultimate Hong Kong/continental buffet and breakfast experience, there is no other choice than Three on Canton. You're also good to go if you're up for only tea and desserts. This one is most definitely worth it for the food and the interior, but expect to pay a lot more for dinner; it teeters on the brink of Splurge.

Haiphong Rd
Three on Canton
Canton Rd
MTR Tsim Sha Tsui
Nathan Rd
Peking Rd

Address: 3/F, Gateway Hotel, Harbour City, 13 Canton Rd, Tsim Sha Tsui, Kowloon
Phone: 2113 7828
Website: www.threeoncanton.com

Oolaa

Gargantuan portions, wide selections from an international menu, and late night hours mean Oolaa is automatically one of the better known restaurants in the busy Central district. You're probably going to be surrounded by many expats – you've been warned.

Address: G/F, Bridges St, Central, HKI (Sheung Wan MTR)
Phone: 2803 2083

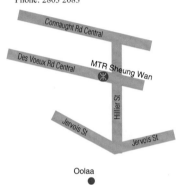

Oolaa

Ammo

Considering the quality of the European fare you'll find under the sexy copper lighting of Ammo, including an excellent menu of tapas, cocktails and Italian mains, it's a little hard to believe the prices are so reasonable. If you want to get pricey here it's possible, but you can easily have a good meal for a mid-range fee, especially if you exclude wine.

Address: Asia Society Hong Kong Centre, 9 Justice Dr, Wan Chai, HKI
Phone: 2537 9888

Ammo

Yamm

Yamm offers a good mix of authentic Chinese and Western dishes. Their tea buffet is excellent for a lazy afternoon, and be sure to try their scones and jam.

Address: Mira Hotel, 118-130 Nathan Rd, Tsim Sha Tsui, Kowloon
Phone: 2315 5111

Watermark

Plopped right on the Star Ferry Pier in Central, Watermark and its solid European selection are complimented superbly by the panoramic views of Victoria Harbour. This spot is almost too perfect for a romantic evening or a cool afternoon lunch. Make sure to try the seafood or the dry aged ribeye.

Address: Shop L, Level P, Central Pier 7, Star Ferry Central, HKI
Phone: 2167 7251

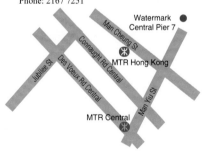

Marriott Café

Probably one of the best bargains for international cuisine in Hong Kong, the Marriott Café's seafood buffet is in a league of its own, and there are drink specials for unlimited wine. Try the abalone – it's a specialty in Hong Kong.

Address: 5/F, JW Marriott Hotel, Pacific Place,

88 Queensway, Admiralty, HKI
Phone: 2810 8366

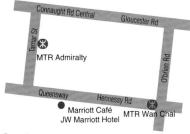

Coast

Convenient and with a reasonable selection of meats, salads, pizzas, burgers and other Western fare, Coast is not the most impressive spot in Hong Kong, but it does have its moments, and it is a decent vegetarian option along Hollywood Road. The interior works like a basic wine bar and – comfortable though it may be – you may have to suffer through some achingly slow service.

Address: 1/F Kinwick Centre, 32 Hollywood Rd, SoHo, HKI
Phone: 2544 5888
Website: www.coast.com.hk

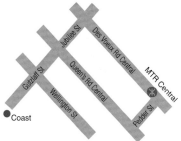

Le Moment

You'll be surprised by this restaurant, hidden somewhat from the main attractions. But once you decide to come here, you will not be disappointed. You can't go wrong with

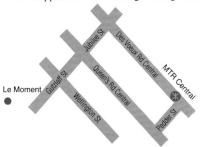

their mouth watering steaks and a bottle of New Zealand imported Pinot Noir.

Address: 55 Peel St, SoHo, HKI
Phone: 3488 0733
Website: www.lemomenthk.com

Mido Café (美都餐室)

Taking it back to classic styles, the interior of Mido is decked out in '50s flare, with antiques strewn throughout the two floors. It's not their curry chicken or pork chops that bring people in, rather the atmosphere and the view. Stop by and find out why it still holds a special place in Kowloon.

Address: G/F, 63 Temple St, Yau Ma Tei, Kowloon
Phone: 2384 6402

Café TOO

The electric ambiance and expansive menu selection (from sushi to Chinese BBQ) means everyone will find something satisfying to eat. Cafe TOO has you covered.

Address: 7/F, Island Shangri-La Hotel, Supreme Court Rd, Central, HKI
Phone: 2820 8571

Grassroots Pantry

Vegetarians and brunch lovers, take note: Grassroots Pantry is one of the few places in Hong Kong that offers an eclectic mix of veggie foods worth salivating over. Just like the name implies, it is almost a secret that only a select few health nuts know about. Detox smoothies, anyone? They're on the menu and perfect for the day after a late night.

Address: 12 Fuk Sau Ln, Sai Ying Pun, Western District, HKI
Phone: 2873 3353
Website: www.grassrootspantry.com

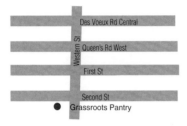

Linguini Fini

▶ PANDA PICK ◀

One of the best budget options for international fare in the city, the casual Italian served up at Linguini Fini rocks a bit too hard for its relatively modest prices, but we're not complaining, and neither will you when you try their home-cured sausages, hand-pulled pasta and local organic veggies. We love the food here, and the art from local graffiti artists along the walls makes it all the more fun.

Address: G/F & 1/F, L Place, 139 Queen's Rd Central, Central, HKI
Phone: 2857 1333
Website: www.linguinifini.com

ToTT's and Roof Terrace

People come here for a few things: the amazing view, the abundance of atmosphere, and the excellent menu. Their Sunday brunches are not bad either. You'd do well to make a reservation beforehand, however, as this place gets pretty packed.

Address: The Excelsior, 281 Gloucester Rd, Causeway Bay, HKI
Phone: 2837 6786

Post 97

If the awesome chargrilled eggplant doesn't sell you, then the duck risotto or spinach and parmesan braised in beer with a truffle mash should probably do the trick. Stop in for brunch, or come in for a late dinner and stick around for some good cocktails.

Address: 1/F, Cosmos Bldg, 9-11 Lan Kwai Fong, Central, HKI
Phone: 2186 1817

Wagyu

Steaks and shakes, come and get'em! Nothing says lovin' (for carnivores, anyway) like a juicy ribeye seasoned with black pepper sauce. Wagyu serves up the quintessential all-American classics as well as other slices of Americana. Wear some baggy clothes because these portions are jumbo-sized.

Address: G/F, 3 The Centrium, 60 Whyndham St, Central, HKI
Phone: 2525 8805
Website: www.wagyu.com.hk

Café Marco (馬哥孛羅咖啡廳)

There's something for everyone here, from the international to the local. The wide selection of entrees on the menu and the speedy service will have your head spinning. All hail their specialty: the Asian breakfast.

Address: 1/F, Marco Polo Hong Kong, 3 Canton Rd, Tsim Sha Tsui, Kowloon
Phone: 2113 3912

Malaysian Chinese Restaurant (馬華餐廳)

Offering up a great selection of Malay cuisine, their satay and chicken curry are our favorites. If you want to be sure to get a table, you might want to make a reservation. Check out their wine menu as well for a great list of imported reds.

Address: G/F, 12 Jordan Rd, Kowloon
Phone: 2367 3552; 2366 5302

Happy Valley Bar & Grill

Situated directly next to the famous Happy

Valley Race Course, the Happy Valley Bar & Grill should be on your list of places to experience before possibly betting on the tracks. You won't have to bet on the food here, however. Come for American food served up with beer and desserts that will give you enough energy to rock a few hours at the track. A great place for a group outing.

Address: 38 Wong Nai Chung Rd, Wan Chai, HKI
Phone: 2250 5722

Feast

Feast is a great place to... well, feast! And you can do so at bargain prices (for Hong Kong). Their buffet includes appetizers and desserts, with an expansive Asian section thrown in for good measure. Try their Tandoori chicken tikka or the eggs Benedict.

Address: 29 Taikoo Shing Rd, HKI East
Phone: 3968 3777

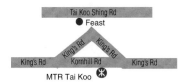

Le Chef

With a great smorgasbord of options to choose from, Le Chef puts tapas, salads, sushi and other dishes at your whim smack dab in the middle of busy Wan Chai. You're going to want to have an empty stomach when you arrive for their appetizers galore.

Address: Metropark Hotel Wanchai, Mezzanine Floor, 41-49 Hennessy Rd, Wan Chai, HKI
Phone: 2863 7345

Butao Ramen (豚王)

Butao Ramen gives Ramen a good name (or a better name than you have for it). If you've been eating that packaged stuff on aisle nine at the back of the store for years, it's time to try out the real deal at this eatery tucked away in Central. This Japanese staple has become popular in Hong Kong for a reason, and once you've had it you may never go down that aisle again.

Address: G/F, 69 Wellington St, Central, HKI
Phone: 2530 0600
Website: www.butaoramen.com

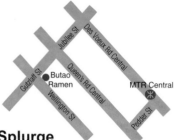

Splurge

Felix

This high-end Western-style restaurant has become well known for its Victoria Harbour views and its steak. A reservation is mandatory, and don't forget to take a few photos of the bathrooms because they're worthy of a few snaps (you'll see why when you come).

Address: 28/F, Peninsula Hotel, Salisbury Rd., Tsim Sha Tsui, Kowloon
Phone: 2315 3188

Lily & Bloom

Lily & Bloom is tucked away in the popular

LKF area of Central, and you will be glad you found it if you venture to eat here. Order the black cod and check that cocktail menu twice. With a nod to New York dining, you'll be impressed with all that is offered.

Address: 6/F LKF Tower, 33 Wyndham St, Central, HKI
Phone: 2810 6166
Website: www.lily-bloom.com

Liberty Private Works

Bar-style seating, stunning décor, and exceptional entrees to choose from, including the notable sea urchin, monkfish and Iberian pork. If you're going to splurge, this is one of the places to do it. Be sure to grab a good bottle of wine off their stunning list. Red or white, you can't go wrong here.

Address: 26/F, 11 Stanley St, Central, HKI
Phone: 5186 3282
Website: www.libertypw.com

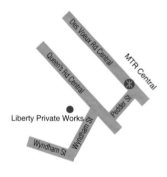

Mandarin Grill & Bar (文華扒房及酒吧)

This restaurant is high end from the atmosphere and ambiance to the menu. Expansive items are available on the menu, and their drinks use some of the best top-shelf liquors available on this side of the world.

Address: 5 Connaught Rd, Central, HKI
Phone: 2825 4004

Kitchen

This bistro is guaranteed to handle all your drooling requests with enough variety to satiate any palate. We suggest the Sunday brunch for the best value, and don't you dare leave without trying the dessert bar. Chocolate is your friend... and also your worst enemy!

Address: W Hotel, 1 Austin Rd West, Kowloon
Phone: 3717 2299

The Market

Known for their selection of international cuisines from Indian to Chinese to European, The Market is a popular destination for people around the world. Drop by for their legendary desserts. It's well worth the trip.

Address: 2/F, Hotel Icon, 17 Science Museum Rd, Tsim Sha Tsui East, Kowloon
Phone: 3400 1308

The Promenade

Reaching The Promenade is an experience in and of itself, before even mentioning their array of cuisines encompassing Asian and European dishes. There's more offered as well with the amazing view and exceptional service. Pricey, but definitely worth every (HK) dollar.

Address: Whampoa Garden, 20 Tak Fung St, Hung Hom, Kowloon
Phone: 2996 8432

Inagiku (稲菊)

If you've got some cash to burn and have a hankering for Japanese, Inagiki is pretty darn hard to beat. The décor is only topped by the Harbour views, and the food is simply world class. It's difficult to recommend anything here because they're all major winners.

Address: Four Seasons Hotel, 8 Finance St, Central, HKI
Phone: 2805 0600
Website: www.fourseasons.com/hongkong

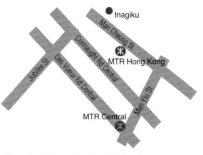

The Peak Lookout (太平山餐廳)

With a smattering of international cuisine (Japanese, Indian, SE Asian to name a few), this place has excellent food and reviews. It's expensive and touristy, but you might want to brave it for the perks of The Peak.

Address: 121 Peak Rd, The Peak, HKI
Phone: 2849 1000
Website: www.peaklookout.com.hk

Flame at Towngas Avenue

This is a restaurant that understands that food is just as much about the journey as it is the final product. You can see the preparation of your food step by step as the chefs busy themselves over your order – you are privy to the recipe of your dish as you watch the full spectacle of culinary brilliance unfold before your eyes.

Address: G/F, 59-65 Paterson St, Causeway Bay, HKI

Phone: 2367 2710
Website: www.towngasavenue.com

TOWNS & VILLAGES

The listings below cover areas outside of Hong Kong's main downtown areas on Northern Hong Kong Island and Kowloon. This includes not only the towns of Aberdeen and Stanley on Hong Kong Island's southern side, but also the towns of the New Territories and smaller villages like those on Lantau Island.

Aberdeen

Budget

Ap Lei Chau Market Cooked Food Center (鴨脷洲熟食中心)

If the stoic name wasn't enough to get you running down to Aberdeen to try this one out, then let us tell you that the food cooked up at the six *dai pai dong* stalls found here is good and tasty enough to be your go-to budget option while hanging out around the Ap Lei Chau area. The seafood selections here are great, and you can find some for around HK$40-60, but if you're feeling more adventurous and need something just a bit fresher, grab something still flipping and flopping from the wet market downstairs and bring it here to be cooked up to perfection.

Address: 1/F, Ap Lei Chau Municipal Services Bldg, 8 Hung Shin St

Tree Café

If you find yourself at the Horizon Shopping Mall, especially if you have kids in tow, consider stopping by the Tree Café (in the furniture shop of the same name) for lunch. Great coffee is served and there is a play area for the kids.

Address: 28/F, Horizon Plaza, 2 Lee Win St, Ap Lei Chau
Phone: 2870 1582
Website: www.tree.com.hk/cafe

Mid-range

Jumbo Kingdom Floating Restaurant (珍寶王國)

The city of lights coming from Aberdeen Harbour has a lot going on, including several floors of cheap and mid-priced food. If you're dining you can grab a free ride on Aberdeen Promenade, and then you should head up to the 3rd floor for solid dim sum. The 2nd floor Dragon Court is hit or miss, so don't buy until you've had a good look around.

Address: Shum Wan Pier Dr, Wong Chuck Hang
Phone: 2553 9111
Website: www.jumbo.com.hk

Aberdeen Fish Market Canteen (香港仔魚類批發市場內的食堂)

PANDA PICK

This *cha chaan tang*-style eatery is run by local fishermen and is one of the best places to eat fresh seafood in the city. How good is it? Well, let's just say you'll need a Cantonese speaker at your hostel or hotel to book a table at least two days in advance (and two weeks early for weekends). Instead of a menu, you just tell the owner your price range and let him select the day's freshest creature to cook up to stunning perfection. To find this place, head to the end of the fish market and look for the single-story yellow building with a green roof.

Address: 102 Shek Pai Wan Rd
Phone: 2552 7555

Prompt

Come for the a la carte dishes and return for the superb service. Not only will the staff help you pick out your foods with detailed descriptions before ordering, but you may get invited for a wine testing or two. We suggest the cheese fondue.

Address: 4/F, Le Meridien Cyberport, 100 Cyberport Rd, Pok Fu Lam
Phone: 2980 7417

Splurge

Crowne Wine Cellars

The fine wine served up at this former WWII bunker works perfectly with the delicious European cuisine cooked up here. It's a good thing, too, because the prices can be steep (and you'll need to sign up for a free one-time "silver" membership to dine), but the glass-house restaurant and its wine cellar are certainly top-notch.

Address: 18 Deep Water Bay Dr, Shouson Hill
Phone: 2580 6287
Website: www.crownewinecellars.com

Chef Studio

Venture into the yet-to-be-refurbished factory that houses Chef Studio and you'll soon be inspired by the spartan-chic interior of this very fine dining establishment. French-inspired dishes crafted by food architect Eddy Leung are beautiful – much of them put together from his rooftop organic garden – and you can watch the preparation action unfold through the open kitchen.

Address: Kwai Bo Industrial Bldg, 40 Wong Chuk Hang Rd
Phone: 3104 4664

Top Deck (珍之寶)

We don't recommend coming for the décor, which borders on cheesy ostentatious, but if you're around on a weekend you can't go wrong with the brunch and free-flowing champagne on Saturday and Sunday. Plus, the food is worth the spicy price, and the breezy deck gets touched with just the right amount of sun.

Address: Top/F, Jumbo Floating Kingdom, Shum Wan Pier Dr, Wong Chuk Hang
Phone: 2552 3331
Website: www.cafedecogroup.com

Cheung Chau

Like all of Hong Kong's Outlying Islands, Cheung Chau eating stays afloat through seafood. To that end, no shortage will ever be found along **Pak She Praya Road**, and nearly all of the places you find here will essentially have mirror image a la carte menus of the ones next door. There is a great night market down on **Praya Sreet** that gets roaring around 22:00 each night with tons of food and snack carts. The best choice for many, however, is to just hop down to **Tai Hing Tai Road** on the other side of the pier and find the food stalls with fish tanks, where you can point a finger of doom to a fish and have the stall owner cook it up just how you like it.

Budget

U Can Cook (自煮食材)

This fine little bistro-style joint on Praya Street serves up tasty Hong Kong fare and good pizzas for very reasonable prices. Excellent sausages and soups are a part of the party, as are nicely cooked meats. When the main course is done and you're ready for a treat, the dessert menu takes things to decadent new levels. Try the cold soba noodles.

Address: G/F, 91A & 82 Praya St
Phone: 2981 6533

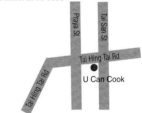

Hometown Teahouse (故鄉茶寮)

The sushi and red bean pastries are killer at this little back-alley grub spot. It's owned by a friendly Japanese couple, and the raving locals are trying to keep this as their best-kept secret. It's closed once a week or so on different nights, so call to make sure they are open.

Address: 12 Tung Wan Rd
Phone: 2981 5038

Kam Wing Tai Fish Ball Shop (甘永泰魚蛋)

This wildly popular Hakka eatery has enough balls for the whole island, and many of them can be yours for an excellent price. Consider

their set of various fish balls on a stick, and don't forget the beer.

Address: 106 San Hing St
Phone: 2981 5038

Katie Dessert

Katie Dessert (師妹甜品)

With creamy crème brulée, deadly-good hazelnut chocolate cake, and a dessert called Flame Snow Mountain (火 焰 雪 山) that lights on fire, it's no small wonder that this excellent sweets and desserts eatery is popular. Katie knows her stuff, and it keeps people coming back time and time again. We're drooling just thinking about it. Unfortunately it's closed on Wednesdays.

Address: 12 Kin Seng Ave
Phone: 9880 3726

Mid-range

Windsurfing Water Sports Centre & Café
〔 長洲滑浪風帆中心露天茶座 〕

If you're a windsurfer or a regular surfer then maybe you've heard of Lee Lai-shan, the professional windsurfer who brought an Olympic gold medal home to Hong Kong for his windsurfing performance in Atlanta. Well….this spot is owned by his uncle, Lai Gun. If that namedrop wasn't enough to blow you ashore to this joint, remember that the fish steak with a beer is perfect after any day at the beach.

Address: 1 Hak Pai Rd
Phone: 2981 8316
Website: www.ccwindc.com.hk

Lamma Island

Seafood is the name of the game on Lamma Island, but you don't have to go marine or go home. In fact, of all the Outlying Islands, Lamma probably has the most eclectic mix of grub. Still, it is a fishy place, especially around Sok Kwu Wan, where restaurants along the waterfront are stocked with seafood and pounded by expats and locals alike on the weekends. (You can take a boat to these shoreline eateries.) For the best variety of restaurants head to **Yung Shue Wan**, the most populous village on the island.

Budget

Best Kebab & Pizza

If you heard that the best Turkish coffee and fruit teas in town can be found here at Best Kebab & Pizza, then you certainly heard right. What you may not realize is that this unassuming little joint also serves up a mean slice of pizza as well as knock-'em-dead kebabs – some might even say the best.

Address: 4 Yung Shue Wan Back St, Yung Shue Wan
Phone: 2982 0902

Waterfront

A small but eclectic mix of fare, including British, Italian and Indian, is served up daily at Waterfront, all within arm's reach of the waving tide. It's a great spot for breakfast or dinner, especially as the sun goes down.

Address: 58 Main St, Yung Shue Wan
Phone: 2982 1168

Bookworm Café (南島書蟲)

Vegetarians, this is your place. From the goat cheese sanga and the shepherd's pie to the dhal and salad combo and the delicious wines, this is the best place in Hong Kong for healthy, eco-friendly eating. It's also a second-hand bookstore.

Address: 79 Main St, Yung Shue Wan
Phone: 2982 4838

Mid-range

Tai Hing Seafood Restaurant (大興海鮮酒家)

Tai Hing, run by Lamma local Cheong Gor, can cater a great meal to your budget. Just tell Cheong what you're willing to spend and he will whip up something seasonal and fresh to make you happy. Reservations are a must, and you shouldn't expect to spend less than HK$250 per head.

Address: 53 Main St, Yung Shue Wan
Phone: 2982 0339

Rainbow Seafood Restaurant (天虹海鮮酒家)

The excellent specialties here, which include steamed grouper, abalone and lobster, are so good that you'll need reservations a day early if you want to get one of their 800 seats. It sits right on the lovely waterfront, and it's possible to take one of the restaurant's ferries straight to their door from Central Pier 9 or Tsim Sha Tsui Public Pier. Check their website for boat times.

Address: 23-25 First St, Sok Kwu Wan
Phone: 2982 8100
Website: www.rainbowrest.com.hk

Han Lok Yuen (閒樂園酒家)

It's on the beach, a stone's throw from the pier, and when the weather is just right, you'll be pinching yourself over your location, as well as their noted pigeon dish. Enjoy both Western and Chinese food from their menu.

Address: 16-17 Hung Shing Ye Beach, Lamma Island
Phone: 2982 0608

Lantau Island

Big ol' Lantau Island has eating aplenty, though much of it is a bit rougher around the edges than the rest of Hong Kong. No problem, though, because that is essentially the idea of Lantau, so enjoy some hikes on this rugged island and then get your eat on in something equally rustic in the villages along South Lantau Road, Mui Wo, Tung Chung, Tai O, Pui O or Discovery Bay Plaza.

Budget

Bahçe

This standout location in Mui Wo is a regular haunt for locals and expats, especially when the weather is warm and they get to hang out on the outdoor patio for awesome kebabs and beers from the brewery next door. Look for it just near the ferry pier.

Address: Shop 19, G/F, 3 Ngan Wan Rd, Mui Wo
Phone: 2984 0222

Spaghetti House (意粉屋)

This unpretentious little Italian dig in Tung Chung has got all an Italian lover could want. Herbivores will jump for joy at their meatless menu, where delicious sauces and creative veggie creations win the day.

Address: Shop G20, G/F, Citygate Outlets, 20 Tat Tung Rd, Tung Chung
Phone: 2109 1297

Solo

Tai O's laidback scenery fits perfectly as it hugs this little terraced café and its satisfying coffee.

Try the tiramisu or the stupidly good apple crumble and ice cream, then take a hike down into Fan Lau to burn off some of that sugar.

Address: 86 Kat Hing St, Tai O
Phone: 9153 7453

Tai O Lookout

If you're hungry, then the Tai O lookout has tasty fried rice and some excellent stuffed buns to make you happy. But what really gets people psyched are the charming old-world décor and stunning panoramic views of the South China Sea from this glasshouse rooftop joint.

Address: Shek Tsai Po St, Tai O Hotel, Tai O
Phone: 2985 8383

Mid-range

Stoep Restaurant

Check out Cheung Sha beach by day, stop in for dinner at this solid Mediterranean restaurant by night. The terrace over the beach is nice, as is the South African *braat* barbecue. They also serve lunch.

Address: 32 Lower Cheung Sha Village
Phone: 2980 2699

Sichuan Back Garden

You'll need to have six people in your party ready to eat at this wild, offbeat joint, and we suggest you round up a crew, because the meals put together by the Cantonese-speaking Norwegian owner Cecilie are Sichuan at its finest. If it sounds interesting, it is, especially when Cecilie's sharp sense of humor gets as fired up as her meals. Better plan on reserving at least three days in advance for this one.

Address: Lo Uk Tsuen, Pui O
Email: cecilie@happyjellyfish.com
Website: www.happyjellyfish.com

Tung Shing Lau (東昇樓海鮮酒家)

This decent Shanghainese restaurant can cook up some massive seafood feasts for fairly reasonable prices, and the chicken, roasted pork and fried rice are surprisingly great. The restaurant has a free shuttle bus to and from the MTR Station in Tung Chung.

Address: G/F, 94 Chun Hou St, Ma Wan Chun, Tung Chun
Phone: 2988 1494

Mui Wo

see Lantau Island

Pui O

see Lantau Island

Repulse Bay

Budget

Saffron Bakery Café

Great organic artisan breads and a cozy atmosphere are cooking daily at Saffron. Also a location in Stanley.

Address: Shop G120, Repulse Bay Shopping Arcade, 109 Repulse Bay Rd
Phone: 2812 2016
Website: saffronbakery.com

Splurge

Verandah (露台餐廳)

Known for their superbly fresh ingredients, off-the-hook cooking and plenty of shucked oysters, Verandah is one of the best places in Hong Kong to experience an amazing buffet, superb brunch and a proper tea set. Book in advance if you want to get a table.

Address: 1/F, The Repulse Bay, 109 Repulse Bay Rd
Phone: 2292 2822
Website: www.therepulsebay.com

Spices Restaurant (香辣軒)

Satay, curry and top-tier seafood dishes are all the rage at Spices. Warm wooden floors, high-ceilings and rattan furniture can swing you away to a beach-bound spot in Southeast Asia, especially if you come to watch the sunset from the open terrace.

Address: 109 Repulse Bay Rd
Phone: 2292 2821
Website: www.therepulsebay.com

Sai Kung Town

Budget

Ali Oli Bakery Café

The perfect refuel spot before or after a hike in Sai Kung Country Park, the Ali Oli Bakery not only pumps out daily, homemade European breads, they'll slap together a great sandwich for you. If that doesn't sound like enough (they are quite filling) then you can still choose something from their set breakfast and lunch menus. Make sure to check out their outdoor patio.

Address: 11 Sha Tsui Path
Phone: 2792 2655

Honeymoon Dessert (滿記甜品)

Branches of Honeymoon Dessert around China and Indonesia are countless – 20 alone in Hong Kong – and if that doesn't say something about the exceptional Chinese-style desserts whipped up here, then let us tell you, they are great. Try their durian pudding or sweet walnut soup for a healthy alternative to heavier, sugar-filled Western desserts.

Address: 9, 10A, B&C Po Tung Rd
Phone: 2792 4991

Mid-range

Chuen Kee Seafood Restaurant (全記海鮮菜館)

With two branches in Sai Kung, Chuen Kee has been making a decent name for itself for several years. Stop in to taste their super creations and find out why this stuff is so good. Look for the major display of crawling sea creatures near their door and pick your favorite.

Location One

Address: 53 Hoi Pong St
Phone: 2791 1195

Location Two

Address: 87-89 Man Nin St
Phone: 2792 6938

Loaf On

With a Michelin star and a "we catch it, you eat it" attitude, life is fun at Loaf On. The midday menu all depends on what was hauled in from the ocean that day, but you can be sure that it is always super tasty. Try their signature fish soup, but come early because it goes quickly.

Address: 49 Market St
Phone: 2792 9966

Splurge

Chez Les Copains

Somewhat on the outskirts of town (take green minibus 1S to Pak Sha Wan), Chez Les Copains is highly worth a trip for its spectacular duck leg confit, French tripe sausage called *andouillette,* and its mouthwatering liver terrine.

Address: 117 Pak Sha Wan
Phone: 2243 1918
Website: www.chezlescopains.com

Sha Tin

For quick eats in Sha Tin swing into the **Shatin New Town Plaza** (新 城 市 廣 場 ; address: 18 Sha Tin Centre St; hours: 10:00-22:00; phone: 2684 9175), which is connected to Sha Tin Station and has a huge amount of chain and fast food restaurants for all tastes and price ranges.

Budget

Shing Kee (盛記盆菜 & 盛記麵家)

Artsy little Shing Kee is a recycled joint: everything, from the tables and chairs to the black-and-white photos on the walls, potted plants, CDs and toys were picked up from wheelie bins and refurbished by the owner. The place is beautiful in an eccentric way, and the daytime noodles are only beat by the by-night hot pot served up here. Walk 15 minutes north of Sha Tin Station or hop on bus 83K.

Address: Shop 5, Lek Yuen Estate Market
Phone: 2692 6611

Lung Wah Hotel Restaurant (龍華酒店餐廳)

The tasty roast pigeon is probably the best thing on the menu, and while the restaurant's other dishes range from passable to good, the real deal here for Bruce Lee pilgrims is the fact that this hotel is where he supposedly stayed during the filming of *The Big Boss*.

Address: 22 Ha Wo Che
Phone: 2691 1828; 2691 1594
Website: www.lungwahhotel.kh

Mid-range

Sha Tin 18 (沙田 18)

Drooled over by locals and expats alike for its superb Peking Duck, Sha Tin 18's popularity seems to grow bigger and badder (in a good way) every day, and that means you'll need to order your crispy-skinned bird at least 24 hours ahead of time. It's worth it, though, especially if you think you'll be in the Sha Tin area at some point for the Ten Thousand Buddhas Monastery or the Sha Tin Racecourse. It's located next to the campus of Chinese University (take the bus to the University stop).

Address: Hyatt Regency Hong Kong, 18 Chak Cheung St
Phone: 3723 1234; 3723 7932

Shek O

Budget

Happy Garden (樂園泰國菜)

Run by a friendly couple and with calming ocean views from its terrace, Happy Garden stays good to its happy name with legit Thai dishes and good seafood.

> Address: 786 Shek O Village
> Phone: 2809 4165

Mid-range

Black Sheep (黑羊餐廳) **PANDA PICK**

A regularly updated blackboard menu, tastefully lighthearted décor, great pizza and refreshing mint-lemonade, Black Sheep brings the chill college town vibe to laidback Shek O. It's all quite fitting really, and we think you'll love this spot as much as we did.

> Address: 330 Shek O Village
> Phone: 2809 2021

Stanley

Budget

Si Yik (泗益)

There's no English signage at this excellent *dai pai dong* eatery with a clanky tin roof (look for long lines and mounds of fruit at the entrance), but putting in the effort to find it will reward you double. The Hong Kong-style French Toast is soft enough to sleep on, and the prices can't be beat. Closed on Tuesdays.

> Address: 2 Stanley Market St
> Phone: 2813 0503

Saffron Bakery Café

Excellent organic breads with artisan touches and standout coffee make the recently renovated

Saffron a perfect timeout in Stanley. There's also a location in Repulse Bay (pg 206).

> Address: G/F, Shop G04, Stanley Plaza
> Phone: 2813 0270
> Website: saffronbakery.com

Mid-range

Lucy's

With fresh food, a flavor-filled menu of both international and local foods, and great desserts, it's no small wonder that Lucy's has become a popular spot for locals and tourists alike. A bit off the main streets, it will feel like a secret cove you'll want to keep all to yourself. Be sure to try one of their famous desserts.

> Address: 64 Stanley Main St
> Phone: 2813 9055

Toby Inn (赤柱酒家)

Toby's, attracts people from all walks of life with good seafood and dim sum. This local haunt is a great place to people watch and get jazzed with some neighborhood color.

> Address: Shop U1 & U2, UG, 126 Stanley Main Street, Stanley
> Phone: 2813 2880

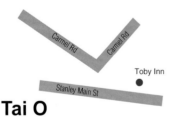

Tai O

see Lantau Island

Tai Po

Check out **Tai Ming Square** in the center of town for decent street food and stalls firing out Hakka-style snacks.

Budget

Wah Fai Restaurant and Cake Shop (華輝餐廳)

Teeming with regulars who come for the draw-card crispy apple pie made with fresh apples and the creamy chicken pies that make this place famous, Wah Fai may be called a cake shop, but it's killing it in the pie department. It certainly had us smiling when we were here.

Address: G/F, 17 Heung Sze Wui Square
Phone: 2656 6420

Tomato Club (蕃滿門)

Do you love tomatoes and tomato-based food? Then boy do we have a place for you! Tomato Club pulls 'em in these days with its saucy creations, and we must say that they do seem to have a green thumb for red food, particularly their array of egg and meat-or fish ball-topped tomato soups, and their curries with ginger rice.

Address: G/F, On Lok Bldg, 1 Mei Sun Lane
Phone: 2667 7277

Yat Lok Barbecue Restaurant (一樂燒臘飯店)

PANDA PICK

Anthony Bourdain fans may want to follow in the celebrity chef's footsteps by making a stop by this great little mom-and-pop eatery for their out-of-this-world roast goose and roast duck. They are beyond the hype, as is pretty much any of the Cantonese barbecue here.

Address: G/F, Po Wah Bldg Block A, 5 Tai Ming Ln
Phone: 2656 4732

Tsuen Wan

If you're heading for Tai Mo Shan Country Park – like many people who come to Tsuen Wan – then stopping off for some breakfast or brunch in Tsuen Wan town is essential. Dim sum is a great pre-hike meal, and you can find two great teahouses – Duen Kee and Choi Lung – just about 5 km (3 mi) northwest of Tsuen Wan town along Route Twisk. For things closer to Tsuen Wan town there are plenty of noodle and Western eateries, especially around **Castle Peak Road**.

Budget

Duen Kee Restaurant

Stop in for Duen Kee's homegrown watercress and compliment it with good dim sum and tea on the rooftop while you check out the caged birds that the old timers like to bring in. Look for the parasols on the ground floor.

Address: 57-58 Chuen Lung Village, Route Twisk
Phone: 2490 5246

Choi Lung Restaurant

This no frills dim sum dig is just down from Duen Kee and puts out self-serve dim sum from the kitchen and make-your-own tea. The restaurant is several decades old, and locals rave about the sweet bean curd made from Tai Mo Shan mountain spring water.

Address: 2 Chuen Lung Village, Route Twisk
Phone: 2415 5041

Nova

A plethora of tasty snacks, meals, desserts and wines makes Nova one of the most popular places in Tsuen Wan New Town. The pizzas are excellent, as are the lox.

Address: G/F, Bayview Garden, 633 Castle Peak Rd, Tsuen Wan
Phone: 2116 4018 / 5119 0090

Gala Cafe (嘉樂冰廳)

Enormous sandwiches, monstrous omelets and wontons galore; this little *cha chaan teng* in Tsuen Wan has good food and huge portions. Because of that it may be better after a good hike, but be aware that this popular place can often have long wait times. Try the milkshakes, which are not too sweet or overly heavy and make a great refresher after a hot day in the park.

Address: G/F, 40B San Chuen St, Tsuen Wan
Phone: 2493 7308

Tuen Mun

Hit the town center for plenty of Chinese options, or skirt the edges for something special.

Budget

Nang Kee Roasted Goose Restaurant (能記燒鵝飯店)

Famous for its succulent and utterly splendid roast goose (whose crispy skin and juicy meat is almost too good to be true), this restaurant is likely the most popular spot in town. It's had over 50 years to built that reputation, but after you taste the food we're sure you'll agree it wouldn't have taken that long.

> Address: 13 Sham Hong Rd, Sun Tsuen, Sham Tseng
> Phone: 2491 0392

Dondonya Shokudo (丼丼屋食堂)

A 70-seat Japanese restaurant in the center of town, Dondonya Shokudo runs a tight shift inside a soft-lit modern décor. Their udon noodles couldn't be fresher, and the green tea latte, tempura and desserts come recommended. A 10% service charge is usually added.

> Address: Shop 2162, 2/F, Tuen Mun Town Plaza, 3 Tuen Lung St
> Phone: 2459 7880

Farmer Restaurant (屯門農家菜)

Staying true to the Cantonese culinary arts, Farmer Restaurant – a Michelin recommended establishment – approaches their food with less salt, less oil and more delicate flavors. The veggies come fresh out of the surrounding farming villages, making this spot one of the most health-conscious choices in Hong Kong.

> Address: Block C, Lam Tei Mei Ling Court, Castle Peak Rd
> Phone: 2461 2381

Tung Chung

see Lantau Island

Yuen Long

Before or after a trip to a nearby walled village, the Ping Shan Heritage Trail, or the surrounding wetlands, get your grub on in **Yuen Long** at the noodle shops or get down on some dim sum in **Tai Wing Wah**.

Budget

Tai Wing Wah (大榮華酒樓)

Tai Wing Wah is easily the most renowned place to eat at in Yuen Long, and that's surprising considering the modest prices. Chef and founder Leung Man-to pulls his veggies from surrounding farms and uses them to cook up some superb creations, including lemon-steamed gray mullet and Malay sponge cake. Walk north from Tai Tong Light Rail Station and turn right on Sai Tai St for another 30 m (98 ft).

> Address: 2/F, Koon Wong Mansion, 2-6 On Ning Rd
> Phone: 2476 9888

Ping Shan Traditional Poon Choi (屏山傳統盆菜)

Poon choi, meaning "basin banquet," is a type of feast traditionally enjoyed in the villages around Hong Kong. It works as a three-level pile of deliciousness, with the priciest and most exquisite treats on the top. You can expect plenty of meats, root and green veggies, and seafood. This one – as the name suggests – is right off the Ping Shan Heritage Trail and will require reservations. Basin meals are made for six or more peeps.

> Address: 36 Tong Fong Tsuen, Ping Ha Rd
> Phone: 2617 8000

Mint Thai House (薄荷葉泰國菜)

The service doesn't always get rave reviews, but the food is decent enough, and the outdoor seating, well-stocked bar, and generally well-done Thai fare all seem to

hold their own for this flashy joint.

Address: Shop 12-13, G/F, Yee Hong Bldg, On
Hong Rd, Yuen Long
Phone: 2475 5872

Farm Milk Co Ltd (農場鮮奶有限公司)

Despite the oddly corporate name and the
isolated location of this little milk farm,
Farm Milk Co Ltd is one of the tastiest
unknown treats in the New Territories. If
you can find the place you will be rewarded
with a selection of silky-smooth flavored
milks straight off the farm. The ginger milk
is stupendous, and there are some simple
snacks here also. You may just want to hire a
taxi and show this address to the driver: 元朗
石崗甲龍村雷公田 78 號 and/or have them call for
directions.

Address: Shek Kong Kap Lung, 78 Lui Kung
Tin, Yuen Long
Phone: 2832 9218

Ho To Tai Noodle Shop (好到底麵家)

Just a five-minute walk south of the Tai
Tong Road Light Rail Station, Ho To Tai is
Michelin rated and prices are surprisingly
easy-on-the-pocket. Saddle up though: this
one has been serving up some of the best
shrimp roe noodles and egg noodles in the
New Territories for some time now, and it
won't be stopping anytime soon. It's great for
a light pre-hike/walk meal. Make sure to ask
the cashier for the English menu.

Address: 67 Fau Tsoi St
Phone: 2476 2495

including excellent scallops and yummy crab
roe on fried rice. The daring can go for the
ostrich meat!

Address: 12 Shan Ting St, Lau Fau Shan
Phone: 2472 3450

Mid-range

Happy Seafood Restaurant (歡樂海鮮酒家)

Cordon Bleu chef Lau Ka-lun has some
creative seafood concoctions for your plate,

How to Use Chopsticks

Don't know how to use chopsticks? While you can find plenty of forks and knives around here, it's always best to do as a local. Plus, Western utensils might be hard to find at delicious hole-in-the-wall retreats or other proud Chinese restaurants. Like anything, you won't learn it in a day, but you might as well go ahead and get started!

4.

Note that many meals in China will be served with a bowl of rice. It is acceptable to place bites of food on top of the rice, so bring the bowl close to your mouth with your left hand and use your chopsticks to shovel the rice and food into your mouth. Using chopsticks as a shovel is easier and it's perfectly OK to do so in Chinese table etiquette.

1.

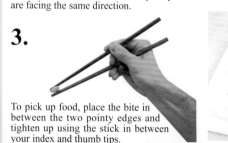

Rest the first stick in between your ring finger and middle finger, and place the back end of the soft area between your index finger and thumb (pointy end facing in the same direction as your fingers). This is your anchor stick and it should not move while eating.

5.

A common misconception is that stabbing the food with your chopsticks like a fork is unacceptable. This is perfectly fine and no one will laugh at your amateur skills. Chinese people do this all the time, especially with hard to eat foods that are slippery, slimy or simply too large to pick up the old fashioned way.

2.

Grasp the second stick with your index finger and thumb tips. This is the stick that moves, and you can position it by simply twisting your thumb and index finger. You can brace it on your middle finger for better control. Make sure both pointy ends are facing the same direction.

6.

Last but not least, practice. After a few meals you'll be a chopstick master!

3.

To pick up food, place the bite in between the two pointy edges and tighten up using the stick in between your index and thumb tips.

Drinking & Nightlife

Are you ready to experience one of the fastest, trendiest and most energetic party cities in Asia? If you said "Absolutely!", you're in the right place. When it comes to cities that move faster than a bullet train, Hong Kong can change tracks faster than you can take a body shot, providing an intoxicatingly edgy vibe to an already enchanting city. As you'll soon learn, Hong Kong is clearly in a league of its own: here, they don't just seize the night – they strangle it!

Where?

The bulk of the bars and clubs that most foreigners and visitors head to are located in Wan Chai, Soho, or Lan Kwai Fong, all on the north side of Hong Kong Island. Wan Chai is known as the seedier side of town, but that has been changing recently over on the western side, where more respectable establishments are taking root. If you're feeling a bit more adventurous and want a more traditional and local experience, take the ferry or taxi across the bridge and head to Tsim Sha Tsui on Kowloon, alternately known simply as TST. This is where you'll find much of the cheaper eats and drinks around Knutsford Terrace in the north.

Lan Kwai Fong, known simply as LKF, has a reputation that ranges from "tourist trap" to "the place to be." At the end of the day, this area of town that was designed as a haven for expats can be anything and everything you want it to be. With so many clubs, bars, restaurants, and shopping outlets within such close proximity to each other, you can pack in a lifetime of partying and decadence without ever leaving LKF.

Clubbing

Some words of caution for clubbing in LKF:
Men, wear a shirt with sleeves or the vast
majority of clubs are going to deny you
entrance. Women, wear those high heels at
your own risk! You're going to be going up
and down hills for most of the night if you
are club/bar hopping. Do like many of the
local girls do and carry a pair of flats or flip-
flops in your purse and put them on when
you change locations; you'll feel a lot better
in the morning (apart from the hangover, of
course).

Wine & Whiskey Bars

Wine and whiskey bars have been picking
up steam in the last decade throughout Hong
Kong thanks to the government removal of
wine taxes in 2008. These places are upscale
and pricey, but they are out there if this is
your bag, and many of them actually offer
tastes or glasses of premium wines (using
"enomatic" technology that preserves the
quality of opened spirits) without having
to take out a bank loan and buy the whole
bottle.

How much?

Drinking in Hong Kong is not cheap.
Before you even think about going out
in Hong Kong, check your wallet and check
it twice. Those on a budget, however, do
have a few options if you don't have any
extra money for entrance into one of Hong
Kong's pricier clubs. One thing you can do if
you want to party like it's 1999 on little more
than a few dimes is to drink like a local by
pounding some drinks with the street partiers.

Hong Kong probably has more 7-11s per
square feet than anywhere else in the world.
In each one, there's a refrigerated area that
sells bargain basement liquors and relatively
cheap beers. For about HK$20, you can
have a little Jack Daniels or a cheap local
brew in your life, which you can take to the
streets and party with other bar-hoppers and
cheapskates. In this way, it's easy to make
the 7-11 and other convenience stores in LKF
or SoHo your very own personalized bar, and
actually one particlarly well-known street-
drinking spot called "Cougar Alley" sits near
a convenience store in SoHo. Not only will
you get alcohol at a fraction of the cost, but
you'll still be mingling with people that are
in the surrounding bars and clubs. No one
stays inside the clubs and bars in Lan Kwai
Fong for long anyway.

NORTH HONG KONG ISLAND & KOWLOON

Hong Kong is loaded with places to wet your whistle, and becuase of the variety, finding a watering hole that suits you and your mood can require some some effort. To expedite the process, our drinking establishments for the north side of Hong Kong Island (HKI) and those of Kowloon are grouped here according to style, i.e. bars, clubs, pubs, gay bars, live music venues, new bars and entertainment. For a drinking spot outside of North Hong Kong Island and Kowloon, just skip past this section to page 222 for a listing of venues in the city's outskirt towns.

Price range:

$ cheap (drinks under HK$50)
$$ moderate (drinks HK$50-150)
$$$ expensive (drinks HK$150 and up)

Bars, Clubs & Pubs

$$$ Dragon I

If you can manage to get into Dragon I, expect to be deluged by the bold and the beautiful. The vast majority of the women here are models, and if they don't directly tell you, it's always easy to find out. Simply go to the back of the club and there they will be, clamoring around the free drink table island

that the club provides exclusively for them. Wear your finest or you may be turned away at the door, and it might be a good idea to bring your plastic, because this place doesn't come cheap in any way, shape or form. Some of the best hip hop in the city can be found here on Monday nights.

> Address: 60 Wyndham St, Lan Kwai Fong, Central, HKI
> Phone: 3110 1222
> Website: www.dragon-i.com.hk
> Hours: 19:00 – late (Mon-Sat)

$$$ Ozone Bar @ The Ritz-Carlton

With top shelf drinks, quality service and an unbeatable view of the city, this upscale urban paradise is *only* 118 floors up (and hundreds of HK$ away) in west Kowloon. If you've got a few dollars burning a hole in your wallet and you want to drink over Hong Kong's amazing vertical skyline, stop over at Ozone Bar for some cocktails. We suggest going for their happy hour specials, then requesting a table outside to get more bang for your buck. The food is not too bad either. Break out your nicest shirt for this one, casual dressers may be turned away.

> Address: 1 Austin Rd West, West Kowloon
> Phone: 2263 2263
> Website: www.ritzcarlton.com/en/Properties/HongKong/Dining/ozone/
> Hours: 17:00–1:00 (Mon-Wed), 17:00–2:00 (Thu), 7:00–3:00 (Fri), 15:00–3:00 (Sat), 12:00–00:00 (Sun)

$$ Tapas Bar

Who doesn't like tapas? Tapas Bar serves them up with their great selection of wines and spirits. Combine that with an ambiance and a bistro décor that is beyond comparison and you have a winner. As you take in the tapas and sangria – an excellent way to unwind after a big day – there's a view of Victoria Harbour that will take your breath away.

> Address: Kowloon Shangri-la Hotel, 64 Mody Rd, Tsim Sha Tsui, Kowloon

Drinking & Nightlife

Phone: 2733 8756
Hours: 15:30–1:00 (Mon-Sat),12:00–1:00 (Sat & Sun)

$$ Cathay Pacific Lounge

For those that are truly using Hong Kong as a speed bump before they move on to their next destination, the Cathay Pacific Lounge should be one of your considerations. If you absolutely cannot get into the city and experience Hong Kong proper, fret not! Cathay Pacific has upgraded its lounge to bring an even better experience to you. Sit at the bar and sip on champagne or order a five-star meal with excellent service provided.

Address: 6F-1 Gate, Chek Lap Kok International Airport
Phone: 2747 7972
Hours: 6:00–23:30 (Mon-Sun)

$$$ Geronimo Shot Bar

Come into Geronimo on the right (or wrong, depending on your alcohol tolerance) night and you might get shot! When that shot drum beats, everyone in the bar gets serenaded with a free shot. Although that might be enough for the average bar hopper, Geronimo goes even further, creating a vibe that has helped it maintain a reputation as one of the go-to bars in LKF, with great music, great crowds, and great drinks. What's not to love?

Address: 2/F, Winner Bldg Block A, 27-39 D'Aguilar St, Lan Kwai Fong
Phone: 2833 9951
Website: www.geronimoshotbar.com
Hours: 17:00-4:00 (Mon-Sun)

$$ Sugar Bar

If you want to escape the hustle and bustle of Lan Kwai Fong for a change, then Sugar Bar might just be the place for you. Located on the 32nd floor of the Island East Hotel, this may be the only place in Hong Kong offering authentic cigars, specialty drinks, and an amazing view of the city from the Kowloon side all wrapped into one. This is a rooftop bar with a down home feel, but with an exclusive touch.

Address: 32/F East, Island East Hotel, 29 Taikoo Shing Rd, HKI
Phone: 3968 3738
Website: www.sugar-hongkong.com
Hours: 17:00–2:00 (Mon-Sat), 12:00–00:00 (Sun)

$$ Trafalgar Bar

If you happen to be on Lockhart Road and want a bit of a change of pace, there's no need to even leave the street – simply look up. On the 5th floor and offering a larger selection of the normal beers than nearly every pub in the vicinity, Trafalgar Bar is indeed a busy bee. From their two projector screens airing sports events to their quiz nights, this English-style pub offers Western food and the opportunity to see the world go by just below.

Address: 5/F, 54-62 Lockhart Rd, Wan Chai, HKI
Phone: 2110 1535
Website: www.trafalgar.com.hk
Hours: 12:00–3:30 (Mon-Sat), 17:00–3:30 (Sun)

$$$ Eyebar

There are several places in Hong Kong to see the impressive skyline, but if you want to admire it with a bit of ambiance and contemporary design thrown in, head over and up, up, up to Eyebar in Tsim Sha Tsui. Their specialty drinks are considered classics and are the perfect combination to a breathtaking view that will have all your friends green with envy for not tagging along. For an even better view, be sure to use their telescope for a closer inspection of your surroundings down below.

Address: 30/F, iSquare, 63 Nathan Rd, Tsim Sha Tsui, Kowloon
Phone: 2487 3988
Website: www.elite-concepts.com
Hours: 11:30-late (Mon-Sun)

$$$ MO Bar

"Like" is definitely not the word you will be using to describe MO Bar, situated in the Landmark Mandarin Oriental Hotel. By the looks of the place – with its jaw-dropping architecture and artwork – you might almost expect foreign dignitaries, superstars and tycoons to waltz in at any minute (and sometimes they just might). What you are more likely to find are Wall Street types networking and mingling over their own specially made drinks, making MO Bar an excellent destination for the traveling businessperson looking to network.

Address: G/F, Landmark Mandarin Oriental, The Landmark, 15 Queens Rd, Central, HKI
Phone: 2132 0077
Website: www.mandarinoriental.com/landmark/fine-dining/mo-bar
Hours: 7:00–1:30 (Mon-Sun)

$$ Hong Kong Brew House

Beer fanatics, take note: if you are a connoisseur of all things brewed, then Hong Kong Brew House is a necessary stop, as they offer the largest selection of beers in the city. So take to their patio, order some good, greasy pub grub and enjoy the suds! Over

100 different beers line the menu, perfect for a brunch after a late Saturday night or during the week when meeting up with friends. Bring your appetite because the portions are big.

Address: LG/F, Lan Kwai Fong Tower, 21 D'Aguilar, Central, HKI
Phone: 2522 5559
Hours: 11:00 – 2:00 (Mon-Thu), 11:00 – 4:00 (Fri-Sat)

$$ Stormies

When you are an establishment firmly nestled between two of the biggest partying streets in the country, people tend to gravitate towards you whether they intend to or not. Stormies itself may be small in size, but its capacity is nearly limitless thanks to the massive amount of people that seep out its doorways and onto the streets of LKF. It's not absolutely necessary to even go inside. Just hover nearby it and someone will come out and serve you.

Address: G/F & 1/F, 46-50 D'Aguilar St, Lan Kwai Fong, Central, HKI
Phone: 2845 5533
Hours: 12:00 – 2:00 (Mon-Sun)

$$ Drop

If you want to be among the hippest and trendiest people in the city on any given weekend (or weeknight), then you simply must drop by Drop. It's known as the place where the cool cats hang out, both international and local, and a bevy of stars have managed to find their way through its doors: The Black Eyed Peas, The Pet Shop Boys, and Robbie Williams to name a few. Here, you'll find a great mix of people while burning your soles up on the dance floor, and if you come late, prepare to stay even later. This place just doesn't let up!

Address: 39-43 Hollywood Rd, Central, HKI
Phone: 2543 8856
Website: www.drophk.com
Hours: 19:00–3:00 (Tue), 19:00–4:00 (Wed-Thu), 21:00–05:00 (Fri & Sat), 21:00–02:00 (Sun)

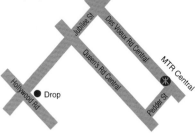

$$ Club Fly

What's the best thing to say about this dance club aside from its great DJs, electric crowds, and intense interior? Probably the large outside square where you can congregate with friends and socialize, because although the music at Fly is some of the best and most consistent to be found in the city on any given night (check out DJ Anil), one of the problems with this club is simply its lack of space. You'll get your house, electro, dubstep, drum & bass, hip hop and a lot more, but you also may cause enough friction with a complete stranger to start a small brushfire (which may or may not be a bad thing). Come before 1:00 if you want to get in and really dance. If you're really feeling it, there's a dancing pole on standby.

Address: G/F, 24-30 Ice House St, Central, HKI
Phone: 2810 9902
Website: www.clubfly.com.hk
Hours: 17:00–late (Tue-Fri), 21:00–late (Sat); closed Mon

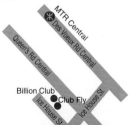

$$ Billion Club

With a name like Billion, it has to live up to the reputation, or suffer the consequences. Luckily for this establishment, it's more than up to the task. The crowd here is mainly young with a few older people thrown into the mix. The DJs are pumping out Top 40 dance music and mash-ups that you've heard before, but there's enough energy pulsing through the crowd that you won't care. You'll also feel like a king or queen once you check out the gold-laced "thrones." For a free admission, be sure to chat up the flyer girls on the main street passing out cards.

Address: 3/F On Hing Bldg, 1-9 Hing Terrace, Central
Phone: 2973 0918
Website: www.billionclub.com.hk
Hours: 17:00-5:00 (Mon-Fri), 22:00-5:00 (Sat)

$$$ Volar

Volar is a venue that attracts just the right mix of foreign and local, with the backdrop sustained by DJs that ensure you will be dancing well into the night. From R&B to house, electro and pop, they've got your genre covered, regularly featuring some of the most acclaimed DJs in the world. And if you know anything about Chinese pop culture, you might recognize a few famous faces thrown in the mix. Plot before you try to trot in here, however, a reservation or booking is usually needed, unless you're prepared to wait.

Address: 44 D'Aguilar St, Central, HKI
Phone: 2810 1510
Website: www.volar.com.hk
Hours: 18:00–2:00 (Tue-Thu), 21:00–6:00 (Fri & Sat)

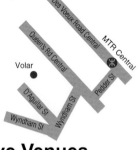

Live Venues

$$ The Wanch

Hankering for a taste of the local music scene? Then The Wanch is definitely a must-

The Fringe Club

see/hear for anyone visiting Hong Kong. Some of the city's best known and most prolific musicians call this venue their home away from home, with live music permeating through their walls every night. Their best night, if we had to choose, might be Sunday, but their Monday night jam sessions are also well worth checking out. And if you Harbour any musical ambitions, you're always invited to jump onstage and rock one out with the musicians.

Address: 54 Jaffe Rd, Wan Chai, HKI
Phone: 2861 1621
Website: www.thewanch.hk
Hours: 17:00–2:00 (Mon-Sat), 15:00–2:00 (Sun)

$$ Hidden Agenda

Just for its industrial look and feel, Hidden Agenda is worth a visit. Its bordering-on-illegal status has never stopped this venue from executing its mission of bringing great music to Hong Kong in dizzying amounts. No genre gets away unscathed. From pop to death metal and punk to Mandarin folk music, you never know who's going to pop up in here (and that's wherein the beauty lies).

Address: 2A Winful Industrial Bldg, 15-17 Tai Yip St, Kwun Tong, Kowloon
Phone: 9651 8567; 9170 6073
Website: www.hiddenagenda.hk
Email: hiddenagendahk@gmail.com
Hours: call to inquire

$$ The Fringe Club

If anyone can be given credit for preserving the history of Hong Kong's local music scene, as well as providing a haven for burgeoning artists, The Fringe Club would be it. You can always hear a great mix of music here, from local Cantonese pop acts to regular performances and established rock bands. If you want to hear the grit of Hong

Kong, The Fringe Club has it in spades.

Address: 2 Lower Albert Rd, Central (MTR: Central Station, Exit D1, D2 or G)
Phone: 2521 7251
Website: www.hkfringe.com.hk
Hours: 12:00-late (Mon-Sun)

$$ *Insomnia*

The spirit of great music never sleeps, and Insomnia is a venue that has been celebrating great music by featuring great musicians for a welcoming crowd every night of the week. The house band hails from the Philippines and knows every song that's ever been on the Billboard Top 40, from rock and pop to old standards. Sit down and have a few drinks while you take it all in. You can stay as long as you want because it never closes!

Address: Ho Lee Commercial Bldg, 30-32 D'Aguilar St, Central, HKI
Phone: 2525 0957
Hours: 24/7

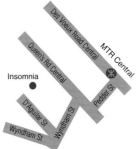

Gay Bars & Clubs

Before we jump into it, we must caution that Hong Kong has a long way to go before it catches up to its gay brethren in America and Europe. Hong Kong may be one of the most liberal cities in Asia, but the gay scene is severely lacking. However, that does not mean there are no options worth visiting and shaking a tail feather at. The scene is picking up fast, and these days there are generally more than enough gay-friendly establishments to accommodate short term visitors.

$$ *Propaganda*

By far the best-known and most visited gay club in Hong Kong, Propaganda stays packed the entire time it is open, particularly because it is one of the few dance clubs that caters exclusively to a gay crowd. It's loud, it's rambunctious and it's not cheap. If you

want to get away from the loud noise for a bit, there's the option of the bar, which is partitioned away from the dance floor. The drink specials will leave a special dent in your wallet and memory, and we suggest going to LKF first and then either walking here later in the night or making it your early morning alternative. Look for the basement.

Address: Basement, 1 Hollywood Rd, Central, HKI
Phone: 2868 1316
Hours: call to inquire

$$ *Volume*

It lacks in name recognition compared to its main competitor Propaganda, but Volume makes up for in delivery. You'll definitely see a more diverse group of people here, all ready to get their groove on 'til the break of dawn. Their DJ lineup is nothing to sneeze at, and on occasion they get a heavy hitter on the decks. Drink specials on Wednesdays are not to be missed for vodka lovers.

Address: LG/F, 62 Jervois St, Sheung Wan, HKI
Phone: 2857 7683
Website: www.volumebeat.com.hk
Hours: 19:00-late (Mon-Sat)

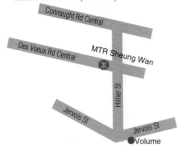

New Bars & Clubs

Bars in Hong Kong spring up, dry up, and close down quicker than you can say "let's take a shot," so before you go out, be sure to check websites and call to make sure that your chosen place is still in existence. The reason is simple: Hong Kongers like to keep it fresh, stay atop the trends and push the envelope in terms of what they think the best nightlife offerings should be.

$$ Rula Bula

Rula Bula is slang in Irish for commotion, and that's exactly what you'll be getting at this new venue, which boasts one of the best sound systems in Lan Kwai Fong. This space already had a guaranteed following before it formally opened its doors, and the selection of stellar DJs ensures that Rula Bula will retain that audience. As the night progresses, watch as the place transforms into a true dance floor and the beautiful crowds begin to congregate. Trust us: you will be assimilated!

Address: 58-62 D'Aguilar St, Lan Kwai Fong, Central, HKI
Phone: 2179 5225
Website: www.rulabula.com.hk
Hours: 17:00–2:00 (Sun-Tue) , 17:00-late (Wed-Sat)

$$$ Havana Bar

At Havana Bar, you will get to experience your own little slice of Cuba. This is one of the best places to chill out on the terrace and enjoy your surroundings, and they are worth taking in as you will be encircled by an attractive crowd that's looking for a good time and better drinks. Havana Bar also can lay claim to some of the most extensive (and

expensive) selections of rum in Hong Kong, so grab your credit card and chase that shot with one of their famous cocktails.

Address: 4/F, The Plaza, 21 D'Aguilar St, Lan Kwai Fong, Central, HKI
Phone: 2851 4880
Website: www.havanabar.com.hk
Hours: 12:00 – 00:00 (Mon-Sat)

$$$ Zanzo

Tai Hang is arguably one of the trendiest neighborhoods in all of Hong Kong and the city's best kept secret. Nestled away from the crowded and beaten paths of Hong Kong, Zanzo sits in a relatively quiet area, and you will quickly notice the calming aspects of its design, which feature simple tones. Choose from a wide selection of sake – much of it produced right here at Zanzo. Their offerings don't end there, however. Also on the menu are sashimi and a slew of other exotic dishes that will have you posting pics on Instagram.

Address: G/F, 15-16 School St, Tai Hang, HKI
Phone: 2750 6490
Website: www.zanzo.hk
Hours: 18:00–01:00 (Tue-Sun); closed Mon

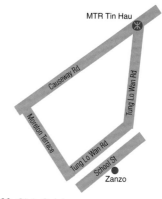

$$$ Club Gala's

Martinis, models and musical mayhem! That's what Club Gala's promises to serve up for anyone that comes onto the premises. With a sound system that will beat you into oblivion, the club constantly brings out the big guns of the local music scene. There's a happy hour six days (excluding Sundays) a week that gives you a few hours to blow off some steam and take a load off. For the weekend, indulge yourself in some of their signature cocktails. It's a bit pricey, but sometimes you've got to splurge, and if you do, this is the best place to do it.

Address: G/F Car Po Commercial Bldg, 18-20 Lyndhurst Terrace, Central, HKI
Phone: 2796 8830
Website: www.clubgalas.com
Hours: call to inquire

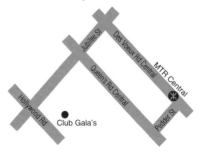

Club Gala's

$$ *Nova & Loft*

My, how things change with a new name. This space was once home to Hyde, but now it has been reborn and re-energized as Nova & Loft through a pimped out DJ station (complete with an elevated stage featuring sexy, scantily-clad dancers performing choreographed sets), new décor and improved seating sections. You probably won't have any time to be anything but vertical on their dance floor, but if you go downstairs, you'll have the option of pool tables or a terrace to drink and enjoy the skyline and the people passing through the streets below. Two floors of pandemonium make the perfect recipe for a great night out.

Address: 2/F & 3/F, Lyndhurst Tower, 1 Lyndhurst Terrace, HKI
Phone: 2522 2608; 6621 7050
Website: www.novaconcepts.hk

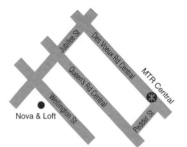

Nova & Loft

Entertainment

$$ *TakeOut Comedy Club*

Craving some humor in English and maybe in Cantonese and Mandarin as well? TakeOut Comedy Club has been bringing on the giggles for years now, with a steady line-up of local talent as well as the occasional star comedian. Come along and you'll for sure be laughing about all those little funny things that get lost in translation.

Address: 34 Elgin St, Soho, Central, HKI
Phone: 6220 4436
Website: www.takeoutcomedy.com
Hours: call to inquire

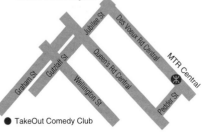

TakeOut Comedy Club

TOWNS & VILLAGES

If you find yourself outside of the party scenes that are northern Hong Kong Island and Kowloon and you're craving a drink, there are still plenty of watering holes to be found in the city's boondock beach towns and New Territories pop-up towns. Whether you're spending a day in fancy Aberdeen and the French Riviera stylings of Stanley on southern Hong Kong Island, kicking back in Sai Kung Town, or beach bumming around Pui O, the listings below will apprise you of our favorites for wherever you find yourself outside of downtown Hong Kong.

Aberdeen

$$-$$$ *LIS Café & Bar*

Located in the suave L'hotel Island South, this chic confection of hotel buffet, modern fine dining and signature cocktail bar sets up quite a show with its minimalist modern black furniture and cozy lighting. A great selection

of imported beers, homegrown cocktails and perfect after-dinner single malts puts LIS near the top of the Aberdeen bar LIST.

Address: Podium Level 3, L'hotel Island South, 55 Wong Chuk Hang Rd
Phone: 3968 8833
Hours: 17:00-00:00 (Sun-Thu), 17:00-1:00 (Fri&Sat)

Cheung Chau Island

$ Hing Kee Beach Bar (興記士多)

Teetering on the edge of Kwum Yum Beach, this uber-casual bar can be picked out by its outdoor plastic tables, strings of lights and the good-natured energy of the patrons outside. Bottled beers and pre-mixed cocktails are available, as are cans of Guinness.

Address: Kwun Yum Beach

Lamma Island

The majority of drinking and nightlife on Lamma Island is situated in **Yung Shue Wan**. The crowds are mostly local expats, and keep in mind that many places operate on club licenses, so you will need to sign a members' book (free) to drink.

$ Fountainhead Drinking Bar

A bar made for drinking? You heard right. If this sounds like just what you're looking for then swing on down to Fountainhead for a guaranteed good atmosphere of local Chinese and expats mixed with good music and agreeable drink prices.

Address: 17 Main St, Yung Shue Wan
Hours: Happy hour all day on weekdays

$$ Island Society Bar

Waiting for you just as you get off the boat, this pier-side expat hangout boasts a good beer selection and kickass local music groups and jam sessions.

Address: 6 Main St, Yung Shue Wan
Hours: Happy hour 16:00-18:00

$$ 7th Avenue

The reasonably-priced grub and alcohol here gets a kick in the pants by the hookahs, and the welcoming atmosphere of this recent addition to the Lamma scene gets a shot in the arm by the fine outdoor seating.

Address: 7 Main St
Hours: 12:00-late

$$ Diesel's Bar

From its home inside of Main Street's oldest building, this local favorite proudly sits as the grungiest bar in town, but for the patrons here that's part of what makes it the best. There's that, and the fact that the courtyard on the side is all too perfect for Hong Kong's countless sunny days.

Address: 51 Main St, Yung Shue Wan
Hours: Happy hour 18:00-21:00 (Mon-Fri)

Lantau Island

$$ Ooh La La

In need of a taste of Thailand while in Hong Kong? According to Ooh La La's website, which proclaims, "Thailand '45 from Central!" all you need to do is post up for a bit at this beachside cocktail bar at Pui O. While it is true that the golden beach and lapping waves do resemble something from China's southern neighbor, the bar and its "audio & video setup for presentations" gets a little too "Phuket" to be as secluded as they say. Still, it's a great place for a frozen margarita or a perfectly mixed mojito when you need to refuel.

Address: Pui O Beach
Phone: 2984 8710
Website: www.oohlala-hk.com

$ China Beach Club

Informal, eclectic and classy ragtag, the China beach club fits right in with Mui Wo, and if you're spending a day at the ocean here it's almost essential to stop by and grab a brew or two for the rooftop overlooking Silvermine Bay Beach. If your stomach starts a-rumbling there are good eats as well, including some good Thai curry, prawns, spring chicken and Greek moussaka.

Address: 18 Tung Wan Tau Rd, Mui Wo
Phone: 2983 8931

$ China Bear (中國熊)

After a long hike around Lantau's rugged terrain or a sunbaked day at Silvermine Beach, there are few better places to pull up, sip a beer in peace and watch the ocean (and the world) go by than the China Bear. Facing the beach and just outside the ferry pier, it's no wonder this is the preferred spot for many visitors to say their hellos or goodbyes (or both) to Lantau Island. Italian and Western comfort food is available as well.

Address: G/F, Mui Wo Centre, 3 Ngan Wan Rd, Mui Wo
Phone: 2984 9720

Mui Wo

see Lantau Island

Pui O

see Lantau Island

Sai Kung

$ Poets

Pub grub and pints puts the spotlight on Poets as a regular Joe kind of place. It's also a great spot to start out your evening before hitting the rest of the bars kicking back just nearby.

Address: 55 Yi Chun St
Hours: Open late; happy hour 12:00-17:00

$ Steamers

In the spirit of the neighborhood and just across the street from Poets, this standout British pub fries up good bar food, and tops it off with well-crafted cocktails and a selection of cold beers and good company.

Address: 66 Yi Chun St
Hours: Happy hour on weekdays 14:00-20:00

Sha Tin

$$ Tin Tin Bar

Part of the hugely popular Sha Tin 18 restaurant, this very classy bar features a standout mix of signature cocktails,

champagnes and malted whiskeys. A regular swing jazz band keeps the atmosphere sophisticated but chill, and the casual dress code and relaxed vibe betray a very high-end core.

Address: 18 Chak Cheung St
Phone: 3723 1234
Hours: 17:00-00:00 (Sun-Thu), 17:00-1:00 (Fri&Sat); happy hour 17:00-20:00 (buy one get one)

Shek O

$ Back Beach Bar (Ben's Bar)

Reclining over on Shek O's beautiful and mellow back beach is this bar that would make even the most Rasta man feel groovy. The ambiance is awesome with thumping reggae music, a few chairs thrown together from old wood, a couple of brick tables facing the ocean and a seaside shrine. Be careful not to melt into that chair while sipping your beer. You can find the place from the Shek O bus terminal if you head down the path that leads past the abandoned school.

Address: 273 Shek O Village, Shek O Back Beach
Hours: 19:00-00:00 (Mon-Fri), 14:00-00:00 (Sat)

Stanley

$$ Smugglers Inn

Finding a good British pub is not always as easy as it should be, considering the area's two centuries of colonial culture. But if that's what you're looking for, and you're in the Stanley area, then Smugglers Inn probably has your number. Its location right on the Stanley waterfront is usually loaded with chaps taking in a rugby match and downing draft ales.

Address: G/F, 90A, Stanley Main St
Hours: 18:00-late; happy hour 18:00-21:00

$$ King Ludwig Beer Hall

The biggest beers in town – period. Combine these imperial-sized steins with traditional oompah tunes, a huge selection of bratwurst and Deutsch eats, and plenty more German kitsch adorning the walls, and you'll be swept off to old Prussia in no time.

Address: Shop 202, Stanley Plaza, 23 Carmel Rd
Phone: 2899 0122
Hours: 12:00-00:00 (Mon-Fri), 11:00-00:00 (Sat), 10:30-00:00 (Sun)

$$ Ocean Bay

For a bit of a more subdued atmosphere, this classy joint has an open front with good ocean views and a selection of alcohol-free mocktails to rival its sleek and tasty cocktails. They have a nice food menu too, including quality oysters.

Address: Shop A2, 92 Stanley Main St
Phone: 2813 6718

$ Squeeze Juice Bar

Fresh-squeezed juices may be a given here, but what you may not realize is that not only do they also put up some sweet-tooth pleasing desserts, they also can shake and stir up some great cocktails with their delicious and healthy juices – something to balance out that potential hangover. Hoegaarden and other bottled beers are available as well.

Address: Shop A, 90A Stanley Main St
Phone: 2813 7273

Tsuen Wan

$$ Social Pub

This decent little pub on Tso Kung Square has a full bar, a good wine selection, and comfort food. It seems to pick up steam around 21:00 each night and rocks to the wee morning hours. We were impressed with the frozen cocktails and ice cream.

Address: 25 Tso Kung Square
Phone: 5318 8802
Hours: 17:00-3:00

$$ Vici Bar

The large, frothy draft beers, cool cocktails and retro décor of Vici Bar have made it and its orange, wood panel-framed walls a major draw card of the Hau Tei Square neighborhood in Tsuen Wan. Late hours, wings and pub grub round out the bonuses here.

Address: Shop A, G/F, 32-36 Hau Tei Square
Phone: 2615 9229
Hours: 17:00-4:00 (Mon-Sat), 18:00-4:00 (Sun)

Tuen Mun

$$ Bar Pacific (太平洋酒吧)

A relative newcomer to the Tuen Mun scene, Bar Pacific has an international feel and a passable selection of beers and mixed drinks. When we were here there were plans for expanding the list.

Address: Shop 4, G/F, Hip Pont Bldg, Tseng Choi St
Phone: 2866 1998
Website: www.barpacific.com.hk

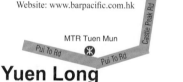

Yuen Long

$$ Unique by M1

If you're in the mood for something unique after visiting outskirt villages around Yuen Long, then stop by this creation by the owners of M1 (which has locations around the city) and check out its flashy, neon-lit interior that looks like something out of Blade Runner or Tron. The bar hosts regular cosplay competitions and has become a particular hit for its scantily-clad parties.

Address: Shop6-8, G/F, Prosperous Bldg, 84-88 Shui Che Kwun St

Shopping

Hong Kong: The Shopper's Paradise

If shopping were an Olympic sport, Hong Kongers would probably always be in the running for the gold. In Hong Kong, it takes stamina, skill and a view to kill (as in killer bargaining, that is) to be a successful shopper. As a city that has more to offer in terms of bargain goods and couture items than most others, Hong Kong is uniquely set up to encompass the passions of all who come into its borders.

Walk the streets of Hong Kong and you will instantly be slapped by fashion at every corner, with every trend present amongst the people. It makes sense, too, as the city has been an international trade hub for centuries. The best way to get the most out of your Hong Kong shopping experience is to know where to go to find what you want and how to haggle the price down to a reasonable deal. So bring your A-game, because Hong Kong is always ready for a bargaining battle!

Before You Haggle

The best strategy for paving your way to a good deal is to arm yourself with information in advance. If there's something in particular that you want, go online and research the hallmarks of authentic goods so you can knowledgably inspect what's for sale. Furthermore, there are relatively simple tests that even non-experts can use to get an idea of the quality of pearls, jade, silk and other items.

Other than knowing what you're getting into, the most important factor in successful bargaining is your attitude. Go into it with a smile and a sense of humor, but above all else, confidence. Get over the idea that you're being rude or pushy. It's all a game and everyone knows it, and you've got to be ready to sidestep statements like, "I guess my family won't eat tonight."

Another factor that will probably help your bargaining skills (and just getting around town for that matter) is hand signals. Chinese people have a unique set of hand signals that are different from the West, where the position of your fingers will resemble the

Chinese character for the numbers of six through ten. You may often see these flashed during bargaining sessions, and it can be very confusing if you've never had it explained. Familiarizing yourself with these before getting into a bargaining session can help a ton. It's pretty straightforward from one to five, and then:

The sign for #6 (六) looks like the old "hang loose" sign, where you make a fist then extend your thumb and pinky.

The sign for #7 (七) is made by touching your thumb to the tips of your middle finger and forefinger (keep your other two fingers curled up tight).

The sign for #8 (八) is the finger gun. This can be confusing since you might assume they mean "2" or "7."

The sign for #9 (九) is made by holding up a fist and then curling your forefinger into a hook shape.

The sign for #10 (十) is shown by making a cross with your forefingers.

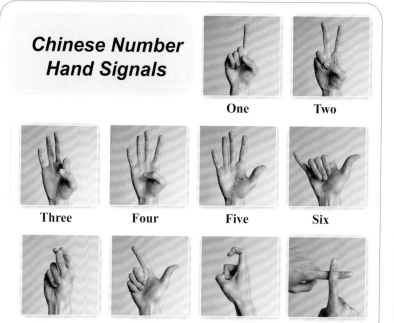

Chinese Number Hand Signals

One	Two
Three	Four	Five	Six
Seven	Eight	Nine	Ten

Haggling: The Art of the Bargain

When it comes to wheeling and dealing on the streets of Hong Kong, you don't need the skills of Donald Trump; rather, just a few pointers to help you get that special something. The first step to becoming an ace haggler all begins with knowing what you want without letting the seller know you have your heart set on the item.

If you see something that catches your eye in a store, don't run over to it immediately. Actually, you should pass it by then discreetly turn and see if anyone else is looking at the product. If you hear a price within your range, go back and try to seal the deal. If that is not an option, ask what the price is and then immediately go down to less than 50% of the quoted price (the actual price is usually about half of what the owners initially ask for).

Also, this is not the time to "have a heart." Remember, this is Hong Kong, only the strong shoppers survive. You may hear every sob story in the book from the seller telling you about his poor family and his rising rent prices, but they are just that, stories. This is all part of the game, one intended to make you spend more money than you should.

If they don't speak English and you don't speak Cantonese, have a pen and pad ready to jot down prices, though most vendors will have a calculator to punch in price numbers. They use this for Chinese speakers as well so that potential customers don't hear the prices they give to others. You might get a better deal if you stick to the paper or the calculator since they will be more reluctant to give you a lower price if everyone around can hear.

Once you've thrown your price out there, there's no turning back, so think about it before you blurt it out or punch it in. If you don't like the last price they give, simply walk away. Most of the time they will shout a lower price at you as you leave, or at least call you to come back so they can discreetly offer you something else. If you head back, quote a price lower than the one they just shouted and do the game all over again until you get the price you wanted (or close to it).

Here's an example of a successful bargaining transaction:

YOU: (Admiring an "I ♥ HK" bag, thinking you'd pay HK$100.)

SELLER: How much you pay?

YOU: I'm not sure... the quality seems fairly low... How much is it?

SELLER: No, it is very high quality, very nice... $200.

YOU: $200??? You're crazy. How about $50?

SELLER: Ha! No way. $200, final offer.

YOU: 60.

SELLER: 175.

YOU: (With a smile on your face) 70

SELLER: $70 I lose money! Final price $140.

YOU: (Walking away.) No, thanks... See ya!

SELLER: Ok, ok, 125!

YOU: 75.

SELLER: 110.

YOU: 85.

SELLER: 100, final price!

YOU: I'll take it. Deal!

You did it! Of course you'll never know how much that HK$100 bag was actually worth, but if you pay what you wanted to pay, you've done alright for yourself.

Clothing Sizes

Diversity is something that Hong Kong has long celebrated, from the fusion of food to the melting pot of people, and it also extends to the shopping selections available throughout the city. Whether you prefer to shop the conventional way or hit up small boutiques, alleys and raucous markets for your goods, you will leave Hong Kong a very happy camper. Wherever you shop in Hong Kong, remember that the sizing is different, so you should always try it on before you decide whether or not you want to buy it. This is easier in department stores or places with fixed prices since, if you try clothes on at a haggling street market, you may be highly pressured to buy anything you try on. As a rule of thumb, whatever size you normally are, go up a half or a full size.

Women's shoe sizes

US	5	5.5	6	6.5	7	7.5	8	8.5	9	9.5	10	10.5	12
China	35.5	36	37	37.5	38	39	39.5	40	41	41.5	42	43	44.5

Men's shoe sizes

US	7.5	8	8.5	9	9.5	10	10.5	11	11.5	12	12.5	13	13.5	14
China	-	42	42	43	43.5	44	44.5	45	45.5	46	46.5	47	47.5	48.5

SHOPPING TIPS ▶

1 If you're not used to bargaining, you might not know when to do it and when to pay the sticker price. Here's where you should bargain really hard: public markets, souvenir stands, and really anywhere that doesn't have marked prices. In restaurants, shopping centers, grocery stores, 7-11s, etc, prices are fixed.

2 If you don't get excited about bargaining, there's a low-energy strategy that can be equally effective. Act like you're bored, in a hurry, or not that interested, and refuse to say a price, no matter how much the seller asks you to. Just walk away after you've worn them down and they'll probably chase after you with an offer.

3 If an item doesn't have a price tag, just know that you're probably going to end up paying more than a local person would. There is an assumption here that foreigners have more money than locals. If you hate the idea of getting "ripped off" by paying foreigner prices, avoid buying anything that doesn't have a stated price. Another sure sign that you're probably paying too much is that the seller speaks very, very good English. The likeliest reason for this is that they cater almost exclusively to foreigners and have built up their skill in order to sweet talk more money out of you. It doesn't have to stop you from buying – maybe that pack of postcards is really worth HK$60 to you – but just know you're not getting the best deal.

4 Don't assume something is a good deal just because it's cheaper than what it would be in your home country. It might still be marked up significantly from the real value. Also consider quality: is getting a pair of jeans for US$10 really a bargain if they fall apart the fourth time you wear them?

5 Take a very good look at your products before starting your bargaining. Important features to look at are zippers, seams and glue (if it has spread farther than the spot requires). Also, look to see if the garment hangs straight or twists or kinks to one side or another.

6 If a seller seems annoyed that you're bargaining really hard, don't be deterred. They're not upset with you personally; they're upset that they won't get a huge profit off of you. In fact, more often than not, they will like you more if you bargain hard (with a smile).

7 The great equalizer in the bargaining war is **hk.taobao.com**, an online shopping Mecca built by Chinese for the Chinese. Use Google translate to navigate your way around the site and find out what similar products are going for before you hit the market. You know that these are the prices they are trying to get Chinese people to pay, and they include delivery. Anything that you buy at the market should be somewhere close to that price.

Hong Kong's Shopping Areas

Hong Kong is a little megalopolis: big in scope, small in actual size. But it is so densely packed with markets and malls you may be a bit unsure where to go for your best shopping experience. That all depends on what you're in the market for, and you should remember that there is no one area that will give you everything you may want or need. While this means that there is always something strange and new to see or buy in this city, it also means that knowing where to start can be tricky. Our shopping destination breakdown below can help get you off on the right foot to the right destination, and don't forget to check the Markets section of our Other Attractions (pg 130) for more.

Hong Kong Island

Admiralty, Central & SoHo Districts

This area is surrounded by some of the tallest skyscrapers on earth, but under the canopy of the concrete jungle lies some of the best shopping to be had on this side of the planet. If you are on the search for high-end fashion and luxury, voila – this is it!

Take the MTR to the Admiralty Station and once you arrive... you have arrived. You will immediately be surrounded by shopping centers: **Pacific Place** (太古廣場 ; 88 Queensway; www.pacificplace.com.hk), **The Landmark** (置地廣場 ; www.landmark. hk), **Exchange Square** (交易廣場), **Jardine House** (怡和大廈) and the world-famous **IFC Mall** (國際金融中心商場) are all within your reach. There are so many high-end shops here that even if you're just window-shopping, you might want to set aside a couple of hours.

Nearby lies **Hollywood Road** (pg 135) and the area of **SoHo** (standing for South of Hollywood Road), which is lined with smaller boutique stores that are just as special as their prices and offer everything from antiques to local artist creations and crafts. Most things here are on the high end scale, but in this area you can see some of the best art galleries, antique shops, and fashionistas (and fashionistos) strolling around, clad in shades and umbrellas in hand – rain or shine.

More impressive shopping lies in Central, where you can see even more of the skyline as you shuffle between luxury shops.

Chun Yeung Street (春秧街)

Chun Yeung Street is home to a large number of wet markets, that sell fruit, vegetables and seafood at a bargain prices. The streets and the people on them move about in a rhythm that is truly its own.

Dried Seafood Street & Tonic Food Street

Selling staple ingredients used in Chinese cooking and in herbal medicine, dried seafood shops can be found in Sheung Wan along Des Voeux Road West, usually referred to as **Dried Seafood Street**. If you're looking for natural or holistic medicine alternatives, this is the area to go to and find dried snakeskin, dried scallops, black moss, and other weird ingredients you thought were only relegated to Harry Potter novels. Nearby, **Wing Lok Street** (永樂街) and **Ko Shing** (高陞大樓) (see our Walking Tour on pg 280) carry ginseng and bird nests, which many Chinese consider the key to a longer, more energetic life, as well as a clearer complexion. See page 133 for more.

Causeway Bay

You'd better be ready to bring it and bring it hard in this district. Causeway Bay is a shopper's dream, and many have had to bow down or bow out, unable to keep up with the mad dash of savings and sales going on all around. For shopping here, you might just want to take an entire day. There are so many malls and markets that some have seen it fit for an entire weekend.

New York isn't the only **Times Square** in the world. Hong Kong has its very own, which commands just as much attention as the original. In fact, in some ways, it surpasses the NYC version. Each month the front foyer is transformed into a new theme, so depending on when you are in the area, you could be walking through a sea of pink trees or a huge Christmas Wonderland theme. Whatever is presented, be sure to bring your camera to take photos as you head up floor after floor of luxury shops like Marc Jacobs and Vivienne Westwood. Around the corner and down the street is the **SOGO Department Store** (崇 光 百 貨 ; www.sogo. com.hk) with more affordable clothes and bargains. Not to be denied, the new **Apple Store** is conveniently located here in case you need a new "i-thingamajig."

Take the MTR to the Causeway Bay section for Times Square and the Causeway Bay shopping area.

Sheung Wan

Eclectic electric would be the best description to apply to this area, which merges the traditional and the unconventional, and spins them on a dizzying axis that makes shopping here all the more fun. For hand-made items you can try your luck in the **Western Market** (pg 131), and then further west there's the **Dried Seafood Street** (pg 133) and Wing Lok Street. On **Bonham Strand West**, there are the famous dried abalone shops, a delicacy that people take photographs of when presented at mealtime. For antique shopping, there's **Cat Street** (pg 132) and for designer furniture and household appliances you can head over to the ever-trendy **Gough Street**.

Kowloon

Tsim Sha Tsui

Bingo! You've hit Hong Kong's 777 jackpot shopping destination. Tsim Sha Tsui is known as a must for the adventurous bargain shopper. The streets here come alive, teeming with peddlers screaming above your head for you to in and find out what bargain they can give you. Have your best haggling skills ready because you'll need them if you want to come out on top. The range of items available is expansive. Anything and everything from Bollywood bootleg DVDs and knock-off cameras to real precious gems and international brands dominate this area. In between all of these small mini-stores are

larger malls like **The One** (www.the-one.hk), **K11** (18 Hanoi Rd; www.k11concepts.com), and **iSquare** (國際廣場 ; 63 Nathan Rd; www. isquare.hk), all of which you may want to drop into. If you're coming to this area, you definitely will want to head back again, so prepare to spend at least a day roaming these streets... maybe even more!

Also in the vicinity are the **Tsim Sha Tsui Centre** (尖沙咀中心 ; www.tsimshatsuicentre. com.hk) and **Empire Centre** (帝 國 中 心), both of which offer Harbour views, cafes and restaurants to sit down in and catch your breath while you revive yourself for the next round of store hunting.

Granville Road (加連威老道 *)*

Do you have a taste for all things couture? Then head over to Granville Road in Tsim Sha Tsui and expect to be barraged by a plethora of budget and modestly priced local and international brands. There's the **Rise Shopping Arcade** (利時商場 ; 5-11 Granville Circuit) and the **Beverly Shopping Centre** (金佰利商場) on Chatham Road, the latter of which features some of Hong Kong's best up and coming designers. Got a marriage on the horizon? Nearby **Kimberly Road** offers some serious bridal dresses at a fraction of what you'd probably pay in your native country.

Address: Granville Rd, Tsim Sha Tsui, Kowloon
Transport: Kwun Tong Line, Tsim Sha Tsui MTR Station, Exit B2, walk along Cameron Rd to Chatham Rd South, turn into Granville Rd

Chungking & Mirador Mansions

What are the Chungking and Miradors Mansions? The more appropriate question may be, "What aren't they?" From budget-hostel city to a place crawling with delicious and cheap South Asian food, Chungking and Mirador are also becoming well known as a place to pick up a bargain. Loaded with currency exchange shops, kitsch memorabilia and dirt-cheap knockoffs, the mansions are a great place for a cheap this or that.

Address: 36-44 Nathan Rd (Chungking), 58-62
Nathan Rd (Mirador), Tsim Sha Tsui, Kowloon
Transport: Kwun Tong Line, Tsim Sha Tsui
MTR Station

Kowloon East & Kowloon West

These areas may be a bit less crowded and noisier than others, but that doesn't mean there aren't loads of bargains and shopping to be had. In fact, Kowloon East and West may be considered the un-sung heroes of shopping in all of Hong Kong. So, expect just as many shopping malls and entertainment options around you, including **ELEMENTS** (圓 方; www.elementshk.com; 1 Austin Rd West, Tsim Sha Tsui), which offers brands in the medium to high-priced range. Next door are the **International Commerce Centre** (環球貿易廣場) and the Airport Express. **Olympia Plaza** (奥都廣場) is another shopping hub, boasting over 250 shops for you to peruse and admire all of the various products on hand.

If you are out in a large group or as a family, options include **MegaBox** (www.megabox.com.hk), the **Wonderful World of Whampoa** (黃埔新天地; www.whampoaworld.com), **Telford Plaza** (德福廣場; www.telford-plaza.com), and **Plaza Hollywood** (荷里活廣場; www.plazahollywood.com.hk).

Temple Street Night Market

Street bazaars like this are hard to come by anywhere in the world, and that is one reason why Temple Street Night Market is an absolute must visit on your trip to Hong Kong. The dizzying mix of fortune tellers next to opera singers and gadget shops next to kama sutra boutiques is something that must be seen up close and personal. The energy here is hectic and a great reminder of what makes Hong Kong such a special city. See page 71 for more.

Jade Market (玉器市場 *)*

The Chinese are admittedly obsessed with jade – the stone has many attributes according to ancient philosophy, including beauty, purity, long life and good health. If you want to take some of this good luck home with you, the Jade Market in Kowloon is the place to go. With over 400 small stores to visit, you will find everything from rings and bangles to earrings and paintings featuring the stone.

The storekeepers will help you select a piece

based on the year you were born and the animal that corresponds with your aura.

Address: Junction of Kansu St and Battery St,
Yau Ma Tei, Kowloon
Transport: Tsuen Wan Line or Kwun Tong Line
Yau Ma Tei MTR Station, Exit C, walk along
Nathan Rd to Kansu St, then continue along
Kansu St until you reach the Jade Market

Mong Kok

If Mong Kok had a motto, it would be "we have everything under the sun." Anything you could possibly want to buy is available somewhere in this dense, crowded area, full of blurring neon signs and congested streets. Actually, just for the energy on the streets alone, it is worth a visit.

However there is more to Mong Kok than just frenetic energy. There are bargains to be had an every corner. One of the most popular is the **Ladies Street Market** (pg 80), where many of the merchants sell only one product. Here, you can see streets filled with stores that will only sell kitchen utensils, birds, shoes, fish or some other wacky product. For those who are a bit less adventurous, you can head to **Langham Place** (朗豪坊; www.langhamplace.com.hk), three blocks west of the Ladies' Street Market.

Sneaker Street (波鞋街 *)*

Trainers, tennis shoes, kicks – there are many names, depending on where you come from. But in Hong Kong, they are referred to as sneakers, and there are entire streets devoted to the footwear. **Fa Yuen Street** is where the trendiest sportswear has been located in Hong Kong since the 1980s. Limited and latest releases are available here, and you can be sure to find a pair that fits your attitude and personality.

Address: Fa Yuen St, Mong Kok, Kowloon
Transport: Kwun Tong or Tsuen Wan Line, Mong Kok MTR Station, Exit D3, walk along Argyle St to Fa Yuen St

Flower Market (花墟)

Exotic plants bloom and overflow in this area that includes over 100 shops offering scents and blossoms year round. During Chinese New Year, this area is inundated with familes looking for those special flowers and plants that are traditionally thought to bring good luck for a new lunar year. Check out their website www.flower-market.hk.

Address: Flower Market Rd, Prince Edward, Kowloon
Transport: Tsuen Wan or Kwun Tong Line, Prince Edward MTR Station, Exit B1, walk east along Prince Edward Rd West until you reach the market
MTR Mong Kok East Station, Exit C, walk to Sai Yee St via the footbridge and follow the signs

Goldfish Market (金魚街)

In Chinese culture, goldfish are thought to bring good luck, so it is not shocking that Hong Kong has an entire area devoted to this popular pet. **Tung Choi Street North** is known as the unofficial Goldfish Market, but you can also find other fish here, as well as other reptiles and amphibians. Even if you're not planning to sneak a frog past customs on the way home, it's worth it to come by and see some of the more colorful fish and other animals on display in the aquariums.

Address: Tung Choi St North, Mong Kok, Kowloon
Transport: Tsuen Wan or Kwun Tong Line, Prince Edward MTR Station, Exit B2, walk east along Prince Edward Rd West until you reach the market.
MTR East Rail Line, Mong Kok East Station, Exit C, walk to Sai Yee St via the footbridge and follow the signs

New Territories & the Outlying Islands

Cheung Chau

Cheung Chau Island and its villages are not brand-name paradises, but there are some small local specialties to be found. One place in particular is **Yuandme** (address: 2 Tung Wan Rd; hours: 10:00-20:00; phone: 2981 8432), a teahouse and shop on Tung Wan Road that is loaded with exceptional Pu'er tea selections and a dazzling collection of Chinese and Western tea antiques.

Lantau

Lantau Island is filled with scores of shops hawking international brands and local art and crafts. Towns like **Mui Wo**, **Pui O** and **Tung Chung** can offer a good variety of local shops, so when you spend your time on Lantau make sure to cruise their laidback lanes and find something special. Other smaller villages like Tai O may have some local crafts on sale as well, but they will be harder to find in such a small fishing village.

New Towns

Hong Kong's New Towns are what make up the developed parts of the New Territories. Though you can find some small boutique shops selling interesting items and clothing, many of them pop up and come down quickly, so it can be difficult to keep a finger on them.

Distractions

The tourist's life is exciting but tiring. Take a break from it all and enjoy the city in the way a local would: in persuit of relaxation and simple fun. The following distactions from a stressful life are all popular with the residents of Hong Kong, and tourists may find them a welcome change of pace from a busy schedule of sightseeing.

Acupuncture

You can find licensed acupuncture professionals at spas and clinics throughout Hong Kong. Generally, acupuncture doesn't cause much pain or many side effects if it's done by a competent professional. But if you have bleeding disorders, a pacemaker or are pregnant, you are at a higher risk of side effects. As with any medicinal practice, make sure you are in the proper condition to receive it and go to a professional who uses proper sanitary procedures.

The acupuncture clinics we have listed below are all known to be professional, clean, and use the utmost care. Still, if you go and anything feels amiss, do not hesitate to leave and find a place that makes you comfortable.

Alive Healthcare & Physiotherapy Centre

Address: Rm 2002, Car Po Commercial Bldg, 18-20 Lyndhurst Terrace, Central
Phone: 2541 8600

International Chinese Medicine Treatment Center

Address: 2/F, Man Hing Commercial Bldg, 79-83 Queen's Rd Central, Central
Phone: 2136 1261

Albert Place Practice

Address: 1103 Luk Yu Bldg, 24-26 Stanley Street, Central
Phone: 2234 9932

Mandarin Oriental Spa

Address: 5 Connaught Rd Central, Central
Phone: 2522 0111

Atlas Chinese Medicine & Physiotherapy Centre

Address: 20/F, Flat 03, Righteous Centre, 585 Nathan Rd, Mong Kok
Phone: 2386 6388

Chuan Spa at Langham Place Hotel

Address: 555 Shanghai St, Mong Kok
Phone: 3552 3388

Compassion Herbal and Acupuncture Clinic

Address: 1/F, Flat 110, 62 Mody Rd, Tsim Sha Tsui

Massage

There are two specialty types of massage that you see frequently in China besides the most common *anmo* (按 摩) massage. These are *tui na* (推拿) and *dian xue* (点穴). *Tui na* is based on Taoist principles and uses deep and focused massage techniques to target specific areas for healing.

Dian xue uses acupressure, i.e. using fingers and knuckles rather than needles to work the meridians and pressure points on the body.

Traditional massage is available at the hotel spas we've listed under acupuncture, as well as many other places. It is also available at countless massage parlors in every district of the city, but some of those may double as brothels, so be careful. The best way to make sure you do not enter a brothel for a "happy ending" is to avoid any massage parlors that only staff women masseuses.

Traditional Chinese Medicine Classes

Traditional Chinese medicine (TCM) has been applied to treat and prevent illness in China for thousands of years. *The Yellow Emperor's Inner Canon*, written during the first century BCE, was the first recorded book to introduce the basic theories of Chinese medicine. It definitely takes more than a few days to master TCM, but getting a taste of this ancient art is a great activity in Hong Kong. The best place to explore TCM is...

Dr & Mrs Hung Hin Shiu Museum of Chinese Medicine

The Dr & Mrs Hung Hin Shiu Museum of Chinese Medicine in Kowloon Tong sits inside a school with over 100 exhibits on traditional Chinese medicine and hosts a free class every Tuesday from 14:30 to 15:30. Participants learn about Chinese medicine and the uses of medicinal herbs. Make sure to bring your passport if you attend.

Address: Ground Floor, Jockey Club School of Chinese Medicine Bldg, 7 Baptist University Rd, Kowloon Tong, Kowloon (Kowloon Tong MTR station)

Martial Arts

Fleeing the destructive forces of the Cultural Revolution, a great many of China's best martial artists (who were persecuted alongside artists and intellectuals) fled to places like Hong Kong. Today, the city holds practitioners of some of China's most traditional, influential and effective lineages. Many styles have come from areas like Foshan in Guangdong, which was the home to Wong Feihung and Ip Man, two legendary martial artists. Wong Feihung, who practiced *hung gar* style, was depicted in over 100 Hong Kong films, while Ip Man popularized *wing chun* in Hong Kong and was one of Bruce Lee's first masters.

There are plenty of schools in Hong Kong opened by students who love to brag that their lineage is the best and comes from one of history's kung fu legends. Stop into one and see their skills for yourself. Few places offer classes in English, so ask the school before you commit.

Lam Chun Fai Hung Gar School

Lam Chun-fai is the son of one of Wong Fei Hung's students. His Hung Kuen school in Hong Kong is open for private lessons by appointment.

> Address: 7/F, Flat D, Aik San Mansion, 355-361 King's Rd, North Point
> Email: cflam@hungkuen.com

Chinese Kung-Fu International School

This school was opened by Sam Lau, one of the students of Ip Man. It holds classes every Tuesday, Thursday, Saturday and Sunday in Tsim Sha Tsui. Tuesday and Thursday night classes are held in the Kungfu Garden Hostel, the guesthouse that Lau operates.

> Address: F4, 3/F, Mirador Mansion, 58 Nathan Road, Tsim Sha Tsui (Kungfu Garden Hostel)
> Phone: 2723 2306
> Website: www.samlau-wingchun.com

Donald Mak International Wing Chun Institute

> Phone: 9132 8162
> Website: www.hkwingchun.com

Shaolin Wushu Culture Centre

This training center in the beautiful Tai O Fishing Village (pg 74) is centered around a courtyard and offers many different classes from dedicated masters. There are dorms for long stays.

> Address: Shek Tsai Po, Tai O Fishing Village, Lantau
> Website: www.shaolincc.org.hk

Cooking Class

One of the highlights of being in Hong Kong is eating dim sum every morning, and no place does dim sum like Hong Kong. What better souvenir to take home than a new dim sum or other Chinese-style cooking ability learned from a bona fide master?

Martha Sherpa's Cooking School

Martha Sherpa's school in Mong Kok, near the Ladies Market (pg 80) holds classes on dim sum, Chinese barbecue, vegetarian, Thai and other styles of cooking.

> Address: Flat B, 1/F, Lee Kwan Bldg, 40-46 Argyle St, Mong Kok (Mong Kok MTR D2 exit)
> Phone: 2381 0132

> Website: www.marthasherpa.com

Towngas Cooking Center

Towngas hosts cooking classes at their Cooking Center. View their schedule of classes at **www.towngascooking.com**. Single classes typically cost HK$380.

Hong Kong YWCA

YWCA hosts cooking classes on different types of food that usually last two to three hours and cost over HK$400. View the schedule at **www.esmdywca.org.hk**.

Easy123 Dining & Cooking Studio

Easy123 also includes classes on dim sum as well as desserts and other styles. Learn more at www.easy123.com.hk.

Language Class

In Hong Kong, Cantonese is the local language, but even though it's only spoken by a modest 59 million people (the same number as Italian), picking up some of the local language while you're here can be a fun challenge that can help you immerse yourself in the culture. Hong Kong also has Mandarin language schools as well.

Q Language

Q Language offers Cantonese, Mandarin, Korean and English courses, including classes and privates. Courses include 15- and 24-hour-per-week Chinese classes.

> Address: 14/F, Wing On Cheong Bldg, 5 Wing Lok St, Central
> Phone: 2540 0552
> Website: www.qlanguage.com.hk

Hong Kong Institute of Languages

Hong Kong Institute of Languages offers classes in Cantonese, Mandarin, Japanese, English, French, German and Spanish.

> Phone: 2877 6160
> Website: www.hklanguages.com

Essential Chinese Language Centre

Essential Chinese Language Centre offers set courses for Mandarin, business Mandarin and Chinese culture, and also individualized courses for Cantonese and Mandarin.

> Address: 8/F, Man On Commercial Bldg, 12-13 Jubilee St, Central
> Phone: 2544 6979
> Website: www.eclc.com

Side Trips

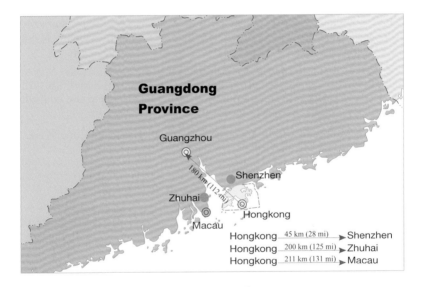

If you've made the most out of your Hong Kong vacation and are looking for an interesting side trip, you're in luck, because around Hong Kong there are some superb destinations for daytrips or even a short weekend away. If you're heading to Macau, remember that it, like Hong Kong, is a Special Administrative Region and not a part of Mainland China, so most nationalities will not need a visa in advance. But there are also several cities in the Mainland's Guangdong Province worth going to. In order to visit Mainland China, though, you must have a visa, and we suggest that you familiarize yourself with some of the differences you will encounter in the Mainland by checking out our Hot Topics section (pg 271).

Visa

Citizens of Japan, Singapore and Brunei can visit Mainland China for up to 15 days without a visa. If your passport is not from one of these three countries then you must apply for a visa for the People's Republic of China, and they are relatively easy to obtain in Hong Kong. You can apply in person at the China Resources Building in Wanchai at 26 Harbour Road.

The office is open from Monday to Friday from 9:00 to 12:00 and 14:00 to 17:00. Applying through an agent saves time and hassle, but you'll need to pay a fee. There are several agents in Tsim Sha Tsui, particularly in the Mirador Mansions, the Chungking Mansions and the Alpha House across the street.

Money

Mainland China uses the *yuan*, whose international currency symbol is ¥. The yuan is also referred to locally as *renminbi*, which means "the people's currency." Most Mainlanders refer to *yuan* as *kuai* (one *kuai* is the same as one *yuan*) and one *yuan* at the time was research is equal to about 1.27 Hong Kong Dollars.

For those heading to Macau, keep in mind that the SAR uses the Macau Pataca (MOP), and its currency symbol is written like this: MOP$10. All casinos in Macau accept Hong Kong Dollars, but for anywhere else you will need to have MOP$. Ferry terminals can exchange currency for you.

Prices in Mainland China are generally cheaper than in Hong Kong. Compared to nearby Guangzhou, for example, prices in Hong Kong are 50% more expensive. If you include rent in the picture, Hong Kong is 160% more expensive. Over in nearby Shenzhen – one of the most expensive cities in the PRC – prices climb a little closer to those in Hong Kong.

Macau Venetian Hotel & Casino

Macau 澳門

When Hunter S Thompson went to Las Vegas looking for the American Dream, what he ended up finding was a dream that had somehow "turned a gun on itself."

We can only speculate on what he would think if he went to Macau today. Hunter died just one year before Macau overtook Vegas as the biggest gambling city in the world, and one wonders whether he would dare venture into the debauchery of the casinos once more or stick to the more relaxing, Mediterranean feel of the old Portuguese neighborhoods. Does Macau represent Xi Jinping's recently touted "Chinese Dream?" Probably not, considering Xi's goal with his much advertized "Chinese Dream" is overtly communist in nature and the opposite of the blatant capitalism on display in Macau.

Besides a rainbow of neon lights, a towering gold hotel shaped like a leaf, a 45,359 kg (100,000 lb) chandelier and HK$1,000 minimum bets on some tables, the city does offer something for those who cannot afford such luxury and excess (which is most of us). Macau is also home to ancient Portuguese culture and architecture dating back 500 years. One of the first (and coincidentally also the last) European-managed territories in Asia, Macau is laden with 16th and 17th century Catholic churches, built among easy-going southern European neighborhoods that predate British Hong Kong by 200 years.

History

The Portuguese explorer Jorge Alvares became one of the first Europeans to reach China when he landed in Guangdong in 1513. In 1557, the Portuguese began renting Macau for 500 taels a year. This continued until Portugal decided to stop paying rent in 1863 and instead joined the onslaught of foreign powers invading China. Control

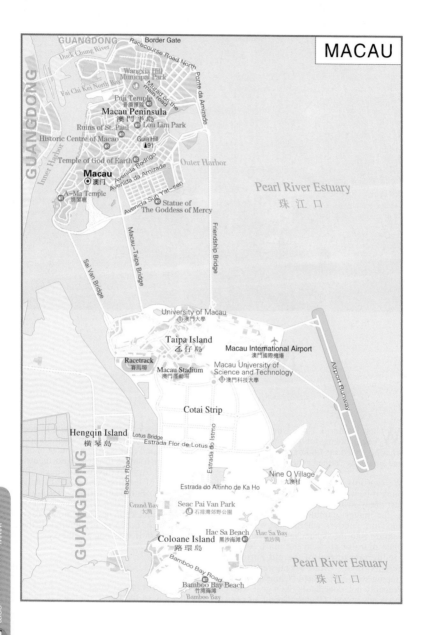

MACAU

GUANGDONG

Border Gate

Racecourse Road North

Duck Chung River

Wangxia Hill
Municipal Park

Mural of the main road

Pui Temple
普濟禪院

Macau Peninsula
澳門半島

Ruins of St. Paul

Lou Lim Park

Historic Centre of Macao

Guia Hill
▲91

Temple of God of Earth

Outer Harbor

Macau
⊙澳門

A-Ma Temple
媽閣廟

Avenida Rodrigo

Avenida da Amizade

Statue of
The Goddess of Mercy

Avenida Sun Yat-sen

Pearl River Estuary
珠江口

Ponte da Amizade

Sai Van Bridge

Macau-Taipa Bridge

Friendship Bridge

University of Macau
① 澳門大學

Taipa Island
氹仔島

Macau International Airport
澳門國際機場

Racetrack
賽馬場

Macau Stadium
澳門運動場

Macau University of
Science and Technology
① 澳門科技大學

Cotai Strip

Hengqin Island
橫琴島

Lotus Bridge

Estrada Flor de Lotus

Estrada do Istmo

Beach Road

Airport Runway

Nine O Village
九澳村

Estrada do Altinho de Ka Ho

GUANGDONG

Grand Bay
大潭

Seac Pai Van Park
① 石排灣郊野公園

Hac Sa Beach
黑沙海灘

Hac Sa Bay
黑沙灣

Coloane Island
路環島

Pearl River Estuary
珠江口

Bamboo Bay Road

Bamboo Bay Beach
竹灣海灘
Bamboo Bay

of Macau was wrestled from the Chinese in 1887 with the Sino-Portuguese Treaty of Amity and Commerce. When Lisbon's Carnation Revolution toppled the Portuguese dictatorship in 1974, the new government took an anti-colonialist position and defined Macau as "a Chinese territory under (temporary) Portuguese administration." In 1986, Portugal signed an agreement with the Chinese government to relinquish Macau, creating the Macau Special Administrative Region (SAR) in 1999.

Politics

Under the provisions of the Basic Law of Macau, the city retains a level of autonomy similar to Hong Kong. A Chief Executive is voted upon by 300 business and political leaders, while their Legislative Assembly consists of 29 members, 12 of whom are directly elected, ten of whom are elected by functional constituencies of business, labour and social groups, and seven of whom are directly appointed by the Chief Executive.

Demographics & Economy

Macau's population density is over three times greater than Hong Kong's. With 582,000 people living in an area of 29 sq km (11 sq mi), Macau is the most densely populated territory in the world (20,069 people/sq km). 92 % of the citizens are listed as Chinese, and the other 8% are actually composed of quite a bit of mixed-blood Chinese. Linguistically, 85% of residents speak Cantonese as their primary language, and 96% speak some dialect of Chinese, be that Mandarin, Cantonese or Hakka. Fewer (0.6%) still speak Portuguese as a first language, and just 1.5% call English a mother tongue. The number of people in Macau has swelled recently, not only because of the 28 million tourists who visit each year, but also from tens of thousands of migrant workers hired for the construction boom.

The population has increased exponentially in recent decades, coinciding with the increased economic output. In 1960, the population was 171,450, and today it has grown to a whopping 582,000. Even more impressive, the GDP per capita has increased five fold since 2002, going from US$14,870 to US$78,275, now the fourth highest in the world. The average life expectancy at birth is the second highest in the world at 84.4 years, according to the *CIA Factbook*.

Stanley Ho: the King of Macau

Macau's takeoff as a gambling center began with Stanley Ho. Nicknamed the "King of Gambling," he began developing Macau as a gaming powerhouse when his Sociedade de Turismo e Diversões de Macau (STDM) company won the bidding for rights to the Macau gambling monopoly in 1962. The Tai Xing Company had controlled the monopoly on gambling since 1934, but they were outdone by Ho and his industry building savvy. It was Ho's STDM which introduced roulette, baccarat and other Western games to Macanese casinos and established TurboJET – a huge hydrofoil ferry service – to cash in on shuffling tourists to and from Macau. Ho currently owns fourteen casinos, including the famous Casino Lisboa.

Visa

Like Hong Kong, Macau is very open to travelers and doesn't require a visa for most of the people who will read this book. Citizens of 66 countries do not require a visa to enter Macau, and citizens of almost every other country will receive a visa upon arrival. At the time of research, the only exceptions were for citizens of Bangladesh, Nepal, Nigeria, Pakistan, Sri Lanka and Vietnam, all of whom must apply for visas in advance.

There is also some difference in the length of stay allowed for different nationalities. Americans, Canadians, Australians, New Zealanders, South Africans, Indians and residents of some other countries are allowed 30 days per visit. Citizens of most European countries are allowed 90 days, and British citizens are allowed 180 days.

◨ Attractions

Casinos

Whether you salivate like dog at the sight of casinos and all that money being thrown around, or you furrow your brow in utter disgust by their gaudiness and visual vulgarity, a trip to Macau is simply not complete without at least bearing witness to the spectacle of its casinos.

There are two main areas of casinos: Macau Island and the Cotai Strip. **Macau Island** is where most ferries arrive, certainly because there are more casinos, including the area's oldest. The majority of the city and cultural areas are also on Macau Island.

The **Cotai Strip** is located on a section of recovered land that joins what used to be the two islands of Taipa and Coloane. It is currently being developed as the so-called "Las Vegas Strip of the East." Already, it includes the largest and second largest casinos in the world, the Venetian Macao and the Sands Cotai Central (both owned by the Sands group). In development are the MGM China and another Wynn casino (in addition to branches of these two casinos on Macau Island).

Minimum bets for mass gaming at Macau casinos averaged HK$1,622 (US$209) in June 2013, according to Deutsche Bank. The Cotai Strip is more expensive than Macau Island. There are cheaper options around, but if you plan to do any gambling in Macau you'd better be ready to throw down some cash.

On Macau Island

The big casinos on Macau Island are the Sands, the Wynn, the MGM, the Casino Lisboa and the Grand Lisboa. If you want some lower betting spots, you'll need to look for the older casinos, most of which have lower minimum bets. At the **Fortuna Casino, Waldo**, **Casa Real** you can find HK$50 buy-ins for black jack, while the **Babylon Casino** runs HK$30 minimums on roulette and the **Emperor Palace Casino** sees roulette go down to HK$20. HK$50 on baccarat can be found at quite a few places around town as well.

At new casinos like **Sands**, the first of the Vegas-style casinos, it can be hard to find a blackjack table for anything less than a HK$200 minimum. Sands has one of the biggest casinos on Macau Island, but others like **Wynn** are more celebrated for their full resort feel. The Wynn's atrium includes the **Tree of Prosperity**, a gaudy, self-indulgent tree with 98,000 24-karat gold leaves that rises out of the floor every seven minutes, basking in a barrage of lights. Out front they have the **Wynn Performance Lake**, where water fountains dance to music.

Baccarat is the name of the game in Macau. 90% of the city's gambling revenue comes from baccarat since most of the casinos don't have poker tables. Wynn and **MGM** are some of the few major casinos with poker tables. Limit and No Limit Texas Hold'em games can be found in these two casinos, and sometimes Omaha if you're lucky. **Casino Lisboa** – which looks like something straight out of Terry Gilliam's film *Fear and Loathing in Las Vegas* – was Stanley Ho's first flagship casino. The dark lighting and cramped space of its interior is a reminder of Macau's early, dingier casinos.

When international players came in and put an emphasis on aesthetics, Ho opened the **Grand Lisboa** across the street from the original Lisboa. Impossible to miss, the 260 m (853 ft) tall tower is shaped like a lotus leaf (although it looks kind of like a pineapple from close up) with its round lobby at the base of the leaf.

By the ferry terminal out east you can find the **Oceanus**, Ho's attempt to cater to lower and mid-range gamblers (loads of HK$100 and HK$200 tables).

On the Cotai Strip

The **Venetian Macau** takes center stage here. With 550,000 sq km (135 million acres) of gaming space, it is the largest casino in the world and one of the top ten largest buildings in the world by floor space, with enough room for nearly 2,000 slot machines and all kinds of games. It mimics the style of the Vegas Venetian, like a Disneyland version of Venice.

Across the street and just a bit smaller is the **Sands Cotai Central**. If the Sands brand name means anything in Macau, it means high bets, especially in Cotai. About one-third of Sands Cotai's tables are in the premium market level, meaning HK$2,000 or higher minimum bets. Sands Cotai is also the home of an ostentatious100,000 pound (45,359 kg), 37 m- (120 ft)-long chandelier.

Next door to the Venetian is the young and hip **City of Dreams**, which includes the Hard Rock Hotel resort. The main casino in City of Dreams is decorated with flashy lights and modern art to the hilt, and the Hard Rock casino is decorated with gorgeous female waitresses and dealers.

Casino Shows

City of Dreams's show **The House of Dancing Water** employs water fountains, props and dancers to create an elaborate Asian-themed show about the "seven emotions" of Confucianism...you know,

since Confucianism and gambling decadence fit so perfectly together. **The Bubble Show** (HK$50), happening every 30 minutes from 11:00 until 20:00, is a family-friendly 3D show about a dragon legend.

Cultural & Historical

The Historic Centre of Macau

With 29 churches, monuments, streetscapes and squares dating back to as early as the 1500s, the Historic Centre of Macau on Macau Island is, in its entirety, a **UNESCO World Heritage Site**. You can get a free map listing of the monuments at the front desk of any of the major resorts and hotels, but we've listed the highlights below.

St Dominic's Church

Portuguese Name: Igreja de São Domingos
Chinese name: 圣母玫瑰堂
Admission: FREE
Hours: 10:00-18:00
Recommended time for visit: 30 min
Address: Largo de São Domingos
Transport: Bus – 3, 6, 26A

This beautiful Baroque-style church was built during the 16th century and is the oldest in Macau. Painted yellow with green doors, it is an early example of the fusion of European and local architecture that defines much of Macau today. Inside is the **Treasure of Sacred Art Museum**, which includes 300 religious works and paintings that are open to the public.

Senado Square

Portuguese Name: Largo do Senado
Chinese name: 議事亭前地廣場
Recommended time for visit: 30 min
Transport: Bus – 3, 3A, 4, 8A, 10, 10A, 11, 18, 19, 21A, 26A or 33 to the Ave De Almeida Ribeiro (San Ma Lo)

The magnificent Senado Square, flanked by St Dominic's Church on one side, is at

the center of the old city, with the historic Avenida de Almeida Ribeiro running through it. It is paved in a traditional Portuguese design that uses small stones of different colors to create warm patterns. In the middle you can find a fountain, and the square is often decorated with lights and lanterns during festival times.

Ruin's of St Paul's

Portuguese Name: Ruinas de Igreja de São Paulo
Chinese name: 大三巴牌坊
Admission: FREE
Hours: 9:00-18:00
Recommended time for visit: 1.5 hours
Address: Travessa de São Paulo
Transport: Bus – 8A, 17 or 26 to Luis De Camoes Garden

Standing on top of a hill in the midst of manicured garden displays, the stunning façade of the old Cathedral of St Paul and St Paul's College is covered with complex carvings and features, including some of the Virgin Mary and the infant Jesus. A few sections of the crypts remain as well.

St Joseph Seminary Church

Portuguese Name: Capela do Seminario Sao Jose
Chinese name: 聖若瑟修院及聖堂
Admission: FREE
Hours: 10:00-17:00
Recommended time for visit: 20 min
Address: Rua Do Seminario
Transport: Bus – 9, 16 or 18

St Joseph Seminary Church is a beautiful yellow and white Baroque building

completed in 1758 with an ornamental exterior and interior columns and bossage.

A-Ma Temple

Portuguese Name: Templo de A-Ma
Chinese name: 媽閣廟
Admission: Donation
Hours: 7:00-18:00
Recommended time for visit: 20 min
Address: Rua de São Tiago da Barra
Transport: Bus – 1, 1A, 5

Pre-dating the Portuguese, this temple dedicated to Tin Hau was built in 1488. Tin Hau is also known as A-Ma, and it is believed that when the Portuguese arrived and asked the name of the area they were told "A-Ma Gau," which means "Bay of A-Ma." This is credited as the origination of the name Macau.

Monte Fortress

Portuguese Name: Fortaleza do Monte
Chinese name: 大炮台
Admission: FREE
Hours: May-Sep 06:00-19:00; Oct-Apr 07:00-18:00
Recommended time for visit: 30 min
Address: East of the Ruins of St Paul's
Transport: Bus – 8A, 17, 18, 19, 26

Built between 1617 and 1626 as part of the College of the Mother of God, Monte Fortress was put up by the Jesuits and was the sight of the Portuguese defense against an aborted Dutch invasion in 1622. Built on top of Monte Hill, it includes a wide open space with a garden landscape, the Macau Museum

and a battery of 17th century cannons along the fortress walls.

Macau Museum

Portuguese Name: Museu de Macau
Chinese name: 澳門博物館
Admission: MOP$15
Hours: Tue – Sun 10:00-17:30
Recommended time for visit: 1.5 hours
Website: www.macaumuseum.gov.mo
Address: East of the Ruins of St Paul's
Transport: Bus – 7 or 8 to Social Welfare Bureau

Macau's excellent museum is ideally situated on the site of the Monte Fortress and provides an outstanding sweep through the history and culture of the city. From the first floor's Genesis of Macau exhibit detailing the formative years of the colony and the city's numerous religions, to the recordings of Macanese poet Jose dos Santos Ferreira reading his poetry in the local dialect, the museum is a big hit that is worth some of your time.

The Macau Tower

Portuguese Name: Torre de Macau
Chinese name: 澳門旅遊塔
Admission: MOP$80 (for observation deck)
Hours: Mon – Fri 10:00-21:00; Sat & Sun 9:00-21:00
Recommended time for visit: 45 min
Website: www.macautower.com
Address: Largo da Torre de Macau
Transport: Bus – 9A, 18, 23

At the south end of Macau Island, west of the

casino district, the Macau Tower stands at 338 m (1,109 ft) and is the 19th tallest tower in the world. It has an observation deck and bungee jumping on the top.

Others: The **Sir Robert Ho Tung Library** was a private mansion built in 1894. Previously owned by Stanley Ho's great uncle, it is now a public library. The **Dom Pedro V Theatre** was one of the first Western-style theatres in China, while the **Holy House of Mercy** is an old medical clinic that was built in 1569. Other notable monuments include the **Moorish Barracks**, **Lilau Square**, the **Mandarin's House**, **St Lawrence's Church**, **St Augustine's Church**, **Casa Garden**, the **Lou Kau Mansion** and the **Old City Walls.**

Coloane Island

A-Ma Cultural Village

Portuguese Name: Estatua da Deusa A-Ma; Estrada do Alto de Coloane
Chinese name: 媽祖文化村
Admission: FREE
Hours: 8:00-19:30
Recommended time for visit: 45 min
Address: Estrada do Alto de Coloane
Transport: Bus – 21A, 25, 50

The religious park at A-Ma Cultural Village is built around the peak (170 m; 557 ft) Alto de Coloane, which is topped by a beautiful 20 m (65 ft) tall white jade statue of A-Ma, the Macanese name for Tin Hau. The park is Macau's highest point, and below the statue you can find a **Tin Hau Temple** (天后古廟), as well as an arboretum, a museum of agriculture and a few hiking trails.

🛏 Sleeping

There is no lack of (luxury) accommodation at each of the resorts in Macau. Just to give you an idea of prices, rooms at the **Wynn** cost about HK$2,000 to HK$4,500 per night. Rooms at cheaper casino hotels like the **Hotel Presidente** cost over HK$700 at the lowest. Definitely book ahead if you plan on staying in one of the casinos. For the cheapest centrally located option in town, try the **San Va Hospedari**a (65-67 Rua da Felicidade; www.sanvahotel.com) for around MOP$150 a night, but lower your expectations. Hotels on **Taipa Island** might be somewhat cheaper than those on Macau Island, but travel to Macau Island takes about 30 minutes.

Hotels book quickly. It's hard to find a room even six months out. For some people, it's definitely more convenient to just take a ferry back to Hong Kong. The ferry runs all night and takes about an hour.

🍜 Eating & Drinking

Macau's local cuisine includes Portuguese, Macanese and Cantonese food, as well as a bit of this and that from around the world. Some of the Macanese specialties include egg tarts, chicken (African-style spicy chicken and Portuguese-style chicken), roasted pigeon and various kinds of curries. You can find these dishes in abundance at cafes around Macau, but you can really only find authentic Portuguese food at more expensive restaurants. **Espaço Lisboa** on Coloane is a delicious and affordable restaurant that features both Macanese and Portuguese-influenced dishes.

Of course, Macau also has a lot of top notch international and Western restaurants within the hotels and resorts. The city has 12 restaurants with stars on the 2012 Michelin guide. The only three-star restaurants in Macau are **Robuchon a Dome** and **The Eight**, both in the Grand Lisboa Hotel. For Cantonese fare, **Tim's Kitchen**, also in the Grand Lisboa Hotel, and **Imperial Court** in the MGM Grand, also made the list.

For a snack, try the jerky given out as free samples by the vendors on the food street leading to the Ruin's of St Paul's. If you like what they offer, it's worth it to hand over some cash and buy some for later.

As you've probably already imagined, you can find a good, stiff drink at any one of Macau's casinos. Following casino theory, the more you drink, the more you spend!

 Events

Feast of the Drunken Dragon

Lunar date: 4th month, 8th day
2014 date: May 6
2015 date: May 25
2016 date: May 14

Carrying dragon heads and tails, the Macanese people dance their way through the streets (starting at the Kuan Tai Temple near Senado Square) as they drink wine and stop at stores along the way to indulge even more. They eventually head to a restaurant for a large meal when the dancing and booze have brought them to exhaustion.

Macau Arts Festival

Date: Throughout May

Throughout May various theaters and other art spaces host promoted events during the Macau Arts Festival. Visit **www.icm.gov.mo/fam/23/en/** for more information.

Macau International Fireworks Display Contest

Dates: Throughout September

Each September some of the best pyrotechnicians in the world come to Macau to represent their countries and compete in the Macau International Fireworks Display Contest. They show off their skills with two shows each Saturday in September and the first week of October. Watch from the waterfront outside the Macau Tower at 21:00 and 21:40 and prepare to be dazzled.

Macau Grand Prix

2014 date: November 13 to 16

The Macau Grand Prix is an annual auto event that involves car and motorcycle races each November. The Macau Formula Three Grand Prix course is known as one of the most demanding circuits in the world.

 **Getting In & Out**

From Hong Kong

The easiest way to get to Macau is to take a boat from the Hong Kong – Macau Ferry Terminal in Sheung Wan. There are so many ferries leaving each day you typically don't need to book in advance, but if you need to book ahead you can either go to the ferry terminal in person or check online at the company website (www.turbojet.com.hk).

TurboJET

TurboJET serves Macau Outer Harbour Ferry Terminal, the main ferry terminal on Macau Island. It runs day service every 15 minutes from 7:00 to midnight and night service once an hour from midnight to 6:00 both ways.

From Hong Kong-Macau Ferry Terminal				
	6-Seat VIP Cabin	4-Seat VIP Cabin	Super Class	Economy Class
Weekdays	HK$1,854	HK$1,236	HK$309	HK$159
Weekends, Holidays	HK$1,982	HK$1,321	HK$330	HK$172
Night Service	HK$2,101	HK$1,401	HK$350	HK$195

From Kowloon Ferry Terminal

From the ferry terminal in Tsim Sha Tsui, the ferry leaves every half hour from 7:00 to 17:30 and then runs night service from 18:00 until 22:30.

	8-Seat VIP Cabin	Super Class	Economy Class
Weekdays	HK$2,574	HK$282	HK$159
Weekends, Holidays	HK$2,574	HK$298	HK$175
Night Service	HK$2,574	HK$314	HK$196

From Hong Kong International Airport

From Hong Kong's airport, TurboJET runs ferries at 10:15, 12:00, 14:00, 15:15, 16:00, 17:50 and 22:00.

	Adult	Children age 2-12	Children under 2 yrs
Economy Class	HK$246	HK$188	HK$133
Super Class	HK$385	HK$287	HK$192

From Shenzhen Airport

From Shenzhen Airport, TurboJET runs ferries at 9:40, 10:30, 12:30, 13:30, 15:30, 16:30 and 19:30. It costs HK$377 for super class and HK$222 for economy class.

Cotai Water Jet

Cotai Water Jet runs from the Hong Kong-Macau Ferry Terminal to Cotai where the big new casinos, including the Venetian Macao, are located. During the day, it leaves at 6:30 and then every half hour from 7:30 to 17:30. Night sailing shifts at 18:00 and runs every hour until midnight. See www.cotaijet.com.mo for more.

Hong Kong-Macau Ferry Terminal to Cotai			
	8-Seat VIP Cabin	Cotai First Class	Cotai Class
Weekdays	HK$1,704	HK$213	HK$160
Weekends, Holidays	HK$1,808	HK$226	HK$172
Night Service	HK$2,000	HK$250	HK$196

Sky Shuttle

Arrive in Macau in style with the Sky Shuttle helicopter. The Sky Shuttle leaves from the heliport at the Hong Kong – Macau Ferry Terminal. Starting at 9:00, flights leave every 30 minutes until 23:00. Tickets must be booked in advance. Book at www.skyshuttlehk.com.

Getting Around Macau

Once you arrive in Macau, it is easy to get to the Macau Island downtown casino area by jumping on one of the free hotel buses at the ferry terminal. Then, you can get around Macau on the public buses or by foot.

The Life & Times of Stanley Ho

 If you visit Macau, you are guaranteed to see something owned by Stanley Ho. They call him "The King of Gambling," but he's much more than that. His business interests also include property, hotels, banking, horse racing, dog racing and TurboJET: the hydrofoil company most people use cross the water to Macau. He's the richest man in Macau, but his rise to the top was hardly along the straight and narrow. His story includes war, smuggling, pirates, concubines and allegations of criminal connections.

The ninth child of 13, Ho was born into a wealthy family. His great uncle was Sir Robert Hotong, a business associate of the Jardine company who financed Sun Yat-sen's revolutionary activities. During the Great Depression, his family lost much of their wealth, and his father left him when Stanley was 13.

Early on, Ho was a poor student. He was assigned to Class D, the lowest in Hong Kong's school system, but supposedly pushed himself hard enough to eventually earn a scholarship to the prestigious Hong Kong University.

Japan's invasion of Hong Kong, however, put a halt to his university education. While fleeing Hong Kong, he was stopped by Japanese soldiers, who suspected him to be European because of his Eurasian appearance. Only by fluently writing a short series of Chinese sentences was he able to resist arrest as a POW.

In Macau, Ho found his first taste of business by smuggling products to Mainland China. Rising quickly through the ranks, he found his wealth increasing as well, but hardly without some serious fights against fellow and enemy smugglers along the way. At one point Ho alleges that he fought off a company of pirates who attacked his ship to steal his loot.

The 1950s were a booming time for Hong Kong construction and provided Ho with the opportunity to start his first construction company. By 1962, he had earned enough money to purchase the rights to the gaming monopoly on Macau by agreeing to boost the city's unimpressive tourism market. Ho made good on the deal, bringing the 26,000 annual tourists of the early 1960s to an astronomical 9 million in 2000.

All this time, Stanley Ho was living a playboy lifestyle that would fall somewhere in between Hugh Hefner and James Bond. He married his first wife in 1942 and was subsequently involved in three more relationships that he considers "wives," fathering a total of 17 children with the four women. Many of his children are involved in Macau business and politics in various forms themselves and are now vying for future control of his empire.

Hussain Ahmad Najadi, a Malaysian businessman, recounts his dealings with Ho in the 1960s: "After spending days and nights in various cabarets and clubs with Stanley, Henry and their various concubines, we managed to tie up a contract for 23 hydrofoils in one go..." Business as usual for the early years of Ho.

His holdings soon expanded to countries like Iran, where he was one of the owners of the Tehran Farahabad Race Course, and North Korea, where he opened the country's only casino. However, after overcoming the Japanese and conquering pirates and Macau's economy, he had yet to face his biggest challenge, one that would hassle him for the three decades of the 1980s, '90s and 2000s: US and Australian regulators.

In 1973 and 1987, the Australian government denied his attempts to invest in casinos in Australia, and later, in 2009, the New Jersey Division of Gaming Enforcement issued a report criticizing MGM for partnering with Ho's daughter, Pansy Ho, on their Macau resort. The report claimed Stanley Ho had "associations with criminal enterprises."

"[T]riads or persons associated with Triads operated the VIP rooms in the SJM casinos," claims the report, citing a private investigation firm.

A review in the May 2007 edition of the *Far Eastern Economic Review* challenged the report's suggestion that such business in Macau could be done any other way, stating, "[M]ost allegations leveled against Mr Ho and his supposed connections to Chinese organized crime fail to take into consideration that it would be almost impossible to run a gambling enterprise in a place like Macau without some kind of understanding with the Triads."

When his Macau monopoly ended in 2002, Ho encountered a slew of new foreign competition. Vegas investors jumped into the development circle. In 2005, his company owned 75% of the market share for gambling. By 2007, it was down to 40%. Meanwhile, Ho, who once had a net value as high as US$9 billion according to *Forbes*, had fallen off the "World's Richest People" list in 2012, as his shares in various businesses became diminished. In the end, however, no one is feeling any pity for Ho, a man who spent US$330,000 on the world's biggest truffle in 2010.

Guǎngzhōu 广州

Guangzhou's location on the Pearl River (Zhū Jiāng; 珠江) made it an ideal trading location between the 1600s and 1800s. Several foreign nations established ports here, and it was through Guangzhou that the majority of opium entered China, eventually leading to the First Opium War and the ceding of Hong Kong. Today, Guangzhou is centered around the factories of Guangdong Province and has grown to boast the third largest GPD in China. Before the Qing Dynasty, Guangzhou wasn't much of a city, so you won't nessecarily find China's oldest monuments here. That being said, it does have some Qing Dynasty-era buildings and some foreign colonial buildings worth visiting, and the growing skyline and malls have made Guangzhou a destination for the moneyed and those into spending money.

Visa

You will need a Chinese visa to get into Guangzhou. See the beginning of this chapter on page 237 for more information.

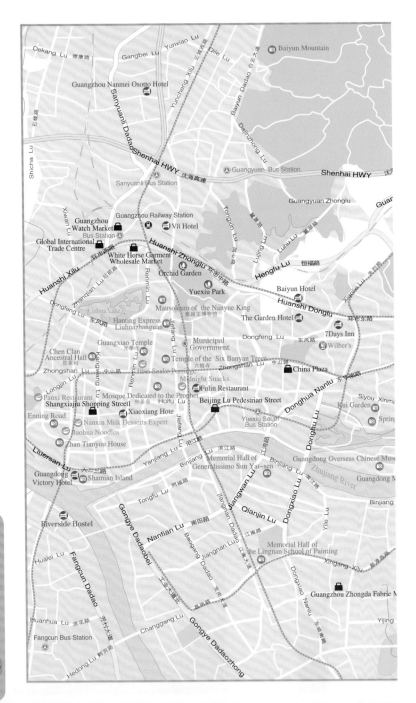

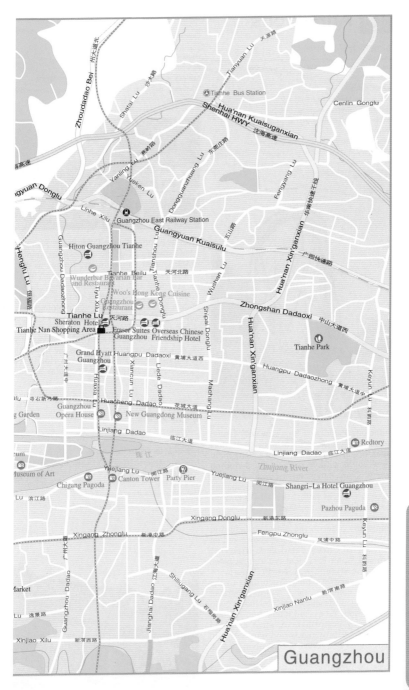

Zhoudadao Bei 州大道北

Shatai Lu 沙太路

Tianyuan Lu 天源路

Tianhe Bus Station

Cenlin Gonglu

Hua'nan Kuaisuganxian
Shenhai HWY 沈海高速

海高速

Guangyuan Donglu

Yanling Lu 燕岭路

Yueken Lu

Dongguanzhuang Lu 东莞庄路

Fangyang Lu

Linhe Xilu 林和西路

Guangzhou East Railway Station

Guangyuan Kuaisulu

Hengtu Lu 恒福路

Guangzhou Dadaozhong

Hiton Guangzhou Tianhe

Tianhe Beilu

Wunderbar Bavarian Bar and Restaurant

Guangzhou Restaurant

Woo's Hong Kong Cuisine

Tianshou Lu 天寿路

Tianhe Donglu

天河北路
Tianhe Beilu

Yushan Lu

Wushan Lu

Shipai Lu

Zhongshan Dadaoxi 中山大道西

Hua'nan Xin'ganxian 华南快速干线

广园快速路

Tianhe Lu 天河路

Sheraton Hotel
Guangzhou

Fraser Suites
Guangzhou

Overseas Chinese
Friendship Hotel

Tianhe Nan Shopping Area

Shipai Donglu

Hua'nan Xin'ganxian

Tianhe Park

Grand Hyatt
Guangzhou

Huangpu Dadaoxi 黄埔大道西

Xiancun Lu

Liede Dadao

Machang Lu

Huangpu Dadaozhong 黄埔大道中

Keyun Lu 科韵路

广州大道中

Huaxia Lu

Garden

Guangzhou
Opera House

Huacheng Dadao 花城大道

New Guangdong Museum

Linjiang Dadao

Linjiang Dadao 临江大道

Redtory

Zhujiang River 珠江

Museum of Art

Yuejiang Lu 阅江路

Canton Tower

Party Pier

Yuejiang Lu

阅江路

Shangri-La Hotel Guangzhou

Lu 滨江路

Chigang Pagoda

Pazhou Paguda

Xingang Donglu 新港东路

Fengpu Zhonglu 凤浦中路

Keyun Lu 科韵路

Xingang Zhonglu 新港中路

Market

Lu 逸景路

Guangzhou Dadao

Jianghai Dadao 江海大道

Shilugang Lu 石榴岗路

Hua'nan Xin'ganxian

Xinjiao Nanlu 新滘南路

科韵南路

Xinjiao Xilu 新滘西路

新滘西路

Guangzhou

Attractions

Chimelong Paradise

Chinese name: 长隆欢乐世界 (Chánglóng Huānlè Shìjiè)
Admission: ¥200
Hours: 9:30-18:00
Recommended time for visit: Half a day
Website: www.chimelongparadise.com (in Chinese)
Address: Yingbin Lu, Panyu District (番禺区迎宾路)
Transport:
Subway – Line 3, Hanxi Changlong (汉溪长隆站) Station
Bus – 129, 303a, 番 125, get off at Hanxi Changlong (汉溪长隆站) Stop

Chimelong Paradise

Chimelong Paradise, China's heavily touted and advertised amusement park chain, has a massive installement here in Guangzhou. It's wrought with 70 attractions, including some of China's most intense roller coasters, and it's a good destination for adrenaline junkies. Case in point: the 10 Inversions Coaster (Shíhuán Guòshānchē; 十 环 过 山 车) is noted for going upside down more than almost any other in the world. In addition to thrill rides, Chimelong has shows and an International Circus, Safari Park, Crocodile Park and Water Park, and it's a great place to see the strange way North Americans are exoticized in China. According to the pamphlet statement, their "North American Lumbering Burlesque Show" includes "wild and exciting, funny and interesting effects" and "crazy performances, such as wood sawing, axe throwing, wood carving" and pretty much everything else involving wood. Besides the entrance ticket price, you can expect to fork over more dough for various other areas in the park.

Shamian Island

Chinese name: 沙面岛 (Shāmiàn Dǎo)
Admission: FREE
Hours: 9:30-18:00
Recommended time for visit: 2-3 hours
Address: riverbank of Bai'etan, Zhujiang (珠江岔口白鹅潭畔)
Transport: **Bus** – 823 from Guangzhou Railway Station to Shi Zhongyiyuan (市中医院) Stop, then walk south 110 m (361 ft)

With its location by the Pearl River, Shamian Island was a part of the concessions granted to the United Kingdom and France as part of the post-Opium War settlement. With its greenery and colonial buildings, it is a popular place for couples to take wedding photos, and among the foreign buildings here you'll see the **Our Lady of Lourdes Chapel** (Lùdé Shèngmǔ Táng; 露 德 圣 母 堂) and the **Christ Church Shameen** (Shāmiàn Táng; 沙 面 堂), both pretty sights from the mid-19th century. The onsite White Swan Hotel (see pg 256) is a luxury hotel popular among foreigners.

Chen Clan Ancestral Hall

Chinese name: 陈家祠 (Chénjiā Cí)
Admission: ¥10
Hours: 8:30-17:30
Recommended time for visit: 1.5 hours
Address: 34 Enlong Li, Zhongshan Qi Lu (中山七路恩龙里 34 号)
Transport:
Subway – Line 1, Chenjiaci Station
Bus – 17 or 88 to Chenjiaci Stop

The large ancestral hall of the Chen Family was built by the clan in 1894 and holds some of the most mesmerizing ancient-style architecture in the city. The 19-hall complex served as an academy for the family, where they studied in preparation for the rigorous Imperial Examinations of the Qing Dynasty. The rich artwork and painstakingly etched wood, stone, brick, and iron carvings throughout its interior are breathtaking by themselves, and make this place highly worth a visit. But there's plenty more: Besides it's superb architecture, gorgeous garden landscaping and stunning screen-door wood carvings, it is also home to beautiful pottery and ceramics – much of which is for sale by local artists – and the standout **Guangdong Folk Art Museum** (Guǎngdōng Mínjiān Gōngyì Bówùguǎn; 广东民间工艺博物馆).

Canton Tower

Chinese name: 广州塔 (Guǎngzhōu Tǎ)
Recommended time for visit: 1.5 hours
Transport:
Subway – Line 3, Chiganta (赤岗塔), Exit B
Bus – 468 or 262 to Guangzhouta Xizhan (广州塔西站) Stop

At 600 m (2,000 ft), the Canton Tower is the second tallest tower (not a skyscraper) in the world. It is lit up at night in rainbow colors. Entrance to the observation deck costs ¥150.

Foshan (佛山)

The cmall city of Foshan, just outside Guangzhou, is accessible by the Guangfo Line, which takes about 1.5 hours from Guangzhou's downtown. It's a pretty ordinary

city, but for the sake of novelty it has the **Toilet Bowl Waterfall** (Mǎtǒng Pùbù; 马桶瀑布) inside the **Shiwan Park** (Shíwān Gōngyuán; 石湾公园) art area. The waterfall is made up of thousands of toilet bowls and sinks and is the headlining attraction of the park, which also has ceramics and antiques on display.

Pedestrian Streets

Guangzhou has a few interesting pedestrian streets that are good for shopping, eating and people watching.

Beijing Road Walking Street (Běijīng Lù Bùxíng Jiē; 北京路步行街)

A crowded road in the heart of downtown Guangzhou, Beijing Road has tasty restaurants, brand name shops and a few hilariously named brand copies (e.g. Piano Boy, with a rabbit for its icon). Beijing Lu holds one of the last remaining sections of the old city wall.

Shangxiajiu Pedestrian Street (Shàngxiàjiǔ Bùxíng Jiē; 上下九步行街)

Similar to Beijing Road, Shangxiajiu is a shopping street, but it's also in the vicinity of some cultural areas, including the **Hualin Buddhist Temple** (Huálín Chánsì; 华林禅寺) to the north and **Guangzhou Cultural Park** (Guǎngzhōu Wénhuà Gōngyuán; 广州文化公园) and Shamian Island to the south.

 Sleeping

Budget

Guangzhou Riverside Youth Hostel (Guǎngzhōu Jiāngpàn Guójì Qīngnián Lǚshè; 广州江畔国际青年旅舍)

About a 15- to 20-minute walk from the metro station, but also accessible by river ferry (until 22:00), this hostel can do the job. Some rooms are provided with free lockers and a small fee is charged for luggage storage. Doubles from ¥178, dorm beds from ¥65.

Address: 15 Changdi Lu (长堤路 15 号) (Metro Line 1, Fangcun- 芳村), Exit B1)
Phone: (020) 2239 2500

Guangzhou Journey House Youth Hostel (Guǎngzhōu Zhēngtú Qīngnián Lǚshè; 广州征途青年旅舍)

This apartment-converted hostel is popular with Chinese job-seekers and is one of the only options in town for budget travelers. However, the area is residential and may be difficult to find for non-Chinese speaking foreigners. Dorm bed ¥55, singles ¥140.

Address: 27/F, Bldg 1, Jiayiyuan Garden, 445 Tianhe Beilu (天河北路445号嘉怡苑1栋27F房)
Phone: (020) 3880 4573
Email: liliwen6@hotmail.com

Mid-Range

Hotel Canton (Guǎngzhōu Dàshà; 广州大厦)

This once glorious hotel is looking a bit outdated these days, but its location in prime position just north of the Beijing Road Pedestrian Street makes it a solid contender. ¥390 and up.

Address: 374 Beijing Lu (北京路374号) (Metro Line 1 or Line 2, Gongyuanqian - 公园前站)
Phone: (020) 8318 9888

Splurge

Guangzhou Baiyun Hotel (Guǎngzhōu Báiyún Bīn'guǎn; 广州白云宾馆)

Call for discounts of up to 75%!

This is one of the city's most famous five-star hotels. The lobby bar is superb and there's no need to count sheep once you lay on their dreamy beds. The bathrooms have also been updated and are top of the line, and the same goes for the excellent spa center. Guangzhou Baiyun sits in the city center near plenty of shops and restaurants. Panda Guides has a special partnership with this luxury hotel. Call ahead to book your reservation and give the code 4074 to recieve massive discounts (up to 75%!).

Address: 367 Huanshi Donglu, Yuexiu District (越秀区环市东路367号)
Phone: (020) 8600 9099
Website: guangzhou-baiyun-hotel.com
Email: sales@guangzhou-baiyun-hotel.com

🥢 Eating

Guangzhou is a good place to try Cantonese fare. Roast goose (shāo é; 烧鹅) and other roast meats are just some of the delicious foods Guangzhou chefs pride themselves on. Others include sweet and sour dishes, spare ribs, won ton noodles and seafood. Keep your eye out for *chángfěn* (肠粉), a tasty snack similar to dumplings but with a larger wrap, something like a dumpling burrito. Cantonese food is famous around China for its light flavor (qīngdàn; 清淡).

Another of Guangdong's culinary styles is Chaozhou cuisine, which includes a variety of balls...and by that we mean fish balls (yú wán; 鱼丸), pork balls (gòngwán; 贡丸), beef balls (niúròu wán; 牛肉丸), and other meats balled up and cooked up in soups and cakes of countless varieties.

🍸 Drinking

Much like everything else in Guangzhou, drinking in this city is not cheap. There are places to drink just about everywhere, but one of the best places to hit up is **Fangcun Bar Street**.

Fangcun Bar Street (Fāngcūn Jiǔba Jiē; 芳村酒吧街)

Fangcun Bar Street (aka Bai-e-tan Street) is the most popular bar street in Guangzhou and sports a good view of the Pearl River. French pub **Amigo** (phone: 020-8155 8173; 荔湾区长堤路白鹅潭风情酒吧街 B03地铺) is one of the most famous bars and is an excellent choice.

✈️ Getting In & Out

Bus

Trans-Island Chinalink buses depart from a number of hotels and other locations to Guangzhou. One place they leave from is Portland Street in Prince Edward (northern

Train Number	Departure Time	Arrival Time
T812	7:25	9:24
T824	8:15	10:12
T820	9:24	11:23
T804	10:52	12:51
T808	11:32	13:26
T814	12:23	14:17
T826	13:11	15:08
T818	14:32	16:31
T810	16:35	18:34
T828	18:00	19:07
T816	18:44	20:43
T802	20:01	22:00

Mong Kok). **China Travel Service (CTS)** is another company that offers buses from Hong Kong to Guangzhou. They leave multiple times per hour from 6:50 to 22:15 from multiple locations, including the CTS branches in Sheung Wan, Mong Kok (62-72 Sai Yee Street), Portland Street, Wan Chai, the Wan Chai Ferry Pier and the Metro Park Hotel in Causeway Bay. For a full list of locations and a timetable, visit **www.ctshk. com/english/bus/zhonglv.htm**. CTS buses cost HK$100 for one way adult tickets.

Train

There are many intercity trains from Hong Kong to Guangzhou. The trains take just less than two hours, but they are expensive (¥190 for adults and ¥95 for children). Train T98B is a cheaper option. It starts from Hong Kong Train Station in Hung Hom at 15:15 and runs to Guangzhou East Station. The train takes two hours and costs ¥21.5 for a seat, ¥50 for a hard sleeper and ¥87.5 for a soft sleeper. A seat on any of the many trains that leave from Shenzhen to Guangzhou is about the same price. You can buy tickets in advance at a travel agency or another in Tsim Sha Tsui.

Ferry

A large boat departs throughout the day from the SkyPier at the Hong Kong International Airport. Besides Guangzhou, it includes several other stops along the Pearl River.

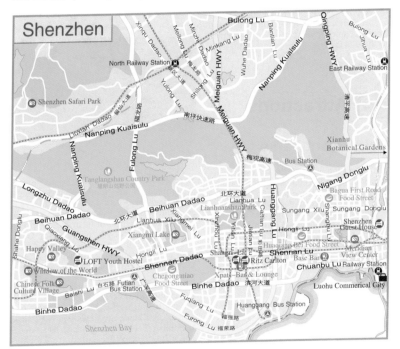

Shēnzhèn 深圳

In Shenzhen you can find people from all over China. The migrant population living here is more than three times greater than the number of people who have permanent residence. That number somewhat betrays Shenzhen's great prosperity, which has come in large part due to its vicinity to Hong Kong. In 1979, it became China's first Special Economic Zone (SEZ), and its stock exchange sits at a market cap of over US$100 billion. And you can believe that the city with the fourth highest GDP of any in China attracts wealth seekers from across the country.

Shenzhen's up-and-coming status has infused within it a very palpable vitality, but there really isn't a whole lot to enjoy here if you don't have some significant cash in the bank. Its shopping, dining and drinking establishments are lauded as among the best north of the Hong Kong border, and it is a superbly welcoming place for outsiders. As their city motto goes, "Once you come to Shenzhen, you are always a Shenzhener."

Visa

Shenzhen offers special five-day Shenzhen-only visas at the Luohu (罗 湖) border checkpoint for citizens of Australia, Canada, New Zealand and most EU countries. The cost is ¥168 for people of most nationalities but ¥469 for UK citizens. Be aware that policies can change at the drop of a hat. For citizens of all other countries, you need to get a Chinese visa through the visa office or an agent.

 **Attractions**

Amusement Parks

Shenzhen is the home of the OCT company, better known as the company behind Happy Valley, a chain of theme parks in China. The OCT company has made Shenzhen one of the leading theme park cities in China with their **OCT East** (Dōngbù Huáqiáo Chéng; 东部华侨城), **Chinese Folk Culture Village** (Zhōngguó Mínsú Wénhuàcūn; 中国民俗文化村), and several others that are too cheesy to mention here.

OCT East

Admission: ¥180 (Knight Valley); ¥160 (Tea Stream Valley)
Hours: 9:30-17:30 (Knight Valley); 9:30-18:30 (Tea Stream Valley)
Recommended time for visit: 1 day
Address: Huaqiao Cheng, Dameisha Dongbu, Yantian (深圳市盐田区大梅沙东部华侨城)
Transport: Bus – 103, 387, J1, M207, M362 or Airport Bus 6 to Daxiagu Stop

OCT East has two sections: **Knight Valley** (aka Ecoventure Valley, Dàxiá Gǔ; 大侠谷) which includes thrill rides and **Tea Stream Valley** (Cháxī Gǔ; 茶溪谷) which is essentially made up of relaxing, smaller themed parks but has no big rides. Knight Valley is located on the side of a hill, providing it some nice views and decent hikes. One of the best rides is the wooden roller coaster on top of the hill.

Chinese Folk Culture Village

Admission: ¥120
Hours: 9:00-18:00 (night show until 22:00)
Recommended time for visit: half day
Address: 9005 Shennan Dadao (深圳市深南大道 9005 号)
Transport:
Subway – Line 1, Huaqiaocheng Station, Exit D
Bus – 21, 26, 101, 105, 113, 201, 204, 209, 210, 222, 223, 230, 232, 233, 234, 301, 311 or 327 to Jinxiu Zhonghua Stop

Spread across China are 56 officially recognized ethnic groups, each boasting a unique culture. Visiting the local villages of an ethnic minority group can be an amazing experience, but most of them live in specific regions, so unless you plan to loop China and see them all first hand (the best choice), your next best option is to visit one of these touristy and bizarre ethnic culture villages.

This one in Shenzhen does a fair job of recreating small scale villages of 22 ethnic groups within its 18,600 sq m (200,000 sq ft) park, but there are times you can't shake the autocratic, borderline racist feel. Among the ethnicities represented are Tibetans, Uighurs, Mongolians, Dong, Naxi, Yi and Miao. They celebrate ethnic festivals such as Water Splashing Festival (spring, Dai people) and Torch Festival (midsummer, Yi people) throughout the year.

Kingkey 100

Chinese name: 京基 100 大厦 (Jīngjī Yībǎi Dàshà)
Address: 5016 Shennan Dong Lu (深南东路 5016 号)
Transport: Bus – 3, 10, 12, 14, 29, 101, 203, 103, 104, 113, K113, 204, K204, 215, 311, 352, 353, and ask the driver to let you get off at the destination: " 我去京基 100 大厦，请到时告诉我下车，谢谢 "

The tallest building in Shenzhen, and one of the 15 tallest in the world as of 2013, Kingkey has an expensive observation deck (¥200) on its top two floors (99 and 100) and a café on floor 96, where you can spend more money to enjoy food with the view.

Xianhu Botanical Gardens

Chinese name: 仙湖植物园 (Xiānhú Zhíwù Yuán)

Admission: ¥20

Hours: 7:00-22:00

Recommended time for visit: 2-3 hours

Address: 160 Liantang Xianhu Lu, Luohu (深圳市罗湖区莲塘仙湖路 160 号)

Transport: Bus – 202, 220, 382, and get off at Xianhu Zhiwuyuan (仙湖 植物园) Stop

The lovely Xianhu Botanical Gardens has trees, azaleas and a petrified forest, providing a nice reprieve from the metallic shininess of the city. Inside the park is the beautiful **Hongfa Temple** (Hóngfǎ Sì; 弘法寺), which has tasty tea. The gardens are to the east of Shenzhen, on the south side of the Shenzhen Reservoir. It takes about 1.5 hours to get there via bus 382.

Wutong Mountain

Chinese name: 梧桐山 (Wútóng Shān)

Admission: ¥20

Hours: 8:00-18:00

Recommended time for visit: 2-3 hours

Address: 2076 Liantang Luosha Lu, Luohu (深圳市莲塘罗沙路 2076 号)

Transport: Bus – 211, "梧桐山假日专线 1," or "梧桐山假日专线 2," and get off at the terminal Wutong Shancun (梧桐山村) Stop

Located about 30 km (19 mi) east of downtown Shenzhen (2.5 hours by public transit), Wutong Mountain, at 944 m (3,097 ft), is the tallest mountain in Shenzhen. There are some lush mountain forests and pavilions along the stairway hiking trail up the mountain, or if you're in a hurry you can take the paved road that is less scenic but faster. Hiking from bottom to top takes about two to four hours.

 **Sleeping**

Like Guangzhou, Shenzhen is a ritzy, expensive place, and budget options are severely limited.

Budget

LOFT International Youth Hostel (Qiáochéng Lǚyóu Guójì Qīngnián Lǚshě; 侨城旅友国际青年旅舍)

A modern place in the YHA China franchise, LOFT sports room keycards, free wifi, and a nearby supermarket. Dorm beds from ¥50-60, doubles from ¥178, bigger suites under ¥400.

> Address: 7 Xiangshan Dongjie, Huaqiaocheng (深圳市华侨城香山东街 7 号)
> Phone: (0755) 8609 5773; 8623 2403
> Email: loftyha@163.com

Shanshui Trends Hotel (Shānshuǐ Jiǔdiàn; 山水酒店)

The Shanshui Trends Hotel in Luohu is a Japanese-inspired hotel with interesting Japanese décor. For the budget conscious traveler, it's unique and affordable. Rooms start at ¥250 per night and go up to ¥303 a night for a deluxe twin room and include free wifi.

> Address: 1098 Yanhe Nanlu, Luohu (沿河南路 1098 号)
> Phone: (0755) 6162 1111

7 Days Inn (Qītiān Liánsuǒ Jiǔdiàn; 七天连锁酒店 *)*

With 12 total locations, most of the 7 Days Inns inside the downtown area of Shenzhen cost close to ¥200 per night for their cheapest rooms. The ones on the outskirts of the city will run you around ¥140 or ¥160. Search at **www.7daysinn.cn** (Chinese only).

Location 1

Address: 1018 Wenjin Zhonglu, Luohu District (罗湖区文锦中路 1018 号)
Phone: (0755) 2582 9869

Location 2

Address: 22 Nanlian Lu, Longgang District (龙岗区南联路 22 号)
Phone: (0755) 8480 4588

Mid-Range

Sunflower Hotel & Residence (Kuíhuā Gōngyù; 葵花公寓 *)*

The Sunflower has apartment style rooms with kitchens and nice furnishings. Some people stay here long term and take advantage of their club and golf course. Amenities include breakfast, internet and a fitness center. Boutique suites cost ¥588 per night, duplex suites cost ¥688 and two-bedroom duplex suites go for ¥988.

Address: 1 Shixia Beiyijie, Futian District (福田区石厦北一街)
Phone: (0755) 3332 8888

Splurge

Futian Shangri-La (Shēnzhèn Fútián Xiānggélǐlā Dàjiǔdiàn; 深圳福田香格里拉大酒店 *)*

Rooms include an in-bathroom TV (you heard right, a TV in the bathroom), internet, iPod connectors, coffee-making facilities, a mini-bar and a safe. They also have a business center, currency exchange, a gift shop, a ticket-booking office, table tennis, fitness room, massage parlor and an outdoor swimming pool. Chinese and Western restaurants, as well as a café and bar, are onsite. Listed rates for doubles are ¥3,000, discounted from ¥1,500.

Address: 4088 Yitian Lu, Futian District (福田区益田路 4088 号)
Phone: (0755) 8828 4088
Email: slft@shangri-la.com

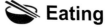 # Eating

Since Shenzhen was only founded in the late 1970s and was merely a small fishing town before that, there's no real authentic Shenzhen dishes. Rather, immigrants from all over China have brought the flavors of their hometowns to the city. For this reason, Shenzhenese food offers a variety from around China.

One unique restaurant is the **Hakka City** (Kèjiā Chéng; 客家城) chain, which serves traditional Hakka food, such as varieties of salted chicken, at affordable fast-food prices. There are branches in Shazui and Bagua.

Another one is **Yinxing Porridge Shop** (Yínxing Zhōudiàn; 银兴粥店), which serves congee with many different kinds of ingredients, including duck.

Drinking

Another reason some people come to Shenzhen is for its bar scene. Shenzhen's bars are perhaps "more Chinese" (anyone who has been to a Chinese nightclub with girls pole dancing on the stage to a random assortment of old club songs knows what this means). But there is a great assortment of drinking venues, from quiet wine bars to raucous and sweaty clubs to match anyone's taste. Dive in.

One particularly famous bar district is the **CITIC Metro Arcade** (Zhōngxin Chéngshì Guǎngchǎng; 中信城市广场) on Nanyuan Lu (南园路), which includes **Circle Bar** (挪威森林酒吧 ; 0755 2598 6260), **D(ay) D(ay) Up** (天天向上 ; 0755 2594 1690), **Before Sunset** (日落之前 ; 0755 2594 6089) and **3D Bar** (三度酒吧 ; 0755 2598 6011).

The **Luohu District**, right across the border, also has its share of bars and restaurants among the shopping, including one of China's most famous clubbing spots among the wealthy, **Baby Face** (0755 8237 3007; 罗湖区江背路国际名园 1 楼 K 室).

 Shopping

Shopping is one of the most popular reasons people come to Shenzhen. Most of the knock-off goods you find in Hong Kong are actually produced in Shenzhen, meaning shrewd shoppers can find excellent deals here, though quality can be hit or miss. Some places pride themselves on maintaining quality, while others define the axiom "you get what you pay for."

Right across the border, **Luohu Commercial City** (Luóhú Shāngyè Chéng; 罗湖商业城) is the first shopping area that targets visitors. It has hundreds of shops over five floors and hawkers are quite intense about wrangling people in. This is a good place to buy fake goods, as long as you know they are fake. Within the city, just two subway stops from Luohu at Laojie, is another popular shopping area at **Dōngmén** (东门; East Gate).

 Getting In & Out

Shenzhen borders northern Hong Kong and is accessible by subway, bus, taxi, or ferry.

By Subway

Subway is the most straightforward way to get to Shenzhen. Just get on the East Rail Line and take it to the end at either Lo Wu (Luohu Checkpoint) or Lok Ma Chau station (Futian Checkpoint; 福 田). Both stations have a checkpoint and a connection to the Shenzhen subway system on the other side. Going to Lo Wu from Central takes an hour and costs about HK$50.

By Bus

A number of city-regulated buses and private buses run to Shenzhen. Minibus 75 runs from outside the Yuen Long MTR station in the New Territories to the Futian Checkpoint, where you will need to walk through and show your documents. **Trans-Island Chinalink** (www.trans-island.com.hk [in traditional Chinese]) operates buses into Shenzhen from Tsim Sha Tsui, Mong Kok, Sheung Wan, Causeway Bay and Portland Street in Prince Edward (northern Mong Kok). **China Travel Service** (CTS) buses leave from Mong Kok outside of their offices at 62-72 Sai Yee Street.

By Taxi

Taxi is the most expensive option. It costs about HK$230 to get from Central to the Futian Checkpoint.

By Ferry

A ferry run by **China Merchant Shekou Ferry Terminal Services Co** (www.szgky. com) goes from Central to Shekou in Shenzhen, leaving weekdays at 9:00, 11:30, 13:00, 15:30 and 17:00. On weekends, the first ferry leaves at 10:00, and the other times remain the same. Standard adult tickets cost ¥110.

Zhūhǎi 珠海

The beach resort/garden city of Zhuhai is clean as a whistle, gleaming from its post just across the border from Macau. It became one of the first Special Economic Zones (SEZ), shortly after Shenzhen, and this popular weekend destination draws a good deal of Hong Kong, Macau and Guangdong tourists, who come for its scenery, its bars and its restaurants. Known as "the city of 100 islands," Zhuhai is a great place to go island hopping, where you can get lost on a number of obscure and secluded island beaches (that are inaccessible from Hong Kong or Macau).

Visa

You need a Chinese visa to get into Zhuhai, but most people can usually get one at the border checkpoints. Special Zhuhai-only visas allow visitors in the city for three days (72 hours).

 **Attractions**

Xianglu Bay

Chinese name: 香炉湾 (Xiānglú Wān)

Admission: FREE

Hours: 9:00 – 21:00

Address: Xiangluwan, Qinglu Zhonglu, Zhuhai (珠海市情侣中路香炉湾)

Transport: **Bus** – 9 or 99 to Zhuhai Yunu (珠海渔女) Stop

Picturesque Xianglu Bay sits on the eastern edge of Zhuhai and is framed by the relaxing Lover's Road (Qínglǔ Lù; 情侣路), which follows the coastline of Zhuhai all the

way from the Macau border. The portion of the road north of **Haibin Park** (Hǎibīn Gōngyuán; 海滨公园) is most famous, and its here that the statue of the **Zhuhai Fisher Girl** (Zhūhǎi Yúnǔ; 珠海渔女) stands on a rock with her hands over her head. Lover's Road – ostensibly named after the legend of the Fisher Girl, an angel who descended to earth and fell in love – continues north along several rocky beaches and some outstanding scenery. Two other big parks are close by: **Jingshan Park** (Jǐngshān Gōngyuán; 景山公园) just north of Haibin Park and **Shixi Scenic Area** (Shíxī Fēngjǐngqū; 石溪风景区) at the very north end of the road.

New Yuanming Palace

Chinese name: 圆明新园 (Yuánmíng Xīnyuán)
Admission: ¥120; ¥60 after 18:00
Hours: 9:00-22:00
Website: www.ymy.com.cn (in Chinese)
Recommended time for visit: 3 hours
Address: Lanpu, Jiuzhou Dadao, Zhuhai (珠海市九洲大道兰埔)
Transport: Bus – 1, 13, 25, 30, 40, 60, 62, 69, 991, 992 to Yuanming Xinyuan Stop

Zhuhai's 146 Islands

Zhuhai has 146 islands, most of which are little visited and sparsely populated – ideal destinations for the adventurous. Some of them are accessible by boats from the Xiangzhou Passenger Port, otherwise you will have to rent your own boat (and driver) if you want to reach the particularly far flung ones. A famous seafood dish of the islands is the "Three Treasures" (sea urchin, goose barnacle and abalone). Some of the most notable islands include:

Guishan Island (Guìshān Dǎo; 桂山岛 **)** – At the fish market on Guishan, you can buy a perch for ¥10 and have it fried at a restaurant across the street.

Dong'ao Island (Dōng'ào Dǎo; 东澳岛 **)** – With clear-water beaches, Dong'ao is considered one of Zhuhai's most beautiful islands.

Wai Lingding Island (Wài Língdīng Dǎo; 外伶仃岛 **)** – One of the closest to Hong Kong, this island provides a view of Hong Kong city from the top of its 311 m (1,020 ft) Lingding Apex.

Zhuhai International Circuit

Chinese name: 珠海国际赛车场 (Zhūhǎi Guójì Sàichēchǎng)
Admission: FREE
Website: www.zic.com.cn/en
Recommended time for visit: half a day
Address: Jinding Zhen, Zhuhai (珠海市金鼎镇)
Transport: Bus – 3a, 3, 10a, 10, 66, 68, 69, get off at Guoji Saichechang (国际赛车场) Stop

The New Yuanming Palace is a replica of the Old Summer Palace Imperial Gardens in Beijing that were destroyed by Anglo-French forces in 1860 (not to be confused with the still-standing Summer Palace). The 1.5 sq km (345 acres) attraction is a themed park with Chinese dance shows and reenactments of ancient lifestyles, so though it may look pretty at first, it's not exactly authentic. On one section of the 80,000 sq m (20 acre) lake, ancient-style sea battles are performed.

The Zhuhai International Circuit was one of China's first international race courses. It holds races, of course, but it also allows ordinary people to ride the course with a professional driver, or have a driver teach you how to operate the race car. Cool!

Around Zhuhai

Jintai Temple

Chinese name: 金台寺 (Jīntái Sì)
Admission: FREE
Hours: 8:00–18:00
Address: Huangyang Shan, Doumen Zhen, Zhuhai (珠海斗门镇黄杨山)
Transport: Bus – K4, 402, 406, 407, 410, 415, 416, 609, get off at Jintaisi Lukou (金台寺路口) Stop

This Buddhist temple at the southern base of the Mt Huangyang Shan stands in the beautiful environment of "the first peak along the gateway to the Pearl River." It's a pleasant scenic area about 1.5 hours away from downtown Zhuhai.

 Sleeping

Budget

7 Days Inn (Qītiān Liánsuǒ Jiǔdiàn ; 7 天连锁酒店)

7 Days Inn typically has very standard rooms with a small table. Their cheapest rooms can be musty and in need of a new coat of paint, but if you just need a place to crash they can get the job done. They also have free internet and cheap Chinese breakfast every morning, which consists of pork buns, spinach buns, hard boiled eggs, congee porridge, tomatoes and soy milk (¥7 for all). Don't expect much English to be spoken. Between ¥150 and ¥300 per room.

Address: 2155 Yingbin Nanlu, Xiangzhou (迎宾南路 2039 号)
Phone: (0756) 686 7777
Prices: Starts at ¥167 for members, ¥206 for non-members

Zhuhai Journey House (Zhūhǎi Zhēngtú Bèibāo Lǚshè; 珠海征途背包旅舍)

This international hostel has very clean rooms, a comfortable atmosphere and friendly and helpful staff. Everything seems to fit well with the surrounding beach environment.

Address: Bldg 2, Section 5, 158 Qinglu Nanlu (情侣南路 158 号海愉半岛花园 2 栋 5 单元 1402 房)
Phone: (0756) 323 2005, 130 1632 0027
¥55 for 10 bed mixed dorm, ¥60-65 for 6 or 4 bed dorm

Mid-Range

Zobon Art Hotel

As the name suggests, Zobon Art Hotel is decorated with modern art-style furniture and paintings. It is also located near the bay, right on Lovers Road. There isn't free internet in the rooms, but there is a Starbucks in the lobby with wifi. Rooms start at ¥590.

Address: 33 Qinglu Zhonglu, Xiangzhou District (情侣中路 33 号)
Phone: (0756) 322 0333
Website: www.zobonarthotel.com

Splurge

Grand Bay View Hotel (Guǎngxin Hǎiwān Jiǔdiàn; 广信海湾酒店)

The Grand Bay View Hotel has a great location, with views of the bay and a location very close to Xianglu Bay Shuiwan Bar Street. The staff is friendly and speaks good English, and there is an onsite café, a restaurant and an exercise gym. Mountain view rooms start at ¥628. Bay view rooms start at ¥1,350.

Address: 1 Leyuan Lu, Xiangzhou District (香洲区乐园路 1 号)
Phone: (0756) 222 3448

 Eating

Street Food

Lotus Road (Liánhuā Lù; 莲花路)

Lotus Road, just north of Macau, is a major food street in downtown Zhuhai. Cheap restaurants and food stalls are everywhere, and the **Gongbei Seafood Street** (Gǒngběi Hǎixiān Jiē; 拱北海鲜街) is also nearby.

Wanchai Seafood Street (Wānzǎi Hǎixiān Jiē; 湾仔海鲜街)

Wanchai (or Wanzai) is an area across the water to the west of Macau and a little bit south of downtown Zhuhai. The seafood street has a lot of cheap restaurants, and the main feature is that you can buy fresh seafood from vendors and then have it cooked at one of the restaurants.

Restaurants

Deyuefang Seafood Restaurant (Déyuèfáng Hǎixiān Jiǔlóu; 得月肪海鲜酒楼)

Deyuefang is a boat-shaped restaurant with bright lights and imperial decorations on a small island in Xianglu Bay (connected to Zhuhai by bridge). The view is superb and the ambience is even better. Its specialties include lobster, crab and pork belly. Reservations are recommended.

Address: Inside Mingting Park, on Qinglu Lu, Xiangzhou District (香洲区情侣路近岸野狸岛名亭公园内)
Phone: (0756) 225 1188; 217 3298
Website: www.deyuefang.net (in Chinese)

Jinyuexuan Restaurant (Jīnyuèxuān Jiǔlóu; 金悦轩酒楼)

One of the most delicious Cantonese restaurants in the city, especially for its morning dim sum, Jinyuexuan has an oceanside view to rival Deyuefang.

Address: 265 Qinglu Nanlu (Rihua Commercial Plaza), Xiangzhou District (香洲区情侣南路 265 号日华广场 1–3 楼)
Phone: (0756) 813 3133

 Drinking

As a tourist city, Zhuhai is known for its nightlife. There are two main bar streets downtown, one with a casual street-food atmosphere, and one with a classic clubbing atmosphere. Watch out for paid bar girls enticing customers to drink at some of the bars, they'll make you pay inflated prices.

Lotus Road

Along with street food, Lotus Road is also packed with carousing tourists at night. The open air cafes and bars are lively and cheap.

Xianglu Bar Street

At Xianglu Bay, Shuiwan Road (Shuǐwān Lù; 水弯路) is the high-end, trendy bar strip and club street. The biggest name here street is 88 Bar (88 酒 吧 ; phone: 0756 871 0188; 221 Shuiwan Lu – 水湾路 221 号), a brand that has bars nationwide and always sports loud music, dancing platforms and a few karaoke rooms.

✈ Getting In & Out

By Land (From Macau)

Zhuhai is accessible by land from Macau. The ancient Barrier Gate of Macau, built in 1871, is located at **Gongbei Port** (Gǒngběi Kǒuàn; 拱北口岸) inside a small park (which you can visit even if you don't go to Zhuhai).

By Ferry

Chu Kong Passenger Transport Co (www.cksp.com.hk) runs ferries to Zhuhai from the China Ferry Terminal in Tsim Sha Tsui and the Hong Kong-Macau Ferry Terminal in Sheung Wan. From the China Ferry Terminal, they leave at 7:30, 8:30, 9:30, 11:30, 13:30, 15:30 and 17:45. From the Hong Kong-Macau Ferry Terminal, they leave at 8:40, 10:30, 12:30, 14:30, 16:30, 19:30 and 21:30.

From Hong Kong, Both Terminals	Adult	Child (Under 5)
VIP Class	HK$325	HK$220
First Class	HK$290	HK$200
Economy	HK$210	HK$135

Five Days in Hong Kong

By Mitchell Blatt

It had been two and a half months since I landed in Shanghai. My visa allowed for 90 days per entry, so I had to get out of the country in two weeks.

At the train station, I asked a friendly Chinese ticket buyer where to buy a ticket for Hong Kong.

"You want to go to Hong Kong?"

"Yeah, I need to get out of China because my visa is about to expire," I said.

"Hong Kong is a part of China!!!" he said. Then he directed me to a special line for Hong Kong where Mainland Chinese need a passport to buy tickets.

I was off to Hong Kong, and I was going to make a trip of it. I wasn't going all the way to this legendary city just to cross the border and then cross it again like so many other visa-running foreigners. Hong Kong deserves more than that.

Day 1

I arrived at Kowloon Station in Hong Kong at 13:00 in the afternoon. After going through the customs checkpoint, I was on my way to switch to the subway when I realized, "Oh, no! I don't have any Hong Kong currency. This *is* a part of China, *isn't* it?"

The subway didn't take Chinese Renminbi, but I was able to exchange some for Hong

Kong Gangbi (HKD) at the customer service desk. I arrived at my hostel in the heart of Mong Kok, the most crowded place in the world, after slowly cutting and dodging through swarms of people on the sidewalk.

My first reaction in Mong Kok was utter astonishment at the sheer number of people. They were everywhere! Looking up from the street, the entire space above my head was filled with a slurry of signs, packing the air to the point they seemed to mix into a thick sludge of colors and Chinese characters. Of course, I couldn't read half of them because they were in traditional Chinese (I can only read simplified Chinese). It was quite a spectacle. After securing my bags in my hostel, I jolted back onto the street to explore this amazingly crowded city.

My first inclination in any new city is just to wander around aimlessly and follow my intuition to whatever looks or feels enticing. Worst case scenario: I find my way back to my hostel and have an interesting walk. Best case scenario: I get lost at the far edge of the city after an epic adventure and eventually find a subway station to take back. It's a win win deal!

From Argyle Street, I started walking north on a random road until I eventually ended up on Shanghai Street. Long signs with single Chinese characters on individual pieces of metal stretched over the alleys; a quintessential image of Chinatown – how fitting.

After walking down a few blocks, I went into

Mong Kok Signs & Mong Kok Street Corner at Night

a shop that was selling traditional Chinese decorations and "hell money" (fake money burned for the dead).

"Do you know where Temple Street is?" I asked.

"What?" the Chinese shopkeeper said.

"Temple Street? Where is Temple Street?"

"What???"

I had no idea how to say Temple Street in Cantonese. Next best idea: I wrote the characters down on a piece of paper and hoped he could read my poorly written traditional characters.

"Oh, Temple Street," he said. "Just south in Jordan."

As the sky darkened my excitement began to mount as I headed towards the famous Temple Street Night Market.

After walking underneath a red gate and strings of red lanterns, I became surrounded by outdoor restaurant tables and merchandise stalls. Soon I was perusing some trinkety crap and saying "*Bu yao*" ("don't want") more times than I could count, and before long I ended up on the north section of the market among the music lounges. An older Chinese man invited me over to his table.

"Nei si naa lei jan?"

I could understand what he was asking me, "Where are you from?" even though I couldn't speak more than two words of Cantonese. We struggled to communicate, but he could understand most of my Mandarin, and I could understand bits and pieces of his Cantonese. Quite a few bottles of beer, several tip box-bound twenty dollar bills and even one song of my own later, I headed back toward Mong Kok in the early morning.

Day 2

The first thing I did the next morning was head straight to the Tsim Sha Tsui waterfront to see the view of the great skyscrapers across the Harbour on Hong Kong Island. The Avenue of Stars juts out from the TST waterfront bearing the handprints of Hong Kong's brightest stars and actors. "Jackie Chan! Wang Kar-wai! Tony Leung!" I thought as I walked. At the end of the walkway there was a Bruce Lee statue just begging me to step up and show my mettle. I must have looked pretty silly in my pitiful pose, trying to emulate Bruce's kung fu awesomeness. But, I always say, if your

Posing with Bruce Lee

Avenue of Stars photos don't look silly then you're not doing it right.

After posing with Bruce I was starting to get pretty hungry, so I went across the Harbour to Central and headed for the Lin Heung Tea House for some dim sum. I was a fool if I thought I was going to get a table without a wait in the middle of *yum cha* (drinking tea) time. The wait was worth it, though, when they brought out the mouth watering rice dumplings and barbecue pork *baozi*. How lucky! I couldn't read the traditional characters on the Chinese-only menu, so I had just picked some at random (a great choice in such a situation) and yanked a few more items off the carts that periodically came by. It was downright heavenly.

Central, as the name suggests, is the center of the city and full of touristic points of interest. I walked around this area after breakfast, going to the Western Market, the Man Mo Temple and the Cat Street Market, then took the Mid-Levels Escalators all the way to the top, where I tried to find my way to Victoria Peak through the botanical gardens. Looking out over the grand landscape, towers and islands seemed to stretch as far as the eye could see, and I savored the view. I had my share of walking to get here, so I took the novelty Peak Tram back down (its an experience to be tried anyway) and back to my hostel for some R&R.

Back at the hostel, I met an English guy named Chris. Who better to go to the crazy Lan Kwai Fong bars with than a heavy drinking Englishman? Hidden among the loud music, thumping bars and people standing on the street drinking, we found the perfect spot (we knew it as soon as we saw the "No Gangnam Style" sign on its jukebox). We met some English investment bankers shortly after and went from bar to bar together drinking, dancing, and getting shot down by beautiful ladies.

Day 3

After two days in the concrete jungle, I wanted to get out of the city. On the third day, I went to Hong Kong's largest island, Lantau Island. The subway took me to a town just on the edge of the island, and then it was onto an island bus and over the bumpy hills and curves up to the Ngong Ping Plateau to see the Po Lin Monastery. Upon getting off the bus, I walked under an entrance gate to find a Starbucks and a souvenir shop. "Quite the corporate monastery!" I thought. It wasn't the monastery, though, it was the Ngong Ping Village, a themed "village" that greets visitors with video theaters and shops. The monastery was down the road in the direction

Temple Street Market

Po Lin Monastery

Tai O Stilt Houses

of the Tian Tan Big Buddha on top of the hill.

The Big Buddha, looking down from his perch on the top of Mount Muk Yue, beckons you with his left hand in his lap. His fingers, positioned in the mudra of "fulfilling wishes," pointed towards the huffing visitors climbing the 240 steps, a vow to bestow happiness and blessings on all who come before him. Taking a look around at the top, I could say for certain that he had fulfilled my wishes for the day.

The monastery was engulfed in manmade nature. A well manicured garden cooed with bright purple flowers, while trails to the east of the monastery led through trees to the base on Lantau Peak.

Fish Drying in Sai Kung

My next stop was Tai O Fishing Village at the far west end of the island. The village is famed for its traditional stilt homes in the water. When I got off the bus, a group of touts surrounded me.

"How about a boat ride to see some dolphins?" one said.

The locals have learned a new kind of fishing – the kind where you troll for tourists.

Everywhere along the narrow village streets, fish were lined up drying in the sun. Walking further along the paved road that leads outside the village center, I could see a bucolic scene with temples and rustic houses perched on the edge of green hills. Sitting down in a cafe, I kicked back and ordered a straight tea. "No milk!" I shouted – Hong Kong people put milk in everything; they even drink milk tea champagne.

I went to bed early that night, tired from the late nights of the past two days and excited to hike to secluded beaches the next morning.

Day 4

Not having set my alarm clock the night before, I woke up later than optimal for my excursion to Tai Long Wan Beach in Sai Kung Country Park. I had a general idea how to get there, but I didn't check the bus time tables in advance. Taking the subway then switching to a minibus, it took about two hours for me to get to Sai Kung town.

Once in Sai Kung, I went to the stop for the 29R bus only to find that I was ten minutes late and it didn't come again for another hour and a half. Sai Kung town was interesting enough to pass some time in. It had a nice promenade with views of islands and boats parked in the sea, as well as seafood restaurants with more kinds of fish and crustaceans out front than I had ever seen. I didn't, however, see enough to warrant spending one and a half hours there.

Luckily, there was another bus that took me to an alternate trailhead from the main bus station. The trail wound through woods and bays. At one point, I had to carefully walk by a herd of cows that was occupying the path. After walking up a hill at the base of Sharp Peak, I descended onto a sandy path, and, through a clearing, I could see the makeshift wood and rope bridge that heralded Ham Tin Wan Beach.

There was almost no one there – just a few hikers like myself coming from the opposite direction – and no development, save for some shack restaurants with plastic tables and chairs.

Bridge to Ham Tin Wan Beach

Continuing along the trail over a rocky ridge with views of the pristine environment, I arrived at the main beach: Sai Wan. There were more buildings there, including some hostels, and I sat down at a restaurant looking at the sea while sipping a beer.

I started talking to some tourists from Canada.

"Want to join our boat to go back to Sai Kung?"

"Thanks for the offer," I said, but for HK$150 a person I passed.

"Do you know when the last bus leaves?" I asked.

"Five o'clock," one of them said. It was 4:40, and the bus stop was some ways down the road. How far, I didn't know.

Running down the path while enjoying quick views of the water reservoir, I made it just in time before the bus left.

Day 5

My time in Hong Kong had come to an end. I was heading back to Mainland China that afternoon. I had seen traditional markets, old fashioned singer lounges, epic cityscapes, beautiful and fragrant temples, fishing villages, secluded beaches, crazy bars and much more. I certainly loved Hong Kong, but after brushing up against so many people on these crowded streets, it felt very claustrophobic at times.

I spent my last half day strolling along the shops of Tsim Sha Tsui. A big green nameplate came into view: the Chungking Mansions. That name sounded familiar. "*Chungking Express*! That's where that movie was filmed," I said to myself. Inside, there were people of all ethnicities standing around.

"Hey, you need a guesthouse?" "Want some hash?" the touts shouted.

I walked through the crowds into the maze of money changers, cell phone sellers and *halal* markets. This place couldn't exist just anywhere, it's special in its own right.

After enjoying a delicious meal of curry and *naan*, I headed to the train station, thoroughly delighted with my time in Hong Kong but ready to get back to the relative peace and tranquility of Shanghai.

Sample Itineraries

Asia's World City has a dizzying array of activities and sights, from gleaming metal forests of shopping, dining and drinking to mountainous Country Parks and beach-framed islands. Among all these destinations sits a peppering of temples and captivating historical sights, and it's no surprise that many people don't know where to begin or end their Hong Kong romp.

Never fear, Panda Guides is here! We've laid out nine of our favorite itineraries to help you formulate some plans of attack. Seven of these routes are themed to help anyone from the shopping addicted to the film obsessed or the beach crazed find their favorites. The last three are walking tours that take you around some of the city's best neighborhoods the cheap and old fashioned way: on foot. So lace up those shoes and remember that you can use these itineraries in whatever way best suits you, be it following them to a tee or mixing, matching and finding your own special places to go AWOL.

Hong Kong Highlights

Victoria Peak→Mid-Levels Escalators→Hollywood Road→Western Market→Star Ferry→Tsim Sha Tsui Promenade

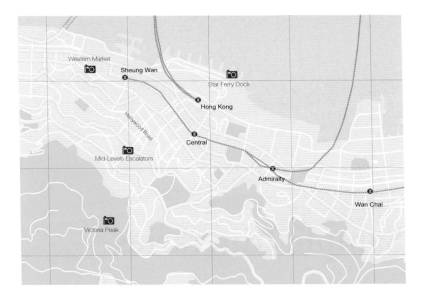

While Hong Kong has a vast amount of superb sights – more than one could visit in a lifetime – there are three that are more or less essential for any worthwhile visit to the city: Victoria Peak, Tsim Sha Tsui Waterfront and the Star Ferry. Certianly everyone has their own tastes, but it's fair to say that if you don't see at least one of these three iconic sights then you have not seen Hong Kong. This itinerary packs all three of them into one great day, and throws a few side destinations in to mix things up.

Get things started off early (around 7:00) with a delicious dim sum breakfast at one of the legendary restaurants of Central, like the Lin Heung Tea House or Maxim's Palace at City Hall. Once you're fueled up, grab the Peak Tram from the Central MTR Station to the top of **Victoria Peak** (pg 49) and get a great morning hike around the many trails that slice the top of the mountain. The Botanical Gardens are just south of Central MTR, and if you want a longer hike you could first walk to the gardens and then get on one of the hiking trails that leads from there up to the top of the peak.

Now that your blood is pumping, say goodbye to the inspirational views from atop the peak and head back down for a ride on the longest series of escalators in the world, the Central to **Mid-Levels Escalators** (pg 52). Hop off off at **Hollywood Road** for a perusal of the plethora of countless antiques that line the shops of this renowned road, then find a place to grab some lunch and afternoon tea before moving on to the antique architecture of the fascinating **Western Market** (pg 131). The warren of shops here selling all manner of textiles, clothes and boutique items is a great way to pass a few hours into the afternoon before the next big highlight of the day.

Make sure to get on the **Star Ferry** (pg 82) at 20:00 so that you can watch the nightly fireworks show over the Harbour. The Star will drop you off right at the **Tsim Sha Tsui Waterfront**, so if you arrive early you can watch the show here, or if there's still daylight, take a walk along the Avenue of Stars to check out your favorite Hong Kong movie stars and directors.

The Nine Dragon Culture Tour

Sik Sik Wong Tai Sin Temple→Kowloon Walled City Park→Shanghai Street→Ladies Street→Temple Street Night Market

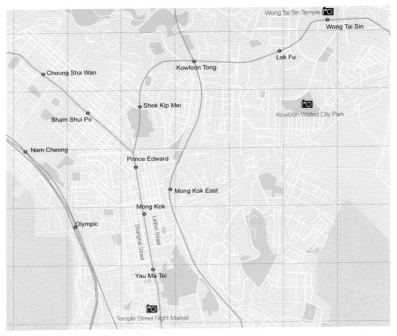

The culture of Kowloon is arguably more vibrant than that of Hong Kong Island, largely because it's closer to the Mainland and fewer expats call the area home. The best way to experience Kowloon's color is by cruising around its streets, and though it's impossible to cover it all in a day, the Nine Dragons (the English meaning of Kowloon) Tour can give you a tantilizing taste of this historic area.

After breakfast, start things off at the beautiful **Sik Sik Yuen Wong Tai Sin Temple** (pg 148), one of Hong Kong's largest and oldest. This popular temple gets packed, so pay an early visit to beat the crowds, then head south to Kowloon City and check out the streets near **Kowloon Walled City Park**. Kowloon Walled City was a Chinese stronghold outside of British rule that was a den of thieves, drugs and other unscrupulous activities for many years. It was destroyed in 1994, but the haunting remnants you can find today are some of the most interesting sights in Kowloon.

Once you've had enough time in the city ruins, take the subway down to the **Ladies Street Market** (pg 80) and enjoy some of Hong Kong's quintessential market culture (and maybe even score some sweet deals) along this famous strip. Neighboring **Shanghai Street** (pg 81) shows off the city's oldest shophouses, and this is a great place for lunch at one of the *sui mei* barbecue stalls that line the street.

Take your time along charming Shanghai Street, then meander your way down to **Temple Street** (pg 71) in the south, making it there in time for a wander through the overflowing street shops and barking salespeople as you walk towards the south end. Stop off for dinner anywhere along the way, then grab some drinks and warm up your vocal chords for a few songs at the outdoor karaoke stalls and lounge bars that make Temple Street so special.

The New Territories Twist

Tsang Tai Uk→Hong Kong Heritage Museum→Ten Thousand Buddhas Monastery→Lam Tsuen Wishing Trees→Fanling Wai→Sha Tin Racecourse

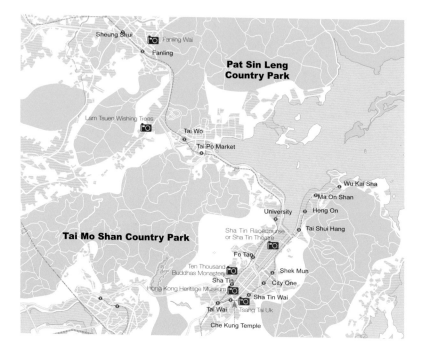

Far away from downtown, the rustic New Territories are some of the most underappreciated areas of greater Hong Kong. From walled villages to beautiful country parks and lovely bucolic scenery, they offer a relaxing respite from the dust of the steel jungle.

After an early breakfast, spend about half an hour scouring the century-old Hakka walled village of **Tsang Tai Uk** (pg 118). Now that your curiosity is peaked, move north to the **Hong Kong Heritage Museum** (pg 139), which will educate you on Hakka culture and the ethnic history of the area.

Get some lunch to recharge those batteries before a walk up the countless stone steps of the **Ten Thousand Buddhas Monastery** (pg 147). The peaceful grounds and the beautiful effigies of Buddha should grant you enough breezy meandering to let your lunch digest. That's good, because next you're taking a

hike through Tai Mo Shan Country Park. Make a quick detour northeast to the **Lam Tsuen Wishing Tree** (pg 93) to string up your own red ribbon of luck before hitting the park's trails on your way to **Fanling Wai** (pg 116), a 17th century walled village of the Pang Clan that is most notable for the awesome Pang Clan Ancestral Hall near the center.

The day has been full of relaxation and sedating country scenery, and that means it's time to kick things up a notch and get some adrenaline flowing to balance out the tour. Grab a quick dinner and then get ready for the **Sha Tin Racecourse** (pg 98) with all the screaming punters throwing down bets on their favorite jockeys. Gambling and drinking are all part of the fun at a Sha Tin horse race, but the dazzling energy means you don't have to do either one to get a buzz at this wild New Territories destination.

The Colonial Conquest

Central Police Station→Legislative Council Building→Clock Tower→1881 Heritage→Afternoon Tea at the Peninsula

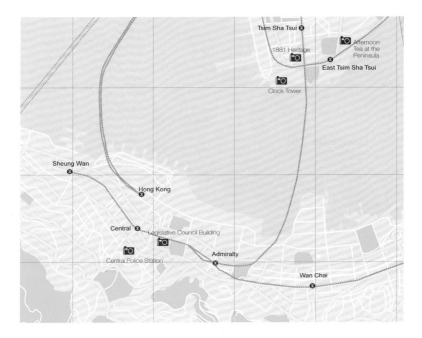

Certainly the highlights of any trip to the former British colony of Hong Kong will include a visit to some of the colonial architecutre that still calls this city home. To make a day of the local Victorian sights, go imperial and follow the Colonial Conquest.

Start in Central, where the British built their first structures, the most impressive of which is the old **Central Police Station** (pg 91) with its grand exterior columns. The Central Police Station is actually a complex of several intriguing colonial administrative and law buildings, and you should make sure you set aside enough time to take in the Victoria Prison, the Headquarters Block and the Barrack block before leaving.

Just down the road is the wonderful neo-classical architecture of the the **Legislative Council Building**, which was built in 1912 and housed Hong Kong's legislative council

from 1985 to 2011. Also known as the Supreme Court Building, it is one of the city's declared monuments and a very handsome sight.

Grab a bite for lunch before crossing the water (by subway or ferry) to Kowloon, where you will be greeted by luxurious colonial hotels and the 19th century **Clock Tower** (pg 92) outside the Hong Kong Cultural Centre. In fact, it's best to take the Star Ferry over the Harbour so that the tower can greet you at the pier, much as it did the thousands of Chinese immigrants coming into Hong Kong via Kowloon Railway Station, which the tower was once a part of.

Next, see the splendid **1881 Heritage** shopping area and then get very British with **afternoon tea at the Peninsula Hotel**, a place where international businessmen have enjoyed tea and lodging since 1928.

Hot Topics

275

Lovely Lantau

Mui Wo→Pui O→Po Lin Monastery→Tai O Fishing Village

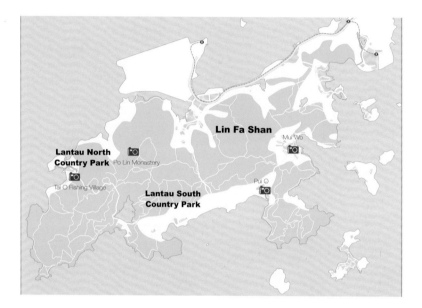

Hong Kong's largest island, Lantau offers up some of the most laidback Bohemian activities in China. There is far too much to do on Lantau to cover in a single day or itinerary, but grooving around these four destinations can certainly give you a great taste of the treat that is Lantau.

Getting to Lantau is part of the breezy adventure. You can board a ferry from the pier at Central, which will bob you over to the quaint beach town of **Mui Wo** (pg 121). Taking it easy rules the day here, and though you should certainly indulge in some beach time and plenty of locals snacks, don't be afraid to wear the tread down in your sandals with a stroll around town.

Muster the energy to tear yourself away from mellow Mui Wo so you can board a bus down the road to **Pui O** (pg 119). The country scenery is sublime here, especially among the water buffalo chewing their cud around the small villages that dot the landscape.

Lunchtime will bring you to the **Po Lin Monastery** (pg 65), where you can fill up on a healthy veggie lunch at the onsite restaurant before ascending the 240 steps to visit the majestic Tian Tan Buddha. The monastery will eat up an hour or two, after which you can put that healthy energy from lunch to good use with a hike through the fine trails that surround the hills of the monastery.

Round out the day with a short ride down to the lovely fishing village at **Tai O** (pg 74), where you can visit a number of historical sights, chat with the superbly friendly locals, and even find a place to have quite possibly the freshest fish dinner you've ever eaten in your life.

Tai O is a great place to watch the sun set over the ocean, but make sure you leave yourself enough time to catch a bus back to the larger towns of Mui Wo or Tung Chung so that you can get a place to rest for the night or hop on a ferry back to the city.

Shopaholics Anonymous

Causeway Bay→Central→Harbour City→1881 Heritage→Golden Mile→Mong Kok

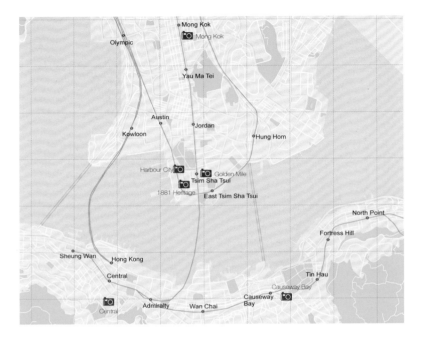

Hong Kong is a "shopper's heaven," and for those of you out there with a possible shopping disorder, we have the perfect treatment for you. It's called Shapaholics Anonymous.

There are literally tens of thousands of stores in Hong Kong, so instead of trying to send you to a list of specific holes-in-the-wall, we will send you to some of the best areas for shopping galore and then let you take the reigns from there. Just make sure you pace yourself and take some breaks here and there. We don't want to be responsible for any side effects of over-shopping.

The first stop is at **Causeway Bay** – this mall mecca has all the brand stores you could ever need. A great place to get started is the Times Square mall, and from there you should make sure to satisfy your addiction along the dozens of boutique stores sporting independent local brands.

The looks you can find in Causeway are quite unique and highly stylish, but don't go too nuts yet, because soon you're off to **Central**, where there are still more luxury fashion stores. If it happens to be Wimbledon time, go to the Ralph Lauren store and get some free champagne and strawberries to keep your shopping fuel burning hot.

Once you've burned enough cash in Central, cross the Harbour to Tsim Sha Tsui, beckoning you with more fine purchasing potential at **Harbour City**. Harbour City boasts hundreds of stores, and if those are not enough for you, the **1881 Heritage** colonial building is nearby. Overtaken by luxury brands today, this site will make fashionistas and fashionistos drool a river.

From here, Nathan Road's **Golden Mile** is lined with more malls and electronic stores than most people can count, and you can walk it all the way up to Mong Kok, where even the most hard-boiled shopper will likely need to call it a day.

Walking Tour – Kowloon City & Temples

Chi Lin Nunnery→Sik Sik Yuen Wong Tai Sin Temple→Hau Wong Temple→Kowloon Walled City Park→Kowloon City Food District

A tour of Kowloon's beautiful temples that's capped off by a trip to a ruined walled city? Sounds like Buddhist heaven on earth. In fact, not only do you get a good taste of Buddhist life in Hong Kong, this tour also brings you through one of the city's most revered temples, the Taoist haven of Sik Sik Yuen Wong Tai Sin. This tour includes plenty of walking, but if you want to save your feet along the 800 m (2,625 ft) first stretch, hop on the MTR.

Get things started off on the right foot with a trip through the gorgeous **Chi Lin Nunnery** and its next-door Nan Lian Garden. Forgo walking busy Lung Cheung Road and take the MTR from Diamond Hill Station to Wong Tai Sin Station, then head out through Exit B3 and follow the signs to the **Sik Sik Yuen Wong Tai Sin Temple,** and consider having your fortune told by the Taoist soothsayers. When you've had your fill, hit the MTR again for a short trip down to Lok Fu Station, where you'll follow Exit B to the signs pointing to the **Hau Wong Temple**.

Hau Wong Temple's origin is shrouded in mystery, but most people believe that it was built to honor a general who aided the last Song Dynasty (960–1279) emperor on his flight south. Whatever inspired the temple, you'll be delighted by the cultural artifacts, including beautiful calligraphy and some superb wall art.

From Hau Wong Temple, cross Tung Tau Tsuen Road for the north gate of **Kowloon Walled City Park**, where there is way too much to see (you should probably save plenty of walking for this one). The area used to be the Kowloon Walled City, a zone outside of British jurisdiction during their colonial days and one hotbed den of depravity and mayhem.

When you get hungry, cross through to the south side of the park, pass through Carpenter Road Park, and cross Carpenter Road to find Nam Kok Road, part of an area called the **Kowloon City Food District**.

Walking Tour – Tsim Sha Tsui

Tak Shing Street & Pak On Building→Hong Kong Museum of History→ Carnival Mansion→Knutsford Terrace→Former Kowloon British School→ Hong Kong Heritage Discover Centre→Avenue of Stars→ Hong Kong Museum of Art→Clock Tower

The area of Tsim Sha Tsui and its excellent waterfront provide some of the best walking material in the urban area. Along the way are old British colonial buildings, some excellent shopping opportunities, Hong Kong's version of Hollywood's Walk of Fame and a fabulous view of Hong Kong Island across the water. If you're up for a half day exploring southern Kowloon, let our walking tour of Tsim Sha Tsui get you off on a good foot.

Get started on the northwest corner of the **Pak On Building** on **Tak Shing Street**, where a liquor store has absinthe for sale. Move south down the building to Austin Road as you peruse the rest of the shops on the main floor. Take a left (east) down Austin Road and admire the architecture, much of which are interesting designs from the 1960s, and veer right as the road splits into Austin Avenue.

After a few minutes you can divert down Chatham Court and across Chatham Road South for the excellent **Hong Kong Museum of History** which is surely worth spending some time in. If you don't have time for the museum, simply continue south along Austin Avenue to check out the **Carnival Mansion** and its courtyard of 1950s homes that feature yellow stairs with funky green railings.

As Austin Avenue turns into Kimberly Road you'll see plenty more mansions along the way worth peeking at, but don't miss the right turn for Observatory Road so that you can visit **Knutsford Terrace** for a sampling of some of the best food options in the city and a reminder of why Asia's World City is so famous for its cuisine. Swing back onto Kimberly Road until you reach Nathan Road, where you'll take a right to move up to the outstanding Victorian Architecture of the **Former Kowloon British School**. Built in 1902, it is the oldest school building in the city, and today it hosts a great collection of Hong Kong antiques.

Head back to Nathan Road and walk south to the mosque, where you can enter Kowloon Park to the right and also visit the **Hong Kong Heritage Discovery Centre**, which was built circa 1910 and once served as a barracks for British soldiers.

Depending on your pace, dusk may be setting in, a perfect time to march down to the **Avenue of Stars** along the waterfront, where you can see tributes to Hong Kong's finest of the silver screen, as well as a bronze statue of Bruce Lee. To get here, just follow Nathan Road south from where you entered Kowloon Park to the MTR East Tsim Sha Tsui Station at Exit L3. Walk through the pedestrian tunnel to Exit J and follow the signs to Avenue of Stars.

Follow the waterfront boardwalk west, stop in the **Hong Kong Museum of Art** if you have time – or just check out its unique architecture from outside – and head over to the 1921-built **Clock Tower** that was once a terminus for the Kowloon-Canton Railway.

Walking Tour – Central

Western Market→Bird's Nest Street & Dried Seafood Street→ Hollywood Road & Cat Street→ Man Mo Temple→Central-Mid Levels Escalator→ SoHo→Central Police Station→Lan Kwai Fong→Duddle Street→Supreme Court Building

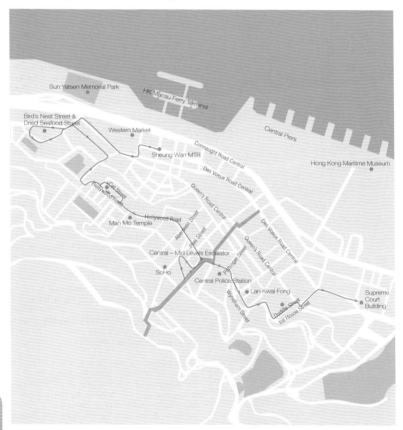

From the traditional to the tailor made, the historical to the high-end, Central mixes modern and old-timey Hong Kong like few other parts of the city. On one hand you can find incense-laden temples and traditional markets and herb shops, while just down the road corporate towers gleam in the sunlight. No matter what you're into, be it luxury brands or old gas lamps, Central has something to interest you, and there's no better way to take it all in than on foot.

Start off admiring the red brickwork of the old **Western Market**, and if you're in the mood for a little shopping you can head inside, though the shops in here are pretty run-of-the-mill since its renovation in 1991. You'll want to save some of that shopping bug anyway as you head south on Morrison Street to make a right on Wing Lok Street, (which is also known as **Bird's Nest Street**) and is where you'll find all manner of traditional Chinese medicines, including, of course, bird's nests and ginseng. Swing left onto Des Voeux Road West and follow it left onto Ko Shing Street for some of the most world-renowned herbal medicine shops, complete with some of the best experts in the world. This will deliver you to Bonham Strand West, where you can get in some of the dried seafood here before moving on.

Take a right onto Possession Street and head up the incline before turning left onto **Hollywood Road** for some of the best antique shopping in Hong Kong. Head east down Hollywood Road or, if the shopping here is not enough, make a detour by turning left at Lok Ku Road and then right onto Cat Street (Upper Lascar Row) for more of the same.

After several minutes down Hollywood Road you will come to the **Man Mo Temple** for a trip back to the middle-19th century. Enjoy the incense coils and have a rest before your walk further down Hollywood Road to the **Central – Mid-Levels Escalators**, where you can cruise them up to the flashy and modern **SoHo** area for a bite to eat and a coffee. Explore on your own, or consider an escalator ride to Elgin Street and walk northwest to Staunton Street, where you can swing back east to the escalator and ride to Hollywood Road again. Make sure to admire the gleaming skyscrapers of modern Hong Kong while you're here.

Further east on Hollywood Road you'll soon come upon the old **Central Police Station**, which is an excellently preserved example of colonial Hong Kong. After taking in the awesome onsite Victorian Prison, move further down Hollywood Road onto Wyndham Street and pass through the nightlife hub of **Lan Kwai Fong**. Wyndham Street winds to Lower Albert Road, where you can follow the signs to **Duddle Street**.

A fitting prologue to the walk through Central, the steps that connect Ice House Street with Duddle Street are part of the original road, built around 1875, and the four lamps that grace the beginning and end of the steps are the only four original gas lamps in the city. At the end of Duddle Street, cross Queen's Road Central and follow Ice House Street to Des Voeux Central, where you'll turn right and march down to the old **Supreme Court Building** for the colonial cap to your walk through Central.

Looking over a statue on the Avenue of Stars

Culture Shock

Language Barrier

Despite being a British colony for about 150 years, Hong Kong still surprises many travelers with its relatively small English-speaking population. That being said, English is still everywhere, and you won't have as hard of a time communicating in English as you would in the Mainland; just keep in mind that it won't be like walking down the street in your hometown where every man, woman, child and dog understands English.

English was the official language of Hong Kong from 1883 to 1974. During the British years, expatriates from Great Britain and those from its colonies like India used English while living in Hong Kong, and even many of the local Chinese learned English. What's more, English signage was everywhere, and still to this day everything from street signs to bus stops is marked with English, making getting around town a lot easier than most other Chinese cities.

However, since Hong Kong's return to China in 1997, the demographics have shifted. There are now more and more Mainlanders moving to Hong Kong each year (either legally or illegally), and most of them only speak Mandarin and not English or Cantonese. This creates a real language barrier for many of the locals.

The current "biliterate and trilingual" policy of Hong Kong, enforced by Beijing, states that the two official languages of the SAR are Chinese and English, and though Cantonese has no official status, roughly 97% of Hong Kongers speak it as their first language. But the amount of Mandarin speakers is growing at lightning speed, and most expats from the Western world, Africa, the Philippines, Pakistan, India, Sri Lanka and Bangladesh will also have a strong command of English.

So how does all this information impact your stay in Hong Kong? For one thing, understanding the complexity of Hong Kong's linguistic web can help you understand what you'll be up against during your stay. English isn't as prominent as it was during British rule, and though many of those who work in hotels, nicer restaurants and the tourism industry usually have some ability with English, you certainly shouldn't expect it wherever you go. While some taxi drivers may know simple English and street names, it appears that the number of English speaking cabbies is becoming smaller by the year. This means it is crucial to carry the card of your hostel or hotel and have the address of your destination written down whenever you go out. Street-side holes-in-the wall and food stalls will mostly have a similar level of English as a cabby. If you speak Mandarin or Cantonese, you will certainly have an easier time getting around, just remember that there are two Chinese language types spoken here; you never know which one the local will speak.

Writing Barrier

That's right, the barriers don't stop at spoken language. With such a mixed bag of tongues, you can also expect to see a plethora of written languages. The big three are English with the Latin alphabet and simplified and traditional Chinese characters. This is quite easy to navigate, however, since, as we mentioned before, nearly all important signage around the city is in English. Cantonese speaking Hong Kong natives use traditional Chinese characters, which are the same characters that have been used for more than 2,000 years all over China. Hong Kong still uses these age-old characters, and it's one of the last places in China to do so.

Mainlanders use simplified Chinese characters, which are simplified versions of traditional characters. Promoted in the 1950s by the communist regime, the reduced forms of over 500 characters became the basis for

a literacy program intended to increase the amount of peasants who could read and write. The program appeared to be a success, with literacy rates around the countryside rising from under 20% in the 1950s to over 90% by 2000. While many of the characters are the same in both the traditional and simplified systems, they can still present a challenge for the reader who isn't familiar with the one he or she is reading. Therefore, if you get something written down with simplified characters, when you show it to a local Hong Konger, they may not be able to understand it (or vice versa), especially if it's not a well-known site.

If your English or Mandarin or Cantonese skills aren't cutting it in this diverse international city, here are a few tips to use while out and about on the streets.

Don't be shy about gesturing. When ordering from a menu or buying things in a store, don't hesitate to simply point at what you want. No one will be offended. Likewise, don't be afraid to use your fingers to show how many you want. You might feel a little silly, but it's a language everyone can understand. That being said, before you head out on your trip, it can't hurt to:

Learn a little Cantonese. As mentioned, 97% of the population speaks Cantonese, so it, even more so than English or Mandarin, is perhaps the best to learn. Even if you only learn a few phrases and numbers, your effort will be recognized and appreciated. Your basic Cantonese may not always get your point across, but it will always earn a little goodwill from whoever you're interacting with. To get a head start on your Cantonese, see page 305 for our Cantonese phrasebook.

Download some helpful language apps. If you have a smart-phone, there are a number of apps that you can use to ease the language barrier. Some apps simply provide Chinese phrases on your phone that you can point to when instructing a taxi driver,or alerting a waitress to your food allergies. Others have cool tools like the ability to trace a Chinese character on the screen with your finger and get an instant English translation. See page 34 for an overview of helpful apps.

Transportation

Hong Kong is organized and Westernized, but at its heart it's still Chinese, and it's only becoming more like the Mainland with each passing day. When it comes to getting from point A to point B in China, sometimes it seems like the only rule is that there are no rules, so read up on the following to feel less shocked when you arrive.

Traffic lights and pedestrian signals are often ignored. Most people in Hong Kong obey the "little red man" and "little green man" walking signs at cross walks. But many don't, making a mad dash for the other end of the curb when the slightest break in traffic opens up. We highly recommend that you wait patiently for the light to change so that you can cross safely. Car accidents here may not happen as much as they do in the Mainland, but they're still common, and Hong Kong's tiny, narrow streets with blind corners make getting smacked easier than you may think.

Also remember that Hong Kongers drive on the left-hand side, making crossings even more difficult for those who aren't accustomed to this. Thankfully, the government has actually written arrows on the road at many crosswalks around town pointing in the direction of the flow of traffic, just to make sure our mates who drive on the right-hand side don't get confused and... well, smashed into playdough.

Flagging down a taxi can be tough. There are thousands of taxis in this city, but for some reason it's always a pain trying to find one. They're kind of like the police: they're always there when you don't need them and never there when you do. When there's a downpour, storm or special event happening in town, it can feel as if it's nearly impossible to hail one down. If you get lucky and land one, remember the piece about the language barrier: some will speak limited English, many won't; and some can read simplified characters, but most won't. (Note: the word "won't" in this case often means "refuse to.")

In all honesty, taxis are rather expensive in Hong Kong. It's best to just take the metro or, for a more peaceful experience, ferries. This way you don't have to worry about the language barrier, paying too much or getting stuck in traffic.

Behavior

When you imagine Hong Kong or other Chinese cities for that matter, do you picture a super-crowded street with hordes of people fighting their way down the road en masse? If you said yes, *ding ding ding*, you are correct! However, what you are imagining of Hong Kong's crowdedness is probably still less than what you'll actually find… even if you've been to the Mainland. This city is one of the most densely populated places on the planet, making it even more packed than its northern neighbors in China (and that's saying a lot!).

Forget your personal space bubble.
Those growing up in an overcrowded place like Hong Kong naturally have a smaller personal space bubble than those growing up in, for example, the Outback. It makes sense: your mind is a blank sheet of paper at birth, so if that page is filled with people, people, and more people at an early age, in your later years people just become another obstacle obstructing you from getting from point A to point B. On a crowded subway car, you can be pressed up against a stranger in a way that you wouldn't expect until after your third date and an elevator will be crammed with twice as many people as it could ever fit. People passing you in the street will brush up against you and not acknowledge it, and you'll get knocked around like a pinball while shopping around at markets. Hong Kong is not for the claustrophobic.

Should I act more Chinese or more Western?
Well, that depends on who you are. The good news about Hong Kong being an internationally diverse city is that the people here will often stereotype you upon first meeting. This sounds discriminatory at first, and maybe there is a bit of prejudice to it, but if you look like a Westerner and walk into an establishment, the staff will give you silverware over chopsticks, greet you in English and use Western etiquette. The same goes for Mainlanders and local Hong Kongers; they will be treated within their cultural realms at most businesses. Remember, the customer is always right.

Don't base your decision off of being "Western" or "Chinese," follow the codes of just being polite and a good person. If you express gratitude (e.g. saying "thank you"), don't go out of your way to deliberately anger someone, and genuinely apologize for any mistakes you have made, the person on the other end of the table will understand that you are not from here and will forgive your cultural misunderstanding. By following the Golden Rule, they will most likely treat you well in return. It's as easy as that!

Regular conversation volume is much louder.
After a few hours in Hong Kong, you may start to wonder why everyone is yelling. It's not your imagination. The Chinese from the Mainland are known to speak at high volumes, so much so that NBA superstar and Chinese native Yao Ming even

coached his fellow countrymen and women that to be good hosts during the Olympics, they should try to speak more softly. The Hong Kongese are no exception to this, and in fact, most people from the Mainland even think the Cantonese are the ones who speak at an ear-piercing volume!

If you get stuck in a linguistic crossfire of Mandarin or Cantonese and can't decipher a single word, remember that by some estimates body language constitutes over 55% of total communication; use this to your advantage. If you think someone is yelling but they have a smile on their face and lax body gestures, they're probably not angry about anything. But if someone is yelling with balled up fists in the air and making erratic motions, that's your sign to get the hell out of Dodge. It may seem like common sense, and it is, so use it.

Mass demonstrations do occur here.
Unlike the Mainland, Hong Kongers have the right to protest. After the handover, much of the protests have taken place to denounce communist rule. Even on Chinese holidays, especially National Day, which celebrates the founding of the People's Republic of China (Hong Kong was not a part of China in those days and many Chinese fled to Hong Kong to escape communism), patriotic Hong Kongers hit the streets to protest Beijing's grip. Protests can turn ugly quickly, so stay clear of them. Even if you agree with whatever they're protesting, it's best to stay away. You're a traveler and are here to experience the happier side of Hong Kong.

Food & Eating

***They will eat everything that swims except a submarine, everything that flies except an airplane, and everything with four legs except tables and chairs."** This famous quote from Prince Phillip on the people of Guangdong Province in southern China is not the most culturally sensitive expression of all time, but it does highlight how funky the food in this part of the world can be to an outsider. You're likely to encounter foods – or parts of animals – being served here that would be totally alien in your culture. Think turtle soup, chicken feet, pig hooves, fish heads, cow stomach and stinky tofu; all of which are common in Mainland China as well. Western culture is actually unique in its refusal to eat many animal parts, so either say a polite "no thank you" or, better yet, give it a shot!

Chinese food in China isn't like Chinese food at home. If you come to

Hong Kong expecting to feast on General Tso's Chicken and fortune cookies, you're in for a letdown. None of these dishes are common here, they're mostly Westernized versions of Chinese food created by immigrants from China. This is a good thing, though. There's a huge and delicious variety of real Chinese food and international favorites waiting for you, from local dim sum to Indian curries to Western burgers. You won't be disappointed and you can surely find anything to suit your palate.

Chinese restaurants can be crowded and noisy. Depending where you eat during your trip, you may encounter restaurants that aren't exactly what you're used to in terms of ambience. Diners are often crowded around small tables and at many dim sum places you will have to share a large round table with complete strangers. You also might notice food being tossed around, chicken bones being spit out onto the table cloth, elbows on the table and maybe even a belch here and there. None of these things mean the restaurant won't be delicious – in fact, if the joint is filled to the brim with clients, it might be a good sign that you've found a popular local spot.

The key word in bold above is "Chinese restaurants." Most Chinese restaurants, whether local Hong Kongese or other specialty cuisine from Mainland China, attract Chinese people, so their rules and etiquette prevail. At Western restaurants, expect Western service, manners and etiquette.

All my drinks are warm! The Chinese believe that drinking too many cold beverages is unhealthy and throws your body out of balance. You might be frustrated to find that everything you order, including soda, juice, water, and beer, arrives at your table room temperature, or in the case of water, steaming hot! Try to have a "when in Rome" attitude about this one. It doesn't happen as often in a city as Westernized as Hong Kong, but you should definitely be prepared to encounter it and request cold drinks at times. While this is true at many Chinese restaurants, Western ones will usually have ice upon request.

Is eating dogs and cats acceptable in Hong Kong? Because of certain stereotypes, Westerners have the notion that Chinese people eat dogs and cats. This is actually true in certain areas where dog, and to a lesser extent cat, can be found on menus in certain regions in China, especially in the southern provinces like Guangdong and Guangxi. And even though Hong Kong's culture is greatly influenced

from the adventurous eaters of neighboring Guangdong, the British made eating dog and cat illegal. That law has upheld to this day, and you won't find these "taboo" animals on any menus. If you want to try dog, you'll need to cross the border over to Guangdong.

Out & About

The air is hazy and polluted. You have undoubtedly read about China's air pollution, but if the pollution is high during your trip, it can take your breath away. Pollution levels are much worse in the Mainland, especially in places like Beijing and the northeastern provinces, but Hong Kong is getting worse. See our section on air pollution (see next page) for more details on how to keep grey days from ruining your trip.

Salespeople and scammers can be very aggressive with tourists. Everyone from fake handbag sellers to rickshaw drivers sees a tourist as a potential money-making opportunity, so don't be surprised if you find yourself being constantly approached or followed by them in touristy areas. If you're not interested, just keep walking and don't make eye contact. If they get too aggressive, don't be afraid to show some anger. Remember that bit we said about body language?

Many girls are carrying umbrellas, but it's a sunny day. Maintaining very white skin is desirable among Chinese women, so they take sun protection seriously. You'll see plenty of girls carrying frilly and cutely-decorated umbrellas to stay in the shade, and you might start to want one yourself if you're visiting Hong Kong in the height of summer.

It seems like everyone's face is constantly buried in a smart-phone, whether they're walking, biking, riding the subway, or even driving! Hong Kong is a wired city and the locals have a bit of an internet obsession. When you consider that non-computer owners have to do all their email, gaming, and chatting on their phone, it makes more sense. On top of that, instant-message programs like WeChat are massively popular in greater China, and many people remain logged in all day to keep in touch with friends.

Bargaining is the rule when shopping at markets. There are good deals to be had in Hong Kong on everything from DVDs to dresses, but you may have to bargain for them. Haggling might be unfamiliar to you and make you feel rude or cheap, but rest assured that it's expected here. See page 228 for tips on successful bargaining.

Nobody wants to tell you "no." You might not notice this right away or at all, but it's an aspect of Chinese culture that you should keep your eye out for, partly because it's fascinating and partly because it could save you a lot of headaches. Chinese people are often reluctant to tell someone "no" or deliver disappointing news, because to do so would mean a loss of face. The meaning of "face" in this context is related to the English phrases "saving face" or "losing face" – face refers to some social status or dignity that we all try to preserve for ourselves.

To the Chinese, directly denying a request means a loss of face, so they will often either fail to give any response at all or will try to subtly say no with a comment such as, "Well, that might not be very convenient." For example, if you ask a staff member at your hotel to help you get tickets for a certain performance and they repeatedly suggest other shows besides the one you requested, it may be because the one you wanted is sold out and they are trying to avoid telling you that they cannot help.

In Chinese culture the context of one's words – like actions, attitude, and body language – bear more weight than the actual words being spoken. For example, when asked a direct question by a Westerner, a Chinese person might say "yes" but act as if they have said "no." This confusing communication is a red flag to alert the Westerner that the real answer is "no" but that they value your relationship and do not want to offend you. Westerners place far more emphasis on the literal meaning of spoken words and can become upset when we feel like we're being "lied to" or "given the run-around."

Pollution in Hong Kong

If your trip to Hong Kong was inspired by colorful photos of the Tiantan Big Buddha on a blue-sky day, or by the chance to stand on Tsim Sha Tsui and behold the neon lit skyscrapers on Hong Kong Island, be prepared for the unfortunate reality: many days in Hong Kong don't look like that. In fact, if you're following the news, you've surely encountered some less-appealing images of the city, like Hong Kongers sporting futuristic face masks and commuting through thick smog.

In the past, Hong Kong was proud of its crystal clear days and blue waterways, as shown by its US$23 million drive to make all buses electric, with the final goal of having "zero emissions" from the road. While Hong Kong does much to promote a green environment, the city unfortunately can't escape its geography and proximity to the world's biggest polluter. The massive economic boom taking place over on the Mainland has made pollution levels skyrocket during the past several years. And Hong Kong isn't the only one getting suffocated. Places like Japan and Korea have been outraged at China's smog blanketing their territories, while countries as far away as the United States even alleging that Chinese pollution has reached California on several occasions.

There's good news and bad news concerning Hong Kong's pollution. The good news is that when compared to Mainland cities (like Beijing), Hong Kong is still very clean. The bad news is that it's getting worse, so much so that the local government pulled a page right out of the "How to deal with Pollution at Tourist Sights" chapter from the Mainland's book and set up large screens of particular attractions on a clean day so tourists can still get the money shot, even on dark, severely polluted days.

What are the causes?

Hong Kong is mainly run on a service based economy, so there aren't many big polluters coming from factories within its territory. Mainland China's toxic air, on the other hand, is the product of a number of factors, with coal-burning industrial operations as the leading cause. Coal provides 80% of China's electricity, and much of the coal used here is a type that is particularly high in sulfur. Meanwhile, Hong Kong's surrounding provinces, in particularly Guangdong, which is home to hundreds of factories and manufacturing plants, produce

so much pollution that a good amount of it regularly seeps over into Hong Kong.

Car exhaust also plays a role in the city's pollution levels. Any multi-million person city is bound to have high levels of carbon (leading to the city's aforementioned plan to erase carbon emissions) but Hong Kong's is also compounded by heavy shipping traffic and construction.

Weather patterns greatly influence the city's atmosphere, as well. If you get a breeze coming from the south, bringing in fresh ocean air, you can have some truly beautiful days. If wind derives from the north, however, it could bring in a wave of pollution that has been collected from every city in Mainland China from Beijing to Shenzhen. That's a scary thought!

Seasonal factors occasionally compound these causes and add up to an even more polluted city. During the winter, coal use increases even further, as most central heating in China is powered by coal. Readings of poor air quality even see a big spike during the Chinese New Year and other special events when the sky fills with fireworks.

How is air quality measured?

There are two types of air pollution measured in China: PM10 (particles less than 10 microns in diameter) and PM2.5 (particles less than 2.5 microns in diameter). The United States Embassy in Beijing and the Chinese government each maintain equipment that provides hourly readings, and both publish their own air quality index that incorporates both PM2.5 and PM10 data. Their hourly readings are reported on

AQI Range	Chinese Ministry of Environmental Protection (MEP)	American Environmental Protection Agency (EPA)
0-50	Excellent	Good
51-100	Good	Moderate Unusually sensitive people should consider reducing prolonged or heavy exertion.
101-150	Lightly Polluted	Unhealthy for Sensitive Groups People with heart or lung disease, older adults, and children should reduce prolonged or heavy exertion.
151-200	Moderately Polluted	Unhealthy People with heart or lung disease, older adults, and children should avoid prolonged or heavy exertion; everyone else should reduce prolonged or heavy exertion.
201-300	Heavily Polluted	Very Unhealthy People with heart or lung disease, older adults, and children should avoid all physical activity outdoors. Everyone else should avoid prolonged or heavy exertion.
301-500	Severely Polluted	Hazardous Everyone should avoid all physical activity outdoors; people with heart or lung disease, older adults, and children should remain indoors and keep activity levels low.

the 1-500 scale used by the World Health Orginization (WHO). Depending on the source you're consulting, the same reading may be described differently; the chart on the left comes from the WHO. For a real time and accurate reading of Hong Kong's (or any other Chinese city's) air quality you can visit this website: **aqicn.org/city/hongkong/**. The local Hong Kong government uses their own air quality rating system, which you can see at their website (http://www.aqhi.gov.hk/en.html), but it differs from the WHO system and is less recognizable to Westerners.

For more information on how to monitor Hong Kong's air quality, see the next page under "What can you do about it?"

What are the health effects?

Depending on the timing of your visit, you may be facing a string of hazardous air days or a week of beautiful blue skies. If the air is polluted while you're in Hong Kong, take heart that the health effects of short-term exposure to polluted air are likely to be limited. On a heavily polluted day, it's possible to develop irritation of the eyes, nose, and throat, coughing, phlegm, chest tightness, and shortness of breath, or to simply feel sluggish and under the weather. Travelers with heart conditions should note that air pollution has been associated with an increased risk of heart attack and an increase in blood pressure.

To put the exposure risk into perspective, Beijing-based family doctor Richard Saint Cyr teamed up with a professor at Brigham Young University to study how the effects of breathing polluted air compare with the effects of smoking cigarettes. He concluded that "a day in Beijing is like smoking one sixth of a cigarette." More specifically, on an average day in Beijing an average adult inhales a total of 1.8 mg of PM2.5 particles from air pollution, which is 1/6 of the average 12 mg of PM2.5 particles inhaled from an average cigarette. This comparison may be reassuring to some, or potentially alarming to travelers with children, the elderly, asthmatics, or those with heart conditions, but pollution levels in Hong Kong are a lot less severe than they are in Beijing. It's always better to be safe than sorry.

Travelers with children may be especially concerned about pollution, and research does seem to suggest that children are more vulnerable. For starters, children take in more air per unit of body weight at a given level of exertion than adults do. But children are considered more at risk mostly because their lungs are still developing. For girls, lungs finish developing at 18 years, while a boy's lungs mature by their early 20's. Luckily, the steps you can take to prevent exposure for children are the same as for adults.

Travelers planning a long-term stay in Hong Kong face more intense, but still manageable, risks. Long-term exposure to polluted air is the number one cause of lung cancer, which is the leading cause of death in China. Cases of lung cancer in China have doubled during the past decade according to some studies, extended exposure to pollutants is associated with depressed lung functions even in healthy people. Studies have tied premature births, birth defects, and low-weight babies to pollution. Overall, the World Health Organization estimated in 2007 that 656,000 Chinese were dying prematurely every year from health conditions caused by indoor and outdoor air pollution.

Hong Kong on a particularly polluted day (top) vs a clear day (bottom)

What can you do about it?

Short-term travelers

Time your visit wisely. Unfortunately, it's difficult, if not impossible, to forecast air quality in advance. But, certain seasons are reliably cleaner than others, so if you're serious about avoiding pollution, shoot to visit Hong Kong in spring or autumn. The weather is nicest then anyway and out of typhoon season.

Check the web or download apps to monitor air quality. You can't make wise decisions about pollution unless you have information. (A sunny, nice-looking day in Hong Kong isn't always an indicator of great air quality either, so it's best to consult an official reading). Again, navigate to **aqicn. org/city/hongkong/** for real-time data from a number of locations in the city, or download one of the many air quality apps available for iPhones, Androids, and other smart-phones (see pg 34). You'll find Hong Kong to be very wifi equipped, so check the air quality early and often during your visit.

Buy a face mask. Inexpensive pollution masks can be had at 7-11s, other chain convenience stores throughout the city and grocery stores. Surgical-type masks will provide no protection from PM2.5, despite the fact that you may see a number of people wearing them on a polluted day. There are cloth masks that have pouches to insert a PM2.5 filter, and though they offer a limited amount of protection; for a short stay they're better than nothing. "N95" type masks are also widely available – search for an "N95" face mask online and you'll get a number of results. Purchasing these at home before you leave is wise, though again, they are available once you arrive. If you're looking for something a little more heavy-duty, try to purchase a mask in advance. One commonly recommended model is a Totobobo (www. totobobo.com), which filters PM10 and PM2.5 and can be easily adjusted to fit a child. On the high end, masks such as a 3M brand 8812 industrial facemask will remove more than 95% of pollutants.

Stay away from heavily-trafficked areas. Harmful pollution is concentrated around Hong Kong's busy roads and highways. When you're exploring the city on foot, choose to walk on smaller roads and streets (they tend to be a lot more interesting, anyway). If you're trying to maintain an exercise routine while on vacation, practice caution: never go running outside without checking the air quality first, and if you choose to run, avoid busy streets.

On a heavily polluted day, limit outdoor activity. You'll most likely have beautiful weather during your stay in Hong Kong. If you don't, don't fight it. On heavily polluted days, plan indoor activities, like trying your hand at cooking classes or visiting one of the city's many excellent museums. Your lungs will thank you. Chances are, the cloud of pollution won't stick around for long, so if you just stick it out for a day or two, the skies will clear up and you can continue on with you outdoor activities.

Long-term travelers

Invest in an air purifier or find accommodations that provide them. If you're going to be in Hong Kong long-term, make an effort to stay somewhere as pollutant-free as possible by keeping an air-purifier in your bedroom. You'll find a wide variety of models of all sizes and prices, but no matter which one you choose, it should have a HEPA filtration system and use activated carbon. IQ Air is the most reputable brand on the market, but can run as much as US$6,000.

Fill your home with green plants.
Household plants are inexpensive and have
been shown to purify air indoors. Place a
few by windows and doors, where pollution
is most likely to enter, and they should be
able to absorb much of the toxins and release
some good oxygen into your room.

**Drink clean water and eat fruits and
vegetables.** If you can't avoid being
exposed to pollution from the air, minimize
your exposure from other sources. Hong
Kong tap water is generally safe to drink,
but to be extra cautious you should boil it.
Purchasing bottled water from a reputable
brand name is also a safe bet. Help your
body fight the harmful effects of pollution
by eating plenty of fruits and vegetables,
which contain antioxidants and enzymes that
counteract pollution damage.

Pollution at the Beaches

Hong Kong's beach water quality has been
a concern for the past few decades, and
you'll want to check with local hostels, hotels
or online for the current conditions of the
beach you'd like to visit. In the 1980s, many
of the beaches had dangerous levels of e-coli
in the water, prompting the government to
start tracking water quality in 1986. They
regularly publish the water quality ratings
online. The system is simple and informative
and you can view their English page here:
**www.gov.hk/en/residents/environment/
water/beachwater.htm**

The beaches with the cleanest water are those
in the island districts like Lantau Island and
the Outlying Islands. Those on Hong Kong
Island and in the Sai Kung District can be
hit or miss; the ever popular Deep Water
Bay and Repulse Bay attract both natives
and tourists on any given day and are two
of Hong Kong Island's most reliable. Your
best bet on beach cleanliness is to go for
the beaches in the Western Areas of the New
Territories (Tuen Mun and Tsuen Wan),
which are uniformly and regularly ranked
"fair" or "good."

Beach water quality always gets worse after
heavy rains, which tend to wash garbage
and runoff towards the coast, so it is advised
that you skip the beach for three days after a
heavy rain. Some beaches to avoid include
those at the Nam Wai seashore, which
has been the subject of lots of reports of
pollution on the seashores, including trash
that is not bio-degradable. Sok Kwu Wan

beach has reports of endangerment to the
sea life in the region, with plastic, aluminum
cans, glass debris, and steel rods on the
seashores. Joss House Bay is not controlled
by the government, so if you venture there
be warned that it may contain substantial
amounts of trash depending on the season.
Cascade Beach is one to be avoided entirely.

Before visiting any beaches in Hong Kong,
be sure to check for typhoon advisories near
whichever beach you decide to visit. The
typhoon season typically lasts from April to
October.

Traveling With Kids

Let's face it: taking your kids to China isn't quite like taking them to the petting zoo down the road in your hometown. But if the thought of long international flights, unfamiliar foods, crazy traffic and rumors of stifling air pollution weren't enough to deter you from visiting Hong Kong with kids, congratulations! You'll find that not only is it cleaner and safer than what you've heard, it's a fascinating and uniquely kid-friendly destination.

But what does the city even offer for kids? In this section, we'll first highlight some kid-pleasing Hong Kong attractions, then get into common concerns and how you can best prepare for a worry-free trip.

Hong Kong's Top Ten Kid-Friendly Attractions

Disneyland (pg 165)

This one may seem like a no brainer, but many people may not realize that Hong Kong has a Disneyland. It does, and it's almost an exact replica of the one in Anaheim, so if all the temple seeing and market mayhem that Hong Kong has to offer is just not doing it for your kids, consider saving one day to give them some time with Mickey.

Ocean Park (pg 166)

This attraction might be a little plastic, and it's not very unique because you can find them all over the West. However, if you still would like to give the kids a day with roller coasters, rides and animals, Hong Kong has its own awesome theme park atop an island mountain that also boasts a small zoo and a marine world. It really can be great fun for kids and adults.

Country Parks (pg 99)

Hong Kong may be known for its gleaming skyline, but don't forget that it has miles and miles of gorgeous mountain wilderness to explore in a series of beautiful Country Parks. Populated by lush forests, secluded beaches and towering peaks, and dissected by webs of hiking trails, these massive areas of the New Territories and the Outlying Islands are some of the best places to get the kids out for some running around.

Hong Kong Heritage Museum (pg 139)

Not only is the Hong Kong Heritage Museum one of the best museums in town (for all ages), its first floor is almost entirely dedicated to children. From the Children's Discovery Gallery for ages four to ten to the Hong Kong Story for toddlers, the kids' areas in this joint are superbly done and will educate your little ones without them even knowing it.

Hong Kong Science Museum (pg 142)

Remember those interactive science museums you used to hit up on fieldtrips as a kid? Remember how much fun you had? Well, this is exactly that kind of place, and it will keep your kids entertained and happy for hours.

Dialogue in the Dark (pg 140)

Dialogue in the Dark runs activities aimed to help the non-blind better understand the world in which the blind live. The main activity is being led through a series of obstacles in a room while blindfolded and then having a discussion afterwards. While it may not be made for a five year old, if you've got some teens rolling with you, Dialogue in the Dark can be a very rewarding for those youngsters of the intellectual persuasion.

Beaches (pg 155)

What kid doesn't like a beach? Sure, there are a few of them out there, but for the vast majority of parents, Hong Kong's sweeping coastline provides some of the best natural kid attractions around. There's absolutely no lack of sand and surf in Hong Kong, so slap some trunks on, grab the sandcastle-making gear, and head out to one of Hong Kong's sandy waterfronts. Just make sure to check the beach conditions of your chosen spot first.

Hong Kong Zoological & Botanical Gardens (pg 86)

Nature is at its finest throughout much of Hong Kong, and that is no exception at the beautiful Botanical Gardens. When this place gets blossoming, which is best in spring but great year-round, it can be surprisingly joyous for children. The plant variety is wondrous, and kids just can't help but have some fun when the refreshing energy of the gardens gets into their blood. To top it off, there is a zoo onsite as well.

Hong Kong Police Museum (pg 143)

Some of you may not feel the displays on Triad narcotics at the police museum are the best for kids, but any budding cops and robbers fan in your family will certainly have some fun checking out the displays on the history of crime fighting in Hong Kong. And the firearms and giant tiger head in the Orientation Gallery are sure to put a spark in the little Dick Tracy in your group.

Star Ferry (pg 82)

One of Hong Kong's oldest institutions and easily one of the best-value cruises in the world, the Star Ferry is a wholesome little treat that kids and adults of all ages enjoy. Besides offering spectacular views of the coasts of Hong Kong Island and Kowloon, kids often think of it like an amusement park ride without the park but with plenty of the amusement. We all know kids love to go for rides, and this one will set you back almost nothing.

Before You Go: How to Prepare

Time your trip wisely. Travel during Chinese holidays? Forget about it. China's 1.4 billion people all seem to travel at the same time: during Lunar New Year (aka Chinese New Year or Spring Festival) every January or February, National Day holiday during the first week of October (even though National Day celebrates the communists' victory over the nationalists in 1949, the Chinese government has amped up celebration efforts in Hong Kong to make the city "more proud to be Chinese"), and Mid-Autumn Festival, generally taking place in September. During these peak travel seasons, lines for tourist attractions can stretch on for hours and train stations are a mess. Adults can barely deal with it, and children definitely struggle to stay sane during these chaotic periods.

Get healthy before you go. Try to ensure that everyone is getting their vitamins and is in good shape before you embark on a long trip. If you're already prone to illness, twelve hours on a packed airplane can do you in.

Prepare in advance for medical issues. Check with your pediatrician or travel clinic to see if kids need extra vaccines or anti-malaria pills. Many pharmacy staples that are easily available in your home town are tough to find in China, so pack accordingly. Also, note emergency contacts for a major hospital, preferably an international one.

Examples of good things to bring include oral hydrating salts or electrolyte solution, hand sanitizer, Aspirin or Tylenol (or whatever anti-fever/pain meds you usually use), anti-itch cream, hydrocortisone cream, Benadryl syrup, and children's sunscreen and mosquito repellent.

Figure out what to bring with you and what to buy in Hong Kong. It's smart to bring your own infant formula when traveling abroad anywhere, since switching brands suddenly can upset a baby's stomach. But if your luggage is lost or you run out while in China, don't panic: family doctors in Hong Kong regularly advise their patients that buying international brands, such as Nestlé, Similac and Enfamil, is safe. Ditto for diapers: unless your baby is very sensitive or has particular needs, you'll find imported diapers with little trouble in Hong Kong. Plus, many brands have Chinese counterparts, like Huggies and Pampers.

They're not exactly like the ones back home, but pretty much OK.

As for food, if your kid is picky, you're better off bringing his or her favorite snacks with you, as they might be hard to find and are expensive. If your kid is a little more easygoing, there's a wide range of treats that they'll probably love. You can buy Heinz brand baby food, but if you're looking for no-sugar-added or organic baby food, it's better to pack it with you. There's a wide variety of safe bottled water brands to give to kids or mix with formula, and a brand called Great Lakes makes 100% apple, orange and tomato juice that is widely available.

Learn a little bit about Hong Kong before you leave. Rent movies that take place in Hong Kong. Your little one might get pumped up to go visit after watching a few Bruce Lee movies (see our Movie List on pg 43 for recommendations). Also, watch the newspaper and TV for stories from Hong Kong, and you and your child might also want to read a book about it (see pg 43 for the Reading List). Have your kids think up questions they have about Hong Kong and try to find the answers on Google. Basically, anything you can do to build excitement and curiosity for the trip will pay off.

Try to pick up a few phrases in Cantonese. Becoming fluent is obviously not a reasonable short-term goal, but learning a few key words can be fun. You might even find a Chinese language camp or class in your neighborhood that your kids could take before you go. Children pick up new languages much more easily than adults, and they might surprise you! An adorable seven year-old with a few phrases in Cantonese is an excellent bargaining tool in the markets of Hong Kong.

Give Chinese food a test run. The good news is that most Chinese restaurants have kid-friendly choices; it's hard to go wrong with pork dumplings or fried rice. But it's smart to hit up a few Chinese spots in your town before the trip. You'll find that Western Chinese food doesn't necessarily resemble Chinese food in Hong Kong, but it's a good warm-up for your kids' taste buds and can help them feel more adventurous.

Time to Travel: The Flight

Time your flight wisely to maximize sleep. It's bound to be a grueling overnight flight to Hong Kong, but you can try to minimize the disruption to your kids' sleep schedules by choosing a flight that leaves later in the evening when they're likely to be asleep.

Check in early to select good seats. Online check-in becomes available 24 hours before departure, so make a point of logging on to check in and choose your family's seats. Some websites even allow you to choose your seat upon purchasing the ticket. Try to avoid sitting near the restrooms, where a lot of foot traffic and doors opening and closing can disturb sleep. The ultimate score for traveling with kids is to be seated in the bulkhead, the row of seats with nothing in front but a wall. There's more legroom (or crawl room) and you won't have to worry about your kids kicking the seat in front of them.

However, some airliners these days are charging for prime seats in economy class. If you have an antsy child, it may be worth coughing up the extra US$100 or so for him or her (and yourself!) on than 10 hour + flight.

Go high-tech. Even if you try to limit your kids' use of electronics at home, now is not the time to take away the iPads or the PSPs. You can confiscate the gadgets once you land and only pull them out again on long bus rides or for the flight home. Older kids might even have homework they need to keep up with if you're traveling during the school year, and the flight is a perfect opportunity to take care of it.

On the Ground: Once You've Arrived

Treat jet lag with patience. The first three nights are the most difficult; and the second night is probably the worst. The best advice is to take it slow and sleep when they do. This might mean slowing down your sightseeing activities for the first couple of days. Don't push everyone too hard. There's a lot to see in Hong Kong, but you can't do it all in two weeks anyway. The time difference is a big adjustment, especially for little ones. Being tired and run down can lead to sickness, so make sure everyone gets rest and try to adjust slowly to the time difference.

Hope for the best, plan for the worst. Fill out an emergency card with your name, contact info, and hotel address, and give it to your child just in case he or she gets separated from you.

Don't leave home without tissues.
Toilet paper is sometimes not provided in
Hong Kong bathrooms, and you never know
when you'll need it. Likewise for Kleenex.
Keep some with you for those times when
you need to blow your nose or wipe your
hands.

Keep hands clean. That's good advice
for all the travelers in your group, no matter
their age. Bring along hand sanitizer and wet
wipes (wipes are readily available in China
too). Wash your hands and your kids' hands
whenever you get a chance – it'll go a long
way toward keeping you healthy.

Watch the traffic. See our Transportation
area of the Culture Shock Section (pg 283)
for more information on how to be a safe
pedestrian in Hong Kong. It's extremely
important to keep an eye on little ones when
you're out and about, and very little kids will
be better off in an infant carrier, in your arms,
or in a stroller. It's not a good place to learn
how to walk.

**Engage your kids in their cultural
surroundings.** Take the time to point
out cultural differences that you notice and
explain the reasons behind them. With a
little guidance, kids tend to appreciate them,
rather than becoming grossed out or upset.
Remember that it's good to get out of your
comfort zone, no matter how old you are,
and Hong Kong's British past might be the
perfect starting point in Asia for your child,
lessening the extremes that are found in other
major Oriental cities like Hanoi, Bangkok
or Beijing. When push comes to shove and
the culture shock is just too much for your
kid, you'll never be too far from a Western
establishment where he or she can cool down
and relax after a long day in the East.

Water, Food & Health

Water Safety

Like in most Western countries, the tap water in Hong Kong is drinkable. However, with pollution on the rise, a factor that can lead to contaminants seeping into city aquifers, along with some older buildings with out-of-date plumbing systems, it may be best to stay clear of tap water.

Boiled Water At mid-range and high end places, it's most likely OK to drink the tap water, even though you should ask before doing so. If not, or to be extra cautious, you should boil it. Boiling will kill any bacteria in the water and make it safe for drinking.

Bottled Water Boiling water will prevent you from getting acutely sick, but your water may contain high concentrations of heavy metals and other chemicals that can't be boiled out. Your healthiest bet is bottled water, which is ubiquitous, inexpensive and available in many street stands, shops, supermarkets, restaurants and hotel stores for very cheap. Check to be sure that the bottle s properly sealed before you drink it.

Other things to consider:

In budget establishments, ice cubes will come from the tap water, so keep this in mind when ordering them for a cold drink.

Using a minimal amount of tap water is generally okay for brushing your teeth.

Alcoholic drinks and drinks made with boiled water, like coffee or tea, are safe to drink.

Food Safety

As with water, there's not too much concern with food contamination in Hong Kong. The Mainland has its fair share of glow in the dark meat, fake eggs, toxic baby formula and many others, but Hong Kong, except for a few minor incidents here and there, has been able to avoid such scandals. The best advice is to not buy any "made in China" food products, but this is taking the extra cautious route.

The only other real warning is food poisoning. If eating out (especially on the street) here's a good chance that you're food will not be as hygienic as you're used to. Especially as a foreigner — who is not used

to the harmless bugs and bacteria that don't affect locals – your chances of getting ill from food increase. Again, you shouldn't be overly concerned, just literally trust your gut and if something tastes or smells off, quit eating it.

Before You Leave

There are a few things you can do before you leave home that will pave the way for a safe eating experience in Hong Kong. It's not a bad idea to put together a mini-medical kit stocked with Immodium, Pepto Bismol, Tums, and other over-the-counter stomach aids. These medicines may be available here, but could be hard to find and expensive, not to mention the time you'd spend scouring pharmacies when you could be sightseeing. Next, ask your doctor to prescribe an antibiotic such as Ciprofloxacin (Cipro) that is effective against traveler's diarrhea. In the event that you do eat something you regret, antibiotics can seriously cut down on the duration of your suffering.

Markets & Shops

If you're hoping to do some self-catering during your trip, keep in mind that not all markets and shops are created equal. In Hong Kong, you'll see small fruit and vegetable carts and mini-markets popping up anywhere and everywhere. Some of these will be more organized outdoor set-ups, while others may simply be a man standing next to a pile of vegetables on the sidewalk. Most are perfectly fine, but if you're really concerned about food safety, the rule "bigger is better" applies when buying food on your own. There are big, well-known, usually foreign-based chains like Tesco (UK), Carrefour (France), and Walmart (US) that you can hit up if you need. These stores have better-developed supply chains and more standardized food storage and food safety practices. Just use caution and common sense, and wash your purchases very thoroughly with purified water.

Disease

While Hong Kong's crime rate is next to none, there is a silent killer in the area that has not only put the town on alert, but the entire world.

SARS and avian flu (aka bird flu or H1N1)

caused minor episodes of panic during the previous decades. The first case of SARS in the Hong Kong SAR (what a coincidence!) occurred in 1997 and the last case was reported in 2003 when nearly 2,000 individuals were infected and there were 299 related deaths. Since then, SARS appears to have been brought under control as the government has taken serious measures to reduce the chance of another outbreak from happening.

H1N1 is another virus that that has struck fear and even death in many countries, especially in East Asia. Similar to procedures againts the spread of SARS, passengers at all points of entry coming into Hong Kong, whether by water, land or air, must go through a temperature screening. Those with a high fever or coming from high risk areas will be quarantined. The moral of the story is think twice before heading to Hong Kong with a high fever, you just might be put in the hole!

If an outbreak were to happen, you'd most likely hear about it before arriving in Hong Kong, allowing you to make adjustments or cancel your trip. In the extremely unlikely event that you're in Hong Kong when an outbreak occurs, there are three likely scenarios. 1) It's a minor outbreak and you'd be able to leave the country if you don't have a fever or symptoms. 2) It's a major outbreak and other countries won't allow you to enter if you're coming from Hong Kong. In this case, advice is hard to give since (luckily) there hasn't been anything reaching this level of severity. 3) You get sick and have to seek treatment. H1N1 and SARS have killed those with weakened immune systems, the elderly and small children, but if you're healthy and get sick, there's a high chance you'll be able to recover based off cases from the past. Hong Kong has top of the line, world class medical facilities too, and the doctors have dealt with this before, so you'd be in good hands.

As a last bit of advice, keep those hands clean. Hand sanitizer seems to be everywhere in this city, so when you see a free stall feel free to go up and disinfect. Also, avoid farms or markets with high concentrations of chickens and other barnyard animals. Unsanitary conditions like these are where many of the diseases get transferred from animals into human populations. Why would you be at a barn in Hong Kong anyway? There's a lot more fun to be had elsewhere in the city!

Hong Kong on a Budget

The cost of living in Hong Kong has shot up in recent years, so it's not really the dirt-cheap destination that it once was. If money isn't a concern, Hong Kong is a limitless playground. But for most of us who need to limit our expenses, Hong Kong can pose a bit of a challenge at times. If you keep to a very tight budget, it's possible to get by on less than US$65 per day. Our example below shows you how, but if you're budget is different you can just use what we have here as a reference. Prices for transportation and attractions are pretty fixed, so the wiggle room in your budget comes from accommodations and food.

* Spend the night in a hostel: HK$250
* Breakfast: steamed bun on the street: HK$20
* MTR to Tsim Sha Tsui: HK$9
* Morning on the waterfront and Avenue of Stars: FREE
* MTR to Jordan: HK$4.5
* Noodle lunch at *dai pai don* food stall on Temple Street: HK$20
* Bottle of water: HK$8
* Walk up and down Temple Street: FREE
* I ♥ Hong Kong T-shirt (well haggled): HK$20
* Walk to dinner at cheap local restaurant: HK$60
* Buy a few beers at a corner store and watch some karaoke: HK$45
* Subway back to hostel: HK$9

TOTAL: HK$495.5 = US$63.80

Tips for saving money

Hong Kong is not the greatest city to visit if you're on a budget. That being said, there are plenty of activities that can be done for free or near free, from marching through the city's markets to hiking through Country Parks or grabbing some cheap noodles at a street-side food stall. In these cases, much of what you'll have to pay for is transportation, but if you know what you're after (hiking or markets) you can hop in a hostel close by and reduce transit times. If you're trying to see Hong Kong without breaking the bank, here are some general rules and tips for maximizing your money.

Accommodation: You want to have a safe and clean place to lay your head at the end of the day. But if you're really getting the most out of Hong Kong, your hotel will just be a place to crash and rest up for the next exciting day. If you're trying to cut costs, start here: the city has several decent, reasonably priced hostels, and as a bonus, you can meet other travelers and exchange stories and information. The centrally located Chungking and Mirador Mansions are also always good budget choices.

Skip cabs, take the subway instead: Though this may go without saying, the subway is by far the cheaper option than taking taxis. In the Mainland, a great way of getting around is on top of a bike, but Hong Kong's narrow roads aren't as bicycle friendly as they are in the Mainland. So, out of all the ways to get from point A to point B, subway is by far the cheapest and most efficient.

Skip tour guides: Generally speaking, you get what you pay for when it comes to tour packages and tour guides. That means that if you have money to drop, you could end up with a knowledgeable, hardworking, and honest tour guide who takes your sightseeing to the next level – but it also means that if you go cheap, you might end up with a dubious tour guide who doesn't add much at all. If you're trying to save money, this is a good place to skip.

Nothing imported: When in Rome, do as the Romans. Your trip to Hong Kong is not a great time to develop a taste for cheese or high-end microbrews if you're on a budget. While both are available here, like all imported products and products targeted at Western tastes, they'll cost you dearly. Indulging once in a while is one thing, but you'll save money and have a more authentic experience if you eat and drink like the locals.

Solo-Female, Disabled, LGBT & Travelers of Color

Solo Female Travelers

If you are a single female traveler in Hong Kong, there's no need for concern, as Hong Kong is one of the safest cities in the world. There is a good deal of respect for women ingrained in the culture, so you are not very likely to experience anything in the way of crime. Of course, you should always exercise common sense and avoid areas or scenes that look dicier than usual, but you are unlikely to come across anything of this nature. The number for emergency is **999**; save it in your cell phone. All phone operators speak English in the case of an emergency, as do most policemen. The biggest warnings if you're a lone woman are to avoid finding yourself alone on Lockhart Road late at night, and maybe don't choose the Chungking Mansions as your accomodation.

Disabled

Although Hong Kong tries to accomodate those with disabilities, the disabled will have some difficulties navigating the city, especially around heavily trafficed areas. There is an app called **Cyberable** (see pg 35) that provides information for those with disabilities. When in doubt, allow about an extra half hour to an hour to arrive at your destination.

LGBT Travelers

Hong Kong has a decent LGBT scene with several prominent night clubs and bars around the city, but compared to cities in the West, they still have strides to make. With one of the lowest crime rates for any large city in the world, you will not have to worry about harassment on the streets as a gay traveler. The areas of SoHo and Lan Kwai Fong (LKF) are very gay friendly and, generally speaking, Hong Kong Island is more liberal and open minded (when compared to the villages of the New Territories, for example).

DS Magazine is the local monthly gay guide for events, and there are also gay and lesbian nights in straight venues as well. If you want to go to a decidedly gay beach, consider Middle Bay. It's a nice alternative to Repulse Bay, because it doesn't tend to get crowded. For some local gay-friendly bars and clubs, see page 220.

People of Color

If you are a black traveler and have never been to Asia before, Hong Kong is one of the few mainstream cities where your presence alone will not cause particular alarm. You will almost certainly be the subject of curiosity at some point, as there are many Chinese – especially vacationing Mainlanders or other Asians – who have never seen a dark-skinned person before. Though the Hong Kongese are generally used to seeing people from all over the world on a very regular basis, to many other Asian people, a black person is a rare sight, and you shouldn't be surprised if you get a few blank stares, requests for photos, pointed fingers or waves. People may also want to touch your hair – so heads up!

Also, be aware that there is a misperception among many Chinese that black people are poor and at the bottom barrel of societies, despite the prominent positions and success of countless black men and women throughout the world. You may be asked where you are from and your nationality, and some Chinese may not believe you if your answer is a first world country. Take it as naïve ignorance, take a few deep breaths, and carry on; you may experience this on many occasions while walking around Hong Kong. When asked about black culture or people, feel free to take the time to kindly explain any discrepancies or misinformation they may have heard, because it is rare for them to get any information from a direct or reliable source.

Hong Kong vs Mainland China

While many of the differences between Hong Kong and Mainland China have been touched upon already in the preceding sections – pollution and transportation for example – there are several more differences of particular note, and those who are planning a trip to the Mainland after Hong Kong should be aware of them. By no means is this list complete – they are just some of the many differences you will find.

Eat Anywhere

Hong Kong has some strict policies when it comes to eating on public transportation. It's a big no-no, and you can be fined up to HK$5,000 for eating on the MTR network or in stations. This is not the case in Mainland China – you see people in the Mainland eating just about anywhere. This kind of behavior is absolutely unacceptable in Hong Kong, and it has actually led to conflicts between vacationing Mainlanders in Hong Kong and locals. If you're headed to the Mainland, be ready for the vision of food and drink being consumed just about anywhere and trash being tossed liberally. That brings us to the next topic.

Trash

One of the biggest shocks for anyone headed to Mainland China for the first time – from Hong Kong or most anywhere in the West – is how dirty much of China can be. Air pollution aside, China has a big problem in many places with trash disposal, or the lack thereof. While you're not likely to encounter mounds of trash in places like downtown Beijing or Shanghai, villages, small towns and the outskirts or suburbs of bigger cities are places where citizens are fine with dumping trash just about anywhere.

Littering is a major problem in Mainland China, and there are few signs of anyone trying to do anything to curb the problem. Where does this attitude to trash the place come from? At least in big cities, much of it seems to stem from the fact that government workers scour the cities picking up trash. While in Western eyes this seems like a poor reason to litter (and it is), to many Chinese the fact that someone is paid to pick up trash means there's nothing wrong with dropping it on the spot. This mindset is beginning to change but the contrast between cleaner Hong Kong and the grubby Mainland can be a shock for many.

Spitting

Before the 2008 Summer Olympics rolled into Beijing a massive campaign was set up by the government to curb the spitting of Mainlanders before the world arrived to a chorus of hacks. Yes, the problem is that bad, and you will notice it practically the moment you set foot in China. While it's hard at this point to say how much spitting was actually reduced during the Olympics, the one thing we know for sure is it's here in force.

Mainlanders are known for spitting all over the place, from street corners, to sidewalks and flowerbeds to gardens. If you're especially unlucky, you might even catch a person or two spitting on the floor of a subway car or station, or even in the lobby of a building! And it's not just a quick "*t'hoo*" to clear the mouth, either; most spitters in the Mainland get guttural with a big "haaawwkk" before releasing whatever was caught down the throat, making for a very unpleasant scene for newcomers.

Another behavior that's completely unacceptable in Hong Kong, spitting is a part of life in Mainland China, and while there are many Mainlanders who abhor the practice of spitting, it's something you're going to have to deal with while over the border.

Smoking

Prohibited in most public areas throughout Hong Kong and never, ever seen in restaurants, smoking is the Mainland's form of indoor pollution, and the problem is just as bad as, if not worse, than the pollution that makes a gray day when the forecast calls for sunny clear skies. The country holds a whopping 350 million regular smokers, more than the size of the entire US population, and that doesn't take into account those who are social smokers: those who smoke at meetings with clients or simply when offered a smoke from a friend (common practices in the Mainland).

Most smokers in China are men. Women smokers are generally frowned upon, especially in more traditional places like villages, but this too is slowly changing, and you're very likely to see women smoking comfortably in big cities, especially in bar or café districts.

Though the government has begun to implement policies to gain some control over the rampant habit, such as banning smoking in hospitals, primary schools, university campuses, restaurants, bars, and office buildings, enforcement of these policies is nowhere to be seen at best. This means that all these places are fair game for smokers. There are a few establishments who may enforce a non-smoking policy, especially Western places, but they do so at the risk of losing a good amount of clientele. Once you're in the Mainland, you'll need to get ready for smokers in most establishments filling the place up with fumes, often right in front of a "NO SMOKING" sign.

Line Cutting

Possibly one of the most irritating behaviors a Westerner or a Hong Konger will encounter in the Mainland, line cutting seems to be the favorite pastime of many a Chinese. Even in big cities like Beijing, Shanghai or Shenzhen, where the local population likes to see themselves as modern, worldly, civilized and sophisticated, line cutting is still a problem among the farmer and migrant peoples who either live in the cities or come in on various daytrips. It can be incredibly frustrating when you're standing in line for a subway or bus, calmly and kindly like the rest of the locals around you, and then a crowd swings up and turns an ordered scene into chaos. Even some of the local city dwellers can't stand it, and sometimes arguments can erupt between those who cut and those who queue.

Pushing

Whose hand is that on your back as you go through the turnstile to board the subway? It's probably a Mainlander, and likely an older person from the countryside. While local Hong Kongese have learned how to pack into crowded areas like champs (there's little choice in a city so densely populated) they still make efforts to be respectful of the people around them, and that means very little unneeded physical contact.

In the Mainland, however, it's not uncommon in the least for people to put a forceful arm or hand on the person in front of them when moving through crowded areas, and if you venture over the Hong Kong border you'll certainly encounter more pushing than you ever thought possible.

Visa Issues &Visa Runs

Any foreigner working in China by law needs a work visa. But, there are still a great many who work under the table without proper documentation, particularly because there are many companies who need foreigners but don't have the means to get them a proper work visa. Instead, the foreigner picks up a multiple-entry travel visa (which does not legally allow one to work) and works for a company with the agreement that both parties keep the employment a tight secret.

The only problem with these multiple-entry travel visas is that most of them require a person to exit China every 30 days. So, when a foreigner is working in the Mainland illegally under a travel visa and that 30 day mark is up, he or she has to leave Mainland China – even if it's only for a few hours. The minute they step foot in, say, Hong Kong, a new 30 day period begins and that person can go back to the Mainland to continue working.

In other cases, some expats and travelers (who actually follow the law) whose visa is about to expire simply want to stay in the country longer and need to get a new visa, and the most convenient place to do that is right here in Hong Kong. So, if you're a foreigner working under the table in the Mainland and just need to pop into Hong Kong for the infamous visa run, or you actually just need a new visa (or to extend your travel visa), a couple-day trip to Hong Kong is in the cards.

Visa services in Hong Kong are fast and efficient, with a quick turnaround, and you can make a great layover holiday out of your three- or four-day visa run. Options for getting here from the Mainland include arriving in Shenzhen and then taking a ferry, bus, or a train directly to Hong Kong, or taking a long, overnight bus from Beijing or Shanghai directly to Hong Kong. The duration of these buses is approximately 20 hours, and both include a night on a small bed.

Flying to Shenzhen is the cheapest option, with bus fees from there only amounting to about ¥150. A great website that has been providing discounted airfare prices for travelers for years is **Ctrip.com**. Using their site, it really is possible to take care of all your traveling needs, from airline tickets to hotel stays. There are packages for airfare or hotel only, or bundled packages for both. Even for last minute trips to Hong Kong, the site is quite popular for bargain tickets.

Ctrip.com

Phone: 400 619 9999
Email: e_service@ctrip.com
Website: www.english.ctrip.com

Normally in Hong Kong there are no difficulties getting a Chinese visa, but if you think you might run into some problems, give yourself two extra days just in case. If you are using a service agency to procure your visa, most companies arrange for a maximum of two days of service, with most receiving their visas the next day. If you decide to get your visa on your own, it could take between three to five days.

Consular Department

The Commissioner's Office of China's Foreign Ministry in the Hong Kong SAR
Address: 6/F, Lower Block, China Resources Building, 26 Harbour Road, Wan Chai

Office hours: Monday to Friday (except Hong Kong public holidays), 9:00-12:00 and 14:00-17:00
Phone: 3413 2300 (24-hour automatic inquiry)
Fax: 3413 2604
Email: fmcovisa_hk@mfa.gov.cn
Website: www.fmcoprc.gov.hk/eng/gywm/gszn/lsbgs/t281583.htm

Less than a five minute walk from the Wan Chai MTR station, this office has some of the most efficient service we have ever seen, but it may take you an hour to submit your application. For cheap housing for your stay, check out the hostel options in Wan Chai (pg 174).

Once you are certain you have secured your next visa, the fun part can really begin. Planning such a short trip can be a bit daunting, but it is totally doable, no matter what your budget is. There are a couple of absolutes that must be experienced in Hong Kong if you are traveling there. A trip to The Peak (pg 49) is one of those. You have the option to take The Peak Tram to the top of Victoria Peak. Although very touristy, it is one of those things that should be seen no matter what. On a clear night, it is a great escape from the boisterous sounds and lights of downtown.

The Star Ferry (pg 82) ride across Victoria Harbour is another great escape, and the city's firework shows during festivals and holidays are always extremely popular with tourists. Another perfect daytrip if you are in Hong Kong for a few days is a quick jaunt to Lamma Island (pg 162); it's actually kind of a getaway from the getaway. And if you want to go where no one knows your name but everyone will by the time you leave, then head over to the Happy Valley Race Course (pg 95). You don't even have to be into horses or betting or even drinking. It's the atmosphere and the people that have made this a staple in Hong Kong for years. By the time you leave, you will be surrounded by friends one way or another.

If you take into consideration these tips and plan accordingly, there is no reason why your trip to Hong Kong to renew your visa should be anything less than a great mini-vacation.

Lockhart Road: The Red Light District

If you find yourself out late one night in the Wan Chai District and you get a whiff of sleaze, the uninhibited, and a slight flash of a red light, do not be alarmed. Do not panic. You've just entered the seedier side of Hong Kong.

Enter Lockhart Road

Every city has to have their seedy area, and Hong Kong's is the area around Lockhart in Wan Chai. Lockhart Road has a three block stretch of treachery that foreigners should be warned about. Though moderate by Western standards, Lockhart Road is still the place where you will see ladies of the night coupled and tripled on the corners whistling at males walking down the streets. It is also the same street where "mama sans" will grab you and try to bring you in to see one of her girls. If you do fall into a club in this area and a woman asks you to buy her a drink that costs an extravagant amount, you'd be right to assume that she is probably a working girl and she's getting a percentage from each drink bought for her. Lockhart is a tricky street, however, because it is lined with some happening clubs and is also more economical than the much pricier Lan Kwai Fong area. For a night out with a group, you shouldn't have any problems at all navigating through the prostitutes and strippers hanging out of doors. Any clubs you go to in this area may have some women "working" however, so be aware of that.

Prostitution in Hong Kong has a thick cloud of smoke surrounding its legality. If there is any real crime in Hong Kong and in this area in general, it is pickpockets. They can be found in all sections of town, but most notably on the Kowloon side and on Lockhart during the evenings. Lockhart Road is lined with small massage parlors and tucked away sex shops, so the two go hand in hand, particularly because in this area there are lots of people walking around with lots of cash on them. If you are walking down this street, be a bit more aware of your surroundings and don't be coerced into going into stores or clubs you don't wish to attend.

Hong Kong Calling Guide

Calling to Hong Kong

• General tips for calling to Hong Kong from abroad

Step 1: Dial the international access code (011 in the US)
Step 2: Dial the country codes of 852
Step 3: Dial the local subscriber number (8 digits)

• Instructions for calling to cities within Hong Kong

For international calls to Hong Kong, always dial the international access code (011 in the U.S), followed by the country code of 852, and, finally, the 8-digit subscriber number. e.g. 011-852-xxxx-xxxx.

If you are calling locally, simply dial the 8-digit subscriber number.

• Instructions for calling to cell phones in Hong Kong

In Hong Kong, cell phone numbers have the same number of digits as land line numbers (8). You don't have to do anything special to reach a cellular number; just dial it as you would a land line.

Making Calls while in Hong Kong

• General Tips for Making Phone Calls within Hong Kong

For any domestic calls within Hong Kong, simply dial the 8-digit subscriber number.

• Mobile phone calls within Hong Kong

Calling cell phones in Hong Kong is no different from calling land lines. Simply dial the 8-digit cell phone number. Cell phone numbers traditionally begin with a 9, but, due to increases in use, many now begin with a 6. e.g. 9xxx-xxxx or 6xxx-xxxx

• Other calls and numbers

Toll-free numbers in Hong Kong begin with 800. Remember that calling an 800 number in Hong Kong from abroad can bring charges as hefty as those for any international call.

Some toll-free numbers are used for public services.

• Tips for Calling Internationally from Hong Kong

For international calls from Hong Kong, dial the access code of 00, country code, area code, and local number. e.g. For a call to San Francisco from Hong Kong, dial 00-1-415-xxx-xxxx.

In Hong Kong, local calls are free and can be made from homes and businesses. You will pay about 10¢ – 15¢ for a 5-minute local call from a public telephone. A similar call from your hotel room will cost about 50¢ -65¢. Long-distance calls can be made from specially marked International Dialing Direct (IDD) public phones. Purchase a phone card or a local card known as an Octopus card. Another card, the PCCW Hello PhoneCard, comes in denominations ranging from HK$50 to HK$300 (US$6.50-US$39), and is available at HKTB information offices, 7-11 convenience stores, machines located beside telephones, and other locations around Hong Kong

Most large hotels in Hong Kong have high-speed dataports that allow guests to use laptop computers. In some hotels, you can purchase an Internet access card for about HK$100 (US$13), valid for anywhere from 100 minutes to unlimited use for 5 days. Other hotels charge a flat rate per day. Hotel business centers also offer computers and Internet access for a fee. Internet cafes are fairly easy to find, and the popular Pacific Coffee chain of cafes offers Internet service.

International country dialing codes:

US & Canada: 1	Australia: 61
China: 86	Hong Kong: 852
Macau: 853	New Zealand: 64
UK: 44	Taiwan 886

Chinese cities' calling codes:

Beijing: 10	Changsha: 731
Chengdu: 28	Chongqing: 23
Fuzhou: 591	Guangzhou: 20
Guilin: 773	Hangzhou: 571
Hefei: 551	Ji'nan: 531
Kunming: 871	Lhasa: 891
Nanchang: 791	Nanjing: 25
Shanghai: 21	Shenyang: 24
Shenzhen: 755	Tianjin: 22
Urumqi: 991	Wuhan: 27
Xiamen: 592	Xi'an: 29

Cantonese Phrasebook

For Westerners, Hong Kong usually proves to be one of the easiest Asian cities to travel through, in large part because the city is so well posted with English signage. In fact, English is one of Hong Kong's official languages thanks to the 150-plus years that Britain ran the show. But that doesn't mean everyone in this city speaks English, and many of those who do are only conversational to a very limited degree. The staff at high end hotels and restaurants will have a strong grasp, but the vast majority of folk you'll encounter in other daily situations – especially those at markets, in taxis or on the street – will not be able to speak English very well, if at all. Brushing up on some Cantonese basics before you arrive will not only help make your trip all the smoother, it will also enrich your stay in Hong Kong by allowing your experience of the culture to be a bit more in depth and personal.

But before we jump into a crash course on spoken Cantonese and begin spitting out tones and strange vowel clusters, let's do a quick breakdown of Cantonese and how it fits into the Chinese language.

The "Chinese" Language

As we mentioned in Hot Topics, Hong Kong's "biliterate and trilingual" policy enforced by Beijing states that the two official languages of the city are Chinese and English. But this is a bit deceptive because, as few people in the West realize, there is no single Chinese language. There are actually ten major varieties of Chinese – Mandarin, Jin, Wu, Hui, Gan, Xiang, Min, Hakka, Cantonese (or Yue) and Ping – spoken throughout the country. Hot debate rages throughout the linguistics community as to whether these are just dialects of a Chinese umbrella language or separate languages altogether, with the majority of experts currently leaning towards the "separate language" camp. The neutral term that has been adopted for these ten is "language variety," but when you consider that the differences between them is something similar to the differences between Italian and French or English and Swedish, you can see why calling them separate languages tends to make the most sense.

The "Chinese" of Hong Kong

So what "variety" of Chinese do they speak in Hong Kong? Well, there are actually two: Mandarin and Cantonese. Because of Hong Kong's location in the heart of Guangdong Province (formerly known as Canton in English) most immigrants to the city throughout its history came from Guangdong. Their language is Cantonese, and today around 97% of Hong Kongese speak Cantonese as a first language. However, this number could be on the decline, as Hong Kong is rapidly filling with Mainland Chinese immigrants, most of whom speak Mandarin as a first language. This means that, although Mandarin and Cantonese are mutually unintelligible, you're likely to encounter both at some point during your stay.

This leads us back to the "trilingual" policy of Hong Kong, which refers to the fact that English, Mandarin and Cantonese are all spoken in the city. The "biliterate" aspect of the policy includes written English and written Chinese, but written Chinese is not the same in Hong Kong as it is in the Mainland. Whereas Mainland Chinese uses the simplified characters implemented by Mao Zedong in the 1950s, Hong Kong still uses traditional characters, the same that have been in use for over 2,000 years. Many characters between the two systems are actually the same, but you will only encounter the traditional set while in Hong Kong.

Cantonese (廣東話)

Whereas Mandarin is only about 700 to 800 years old, having come about as an official language during the Ming Dynasty, Cantonese traces its roots back a good 2,000 years. Many Hong Kongese and some experts maintain that Cantonese is actually far closer to Old Chinese than Mandarin, but what actually constitutes Old Chinese is difficult to define because it too would have had a large number of dialects and varieties.

Cantonese does include more final consonants (consonants that fall that the end of a word, such as the "t" in "bat") than Mandarin, and this is very similar to what experts are piecing together about Old Chinese, which is believed to have had a great many words that ended in consonants. What makes Cantonese particularly difficult – in many people's opinions more difficult than Mandarin – are the tones and the vowel clusters.

Tones

Cantonese, like all Chinese languages, is tonal. This means that every syllable has multiple meanings depending on the tone. A tone is essentially the pitch of the syllable, which can rise, fall, or stay flat/even. You can hear an example of a tone if you make a one-word question in English, such as "Really?" Here, the pitch starts low and rises sharply by the end of the word, creating a rising tone. While English and most other languages in the West use tones to indicate things like questions or emotion, Chinese languages use tones to differentiate the meaning between homophones (words that sound exactly the same).

Is Cantonese dying?

Spoken by around 100 million people throughout the world, Cantonese is the lingua franca of China's southern provinces of Guangdong and Guangxi. It also enjoys a status as the first or second language of many people throughout Singapore, Malaysia, Thailand and Vietnam, and is the majority language of Chinese communities throughout the world, especially the Chinatowns of major cities in the US, Canada, Europe and Australia. This is because the majority of the immigrants who built these global Chinese communities came from Guangdong.

Today, however, one of the world's oldest languages may be on the decline due to two major competitors: Mandarin and English. On the home front, Cantonese still sits comfortably as the de facto language of the adult populations in Guangdong, including Hong Kong, but Mandarin is taking root in the younger population, and that means Cantonese could be pushed out of prominence in a generation or two. Consider this statistic: of the ten major languages in the Chinese family, Yue (the term for the many dialects of Cantonese) accounts for only around 60 million native speakers in China, or about 6% of China's population. Compare that with Mandarin, which boasts a whopping 848 million first language speakers – 70% of China's population – and you begin to see just how minor Cantonese is compared to its government approved cousin.

The growing number of Mandarin speakers is due in no small part to the directives of Beijing, who promotes Putonghua, or "standard speech," China's official form of Mandarin, as the first language of the country's population. In pockets of China where Mandarin is not a first language, such as Shanxi (where Jin is the native tongue) or Guangdong, children may speak their local language or dialect at home, but in school Mandarin rules the day. All official affairs in China are conducted in Putonghua, and the only way two people from different linguistic regions, say, a businessman from Hong Kong and one from Xi'an, can communicate is through this standard language. While this standardization of Mandarin is clearly important for the development of the country, the tradeoff is that China's fascinating minority languages and dialects are seeing less and less use.

Abroad, Cantonese is facing a similar problem. Much of the Yue speaking populations in the Chinatowns of places like New York, Toronto, London and Paris are aging, and their children and grandchildren are less and less inclined to add spoken (and especially written) Cantonese to the list of things they need to study. Much of these overseas populations are first or second generation transplants, so the language they carried with them is still strong. However, much as fourth or fifth generation Italian Americans speak little to no Italian, the later generations of Chinese Americans (or Chinese Canadians, Chinese French, etc) will likely see Cantonese fade into their familial past as well.

So, is Cantonese on the decline? Probably, though it will be another ten years before the extent of its decline can be known for sure. Does this mean Cantonese is dying? Not exactly. Decline and death are not the same things, and when you consider that languages like Basque (an obscure ancient language of small regions in France and Spain) and Gaelic in Ireland and Scotland still survive amidst the dominant national languages of their countries, it appears unlikely that Cantonese will be leaving us any time soon.

Every Chinese language also has a multitude of dialects, and Cantonese is no different. Some Cantonese dialects make use of more than ten tones, but the standard Cantonese spoken in Hong Kong distinguishes six different tones:

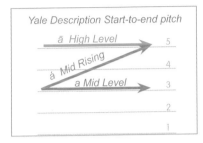

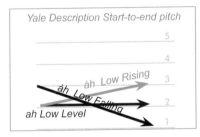

There are two things you should notice about the tone charts. The first one is that these six tones are actually simpler than what you might have initially thought since three of them are straight/flat tones and two are rising tones that simply begin from a higher or lower register. The second thing to notice is the letters next to each tone. Rising tones are marked with an up stroke over the vowel, while the falling tone has a down stroke. A high flat tone has a straight line over the vowel, and mid- or low-level flat tones have no marking. What's more, tones that begin from a mid to high pitch have a lone vowel (top chart), while those that begin from a low pitch have a vowel followed by an "h" (bottom chart). This may seem very daunting at first, but if you take just a few minutes to practice them each day you can be surprised by how quickly you can memorize this system. See the Yale Romanization on the right for more information on the pronunciation of Cantonese vowels and consonants.

For most Westerners, tones are the most difficult part of Cantonese. In daily speech they come quickly and are very difficult for the untrained ear to identify. Doing your best to pronounce and understand them is

really all that is needed, and most people will be able to get the meaning of what you are saying even if your tones are off. What's more, any local will appreciate you simply making an effort to communicate in their language, so don't sweat those tones.

The simplest way to distinguish the three types of tones in Cantonese – i.e. flat, falling, and rising – is to think about when you use them in English and try to emulate that. As mentioned, a rising tone is like a one word question ("Really?" or "What?"). Make a flat tone by singing a single musical note with different vowels, such as "aaa" or "ei" (but only hold the note for a split second). A falling tone is similar to a command, as if you told your dog to "Sit." Now just practice the flat tone in a low, mid and high level, and the rising tone from a low and high level, and you're on your way to being a Cantonese tone master!

Grammar

The difficulty of Cantonese tones is largely evened out by the ease of the language's grammar. There are no verb conjugations, no plurals, and the order of the words in the sentence is generally very similar to English. Most basic sentences use subject + verb + object. In English, this order can be seen in the sentence "I love you." The order is exactly the same in Cantonese: "Nngóh oi néih." "Nngóh," meaning "I" is the subject; "oi" as "love" is the verb; and the object "néih" means "you." But if we want to say "He loves you" in Cantonese, the verb will stay exactly the same as in the first sentence: "Ta oi néih." This grammatical simplicity is a welcome difference from Indo-European languages, especially Romance languages like French, Spanish or Italian, where verb conjugations change drastically depending on the subject and tense.

Yale Romanization

Romanization is the act of transliterating a language into the Roman alphabet used in the English speaking world. Unlike Mandarin, which uses the effective and well-designed system of pinyin to write Chinese pronunciations in the Roman alphabet, Cantonese does not have one ubiquitously accepted system for writing its pronunciation. However, the system that is considered easiest for Westerners to become familiar with is called Yale Romanization, and this is the one we use as well. All pronunciations below are approximate, and the best way for you to really master the sounds of Cantonese, including the tones, is to hang out with native speakers and try to mimic their speech. It's a good thing you're on your way to Hong Kong – there are plenty of native speakers here!

Consonants

Notice that some consonants do not have a burst of air following them as they normally do in English. To tell the difference, hold your hand in front of your mouth and say "park" and "spark." Notice that following the "p" sound in "park" there is a slight burst of air, whereas there is little to no burst following the "p" of "spark." You will notice this difference in several pairs of consonants below.

b – p in "sport" (like making a "p" sound with no burst of air following it)
p – p as in "pat" (a regular "p" sound with the light burst of air that follows)
m – m as in "mom"
f – f as in "foot"
d – t in "stop" (like making a "t" sound with no burst of air following it)
t – t as in "top" (a regular "t" sound with the light burst of air that follows)
n – n as in "not"
l – l as in "lap"
g – k in "sky" (like making a "k" sound with no burst of air following it)
k – k as in "kite" (a regular "k" sound with the light burst of air that follows)
ng – ng as in "singer"
h – h as in "hot"
j – zz as in "pizza"
ch – ts as in "tsunami"
s – s as in "sleep"
gw – qu as in "square" (like making a "kw" sound with no burst of air following it)
kw – qu as in "quark" (a regular "kw" sound with the light burst of air that follows)
y – y as in "yard"
w – w as in "want"

Finals

The final consonants p, t, and k are unreleased. This means that they are virtually silent and you hear no "puff of air" at the end of the syllable. The same sounds can be heard if you say "cap," "cat," and "track" in a very casual way. Say them in a sentence, and you should get the right sound (it's almost as if the words are cut off in your throat before the consonant can be uttered).

Vowels

The vowel chart below is meant to help you become familiar with Cantonese pronunciations. They do not have tones, so

remember that when you begin practicing words, phrases and sentences in the pages that follow, many vowels will have tonal markings (including the "h" after some vowels to show a tone that begins in a low register) that you will need to take into consideration.

aa – a as in "spa"
aai – igh as in "sigh"
aau – ow as in "how"
aam – am as in "Vietnam"
aan – an as in "Taiwan"
aang – combination of aa and ng
aap – ap as in "tap"
aat – at as in "hat"
aak – ack as in "back"
ai – i as in "kite"
au – ou as in "scout"
am – ome as in "some"
an – un as in "sun"
ang – ung as in "lung"
ap – up as in "cup"
at – ut as in "cut"
ak – uc as in "suck"
e – e as in "bet"
ei – ay as in "say"
em – em as in "temple"
eng – eng as in "length"
ek – eck as in "peck"
i – ee as in "tee"
iu – ew as in "few"
im – eem as in "seem"
in – een as in "seen"
ing – ing as in "sing"
ip – eep as in "sleep"
it – eet as in "meet"
ik – ick as in "sick"
o – aw as in "paw"
oi – oy as in "boy"
ou – oe as in "toe"
on – awn as in "pawn"
ong – ong as in "song"
ot – aught as in "caught"
ok – alk as in "walk"
u – oo as in "coo"
ui – ooey as in "gooey"
un – oon as in "soon"
ung – ung as in "Bandung"
ut – oot as in "boot"
uk – ook as in "book"
eu – er as in "her" (Britsh English, with rounded lips)
eung – combination of eu and ng
euk – ork as in "work" (British English)
eui – o as in "no" (British English)
eun – on as in "person"
eut – ot as in "carrot"
yu – Somewhat like ew as in "few"
yun – Somewhat like une as in "tune"
yut – Somewhat like ute as in "cute"
m – mm as in "hmm"
ng – ng as in "sing"

Basic Phrases

Welcome	fūnyìhng	歡迎
Hello.	Néih hóu.	你好。
How are you?	Néih hóu ma?	你好嗎?
What is your name?	Néih giu māt'yéh mèhng a?	你叫乜嘢名呀?
What is your name (formal)?	Chíngmahn dím chīngfū?	請問點稱呼?
My name is	Ngóh go méng giu	我個名叫 …
Nice to meet you.	Hahng'wúih.	幸會。
Please.	Chíng.	請。
Thank you. (when someone helps you)	Ṁh'gōi.	唔該。
Thank you. (when someone gives you a gift)	Dōjeh.	多謝!
You're welcome.	Ṁh'sái haak-hei.	唔使客氣。
Excuse me. (getting attention)	Ṁh'hóu yisi	唔好意思。
Excuse me. (to get past)	Ṁh'gōi(Ṁh'gōi jeje).	唔該 (唔該借借)。
Sorry.	Deui-ṁh-jyuh.	對唔住。
Goodbye (formal)	Joigin.	再見!
Goodbye (informal)	Bāaibaai.	拜拜!
just so-so	màh má déi	马马虎虎
a little	síusíu	少少
I can't speak Cantonese.	Ngóh ṁh'sīk góng Gwóngdōngwá.	我唔識講廣東話。
Do you speak English?	Néih sīk-ṁh-sīk góng Yīngmán a?	你識唔識講英文呀?
Is there someone here who speaks English?	Nīdouh yáuh móuh yàhn sīk góng Yīngmán a?	呢度有冇人識講英文呀?
Help!	Gau mehng ā!	救命呀!
Look out!	Síusām!	小心!
Good morning.	Jóusàhn.	早晨。
I don't understand.	Ngóh ṁh'mìhng.	我唔明。
Where is the toilet?	Chi só hái bīn douh a?	廁所喺邊度呀?
Where are you from?	Néih haih bīndouh yàhn a?	你係邊度人呀?
Pleased to meet you!	Hóu hòisàm yìhngsīk néih!	好開心認識你!
Good luck!	Jūk néih hóuwahn!	祝你好運!
I love you!	Nngóh oi néih!	我爱你!
Cheers!	Yámbūi!	飲杯!

Numbers

1	yāt	一
2	yih	二
3	sāam	三
4	sei	四
5	ńgh	五
6	luhk	六
7	chāt	七
8	baat	八
9	gáu	九
10	sahp	十
11	sahpyāt	十一
12	sahpyih	十二
13	sahpsāam	十三
14	sahpsei	十四
15	sahpńgh	十五

Numbers

16	sahpluhk	十六
17	sahpchāt	十七
18	sahpbaat	十八
19	sahpgáu	十九
20	yihsahp	二十
30	sāamsahp	三十
40	seisahp	四十
50	ńghsahp	五十
60	luhksahp	六十
70	chātsahp	七十
80	baatsahp	八十
90	gáusahp	九十
100	yātbaak	一百
1,000	yātchīn	一千
10,000	yātmaahn	一萬

Time & Dates

now	yīgā	而家
late	chìh	遲
early	jóu	早
morning	jīujóu	朝早
afternoon	ngaanjau	晏晝
evening	yeh máahn	夜晚
one o'clock	yāt dím	一點
two o'clock	léuhng dím	兩點
today	gām'yaht	今日
yesterday	chàhm'yaht	尋日
tomorrow	tīngyaht	聽日
the day before yesterday	chìhnyaht	前日
the day after tomorrow	hauh'yaht	後日
this week	gām go láihbaai	今個禮拜
last week	seuhng go láihbaai	上個禮拜
next week	hah go láihbaai	下個禮拜
Sunday	Láihbaai yaht	禮拜日
Monday	Láihbaai yāt	禮拜一
Tuesday	Láihbaai yih	禮拜二
Wednesday	Láihbaai sāam	禮拜三
Thursday	Láihbaai sei	禮拜四
Friday	Láihbaai ńgh	禮拜五
Saturday	Láihbaai luhk	禮拜六
January	Yāt'yuht	一月
February	Yih'yuht	二月
March	Sāam'yuht	三月
April	Seiyuht	四月
May	Ngh'yuht	五月
June	Luhk'yuht	六月
July	Chāt'yuht	七月
August	Baat'yuht	八月
September	Gáuyuht	九月
October	Sahpyuht	十月
November	Sahpyāt'yuht	十一月
December	Sahpyih'yuht	十二月

Colors

black	hāk sīk	黑色
white	baahk sīk	白色
gray	fūi sīk	灰色
red	hùhng sīk	紅色
blue	làahm̀ sīk	藍色
yellow	wòhng sīk	黃色
green	luhk sīk	綠色
orange	chàahng sīk	橙色
purple	jí sīk	紫色
brown	fē sīk	啡色
pink	fán hùhng sīk	粉紅色

Shopping

I need…	Ngóh yiu…	我要…
Expensive	gwai	貴
Cheap	pèhng	平
Toothpaste	ngàh gōu	牙膏
toothbrush	ngàh chaat	牙刷
tampons	waihsāng gān	衛生巾
soap	fāangáan.	番梘
shampoo	sáitàuhséui	洗頭水
razor	taisōudōu.	剃鬚刀
postcard	mihngseunpín	名信片
postage stamps	yàuhpiu	郵票
battery	dihnchìh	電池
writing paper	seunjí	信紙
pen	bāt	筆
English-language books	Yīngmàhn syū	英文書
English-language magazines	Yīngmàhn jaahpji	英文雜誌
English-language newspaper	Yīngmàhn bouji	英文報紙
Do you have this in my size?	Nī gihn yáuh-móuh ngóh go má a?	呢件有冇我個碼呀?
How much?	Géidō chín a?	幾多錢呀?
Do you ship (overseas)?	Néihdeih sung-m̀h-sung fo (heui ngoihgwok) gah?	你哋送唔送貨 (去外國) 嘎?
That's too expensive.	Taai gwai la.	太貴啦。
I can't afford it.	Ngóh béi m̀h héi.	我俾唔起。
I don't want it.	Ngóh m̀h séung yiu.	我唔想要。
You're cheating me.	Néih āk gán ngóh gé.	你呃緊我嘅。
I'm not interested.	Ngóh móuh hing cheui.	我冇興趣。
OK, I'll take it.	Hóu, ngóh yiu nī gihn.	好, 我要呢件。
Can I have a bag?	Hó-m̀h-hó'yi béi go dói ngóh a?	可唔可以俾個袋我呀?

Problems

I'll call the police.	Ngóh wúih giu gíngchaat.	我會叫警察。
Police!	Gíngchaat!	警察!
Stop! Thief!	Máih jáu! Chaahkjái!	咪走! 賊仔!
Please help me.	M̀h'gōi bōng ngóh.	唔該幫我。
It's an emergency.	Hóu gán'gāp.	好緊急。
I'm lost.	Ngóh dohngsāt louh.	我蕩失路。
I lost my bag.	Ngóh m̀h'gin jó go doih.	我唔見咗個袋。
I don't feel well.	Ngóh m̀h syūfuhk.	我唔舒服。
I've been injured.	Ngóh sauh jó sēung.	我受咗傷。
Please call a doctor.	M̀h'gōi bōng ngóh giu yīsāng.	唔該幫我叫醫生。
Can I use your phone?	Hó-m̀h-hó'yi je go dihnwáh yuhng a?	可唔可以借個電話用呀?

Transportation

train	fóchē	火車
bus	bāsí	巴士
Taxi!	Tda-síh!	的士!

Transportation

railway station	fóchē jaahm	火車站
bus station	bāsí jaahm	巴士站
airport	gēichèuhng	機場
How much is a ticket to _____?	Heui _____ jēung fēi yiu géidō chín gah?	去 _____ 張飛要幾多錢嘎?
One ticket to _____, please.	Yāt jēung fēi heui _____, m̀h'gōi.	一張飛去 _____, 唔該。
Where does this bus go?	Nī ga bāsí heui bīn?	呢架巴士 去邊度呀?
Take me to _____, please.	Joi ngóh heui _____, m̀h'gōi.	載我去 _____, 唔該。
How much does it cost to get to _____?	Heui _____ yiu géidō chín gah?	去 _____ 要幾多錢嘎?
Take me there, please.	Joi ngóh heui gódouh, m̀h'gōi	載我去嗰度, 唔該。

Accommodation

youth hostel	chīngnihn léuihséh	青年旅舍
hotel	jáudim	酒店
Do you have any rooms available?	Néihdeih yáuh-móuh hūngfóng a?	你哋有冇空房呀?
How much is a room for one person/two people?	Dāanyàhnfóng/Sēungyàhnfóng yiu géidō chín a?	單人房 / 雙人房 要幾多錢呀?
bedsheets	chòhngkám	床襟
bathroom	yuhksāt	浴室
telephone	dihnwah	電話
TV	dihnsih	電視
May I see the room first?	Hó-m̀h-hó'yi tái-háh gāan fóng sīn a?	可唔可以睇下間房先呀?
quieter	jihngdī	靜啲
bigger	daaihdī	大啲
cleaner	gōnjehngdī	乾淨啲
cheaper	pèhngdī	平啲
OK, I'll take it.	Hóu, ngóh yiu nī gāan.	好, 我要呢間。
I will stay for _____ night(s).	Ngóh húi háidouh jyuh _____ máahn.	我會喺度住 _____ 晚。
lockers	chyúhmahtgwaih	儲物櫃
Is breakfast/supper included?	Bāau-m̀h-bāau jóuchāan/máahnchāan gah?	包唔包 早餐 / 晚餐 嘎?
What time is breakfast/supper?	Géidím yáuh jóuchāan/máahnchāan gah?	幾點有 早餐 / 晚餐 嘎?
Please clean my room.	M̀h'gōi bōng ngóh jāp-háh gāan fóng.	唔該幫我執下間房。
Can you wake me at _____?	Hó-m̀h-hó'yi _____ giuséng ngóh a?	可唔可以 _____ 叫醒我呀?
I want to check out.	Ngóh séung teuifóng.	我想退房。

Places around the world

Japan	Yaht Bún	日本
Mainland China	Daaih Luhk	大陸
People's Republic of China	Jùng Wàh Yàhn Màhn Guhng Wòh Gwok	中華人民共和國

Places around the world

China	Jùng Gwok	中國
North America	bàk méih jàu	北美洲
South America	nàahm méih jàu	南美洲
South China	Wàh Nàahm	華南
Hollywood	Hòh Léih Wuht	荷理活
San Francisco	Sàam Fàahn Síh	三藩市
Beijing	Bàk Gìng	北京
Osaka	Daaih Báan	大阪
Tuen Mun	Tyùhn Mùhn	屯門
Guangzhou	Gwóng Jàu	廣州
Sydney	Sik Nèih	悉尼
Las Vegas	Lāai Sī Wàih Gā Sī	拉斯維加斯
Tokyo	Dùng Gìng	東京
Kweilin or Guilin	Gwai Làhm	桂林
Shenzhen	Sàm Jan	深圳
New York	Náu Yeuk	紐約
Washington DC	Wàh Sihng Deuhn	華盛頓
Russia	Ngòh Gwok	俄國
Canada	Gā Nàh Daaih	加拿大
Hungary	Hūng Àh Leih	匈牙利
Italy Yi	Daaih Leih	意大利
The Czech Republic	Jiht Hāak	捷克
France	Faat Gwok	法國
Haiti	Hói Deih	海地
Australia	Ou Daaih Leih A	澳大利亞
Australia	Ou Jàu	澳洲
U.S.A.	Méih Gwok	美國
U.K.	Yìng Gwok	英國
Portugal	Pòuh Tòuh Áh	葡萄牙
New Territories	Sàn Gaai	新界
Outlying Islands	lèih dóu	離島
Lantau Island	Daaih Yùh Sàan	大嶼山
Sha Tin	Sā Tìhn	沙田
metropolis	daaih dòu wùih	大都會
Central	Jùng Wàahn	中環
Kowloon	Gáu Lùhng	九龍
Kowloon Tong	Gáu Lùhng Tòhng	九龍塘
Yuen Long	Yùhn Lóhng	元朗
Mid-level Bun	Sāan Kèui	半山區
peninsula	bun dóu	半島
Lamma Island	Nàahm Ngā Dóu	南丫島
Tolo Harbour	Tou Louh Góng	吐露港
China Town	Tòhng Yàhn Gāai	唐人街
districts	deih kèui	地區
address	deih jí	地址

Places around the world

place	deih fōng (fòng)	地方
Big Wave Bay	Daaih Lohng Wāan	大浪灣
East Tsim Sha Tsui	Jīm Dùng	尖東
Tsim Sha Tsui	Jīm Sà Jéui	尖沙咀
Victoria Peak	Sāan Déng	山頂
Mandarin Oriental Hotel	Màhn Wàh Jáu Dim	文華酒店
Mong Kok	Wohng Gok	旺角
Beaches	hói tāan	海灘
Deep Water Bay	Sàm Séui Wāan	深水灣
Repulse Bay	Chín Séui Wāan	淺水灣
Macau	Ou Mún	澳門
dock, pier	máh tàuh	碼頭
Mai Po	Máih Bou	米埔
Victoria Harbour	Wàih Dò Leih A Góng	維多利亞港
Victoria Harbour	Wàih Góng	維港
Garden Road	Fà Yùhn Douh	花園道
intersection	gàai háu	街口
Sai Kung	Sài Gung	西貢
Happy Valley	Páau Máh Déi	跑馬地
Causeway Bay	Tùhng Lòh Wàan	銅鑼灣
Cheung Chau	Chèuhng Jàu	長州
Aberdeen	Hèung Góng Jái	香港仔
Lei Yue Mun	Léih Yùh Mùhn	鯉魚門
Wong Tai Sin	Wòhng Daaih Sìn	黃大仙
Guangsi	Gwóng Sài	廣西
Yunnan	Wàhn Nàahm	雲南
Asia-Pacific	A Taai	亞太
Asia	Nga Jàu	亞洲
East Asia	Dūng A	東亞
The East	Dūng Fòng	東方
Eastern Europe	Dūng Àu	東歐
the East and the West	dūng sāi fòng	東西方
Europe	Àu Jàu	歐洲
America	Méih Jàu	美洲
Africa	Fèi Jàu	非洲
Pearl River	Jyū Gòng	珠江
Yangtze River	Chèuhng Gòng	長江
Vermont State	Faht Mùhng Dahk Jāu	佛蒙特州
California	Gā Jāu	加州
George Town	Kiuh Jih Sihng	喬治城
Germany	Dāk Gwok	德國
London	Lèuhn Dèui	倫敦
Greece	Hèi Laahp	希臘
Vietnam	Yuht Nàhm	越南
Thailand	Taai Gwok	泰國

Places around the world

India	Yan Douh	印度
Philippines	Fèi Leuht Bàn	菲律賓
Syria	Jeuih Leih A	敍利亞
Egypt	Oì Kahp	埃及
Korea	Hòhn Gwok	韓國
South Korea	Nàahm Hòhn	南韓
North Korea	Bầk Hòhn	北韓
Spain	Sài Bàan Ngàh	西班牙
Capital	Sáu Dòu	首都

The Chinese Menu

fried	jīn	煎
stir-fried	cháau	炒
boiled	jyú	煮
deep-fried	ja	炸
simmered	mān	炆
stewed	dahn	燉
baked	guhk	焗
steamed	jīng	蒸
menu	châan-páai	餐牌
bill please	màaih-dâan	埋單
Drink Tea	Yám Chàh	飲茶
jasmine tea	hēung-pín	香片
lung-ching tea	lùhng-jéng	龍井
Pu-er tea	Bóu-léi	寶利
chrysanthemum with Pu-er	gūk-bóu	菊寶
freshly cooked	sân-sìn chêut-lòuh	新鮮出爐
menu for today	sih-yaht châan-páai	是日餐牌
same price	tùhng-ga	同價
soup of the day is included sung	laih-tông	送例湯
soup of the day	laih-tông	例湯
breakfast	jóu-châan	早餐
dinner (more formal)	máahn-châan	晚餐
dinner	maáhn-faahn	晚飯
lunch (more formal)	çgh-châan	午餐
lunch	çgh-faahn	午飯
simple set menu	faai-châan	快餐
afternoon tea set	hah-çgh-chàh châan	下午茶餐
deliver the food sung	ngoih-maaih	送外賣
hall dinning	tòhng-sihk	堂食
take away / deliver the food	ngoih-maaih	外賣
take away by oneself	jih-chéui	自取
telephone	dihn-wá	電話
salty	hàahm	咸 / 鹹
sour	syûn	酸

The Chinese Menu

spicy	laaht	辣
sweet	tìhm	甜
sweet and sour	tìhm-syûn	甜酸
fresh squid	sìn-yáu	鮮魷
shelled shrimp	hâ-yàhn	蝦仁
bar	jáu-bâ	酒巴
Chinese restaurant	jáu-làuh	酒樓
restaurant	châan-tēng	餐廳
Hong Kong style café	chàh-châan-tēng	茶餐廳
Western restaurant	Sâi-châan-tēng	西餐廳
barbecue	sìu-hâau	燒烤
hot pot	fó-wô	火鍋
hot pot (spoken)	dá-bîn-lòuh	打邊爐
Korean barbecue	Hòhn-gwok sîu-hâau	韓國燒烤
McDonalds	Mahk-Dông-Lòuh	麥當勞
Spaghetti House	Yi-fǎn-ûk	意粉屋

Meat

meat	yuhk	肉
beef	ngàuh-yuhk	牛肉
mutton / lamb	yèuhng-yuhk	羊肉
pork	jyû-yuhk	豬肉
chicken	gâi	雞
duck	aap	鴨
goose	ngòh, ngó	鵝
pigeon	gaap	鴿
quail	âm-chêun	鵪鶉
turkey	fó-gâi	火雞
bacon	yîn-yuhk	煙肉
ham	fó-téui	火腿
sausage	hêung-chéung	香腸
diced chicken	gâi-dîng	雞丁
diced pork	yuhk-dîng	肉丁
minced beef	míhn-jih ngàuh-yuhk	免治牛肉
beef fillet	ngàuh-láuh	牛柳
chicken fillet	gâi-láuh	雞柳
fish fillet	yùh-láuh	魚柳
pork fillet	jyû-láuh	豬柳
chicken steak	gâi-pá	雞扒
lamb steak	yèuhng-pá	羊扒
pork chop	jyû-pá	豬扒
steak	ngàuh-pá	牛扒

Seafood

seafood	hói-sìn	海鮮
salmon	sâam-màhn-yú	三文魚

Seafood

shrimp/prawn	hâ	蝦
crab	háaih	蟹
oyster	hòuh	蠔
lobster	lùhng-hâ	龍蝦
abalone	bâau-yùh	鮑魚
dried scallop	gôn-yiuh-chyúh	乾瑤柱
dried shrimps	hâ-máih	蝦米
fish maw	yùh-tóuh	魚肚
sea cucumber	hói-sâm	海參
shark fin	yùh-chi	魚翅

Vegetables

tofu	dauh-fuh	豆腐
string bean / long bean	dauh-gok	豆角
chilli / pepper	laaht-jîu	辣椒
chives	gáu-choi	韭菜
garlic	syun-tàuh	蒜頭
ginger	gêung	薑
green pepper	chêng-jîu	青椒
onion	yèuhng-chûng	洋蔥
chestnut	leuht-jí	栗子
corn	sûk-máih	粟米
tomato	fâan-ké	蕃茄
cabbage	yèh-choi	椰菜
celery	kàhn-choi	芹菜
Choi Sum	Choi-sâm	菜心
lettuce	sâang-choi	生菜
bok choi	baahk-choi	白菜
pea shoots	dauh-mìuh	豆苗
spinach	bô-choi	菠菜
melon	gwâ	瓜
bitter melon	fú-gwâ	苦瓜
cucumber	chêng-gwâ	青瓜
eggplant	ké-jí	茄子
pumpkin	nàahm-gwâ	南瓜
winter melon	dûng-gwâ	冬瓜
bamboo shoot	séun	筍
carrot	hùhng-lòh-baahk	紅蘿蔔
green radish	chêng-lòh-baahk	青蘿蔔
lotus root	lìhn-ngáuh	蓮藕
potato	syùh-jái	薯仔
sweet potato	fâan-syú	番薯
button mushroom	mòh-gû	磨菇
Chinese mushroom	dûng-gû	冬菇
straw mushroom	chóu-gû	草菇

Fruit

fruit	sâang-gwó	生果
aloe	lòuh-wuih	蘆薈
apple	pìhng-gwó	蘋果
banana	hêung-jîu	香蕉
cherry	chê-lèih-jí	車厘子
coconut	yèh-jí	椰子
grape	pòuh-tàih-jí	葡提子
honey melon	maht-gwâ	蜜瓜
kiwi fruit	kèih-yih-gwó	奇異果
lemon	lìhng-mûng	檸檬
lichee	laih-jî	荔枝
longan	lùhng-ngáahn	龍眼
mango	mông-gwó	芒果
olive	gaam-láam	橄欖
orange	cháang	橙
papaya	muhk-gwâ	木瓜
peach	tóuh	桃
honey peach	maht-tòuh	蜜桃
pear	léi	梨
pineapple	bô-lòh	菠蘿
strawberry	sih-dô-bê-léi	士多啤梨
sugar cane	gâm-je	甘蔗
Mandarin orange	gâm	柑
watermelon	sâi-gwâ	西瓜

Staple Food & Eggs

congee/porridge	jûk	粥
noodles	mihn	麵
oatmeal	mahk-pèih	麥皮
rice noodles	mai fán	米粉
buns with egg yolk and cream	náaih-wòhng bâau	奶黃包
buns with lotus seed filling	lìhn-yùhng bâau	蓮蓉包
rice-noodle rolls filled with shrimp	sîn-hâ chéung-fán	鮮蝦腸粉
rice-noodle rolls filled with BBQ pork	châ-siu chéung-fán	叉燒腸粉
rice	faahn	飯
pre-deep-fried noodles	yì-mihn	伊麵
fine noodles	yau-mihn	幼麵
flat noodles	chôu-mihn	粗麵
instant noodles	gûng-jái-mihn	公仔麵
instant noodles	jîk-sihk-mihn	即食麵
Udon	wû-dûng	烏冬
fine rice noodles	máih-fán	米粉
flat rice noodles	hó-fán	河粉
thick rice noodles	laaih-fán	瀨粉

Staple Food & Eggs

macaroni	tûng-sâm-fán	通心粉
spaghetti	yi-daaih-leih-fán	意大利粉
egg	dáan	蛋
chicken egg	gâi-dáan	雞蛋
quail egg	âm-chêun-dáan	鵪鶉蛋
egg white	dáan-báak	蛋白
egg yolk	dáan-wóng	蛋黃

Dish & Drink Names

pork dumpling	sîu-máai	燒賣
shark fin dumpling	yùh-chi gáau	魚翅餃
shrimp dumpling	hâ-gáau	蝦餃
soup dumpling	gun-tông gáau	灌湯餃
chicken feet	fuhng-jáau	鳳爪
ox tripe	ngàuh-paak-yihp	牛柏葉
ox stomach	gâm-chìhn-tóuh	金錢肚
pork ribs	pàaih-gwât	排骨
barbecued pork bun	châ-sîu-bâau	叉燒包
chicken bun	gâi-bâau	雞包
crystal bun	séui-jîng-bâau	水晶包
egg custard bun	náaih-wòhng-bâau	奶皇包
small chicken bun	gâi-bâau-jái	雞飽仔
lotus seed bun	lìhn-yùhng-bâau	蓮蓉包
pan-fried rice roll	jìn chéung-fán	煎腸粉
turnip cake	lòh-baahk-gôu	蘿蔔糕
water chestnut cake	máh-tàih-gôu	馬蹄糕
multi-layered steamed cake	chìn-chàhng-gôu	千層糕
sesame roll	jî-màh-gyún	芝麻卷
sesame cake	jî-màh-gôu	芝麻糕
Shanghainese pork dumpling	síu-lùhng-bâau	小籠包
diced chicken with cashew	yîu-gwó gâi-dîng	腰果雞丁
roasted pigeon	sîu-yúh-gaap	燒乳鴿
red-cooked pork	hùhng-sîu-yuhk	紅燒肉
sweet and sour pork	gû-lôu-yuhk	咕嚕肉
Spicy tofu with ground pork and black bean sauce	màh pòh dauh fuh	痲婆豆腐
deep-fried pork ribs with peppered salt	jîu-yìhm-gwât	椒鹽骨
braised crab in ginger and spring onion	gêung-chûng guhk háaih	薑蔥焗蟹
curry stir-fried crab	ga-lêi cháau háaih	咖喱炒蟹
eggplant with minced pork	yùh-hêung kkéé-jí	魚香茄子
water spinach with fermented bean curd	fuh-yúh tûng-choi	腐乳通菜
hot dog	yiht-gáu	熱狗

fried rice noodles	cháau-fán	炒粉
fried noodles	cháau-mihn	炒麵
fried fine rice noodles	cháau-máih	炒米
fried flat rice noodles in Thai style	cháau-gwai-díu	炒貴刁
fried flat rice noodles with beef	gôn-cháau-ngàuh-hó	乾炒牛河
fried noodles with shredded chicken	gâi-sî cháau-mihn	雞絲炒麵
satay beef with rice	sa-dê ngàuh-yuhk faahn	沙嗲牛肉飯
Portuguese chicken with rice	pòuh-gwok-gâi faahn	葡國雞飯
sweet corn and diced chicken with rice	sûk-máih gâai-lâp faahn	粟米雞粒飯
ham and fried egg with rice	fó-téui jîn-dáan faahn	火腿煎蛋飯
pork chop with rice	jyû-pá-faahn	豬扒飯
scrambled egg and shelled shrimps with rice	waaht-dáan hâ-yàhn faahn	滑蛋蝦仁飯
fried rice with shrimp and diced meat	Yèuhng-jâu cháau faahn	楊州炒飯
baked rice	guhk faahn	焗飯
baked pork chop with rice	guhk jyû-pá faahn	焗豬扒飯
Chinese sausage and preserved meat with glutinous rice	laahp-méi noh-máih faahn	臘味糯米飯
barbecued pork	châ-sîu	叉燒
roasted suckling pig	yúh-jyú	乳豬
roasted pork	sìu-yuhk	燒肉
roasted duck	sìu-aap	燒鴨
roasted goose	sìu-ngó	燒鵝
soya sauce chicken	yàuh-gâi	油雞
barbecued pork with rice	châ-sîu faahn	叉燒飯
soya sauce chicken with rice	yàuh-gâi faahn	油雞飯
steamed chicken with rice	chit-gâi faahn	切雞飯
dumpling	séui-gáau	水餃
wonton	wàhn-tân	雲吞
beef ball	ngàuh-yún	牛丸
fish ball	yùh-dáan	魚蛋
wonton noodle	wàhn-tân mihn	雲吞麵
stewed beef with noodles	ngàuh-náahm mihn	牛腩麵
hot and sour soup	syún-laaht tong	酸辣湯
trolley style noodles	chê-jái mihn	車仔麵
sliced fish congee	yùh-pín jùk	魚片粥
deep fried bread stick	yàuh-ja-gwái	油炸鬼
sweet flour oval cake	ngàuh-leih sôu	牛脷酥
rice roll filled with deep fried bread stick	ja-léung	炸兩
mango pudding	mông-gwó bou-dîn	芒果布甸

Dish & Drink Names

sweet soup	tòhng-séui	糖水
Russian borsch soup	lòh sung tòông	羅宋湯
pizza	yi-daaih-leih bohk-béng	意大利薄餅
wine / alcohol	jáu	酒
beer	bê-jáu	啤酒
soft drinks	hei-séui	汽水
fruit juice	gwó-jâp	果汁
milk	náaih	奶
cold drinks	dung-yám	凍飲
whisky	wâi-sih-géi	威士忌
Blue Ribbon	Làahm-dáai	藍帶
Carlsberg	Gâ-sih-baak	嘉士伯
Heineken	Héi-lihk	喜力
Tsing Tao	Chîng-dóu	青島
Maotai	màauh-tòih	茅台
brandy	baahk-lãan-déi	白蘭地
champagne	hêung-bân	香檳
coffee	ga-fè	咖啡
black tea	hùhng-chàh	紅茶
green tea	luhk-chàh	綠茶
lemon tea	lìhng-mùhng chàh	檸檬茶
milk tea	náaih-chàh	奶茶
soya milk	dauh-jêung	豆漿
7 Up	Chât-héi	七喜
Coca Cola	Hó-háu hó-lohk	可口可樂
coke	hó-lohk	可樂
Fanta	fân-daaht	芬達
Pepsi	Baak-sih	百事
Sprite	Syut-bîk	雪碧
apple juice	pìhng-gwó jâp	蘋果汁
orange juice	cháang jâp	橙汁
tomato juice	fâan-ké jâp	番茄汁
plum soup	syûn-mùih tong	酸梅湯
red bean with ice	hùhng-dáu bîng	紅豆冰
hot water	yiht-séui	熱水
cold water	dung-séui	凍水
iced water	bîng-séui	冰水
bread	mihn-bâau	麵包
cake	daahn-gôu	蛋糕
coconut tart	yèh-tâat	椰撻
egg tart	daahn-tâat	蛋撻
moon cake	yuht-béng	月餅
oyster sauce	hòuh-yàuh	蠔油
salad dressing	sâ-léut jeung	沙律醬
soya sauce	sih-yàuh	豉油

Dish & Drink Names

soya sauce – dark color	lóuh-châu	老抽
soya sauce – light color	sàang-châu	生抽
spicy sauce	laaht-jeung	辣醬
sweet sauce	tihm-jeung	甜醬
sugar	tòhng	糖
vinegar	chou	醋
butter	ngàuh-yàuh	牛油
cheese	jìjì-sí	芝士
yogurt	yúh-lohk	乳酪
ice-cream	syut-gôu	雪糕
bird's nest	yin-wô	燕窩
peanut	fâ-sàng	花生
thousand-year egg	pèih-dáan	皮蛋
chocolate	jyŭ-gŭ-lĭk	朱古力
tablespoon	tông-chìh	湯匙
teaspoon	chàh-chìh	茶匙
spoon	chìh-gàng	匙羹
bowl	wún	碗
chopsticks	faai-jí	筷子
glass / cup	bûi	杯
plate	díp	碟

Glossary

A

Anita Mui (梅艶芳) (1963 – 2003) – Hong Kong singer and actress who became a Cantopop legend and was known as the "Madonna of Asia," among her many influential songs "Bad Girl" is perhaps her best known

arhat (羅漢) – Sanskrit for a Buddhist, especially a monk, who has attained enlightenment and is freed from the cycle of rebirth

B

bodhisattva (菩薩) – Buddhist who has reached nirvana but remains on earth to help others achieve enlightenment

C

CAAC – Civil Aviation Administration of China

CCP – Chinese Communist Party

cha chaan tang (茶餐廳) – small cafes that serve Western style dishes

cheongsam (旗袍) – known as a qípáo in Mandarin, a tight-fitting and fashionable dress with a slit up the side that was especially popular in 1920s Shanghai

Chiang Kai-shek (蔣介石) (1887-1957) – anti-communist leader of the Kuomintang and head of the nationalist government from 1928 to 1949

CITS – China International Travel Service

Confucius (孔子) (551-470 BCE) – legendary thinker, philosopher and scholar who developed the philosophy of Confucianism, a system of rules, moral values and code of conduct for civil and obedient society

D

dai pai dong (大排檔) – open-air, street-side eating stall, especially at night in street markets

Deng Xiaoping (鄧小平) (1904-1997) – paramount leader of the Chinese Communist Party from 1978 to 1992

dim sum (點心) – a Cantonese specialty that means "touch the heart" and consists of various small dumpling or snack-like dishes wheeled around on carts and eaten for breakfast, brunch or lunch; see also yum cha

dragon boat (龍舟) – a long, narrow boat in the shape of a dragon used in dragon boat races

dry market (乾貨市場) – an often outdoor market that sells dry goods, including those that sell clothing, herbs, tonics and dried seafood, meats and veggies

E

erhu (二胡) – the Chinese fiddle; a two-stringed bow instrument originally used in folk music and now being applied to a spectrum of musical genres

F

feng shui (風水) – also called geomancy, literally "wind and water"; the ancient art of arranging a space (i.e. buildings and objects) to maximize the flow of qi and harmonize humans with the surrounding environment

Five Great Clans (新界五大氏族) – **Tang** (鄧), **Hau** (侯), **Pang** (彭), **Liu** (廖), **Man** (文); five familial clans that settled ancient Hong Kong, built walled villages and whose families today have tens of thousands of descendants in the Hong Kong area and abroad, many of whom still hold high political and social clout

G

Guanyin (觀音) – Chinese bodhisattva and Goddess of Mercy revered at Buddhist temples throughout Hong Kong, Guanyin was originally depicted as a man and to this day is considered to be largely asexual; also known as Kwun Yam

H

Hakka (客家) – a Chinese ethnic group who settled Hong Kong millennia ago and speak a different language than the Cantonese

hell money (冥幣) – mock currency that is burned in offering to spirits of the deceased

HKTB – Hong Kong Tourism Board

J

Jardine, William (1784 – 1843) – Scottish-born surgeon-turned-merchant who co-founded the conglomerate Jardine, Matheson & Co and had a strong hand in the distribution and illegal sale of opium in Qing-era China and the start of the First Opium War; many places in Hong Kong are still named for him

junk – ancient, square-sailed Chinese war or fishing vessels; also diesel-run wooden recreational yachts often seen in Victoria Harbour

K

kaido – small or medium ferry that runs short or non-scheduled trips to various small islands and fishing villages

Kwan Tai (關帝) – alternate name for Kwan Yu

Kwan Yu (關羽) – Chinese God of War, Integrity, Honor and Righteousness, he is often paired with Man Cheong in Man Mo temples around Hong Kong; also called Kwan Tai

Kwun Yam (觀音) – see Guanyin

Kuomintang (國民黨) – the Nationalist Party under Chiang Kai-shek who were dominant for a time after the fall of the Qing Dynasty

kung fu (功夫) – western word for the Chinese martial arts

L

Leslie Cheung (張國榮) (1956 – 2003) – Hong Kong singer and actor largely considered one of the founding fathers of Cantopop, he worked closely with friend Anita Mui for much of their careers and committed suicide the same year she died

M

mahjong (麻將) – a hugely popular Chinese game that involves engraved tiles and rabid gambling

Man Cheong (滿寵) – Chinese God of Literature and Civility, Man Cheong is often seen paired with Kwan Yu at Man Mo temples around Hong Kong

Mao Zedong (毛澤東) (1893 -1976) – the early leader of the communist forces and founder of the PRC, he stood as the Chairman and de facto ruler of the Communist Party until his death.

MTR – Mass Transit Railway

N

nullah – a word used only in Hong Kong in place names and sometimes to refer to a drain or gutter

P

Punti (本地人) – roughly meaning "locals," this was the first Cantonese speaking ethnic group to settle around Hong Kong

Q

qi (氣) – vital energy; universal energy

R

renminbi (人民幣) – literally "the people's currency"; the official name of Mainland Chinese currency

RMB – abbreviation of renminbi

S

SAR (特別行政區) – Special Administrative Regions

SARS – Severe Acute Respiratory Syndrome

si yau sai chaan (豉油西餐) – also called "soy sauce Western," a cuisine originally from the 1950s featuring Western dishes prepared in a Chinese style

Sun Yat-sen (孫中山) (1866 -1925) – first president of the Republic of China; considered by many to be the father of modern China, he is adored by communists and republicans alike

T

tai chi (太極) – a slow -moving martial art that also functions as a moving meditation

Teresa Teng (鄧麗君) (1953 – 1995) – Taiwanese pop singer who became a sensation in Hong Kong and recorded folk songs and romantic ballads in Mandarin, Taiwanese Hokkien, Japanese, Indonesian and English, her best known song is "The Moon Represents My Heart"

Tin Hau (天后) – Chinese Goddess of the Sea venerated at dozens of temples around Hong Kong, she traditionally wore a red dress and is said to help those in trouble at sea

Triads (三合會) – a Chinese secret society equivalent to the Mafia, originally they were founded as patriotic groups to fight against Manchurian Qing usurpation of China

W

wan (灣) – bay

wet market (濕貨市場) – outdoor market that sells produce, meat and fish

wushu (武術) – Mandarin Chinese word for martial arts, today it mostly refers to martial-based performance acrobatics

wuxia (武俠) – Mandarin word for martial hero and the focus of wuxia films

Y

yum cha (飲茶) – literally meaning "drink tea," a Cantonese expression that refers to dim sum

Travel Resources

Consulates

Hong Kong and Macau have several consulates with jurisdiction within both.

Australia

Address: 23/F, Harbour Centre, 25 Harbour Rd, Wan Chai
Phone: 2827 8881
Email: enquiries.hongkong@dfat.gov.au

Bangladesh

Address: Suite 4007, China Resources Bldg, 26 Hourbour Rd, Wan Chai
Phone: 2827 4278; 2827 4279
Email: bangladt@netvigator.com

Cambodia

Address: Suite 1819, Star House, 3 Salisbury Rd, TST
Phone: 2546 0718
Email: cacghk@netvigator.com

Canada

Address: 12-14/F, One Exchange Sq, Central
Phone: 3719 4700

Finland

Address: Suite 2405-2408, 24F, Dah Sing Financial Centre, 108 Gloucester Rd, Wan Chai,
Phone: 2525 5385

France

Address: 26F Admiralty Centre II, 18 Harcourt Rd, Wan Chai
Phone: 3752 9900

Germany

Address: 21F United Centre, 95 Queensway
Phone: 2105 8788

Greece

Address: Suite 1208 Harcourt House, 39, Gloucester Rd, Wan Chai
Phone: 2774 1682; 9120 0768 (Emergency)
Email: grgencon.cg@mfa.gr

Grenada

Address: Building No. 7, Suite 2704, Nine Queen's Rd Central
Phone: 3656 2838

India

Address: 16/F, United Centre, 95 Queensway, Admiralty
Phone: 3970 9900

Indonesia

Address: 2/F, Indonesian Bldg, 127-129 Leighton Rd, Causeway Bay
Phone: 3651 0200; 2890 4421
Email: imigrasi@kjrihkimigrasi.org
Website: www.kjrihkimigrasi.org/web/html/imigrasi/visa/visa.htm
Office Hours:
Mon-Fri: 9:30-12:30 (submission); 14:30-16:30 (collection)

Ireland

Address: Ste 1408, Two Pacific Place, 88 Queensway
Phone: 2527 4897

Italy

Address: Suite 3201, Central Plaza, 18 Harbour Rd, Wan Chai
Phone: 2522 0033; 2522 0034; 9010 7875 (Emergency)
Email: consolato.hongkong@esteri.it

Japan

Address: 46-47F, One Exchange Sq, 8 Connaught Pl, Central
Phone: 2522 1184

Malaysia

Address: 24/F, Malaysia Building, 50 Gloucester Rd, Wan Chai
Phone: 2821 0800
Email: malhkong@kln.gov.my
Office Hours: 9:00-13:00 and 14:00-17:00

Myanmar (Burma)

Address: Suite 2401, Sun Hung Kai Centre, 30

Harbour Rd
Phone: 2845 0810

The Netherlands

Address: Suite 5702, Cheung Kong Center, 2 Queen's Rd, Central
Phone: 2522 5127
Email: information@netherlands-cg.org.hk

New Zealand

Address: 6501 Central Plaza, 18 Harbour Rd, Wan Chai
Phone: 2525 5044
Email: nzcghkg@biznetvigator.com

Pakistan

Address: Suite 803-4, Tung Wai Commercial Bldg, 109-111 Gloucester Rd, Wan Chai
Phone: 2827 0295; 2827 0245; 2827 0681
Email: pakconhk@netvigator.com

Philippines

Address: 14/F, United Centre Building, 95 Queensway, Admiralty
Phone: 2823 8501
Email: hongkong.pcg@dfa.gov.ph; hongkongpc@philcongen-hk.com
Website: www.philcongen-hk.com

Poland

Address: Suite 2506, Hopewell Centre, 183 Queen's Rd E, Wan Chai
Phone: 2840 0779; 9366 3262
Email: hongkong.kg.info@msz.gov.pl
Website: www.hongkong.msz.gov.pl

South Africa

Address: Suites 2706-2710, Great Eagle Centre, 23 Harbour Rd, Wan Chai
Phone: 257 73279
Email: sacghgk@netvigator.com

Spain

Address: Suite 5303, Central Plaza, 18 Harbour Rd, Wan Chai
Phone: 2525 3041
Email: cog.hongkong@mae.es
Website: www.exteriores.gob.es/consulados/hongkong
Office Hours: 9:00-13:00 (Visa application and collection)

Sri Lanka

Address: 22/F Dominion Centre, 43 Queens Rd E, Wan Chai
Phone: 2876 0828

Thailand

Address: 8/F Fairmont House, 8 Cotton Tree Dr, Central
Phone: 2521 6481

United Kingdom

Address: 1 Supreme Court Rd
Phone: 2901 3000; 2901 3222
Email: hongkong.consular@fco.gov.uk
Office Hours:
Mon-Friday: 9:00-14:00 for personal callers; Mon-Thu: 9:00-16:30 and Fri: 9:00-16:15 for telephone enquiries.

United States of America

Address: 26 Garden Rd
Phone: 2523 9011
Email: information_resource_center_hk@yahoo.com; acshk@state.gov
Website: hongkong.usconsulate.gov
American Citizens Services
Phone: 2841 2211
Email: acshk@state.gov

Visa Inquiries

Phone: 5808 4666 (8:00-20:00, Mon-Fri)
Email: support-hongkong@ustraveldocs.com.

Venezuela

Address: Suite 5405, Central Plaza, 18 Harbour Rd, Wanchai
Phone: 2730 8099
Email: dep.consular@consulvehk.org

Representative office of China (The Commissioner's Office of the P.R.C. Foreign Ministry)

Address: 7/F, Lower Block, China Resources Bldg, 26 Harbour Rd, Wan Chai (Use Wanchai MTR station and walk from there)
Phone: 3413 2300
Email: fmcovisa_hk@mfa.gov.c
Website: www.fmcoprc.gov.hk/eng
Office Hours: 9:00-12:00 and 14:00-17:00 (Mon-Fri)

Visas to Mainland China can be obtained from here. The normal visa service takes four working days including the day when the application is submitted but an express service of two or three working days is available for an extra fee. Nationals of the Schengen countries pay $200 for single entry visas.

Taiwan (Taipei Economic and Cultural Office)

Address: 4/F, Tower One, Lippo Centre, 89 Queensway, Central
Phone: 2530 1187

Useful Links & Numbers

Hong Kong International Dialing Code is 852, further area code is not required.

Transport in and around Hong Kong

Hong Kong International Airport (www.hongkongairport.com)

Airport Enquiry Hotline: 2181 8888
Car Parks: 2183 4360
MTR Corporation (www.mtr.com.hk): 2881 8888

Bus Services

Citybus (www.citybus.com.hk): 2873 0818
Long Win Bus (www.kmb.hk): 2261 2791
New Lantao (www.newlantaobus.com): 2984 9848

Residents' Coaches

Discovery Bay Transit Services (www.hkri.com): 3651 2345
Park Island Transport Company (www.pitcl.com.hk): 2946 8888

Airport-Hotelink: 3193 9333

Rehabus: The Hong Kong Society for Rehabilitation (www.rehabsociety.org.hk): 2817 8154 (Hong Kong residents); 8100 8655 (overseas visitors)

Ferry Transfer

Hong Kong International Airport Ferry Terminal Services: 2215 3232
CKS (Services to / from Shenzhen Shekou and Fuyong, Dongguan Humen, Macao (Maritime Ferry Terminal & Taipa), Zhongshan and Zhuhai Jiuzhou) (www.cksp.com.hk): 2858 3876
TurboJET (Services to / from Macao (Maritime Ferry Terminal & Taipa), and Guangzhou Nansha) (www.turbojetseaexpress.com.hk): 2859 3333

Mainland Coaches

China Travel Tours Transportation (ctsbus.hkcts.com): 3559 1474
Eternal East Cross-Border Coach (www.eebus.com): 3760 0888
Go Go Bus (www.trans-island.com.hk): 2261 2555

Sinoway (HK-China) **Express** (www.168zght.com): 3197 9309

SkyLimo (Mainland Limousines)

China Travel Service: 2261 2169
Eternal East Tours (www.eebus.com): 3760 0888
KCI Travel: 2261 2636
S.T. Travel (www.st166.net): 3197 9312
Sinoway (www.168zght.com): 3197 9310
TIL Travel: 2261 2636

Government Departments

Hong Kong Government (www.gov.hk): 1823
Consumer Council (www.consumer.org.hk): 2929 2222 – To protect the interest of consumers
Transport Department (www.td.gov.hk):

2804 2600 To plan and regulate Hong Kong's transport systems
Leisure and Cultural Services Department (www.lcsd.gov.hk): 2414 5555 – To provide quality leisure and cultural services, such as sport centers, museums and libraries etc
Hong Kong Tourism Board (www.discoverhongkong.com): 2508 1234 – To promote Hong Kong as a tourism destination
Immigration Department (www.immd.gov.hk): 2824 6111 – Facilitating the visit of travelers and exercising immigration control
Hong Kong Observatory (www.hko.gov.hk): 187 8066 – To provide weather forecasting, services in climate, radiation, time standard, seismology, oceanography, astronomy and others
Check the time and weather: 18501 for English; 18508 for Mandarin

Other Numbers

Emergency services (police, fire, ambulance): 999
Police Hotline: 2527 7177
Travel Industry Council of Hong Kong: 2807 0707
Hong Kong Tourism Board Visitor Hotline: 2508 1234
Department of Health: 2961 8989
Customs and Excise Department 24-Hour Hotline: 2815 7711
Hong Kong Post: 2921 2222
Hong Kong Hotels Association Hotel Reservation Hotline: 2383 8380; 2769 8822
Telephone directory enquiries: 1081

Lost passport

If you lose your passport, make a "lost report" at the nearest police station – call the Police Hotline 2527 7177 for locations or refer to their website (www.police.gov.hk) to find a Report Room. You will also need to contact your consulate to have your passport replaced.

Lost or stolen wallet

If your wallet or valuables are lost or stolen, notify your hotel immediately and report the theft to police. Keep a separate record of your credit card numbers and report the loss to your card issuers as quickly as possible. Check with your credit card issuers or insurance company for emergency assistance. Most issuers have toll-free numbers and 24-hour services to deal with such emergencies.

Index

A

Aberdeen 120
Aberdeen Fish Market Canteen 120
Aberdeen Floating Village 120
accommodation, see sleeping
airport 44
A-Ma Cultural Village 245
A-Ma Temple 244
Allen Fong 20
Ani-Con & Games 36, 39
Anita Mui 14, 15, 21, 24-26, 43, 67, 72, 140, 323
antiques 54, 132, 230
Apliu Street Flea Market 136
Apps 34-35
Avenue of Stars 55-58

B

Bank of China Tower 89
bargaining 226-229, 286
bars & pubs, see drinking
beaches 155-158
 Big Wave Bay Beach 156
 Cheung Sha Beach 158
 Hap Mun Wan Beach 156
 Long Ke Wan Beach 157
 Repulse Bay 59-61
 St Stephen's Beach 63
 Stanley Main Beach 63
 Turtle Cove Beach 158
Beacon Hill 113
Big Wave Bay Beach 156
Bird Market 82
Birthday of Tin Hau 36, 38
boat travel, see ferry
books 43
Bride's Pool Waterfall 106
Bruce Lee 19, 43, 56-57, 235
Buddha's Birthday 38
Buddhism 30, 38-39, 66, 70, 145, 146
Bun Festival 36, 38, 161
buses 44, 46

C

calling guide 304
Cantonese 305-322
Cantonese cuisine 182-183
Cantonese Opera 22-24
Cantopop 24-26
Carnival Mansion 279
Casa Garden 245
casinos 242
Cat Street 132
Cat Street Galleries 132

CCP 14, 18, 38, 63, 183, 323
cell phones 304
Central Library 147
Central Plaza 325, 326
Central Police Station 91
cha chaan teng 10, 14
Chatham Court 279
Che Kung Temple 37, 45, 129
Chek Keng 105
cheongsam 323
Cheung Chau Island 161
Cheung Sha Beach 158
Chi Lin Nunnery 68-70
children, travel with, see kids
Chinese medicine 133, 235
Chinese New Year 36, 239
Chinese opera 23, 261
Chinese Permanent Cemetery 120
Ching Chung Temple 126
Ching Ming Jie 37
Christianity 31
Christian 41
Chuk Lam Sim Monastery 151
Chungking & Mirador Mansions 231
Chungking Mansions 168-169
Chung Yeung Festival 36, 40
Chun Yeung Street Wet Market 136
chopsticks 212
climate 33-34
Clockenflap Music Festival 36, 40
Coloane Island 245
Confucianism 30-31, 145, 150, 243
consulates 325-326
country park 100-113
 Lantau Island Country Parks 110-112
 Ma On Shan Country Park 113
 Plover Cove Country Park 106-107
 Sai Kung Country Park 104-105
 Shek O Country Park 108-109
 Tai Mo Shan Country Park 100-101
 Tai Tam Country Park 102-103
cooking 236
crime 41
credit cards 35
Cultural Revolution 14, 159, 183, 235

culture shock 282-286
currency, see money
customs 34, 327

D

Deep Water Bay 61
Des Voeux Dried Seafood Street 133
Dialogue in the Dark 140
Diamond Hill 45, 69
dim sum 185
disabled travelers 299
discounts 34
Discovery Bay 30
disease 297
Disneyland 165
distractions 234-236
districts 16-18
Dr Sun Yat-sen Museum 144
dog racing 249
Dom Pedro V Theatre 245
Dragon Boat Festival 36, 38, 76
Dragon's Back 108-109
Dried Seafood Street & Tonic Food Street 230
drinking 213-225

E

eating 182-212
economy 27-28, 241
Edward Youde Aviary 87
Embassies, see consulates
events 36-40
exchange rates 35
Exchange Square 230
expats 29-30

F

Fa Yuen Street Market 137
Fan Lau Fort 111
Fanling Wai 116
female travelers 299
feng shui 60, 69, 89, 116, 323
ferry 47
festivals 36-40
 Ani-Con & Games 36, 39
 Birthday of Tin Hau 36, 38
 Buddha's Birthday 38
 Bun Festival 36, 38, 161
 Chinese New Year 36-37
 Ching Ming Jie 37
 Clockenflap Music Festival 36, 40
 Chung Yeung Festival 36, 40
 Dragon Boat Festival 36, 38, 76

Food Expo 36, 39
Hong Kong Art Walk 36-37
Hong Kong Book Fair 36-38
Hong Kong Cricket Sixes 36-40
Hong Kong Fashion Week for Spring/ Summer 36, 38
Hong Kong Film Festival 36-37
Hong Kong Rugby World Cup Sevens 36-37
Hong Kong SAR Establishment Day 38
Hong Kong Wine & Dine Festival 40
Hong Kong WinterFest 40
Hungry Ghost Festival 36, 39
Hung Shing Festival 36, 37
Mid-Autumn Festival 36, 39-40, 293
Monkey God Festival 36, 40
Spring Festival 36-37
Standard Chartered Hong Kong Marathon 36-37
film 14, 18-22, 43, 56,
finance 28
First Opium War 43, 250, 324
fishing 74-76
Five Great Clans 10, 77, 114, 116, 323
Flagstaff House Museum of Teaware, The 144
Flower Market 233
food 286-297, see also eating
Food Expo 36, 39
food safety 296-297
Former Kowloon British School 279
Foyer of Cheung Kung Hai Conference Centre 88
fortune telling 71

G

gambling 239, 241, 242, 249, seealso casinos
gay travelers 299
geography 16-18
giardia 292
glossary 323-324
Goldfish Market 233
Golden Bauhina Square 94
Good Wish Gardens 148
Granville Road 231
Guangzhou 250-257

H

Hakka people 11, 38, 105, 107, 114, 118, 125, 139, 141, 142, 144, 241, 323
Han Chinese 10, 74, 75
Han Dynasty 75, 146
Hap Mun Wan Beach 156
Happy Valley Racecourse 95
Harbour City 58, 277
health 296-297
Hebe Haven 17
Hepatitis34
High Island Reservoir 105

history 10-16
HKI 185
   see also Hong Kong Island
holidays, see festivals
Hollywood Road 135
Hollywood Road Man Mo Temple 149
Hong Kong Art Walk 36-37
Hong Kong Book Fair 36-38
Hong Kong City Hall 24
Hong Kong Coliseum 26
Hong Kong Convention & Exhibition Centre (HKCEC) 94
Hong Kong Cricket Sixes 36-40
Hong Kong Dolphinwatch 76
Hong Kong Fashion Week for Spring/ Summer 36, 38
Hong Kong Film Festival 36-37
Hong Kong Heritage Discovery Centre 140
Hong Kong Heritage Museum 139
Hong Kong Island 16-17,
Hong Kong Marathon 37
Hong Kong Maritime Museum 144
Hong Kong Mountain Bike Association 112
Hong Kong Museum of Art 138
Hong Kong Museum of History 141
Hong Kong Observatory 327
Hong Kong Overview, see overview
Hong Kong Park 87
Hong Kong Polytechnic University 141, 142
Hong Kong Racing Museum 95
Hong Kong Railway Museum 128
Hong Kong Rugby World Cup Sevens 36-37
Hong Kong SAR Establishment Day 38
Hong Kong Science Museum 142
Hong Kong Shaolin Wushu Culture Centre 76
Hong Kong Space Museum 58
Hong Kong SAR 297, 302, 3241
Hong Kong Trail 51-52
Hong Kong University 88
Hong Kong University Heritage Buildings 88
Hong Kong Visual Arts Centre 87
Hong Kong Wetland Park 97
Hong Kong Wine & Dine Festival 40
Hong Kong WinterFest 40
Hong Kong Zoological & Botanical Gardens 86
Hongkongers 31-32
horse racing 17, 249
HSBC Building 89
Hungry Ghost Festival 36, 39
Hung Hing Ying Building 88
Hung Shing Festival 36, 37

Hung Shing Temple 75-76
Hung Shing Yeh Beach 179
Hungry Ghost Festival 36, 39

I

Ice House Street 280-281
Immigration Department 327
internet access 304
Islam 31
Islands 159-164
   Cheung Chau Island 161
   Lamma Island 162
   Lung Kwu Chau 164
   Ninepin Islands 163
   Po Toi Island 160
   Sha Chau 164
   Soko Islands 164
   Tap Mun Chau 163
   Tung Lung Chau 163
   Tung Ping Chau Island 159
itineraries 271-281

J

Jackie Chan 18-19, 56-57, 59, 94
Jade Market 232
Jamia Mosque 154
Jardine House 230
Jet Li 18, 21, 57
Jewish 41-42
Joss House Bay Tin Hau Temple 146

K

Kadoorie Farm & Botanic Garden 97
Kam Tin 77, 115, 124
Kangxi Emperor 11
Kat Hing Wai 115
Kau Ling Chung Campsite 111
Kau Sai Chau 122
kayaking 63, 158
kids 292-295
King Yin Lei Mansion 117
Kiu Tsui Chau 156
Knutsford Terrace 279
Kowloon 16-17
Kowloon City Wet Market 137
Kowloon Mosque & Islamic Centre 42
Kowloon Park 42, 140, 279
Kowloon Peak 113
Kowloon Tong 42, 313
Kowloon Walled City Park 273, 278
Koxinga 11, 114
kung fu 18-19
Kwan Tai Temple 75
Kwun Yam Shrine 61

L

Ladies Street Market 80-82
Lam Tsuen Wishing Tree 93
Lamma Island 162
Lan Kwai Fong 213-214
Lantau Island Country Parks 110-112
Lantau Link 67
Lantau Peak 68, 111

Lantau Trail 63, 111
Lau Fau Shan & Pak Nai 123
Legislative Council Building 275
Lei Yue Mun 144, 314
lesbian travelers 299
Leslie Cheung 14, 15, 21, 24-25, 43, 324
Leung Shuen Wan 105
light rail 47
Li Ka-shing 28-29
Lin Fa Kung Temple 147
Lin Zexu 12
Liu Man Shek Tong Ancestral Hall 123
Lo So Shing Beach 162
Lockhart Road 303
Long Ke Wan Beach 157
Longevity Bridge 61
Lou Kau Mansion 245
Lung Kwu Chau 164

M

Ma Hang Park 64
Ma On Shan Country Park 113
Macau 239-249
    history 239
    politics 241
    demographics & economy 241
    visa 241
    casinos 242
Macau Arts Festival 246
Macau Formula 3 Grand Prix 246
Macau International Fireworks Display Contest 246
Macau Tower 245
MacLehose Trail 100-101, 104-105, 113
Mai Po Marshes 96
Mai Po Nature Reserve 96, 97
Man Cheung Po Campsite 111
Man Mo Temple 121, 128, 149
Maritime Museum 144
Markets 130-137
    Apliu Street Flea Market 136
    Cat Street 132
    Chun Yeung Street Wet Market 136, 230
    Chungking & Mirador Mansions 231
    Des Voeux Dried Seafood Street 133
    Dried Seafood Street & Tonic Food Street 230
    Flower Market 233
    Fa Yuen Street Market & Cooked Food Stalls 137
    Goldfish Market 233
    Granville Road 231
    Hollywood Road 135
    Jade Market 232
    Kowloon City Wet Market 137
    Ladies Street Market 80-82
    Queen's Road Ladder Street Markets 137
    Sneaker Street 232
    Stanley Market 63
    Temple Street Night Market 71-73

Western Market 131
Yau Ma Tei Wholesale Fruit Market 134
martial arts 18, 22, 235, 324
Mass Transit Railway (MTR) 44, 45, 324
massage 235
Mid-Autumn Festival 36, 39-40, 293
milk tea 183-184
Mid-Levels Escalators, the 52-54
Ming Dynasty 11, 40, 135, 144
minibuses 47
Miu Fat Monastery 153
mobile phones, see cell phones
money 35, 228-229, 238
Mongol 11
Monkey God Festival 36, 40
Monte Fort 244
Moorish Barracks 245
Mormon 42
mountain biking 110, 112
movies 43, see also film
Murray House 64
Museums 138-144
    Dialogue in the Dark 140
    Dr Sun Yat-sen Museum 144
    Flagstaff House Museum of Teaware, The 144
    Hong Kong Heritage Discovery Centre 140
    Hong Kong Heritage Museum 139
    Hong Kong Maritime Museum 144
    Hong Kong Museum of Art 138
    Hong Kong Museum of History 141
    Hong Kong Racing Museum 95
    Hong Kong Railway Museum 128
    Hong Kong Science Museum 142
    Hong Kong Space Museum 58
    Museum of Coastal Defence 144
    Police Museum 143
    Sam Tung Uk Museum of Hakka Culture 125, 142
    Sheung Yiu Folk Museum 105
music 24-27
Muslim 42
Mui Wo 121

N

Nathan Road 36, 279
New Territories 16-17
Ngong Ping 360 68
nightlife see drinking
Ninepin Islands 163
North Point 17, 136

O

Ocean Park 166
Ocean Terminal 55, 58
Octopus Card 44

Ohel Leah Synagogue 41
opium 11-13, 43, 102, 141, 159, 164, 250, 254, 324
Outlying Islands 17, 18, 159, 233
overview 10
    Cantonese Opera 22-24
    economy 29-32
    expats 29-30
    film 18-22
    geography and districts 16-18
    history 10-16
    Hongkongers 31-32
    music 24-27
    religion 30-31

P

Pak On Building 279
Pak Tai Temple 90, 161
Pak Tam Chung Nature Trail 105
Panda Ambassadors 335
Pang Clan Ancestral Hall 116
parks & gardens
    Edward Youde Aviary 87
    Good Wish Gardens 148
    Hong Kong Park 87
    Hong Kong Wetland Park 97
    Hong Kong Zoological & Botanical Gardens 86
    Kadoorie Farm & Botanic Garden 97
    Kowloon Park 42, 140, 279
    Kowloon Walled City Park 273, 278
    Lantau Island Country Parks 110-112
    Ma On Shan Country Park 113
    Plover Cove Country Park 106-107
    Sai Kung Country Park 104-105
    Shek O Country Park 108-109
    Tai Mo Shan Country Park 100-101
    Tai Tam Country Park 102-103
    Victoria Park 38, 176
passports 327
Pat Sin Leng Nature Trail 107
Peak Galleria 49-52
Peak Tower 49-52
Peak Tram 49-52
Peak, the 49-52
Peninsula Hong Kong 173
phones 35
pineapple bun 184
Ping Shan Heritage Trail 77-79
pink dolphins 74, 76
Plover Cove Country Park 106-107
Plover Cove Reservoir Hike 106
Po Lin Monastery 65-68
Po Toi Island 160
Police Museum 143
politics 241
pollution 287-291
population 241, 301, 306
Possession St 281
public holidays, see holidays
pubs, see drinking

Pui O 119
Punti people 11, 114, 142, 324

Q

Qing Dynasty 11, 13, 38, 107, 114, 135, 138, 161, 250, 255,
Queen's Road Ladder Street Markets 137

R

red light district 303
religion 30-31
Repulse Bay 59-61
restaurants, see eating

S

Sai Kung Country Park 104-105
Sai Kung Town 122
sailing 158, 247
Sam Tung Uk Museum of Hakka Culture 125, 142
sampans 75, 83, 120, 156, 163, 164
scams 147, 286,
sculpture 86, 135
Second Opium War 13
Senado Square 243-244
SEZ (Special Economic Zone) 257, 262
Sha Chau 164
Sha Tin 129
Sha Tin Racecourse 95, 98
Sham Wan 162
Shanghai Street 81
Sharp Peak 104-105
Shau Kei Wan 102, 108
Shek O Country Park 108-109
Shenzhen 257-261
Sheung Shui 123
Sheung Yiu Folk Museum 105
shopping 226-233
Shui Tau Tsuen 124
Sik Sik Yuen Wong Tai Sin Temple 148
Silvermine Bay Beach 121
Silvermine Waterfall 121
sleeping 168-181
smoking 34, 301
snakes 133
Sneaker Street 232
Soko Islands 164
Sok Kwu Wan 162
Spring Festival, see Chinese New Year
St Stephen's Beach 63
Standard Chartered Hong Kong Marathon 36-37
Stanley 62-64
Stanley Ho 241, 249
Stanley Main Beach 63
Stanley Market 63
Stanley Military Cemetery 63
Stanley Plaza 64
Stanley Promenade 64
Star Ferry 82-84
Statue Square 40
subway 44-45
Sun Yatsen, Dr 88, 144, 249, 324

Sun Yatsen Place 88
Sunset Peak 111-112
Supreme Court Building 275, 280-281
sweet rolls 184
swimming 63, 99, 110

T

tai chi 324
Tai Mo Shan Country Park 100-101
Tai O Fishing Village 74-76
Tai Po 128
Tai Po Market 106, 128
Tai Tam Country Park 102-103
Tanka people 74
Taoism 30, 39, 145, 150
Tap Mun Chau 163
Tate's Cairn 113
taxi 47
temples 145-154
   Chi Lin Nunnery 68-70
   Chuk Lam Sim Monastery 151
   Hollywood Road Man Mo Temple 149
   Jamia Mosque 154
   Joss House Bay Tin Hau Temple 146
   Lin Fa Kung Temple 147
   Miu Fat Monastery 153
   Po Lin Monastery 65-68
   Sik Sik Yuen Wong Tai Sin Temple 148
   Ten Thousand Buddhas Monastery 147
   Tin Hau Temple 72-73, 124, 146, 163, 246
   Tsing Shan Monastery 152
   Yuen Yuen Institue 150
Temple Street Night Market 71-73
Ten Thousand Buddhas Monastery 147
Tian Tan Big Buddha 67
Tin Hau Temple 72-73, 124, 146, 163, 246
toilets 295
tong yuen 183
towns & villages 119-129
   Aberdeen 120
   Lau Fau Shan & Pak Nai 123
   Mui Wo 121
   Pui O 119
   Sai Kung Town 122
   Sha Tin 129
   Sheung Shui 123
   Shui Tau Tsuen 124
   Tai Po 128
   Tsuen Wan 125
   Tuen Mun 126
   Yuen Long 127
trade 27-28
trams 47
transportation 44-47
   airport 44
   buses 44, 46
   ferry 47
   light rail 47

minibuses 47
subway 44-45
taxi 47
trams 47
Treaty of Nanking 12
Triads 10, 14, 19-20, 43, 72, 80, 134, 137, 143, 145, 249, 324
Tsang Tai Uk 118
Tsim Sha Tsui Clock Tower 92
Tsim Sha Tsui Waterfront 55-58
Tsing Shan Monastery 152
Tsu Hsing Monastery 111
Tsuen Wan 125
Tsuen Yue Wan Campsite 111
Tuen Mun 126
Tung Lung Chau 163
Tung Ping Chau Island 159
Turtle Cove Beach 158
Typhoon 33, 290-291

V

vaccines 34
Victoria Harbour 314
Victoria Park 38, 176
Victoria Peak 49-52
villages, see towns
visa 41, 237, 241, 250, 258, 262, 302-303, 325-327, see also passports
Violet Hill 102
visual arts 87

W

walking tours
   Central 280
   Kowloon City & Temples 278
   Tsim Sha Tsui 279
Walled Villages 114-118
   Fanling Wai 116
   Kat Hing Wai 115
   King Yin Lei Mansion 117
   Tsang Tai Uk 118
Wan Chai Historic Buildings 90
water safety 296-297
weather 33, 327
Western Market 131
windsurfing 110, 122, 158, 204
Whampoa 232
Wong Kar-wai 20-22, 57
Wong Tai Sin 17, 148, 314

Y

Yau Ma Tei Wholesale Fruit Market 134
Yuen Long 127
Yuen Yuen Institue 150
Yueng Hau Temple 75
yum cha 185, 268, 324, see also dim sum

Z

Zedong, Mao 305, 324
Zhuhai 262-265

Notes

Notes

Behind the scenes

This is the first edition of Panda Guides' *Hong Kong* guidebook and it was written by a team of expert Hong Kong expat writers who come from all corners of the English speaking world. Apart from their writings, this book was produced in Panda Guides' Beijing office with assistance from the Panda Guides' headquarters in Toronto, Canada. It was produced by the following:

Commissioning Editor – **Robert Linnet**

Managing Editors – **Trey Archer, Grant Dou**

Editor – **Jessica Suotmaa**

Managing Layout Designers – **Liu Qingli, Alice Harris**

Coordinating Cartographer – **Yan Laiyong**

Managing Cartographers – **Ding Zhicheng, Jessie Li**

Assistant Cartographers – **Feng Lili, Paul Taylor**

Chief Proofreader – **Jessica Suotmaa**

Proofreaders – **Elmer Chen, Robynne Tindall, Douglas Smith, Tina Johnson**

Internal Image Research – **Ellen Wong, Aaron Clarke**

Cantonese Content – **Alex Lau**

Other Contributors – **Sam Gussway, Grant Dou**

Office Assistant – **Li Lan, Zhang Qin, Suriguga**

Writers – **Mitchell Blatt, Robert Linnet, Triston Brewer, Trey Archer**

A special thanks also goes out to **Chen Chen, Chang Zhengong, Ellen Hou, Jason Yu, Lauren Hou, Danny Shao, Han Fei, Liu Quanzu, Zhao Yong, Li Weixing, Yang Haibin, Wang Lei, Abel Thompson, Jeffery Scott, Lawrence Anderson** and **Jackie Lee**. Your work is greatly appreciated.

And last but not least, thank you to everyone along the way who helped us research this book. From the farmer on the street who pointed us in the right direction to the business man who gave us a ride when it was raining outside; none of this would have been possible without the people of China. 多谢！ Dojeh!

PANDA GUIDES

The Panda Ambassadors Program

Do you want an all-inclusive paid trip to China? Of course you do! By following the Panda, you can win that dream China trip, so keep reading to learn about the incredible Panda Ambassadors Program.

Once a year we will choose 20 lucky individuals to have the Chinese adventure of a lifetime. The selection process is simple. All you have to do is buy any Panda Guides travel book (*Beijing, Shanghai, Hong Kong* or *China*), go to our website to enter the six-digit code found on the inside of the front cover, then wait to see if your number is selected. All winners will be announced on our website and contacted through email in April. That's it!

Each winner gets a free two-week trip to China – transportation, accommodation and meals will be paid for by Panda Guides Publishing Inc. The only thing you have to do is purchase your visa, a flight and any extra souvenirs you'll want during your visit. The total value of this amazing package is ¥15,000 (roughly US$2,500).

A certified Panda Guides tour guide will bring the selected winners on a journey through a fascinating part of the country. It could be the ancient Silk Road along China's great northwest, a tropical retreat in the southern Canton region, or a river cruise through the Yangtze River. The journey will change once a year to ensure the scenery stays fresh, but no matter where you end it up, we guarantee it will be a wonderful trip!

Unfortunately, sometimes the real world gets in the way of our leisure time. But don't worry, all winners will have a three-year window to take their trip. If the winner still cannot take their free trip during this time, they can give it to someone else.

As you can see, through our Panda Ambassadors Program, Panda Guides is more than just a guide, it's an experience. In fact, we want you to enjoy your travel experience so much that we're willing to pay for it. So come along and let us welcome you to China, we hope to see you here soon.

See our website **www.pandaguides.com/pandaambassadors** for more.

123456

The Authors

Mitchell Blatt

Mitchell grew up in Cleveland, OH and graduated from Indiana University with a B.A. in journalism. He has written about sports, travel and culture. Since he began studying Chinese, he has become obsessed with Chinese culture and travel. Living in Hong Kong, he contributes to outlets such as ChinaHush, eChinaCities, and TheChinaChronicle.com, where his coverage includes stories on Hong Kong arts, film, and music, and a guide for Go Nomad on traveling on a budget in Hong Kong. In his free time, he enjoys visiting Hong Kong's beautiful Country Parks.

Triston Brewer

Born in Dallas, Texas, Triston moved to Europe over ten years ago, working as a performance artist and writer in several countries. Fluent in English, German, Spanish, and Dutch, he has lived in the cities of Barcelona, Berlin and Istanbul, just to name a few. He has been published in The Huffington Post, Trespass (London), Adaras Magazine (Miami) as well as featured in publications such as the New York Times, Vogue Italia, Turkish Huriyet and other online and print magazines in the U.S. and internationally. He recently released his first novel on life abroad. Currently, he resides in Hong Kong, and is working on his next novel.

Robert Linnet

Born in Denver, CO, Robert received his B.A. in Linguistics from the nearby University of Colorado. After spending four months of the 2009 summer in China training in martial arts and traveling, Robert packed up and moved into the Middle Kingdom the following year. It was the summer of 2010 when he spent an unforgettable week in Hong Kong, prompting him to make the city his home for the long four months of the following winter, and since then he has been sure to visit the city regularly. In addition to Hong Kong, Robert has traveled to more than 15 cities throughout China and loves practicing kettlebell, Baji Chuan kung fu, and is obsessed with adding to the thousands of Chinese characters he currently reads and writes. Though he currently resides in Beijing, he recently made a trip back to Xi'an to marry his girlfriend Chen Chen.

Trey Archer

Trey Archer is from Lake Charles, Louisiana and studied International Affairs at the George Washington University. While backpacking Latin America in 2007, he declared while hitchhiking by boat from Colombia to Panama that he'd pursue a career in travel writing after graduation instead of entering the world of diplomacy. Since then he has traveled to nearly 100 countries, speaks Spanish, Portuguese and Mandarin fluently, and has lived in nine different nations. Though he currently resides in Beijing, he's always going to Hong Kong to visit his sister Adri and brother-in-law Andrew who live there. In his free time, Trey trains muay Thai, supports the New Orleans Saints, cycles and travels as much as humanly possible.

Table of Co

Hong Kong Overview 10

Getting Prepared 33

Transportation 44

Top Attractions 48

  Victoria Peak.....................................49

  The Mid-Levels Escalators..............52

  Tsim Sha Tsui Waterfront &
  the Avenue of Stars 55

  Repulse Bay.....................................59

  Stanley..62

  Po Lin Monastery.............................65

  Chi Lin Nunnery...............................68

  Temple Street Night Market 71

  Tai O Fishing Village 74

  Ping Shan Heritage Trail 77

  Ladies Street Market........................80

  Star Ferry..82

Other Attractions 85

  Parks & Heritage Buildings 86

  Country Parks 99

  Walled Villages..............................114

  Towns & Villages............................119

  Markets 130

  Museums 138

  Temples & Monasteries 145

  Beaches..155

  Islands 159

  Amusement Parks..........................165

Sleeping..168

Eating..182

Drinking & Nightlife 213

Shopping.......................................226

Distractions...................................234

Side Trips......................................237

  Macau 239

  Guangzhou ....

  Shenzhen.......................................257

  Zhuhai...262

Travel Stories 266

Hot Topics.....................................271

  Culture Shock 282

  Pollution in Hong Kong...................287

  Traveling With Kids.........................292

  Water, Food & Health.....................296

  Hong Kong on a Budget..................298

  Solo-Female, Disabled, LGBT &
  Travelers of Color...........................299

  Hong Kong vs Mainland China 300

  Visa Issues &Visa Runs.................302

  Lockhart Road:
  The Red Light District 303

  Hong Kong Calling Guide 304

Cantonese Phrasebook.................305

Glossary 323

Travel Resources 325

Index 328

erview – The Overview is the place to start. Here you can learn about the history and culture of Hong Kong, as well as get a background on what makes this wonderful city so vibrant. There are plenty of fun facts too, as well as the Hong Kong reading and movie list.

2. **Hot Topics** – Mentally prepare with Hot Topics. Everything you need to know about how to travel with kids, protect yourself against pollution, stay safe and healthy, and more is touched on in this chapter. There are also a few sample itineraries to help with planning your trip.

3. **Getting Prepared** – First decide which season is best for your trip and which festivals are going on during your visit, then pack those bags, get your visa and buy a ticket through the help of our user-friendly Getting Prepared section.

4. **Top Attractions & Other Attractions** – Learn about Hong Kong's many world-class attractions through vivid descriptions, histories and vibrant full-color pictures. If your trip is limited in time, the hardest part will be narrowing down the list! It's also a good idea to bring this guidebook to these sites to stay fresh on their details – it's certainly cheaper than hiring an overpriced tour guide.

5. **Side Trips** – If you have time to spare after seeing it all, go for one (or a few) of our Side Trips. Whether it's an overnighter to the old Portuguese quarter and casinos of Macau, a shopping and dining romp through Shenzhen, or a foodie feast through the birthplace of Yue cuisine in Guangzhou, we've got options for every kind of traveler.

6. **Sleeping** – Book the perfect lodging via the Sleeping chapter. You can even use the customized pull-out city map to ensure your hotel or hostel is close to all of your desired sights.

7. **Eating and Drinking & Nightlife** – Reserve a five-star restaurant or do as the locals do and chow down at a hole-in-the-wall using our comprehensive restaurant list. After your meal, paint the town red at the city's hottest bars, clubs and live music venues.

8. **Distractions** – When you need a break from all the sightseeing, flip through Distractions to see which massage parlor can best spoil you. Perhaps a kung fu class, cooking lesson, or even a crash course on Traditional Chinese Medicine is calling your name? We have tons of pleasant activities to "distract" you along the way.

9. **Travel Resources** – Lost your passport and need a new one? Decided to continue traveling and need visas for other countries? Travel Resources can be your best friend and a lifesaver if a problem arises.

10. **Cantonese Phrasebook** – By speaking the local lingo and learning more about one of the world's oldest and most fascinating languages, not only will you enlighten your soul, but you'll also find traversing the town a lot easier. Get started with our Cantonese Phrasebook.

PANDA GUIDES

THINK CHINA THINK PANDA

HONG KONG

THIS EDITION WAS RESEARCHED AND WRITTEN BY

Mitchell Blatt
Tristan Brewer
Robert Linnet
Trey Archer